CW01522112

THE HISTORY OF BRITAIN
John Milton

Gul. Faithorne ad Vivum.   Delin. et sculpsit.

Ioannis Miltoni Effigies Ætat: 62.
1670.

THE HISTORY
OF BRITAIN

John Milton

A facsimile edition
with a critical Introduction
by
Graham Parry
University of York

PAUL WATKINS
STAMFORD, 1991

© New Introduction, Graham Parry 1991

Published in 1991 by
PAUL WATKINS,
18, Adelaide Street,
Stamford,
Lincolnshire,
PE9 2EN.

ISBN
1 871615 25 9

The *Digression* appears by permission of the Syndics of
Cambridge University Library

The frontispiece portrait of Milton is taken from the
first edition of 1670 and is reproduced with the
permission of the Bodleian Library, Oxford.

Issued in a limited edition of 500 copies only.
This is copy number

306

New material typeset in Garamond by
Paul Watkins *Publishing*
Printed (on long-life paper) and bound by Woolnoughs
of Irthlingborough

CONTENTS

NOTE FROM THE PUBLISHER

The first edition of Milton's famous *History of Britain* was published in 1670. This facsimile is taken from the first impression of the second edition, of 1677. The second edition was chosen because it is in a more convenient octavo format than the quarto first edition.

The editions vary in a few minor details: variations of spelling and punctuation as well as in a few changes of expression. There were no illustrations in the second edition, but the first included a fine portrait of Milton which we have used as a frontispiece. Thanks are due to the Bodleian Library, Oxford, for permission to use their copy of the plate for the purposes of reproduction.

Milton's interpretation of early Britain has made his work famous, but although it has been edited many times for editions of the complete works of Milton, this is the first edition in the form of a separate book since 1818. The new edition also contains the important *Digression* (missing from the seventeenth-century editions) and a list of ideas for historical dramas which Milton compiled while he was writing the *History*. Thanks are due to the Syndics of Cambridge University Library for permission to reproduce the copy of the Digression in their possession.

Thanks are also due to many people for their advise, enthusiasm and encouragement, including Mark English, Simon Keynes, Philip Riley, David Roffe, Margaux Stocker and Anne Wilkins; but especially to Graham Parry for writing his informative Introduction.

Shaun Tyas

INTRODUCTION

What surprises about Milton's *History of Britain* is what it is not. It is not a patriotic record of the origins of the nation, nor an illustration of divine providence at work in the shaping of Britain's destiny. Milton shows little interest in the spread of Christianity in these islands, or in the doctrine and discipline of the early church. He fails to enquire into those highly charged antiquarian topics, the origins of parliaments, the government of the Anglo-Saxons, and the character and content of Anglo-Saxon law; there is no concern for an Ancient Constitution in England before the Normans. All these topics, which one might expect to be exercising Milton in the 1640s when he composed the greater part of the *History*, are scarcely addressed. Instead, he produced a dense narrative of events from mythical times to the Norman Conquest. He concentrated on the succession of rulers, the insurrections and convulsions that were endemic in a country that was at first tribal, and then divided into many kingdoms, and reflected on the vices that seem engrained in British political life throughout its history. What, one may well ask, were Milton's serious intentions in writing this book, and how does it fit into his career as polemicist?

From Milton's own account in his *Second Defence of the People of England* (*Defensio Secunda*,

1654), a tract that contains a lengthy auto-biographical sketch and an apologia for his role in defending the execution of Charles I, as well as a vigorous justification of the course that the English revolution had taken, we know that he had written four sections by early 1649: 'I turned my thoughts to a continued history of my country from the earliest times to the present period. I had already finished four books, when, after the subversion of the monarchy and the establishment of a republic, I was surprised by an invitation from the Council of State, who desired my services in the office for foreign affairs.' Milton claims that he set about his task after the writing of *The Tenure of Kings and Magistrates*, and that it was interrupted by an offer of a post from the Council of State. This would only allow two or three months for a complicated scholarly exercise, a period patently inadequate, and the critical consensus now assumes that Milton must have been working on the project from some time after 1645. Such a view is in harmony with the evidence of Milton's Commonplace Book, which indicates that he was reading the sources of British history intensively during the years 1640-44. It is worth noting that in the passage from the *Second Defence*, Milton expressed his intention of bringing his history down to his own age; in addition, the same section suggests that the *History* was composed as a private exercise, but one tending to the public good.

Certainly one can understand why Milton felt the need to write a national history. For a country

8

so proud of its achievements, and indeed so prolific in the writing of histories, there were few books that offered a comprehensive and judicious account of Britain from its beginnings until present times. William Camden, who contemplated writing a national history to complement his great topographical survey *Britannia*, and who was best qualified to write such a history, turned aside from the task as too vast and settled instead for editing a collection of chronicle sources in 1603. For the early Stuart reader, ambitious of a complete account of his country's past, John Speed's *Historie of Great Britaine* (1611), dominated the field, a volume so large that it needed a servant to carry it. Speed had been able to benefit from Camden's admirable treatment of Roman Britain in *Britannia*, and he could supplement the medieval chroniclers with new manuscript material from Sir Robert Cotton's collection. His history was pleasingly narrated in a loosely descriptive style, but it was deficient in causality, analysis, and in political savoir-faire. The more trenchant historians, who had an understanding of the critical methods of Italian historiography as exemplified by Machiavelli and Gucciardini, were inclined to concentrate on individual reigns rather than attempt to evaluate the whole panorama of Britain. Sir Thomas More's *Richard III*, Camden's *History of Elizabeth*, Sir Francis Bacon's *Henry VII*, Lord Herbert of Cherbury's *Henry VIII*, Sir John Hayward's *Edward VI*, and John Habington's *Edward IV* are typical examples of the highly focussed study of a monarch in his political setting. Bacon, so alert to the deficiencies of English intellectual culture, had complained in *The Advancement of Learning* of the 'indignity and unworthinesse of the History of England, as it now is', and had proposed to James I 'that it would be honour to your Majesty, and a work acceptable with Posterity, if this Iland of Great Britany, as it is now joyned in a Monarchy for the Ages to come, so were joyned in one History for the times past, after the manner of the sacred History'. Bacon believed that with the union of the kingdoms under James, making Britain a political entity for the first time since mythical antiquity, the time was right for a history that would clarify the pattern of events that had led to this culmination.

A culmination of a different kind probably moved Milton to embark on his history. The Civil War was a crisis that forced men to think about the past in order to understand the present. Here was a struggle for liberties both civil and religious, in which not only were ancient forms of oppression being challenged, but the Christian spirit of the nation being tested. Surrounded by a disintegrating kingdom in the 1640s, Milton may well have been moved to compose a history of Britain in order to explore the nature of the British people, to see how it was revealed and expounded by the course of events over the whole span of the national existence. In the momentous circumstances of the Civil War, the philosophic mind might attempt to view the present troubles in long perspective, the climax of centuries of violence and war in which the generations of Englishmen had fought over the control and exercise of authority. As Bacon had suggested that a British history might have analogies with sacred history, perhaps Milton hoped to discover secret coherences between character and destiny operating through the ages under the vicissitude of events.

Is there such a thing as national destiny? Milton evidently thought that there was, and that its nature could be found in history. In his first tract against episcopacy, *Of Reformation in England*, a work heavy with ecclesiastical history, he had traced the providences of God towards the English nation since the breaking out of the Reformation in the reign of Henry VIII, and depicted the transformation of the English into the godly people who would be the instrument of the divine will in the last age of the world. In the rhapsodic close to that work he had expressed the hope that someone - perhaps Milton himself - 'may perhaps be heard offering at high strains in new and lofty measure to sing and celebrate thy divine mercies and marvellous judgements in this land throughout all ages'. That was written in the unrestrained mood of 1641, before the country fell into civil war, and the expectation was of a heroic poem, suiting the elevated theme. With the warfare and confusion of the 1640s, Milton's early optimism dimmed, but the preoccupation with a national history persisted, to be written now in prose, and with less assurance of divine guidance.

11

This desire to set down the history of Britain superseded to a large extent Milton's earlier intention to write a patriotic poem celebrating the deeds of British heroes, an ambition that seems to have been quickened by his Italian visit in 1638-9. In the poem 'Epitaphium Damonis', on the death of his friend Charles Diodati, and in that addressed to Manso, the Italian patron of poets, Milton had sketched brief outlines of poems that would praise the legendary figures in the line of Trojan Brutus, or recount the exploits of King Arthur against the Saxons. These airy projects faded as the political events of the Long Parliament turned Milton's thoughts to immediate matters of liberty and reform. Nonetheless, when it came to compiling *The History of Britain*, Milton found it hard to reject the fabulous stories of British antiquity that had roused his imagination in younger days.

In beginning his narrative, Milton straight away came up against the problem that baffled all seventeenth century historians: what had happened in Britain before Caesar's invasion had brought these islands to the attention of the classical world, and into the realm of civilised discourse? Who indeed were the British, and could they legitimately be said to possess a history while they were sunk in the night of oblivion? Given the absence of written records, and the rudimentary state of archaeology (an area in which he had no interest at all), Milton was faced with the alternative of a dismal blank of pre-history, or the colourful fictions of the medieval chroniclers who had embroidered the inventions of Geoffrey of Monmouth. Writing in the mid-twelfth century, Geoffrey had first set out the story of the settlement of Britain by Brutus and his Trojan followers who, after the destruction of the indigenous giants, had founded the city of Troynovant, the forerunner of London, and had spread their chivalric culture throughout their new home. Geoffrey too had described in plentiful detail the succession of kings and princes down to Arthur, terminating with the reign of Cadwallader, when the remnant of the British had been forced by the Saxons into the mountains of Wales, there to await the time when they should once again occupy their lost kingdom. Full of incident, and with a cast of thousands, Geoffrey's history was hard to resist. It had been subjected to varying degrees of scepticism from the time of Polydore Vergil's *Anglica Historia* (1534), and Camden had declared it to be unworthy of serious consideration, yet it had endeared itself to so many generations of Englishmen, and had been the source of so much poetry and romance, that it had become the indispensable record of British identity, giving the nation a noble and distinguished antiquity comparable with that of Rome. Even the polymathic Selden, who totally disbelieved the whole corpus of this so-called 'British History', was willing partially to suspend that disbelief when he came to annotate Drayton's *Poly-Olbion* in 1612. In order to humour his friend's poetic fancies he acknowledged the power of 'that universal desire, bewitching our Europe, to derive our blood from

Trojans'. Milton also found himself bewitched, against his better judgement. The poet in him overcame the historian.

He notes 'the obscure beginning which truest antiquity affords the nation', knows that 'the greater part of judicious antiquaries' have long rejected Geoffrey's account 'for a modern fable'. Nevertheless, he reflects, there may be germs of truth in the old stories, just as, when he came to write *Paradise Lost*, he was inclined to think that the Greek mythologies might preserve distorted memories of primeval events:

> oft-times Relations heretofore accounted Fabulous have bin after found to contain in them many footsteps, and reliques of somthing true, as what we read in Poets of the Flood, and Giants little beleev'd, till undoubted witnesses taught us, that all was not fain'd; I have therefore determin'd to bestow the telling over ev'n of these reputed Tales; be it for nothing else but in favour of our English Poets, and Rhetoricians, who by thir Art will know, how to use them judiciously. (p.7)

'Our English Poets' scarcely needed Milton's retelling of the Brutus legends, for they were readily available in most of the printed chronicles, in Spenser, Speed and Drayton. But Milton is determined to proceed, and softens his initial expression of disbelief by remarking that these tales are 'defended by many, denied utterly by few'. He reserves his scorn for an alternative version of British origins, the settlement of the islands by a

14

younger son of Japhet called Samothes, a figure regrettably not mentioned in the Bible, who was put into circulation in the fifteenth century by a Dominican monk, Annius of Viterbo. Annius published a number of works which he claimed to have recovered from old manuscripts, among which was an account of the peopling of the world written by the Chaldean historian Berosus. Berosus was immediately detected as a forgery, and Annius denounced as a cheat, but the stories, like genies escaped from a bottle, were hard to stop up again. Milton repudiates this 'outlandish figment' with some vigour, and prepares to retell the British History of Geoffrey of Monmouth. First, however, even his plain prose narrative requires God's blessing, and we find Milton 'imploring Divine Assistance, that it may redound to his Glory, and the good of the British nation' (p.8).

So Milton, though wishing to write a 'true history', begins with fables. He accepts, in effect, that the traditional stories have acquired a privileged status for many of his readers, and that legends that fill the gaps in the documentary record eventually become a form of alternative history sustained by popular belief. It is noteworthy, however, that Milton makes no attempt to engage in modern methods of enquiry into the origins of the nation. Philology was a relevant instrument of research, used variously and successfully by William Camden in *Britannia,* and *Remains Concerning Britain,* and by Richard Verstegan in his *Restitution of Decayed Intelligence in Antiquities* to demonstrate the kinship of the Ancient Britons and the northern European tribes in Gaul and Germany. Milton was not alert to the potential of what we would now call comparative anthropology as a means of recreating lost societies. Encounters with the Virginian Indians in particular had prompted several thoughtful writers to draw analogies with pre-Roman Britons: Thomas Hariot's *The New Found Land of Virginia* (1588), Speed's *History* (1611) and John Aubrey in his writings on Wiltshire (though these remained unpublished) had made some useful advances here. Field monuments such as standing stones and barrows might give clues to population centres and social customs, but in Milton's time few scholars were prepared to assign these monuments to the Ancient Britons: they were generally considered to be contemporary with the Romans, or Danish. Even the classical historians, carefully sifted, could provide information about Ancient Britain as reported by travellers' tales or rumour. But though these approaches might throw light on a primitive society, they could not provide a history. Hence Milton's preference for Geoffrey.

Brutus receives an elaborate presentation, as do the violent exploits of his descendants. Milton finds time to recount the story of Sabrina, the 'damsel' drowned in the Severn, which he had inserted into 'Comus'; he devotes a great deal of space to King Lear and his daughters, though whether he chooses to linger on this story in order to allow the reader to reflect on the liberties that Shakespeare had taken with these scenes must remain an open question. The Lear story was moderately well known, but Milton was a great admirer of Shakespeare, and his decision to give Lear such prominent treatment may have stemmed from his interest in the play. He reminds his reader that, according to legend, Cordelia survived to rule in peace until overthrown by her sisters' sons, whereupon she committed suicide. These events took place, according to Geoffrey's history, a little after Solomon and shortly after the founding of Rome.

Milton parades his grandly named nonentities splendidly before the reader: Cunedagius, Gurguntius Barbirus, Guitheline, Gorbonian, 'than whom a juster man lived not in his age', and Elidore, 'a mind so noble, and so moderate as almost is incredible'. We are cheered to learn that Lud, who rebuilt Troynovant and made it London, 'was hardy, and bold in war; in peace a jolly feaster'. Somewhat shamefacedly, as he concludes the catalogue of British worthies, Milton remarks 'I neither oblige the beleif of other person, nor over-hastily subscribe mine own' (p. 37). With palpable relief, he approaches the Roman invasion: 'like one who had set out on his way by night and travail'd through a Region of smooth or idle Dreams, our History now arrives on the Confines, where day-light and truth meet us with a cleer dawn, representing to our view, though at a farr distance, true colours and shapes' (pp.37-8). Caesar is at hand.

Having almost forfeited the right to be considered a serious historian in his first book, Milton recovers his poise when dealing with the Roman invasion and the Roman occupation in Book II. Now he can draw on the first hand accounts of Caesar and the precise observation of Tacitus, as well as the dozen or more Roman historians who noted British affairs during the long Roman domination. Indeed, Milton's critical spirit is so revived by contact with classical authorities that he is emboldened to question Caesar's assertion that virtually nothing was known of Britain amongst the Gauls before the invasion: if as Caesar states the British Druids were so honoured for their learning that Gallic priests came regularly to Britain for instruction, then there must have been a certain traffic between the two nations, and knowledge of Britain must have been more extensive than Caesar estimated. From Caesar's *Commentaries*, Milton projects a picture of the Ancient Britons as a primitive people, hardy, warlike and savage. He can easily envisage Caesar's Britons and the rude nature of their life:

> thir Towns and strong Holds were spaces of ground fenc't about with a Ditch and great Trees fell'd overthwart each other, thir buildings within were thatch't Houses for themselvs and thir Cattell: In peace the Upland Inhabitants besides hunting tended thir flocks and heards, but with little skill of Countrie affaires; the making of Cheese they commonly knew not, Woole or Flax they spun not, gard'ning and planting many

of them knew not; clothing they had none, but what the skins of Beasts afforded them, and that not alwaies; yet gallantrie they had, painting thir own skins with several Portratures of Beast, Bird or Flower, *A Vanitie which hath not yet left us, remov'd only from the skin to the skirt behung now with as many colour'd Ribands and Gewgawes*; towards the Sea side they till'd the ground and liv'd much after the manner of *Gaules* thir Neighbours, or first Planters. (p.59)

How different is all this from the glamorous Trojans with their chivalry and high culture. Saturated as he was in classical learning, Milton instinctively adopted the viewpoint of Caesar, and probably found it easier to accept the idea that the Britons had been a grim, primitive people, rather than some noble transplant of antiquity, because he could look on them through Caesar's eyes. He could even make fun of their barbarism, imagining the half-naked painted warriors, when 'poursu'd by Enemies, not nice of thir painting to run into Bogs, worse than *wild Irish* up to the Neck'. He could be scornful of the reputation that the Druids had accumulated for wisdom and arcane lore: 'yet Philosophers I cannot call them, reported men factious and ambitious, contending somtimes about the Archpriesthood not without Civil Warr and slaughter'. All in all, considering the crude practices of the Ancient Britons, Milton judged they were 'Progenitors not to be glori'd in'.

Milton welcomed the Roman invaders in that 'they beate us into som civilitie'. One might have expected Milton to trace the growth of this civility, but he devotes no enquiry to the cultural consequences of Britain's assimilation into the Roman empire, preferring to trace instead the numerous revolts and disturbances that prevented the Romans from ever fully mastering the island. Milton faces a dilemma here: as a humanist proud of his classical inheritance, he approves of the civilising influence of the classical world, yet he also wants to present the British as a people with a native love of freedom and independence. So he finds himself in Book II describing the long history of resistance to Roman rule by revolting chieftains who are represented as stalwarts for British liberty, and disparaging the growth of Roman culture as an insidious form of servitude. He is in fact silently paraphrasing Tacitus in *Agricola* when he writes how Agricola, after effectively subduing Britain, set about introducing the amenities of Roman life:

> He caus'd moreover the Noblemens Sons to be bred up in Liberal Arts; and by preferring the Witts of *Britan*, before the Studies of *Gallia*, brought them to affect the Latine Eloquence, who before hated the Language. Then were the *Roman* fashions imitated, and the Gown; after a while the incitements also and materials of Vice, and voluptuous life, proud Buildings, Baths, and the elegance of Banqueting; which the foolisher sort call'd Civilitie, but was indeed a secret Art to prepare them for bondage. (p.85)

Though impressed at 'the native and naked British valour defending their country', Milton had difficulty in finding adequate representatives to display British valour combined with virtue. Caractacus had obvious merits, and in rehearsing his history, Milton broke his self-imposed rule of not introducing fictitious speeches after the manner of the ancient historians. Such speeches, he knew, lacked authenticity and imposed a later interpretation on events. 'I affect not set speeches in a Historie, unless known for certain to have bin so spok'n in effect as they are writt'n... and to invent such, though eloquently, as som Historians have done, is an abuse of posteritie, raising, in them that read, other conceptions of those times and persons than were true' (p.79). Caractacus is allowed to speak and express his nobility of mind and honourable bearing, but he is the only character who enjoys this privilege in the book. By denying himself the use of the convention of the set speech, Milton lost an invaluable means of enlarging a character from the meagre details of his sources. In consequence, his British figures develop little substance, in contrast with the agents of Rome whose exploits are extensively reviewed by the classical historians.

Boadicea, who might have served as an exemplary figure of the British desire for liberty, fares ill with Milton. A national heroine in Elizabethan times, praised by Camden and Speed, and the subject of a tragedy by Fletcher, Boadicea repels Milton. Her remorselessness, and the barbarity of her treatment of her victims, disqualified her from any admiration or respect. In her last battle, 'the *Britans* never more plainly manifested themselves to be right *Barbarians*; no rule, no foresight, no forecast, experience or estimation, either of themselves or of thir Enemies; such confusion, such impotence, as seem'd likest not to a Warr, but to the wild hurry of a distracted Woeman, with as mad a Crew at her heeles' (p.80).

Milton's hostility is complicated by his dislike of female leaders, a prejudice that emerges time and again in his *History*. Writing of Cartismunda, Queen of the Brigantes, he had remarked on 'the uncomliness of thir Subjection to the Monarchie of a Woman' (p.73). He expressed his disapprobation of the Empress Agrippina sitting in state with her husband when Caractacus was judged: 'a new and disdained sight to the manly eyes of *Romans*, a Woman sitting public in her Female pride among Ensignes and Armed Cohorts' (p.71). Later on in the *History*, Saxon women who become prominent in public affairs will be frowned upon.

In one area where Milton might be expected to exert his critical faculties most strenuously, he is surprisingly incurious. The subject in question is the origins of Christianity in Britain. It was in Milton's interest to be as well informed in this matter as possible, for the more evidence of the primitive church in Britain that could be found, the more cogently the case for continuing reformation could be fought in the 1640s, as later accretions of doctrine, government and ceremony could be attacked as having no basis in the early church. Faith, patriotism and the antiquarian spirit came together in the seventeenth century to search for the earliest traces of Christianity in Britain, it being a point of honour that the gospel should have reached here at an exceedingly early time. And of course, evidence that self-regulating Christian communities were established in Britain before the Church of Rome stretched its dominion over the West was eagerly sought for, to provide a model and an inspiration for the reformed Christians of the modern age. In the seventeenth century, James Ussher, the Archbishop of Armagh, had extended his prodigious scholarship into the obscurities of Christian beginnings, resulting in his *Britannicarum Ecclesiarum Antiquitates* (1639). Milton used this book, as his marginal notes to the *History* testify, yet he neither employs it to sharpen his own critical enquiries nor does he bother to build up a picture of early Christian life in Britain. He accepts without debate the old story (which at least had Bede for its source, even if its elaboration was provided by Geoffrey) that the dubiously historic Lucius, a British king under the Romans in the late second century, had requested the bishop of Rome to send missionaries to himself and his people. All Milton makes of this episode is to praise Lucius for his voluntary acceptance of the gospel, whilst being cynical of any popular conversion, observing with characteristic suspicion that the nation's 'first professing by publick Authority was no real commendation of thir true faith; which had appear'd more sincere and praise-worthy, whether in this or other Nation, first profess'd without publick Authority or against it, might else have bin but outward conformity' (pp.94-5).[1] He mentions the letter purportedly sent by Lucius to Pope Eleutherius asking for Christian instruction, a letter preserved in a manuscript in Sir Robert Cotton's library, the authenticity of which had been passionately argued over by Stow, Speed, Spelman and Ussher; yet Milton cares little one way or the other, and moves on to cite other stories of the first propagation of the Gospel in Britain, back to Joseph of Arimathea. Milton disclaims responsibility for pronouncing on these matters as being the province of the ecclesiastical historian, but even so, his lack of zeal in trying to establish some critical guidelines in early Christian history must cause one to question Milton's intellectual integrity in writing this work. There is a casualness, a lack of rigour, a failure in the end to seek after truth in the light of reason, that must have helped to discourage Milton from publication for many years.

A similar indifference attends Milton's coverage of the spread of Arianism in late Roman Britain, and the flourishing of Pelagianism, the heresy that was Britain's first contribution to ecclesiastical affairs. Pelagius had been a fourth

[1] It is a typically Miltonic sentiment that he would be more impressed if people had accepted Christianity without official encouragement, or in the face of public authority, than if they had merely followed the lead of the king.

24

century Briton living in Rome who had propounded a doctrine that denied the inheritance of original sin, insisted that man enjoyed the exercise of free will, cast doubt on the theory of strict predestination, and held out the hope of universal redemption. St. Augustine had denounced all these propositions, but Pelagianism had a strong hold on late Roman and early Saxon Britain. In the seventeenth century these ideas had enjoyed a revival, and contributed much to the doctrinal position of the Arminians, whose theology was attractive to Milton in some respects. In reviewing the events of the fourth century, Milton passed over the opportunity to look at the historical sources of the Pelagian controversy, or to represent it as a British challenge to a conservative orthodoxy, with an emphasis on the free will of the individual conscience. It is true that Milton makes it clear that he is not writing an ecclesiastical history, but the heresy did cause disruption in British society, and Milton's slight, rapid allusion to these events seems an odd suppression of interest in matters that were so alive in the mid-seventeenth century.

Milton takes Book II up to the fall of Rome and the withdrawal of the Roman legions from Britain. His closing reflections express the sadness of the classical humanist at the extinction of ancient virtue and the regret of the scholar at the demise of reliable historiography: '...with the Empire fell also what before in this Western World was chiefly *Roman*; Learning, Valour, Eloquence, History,

Civility, and eev'n Language it self, all these together, as it were, with equal pace diminishing, and decaying. Henceforth we are to stear by another sort of Authors...' (pp.115-16). Milton's humanism is offended by the Britons' reluctance to seize their liberty; his scholarly spirit is appalled at his need now to depend on the imperfect writers of the dark ages: '...we must expect, in civil matters to find them dubious Relaters..., in most other matters of Religion, blind, astonish'd, and strook with Superstition as with a Planet; in one word, Monks' (p.116).

However unreliable, unmethodical and frustrating these monkish writers of the Saxon era might be, they were at least readily available to Milton in excellent modern editions. The flourishing of Saxon studies in Elizabethan and Stuart times had been caused by a need to know more about the character and condition of the Anglo-Saxon church, with all the implications this subject had for the recreation of an English church after the Reformation. Further impetus came from lawyers, antiquarians and politicians eager to know about the laws, institutions and modes of government of Anglo-Saxon England as they struggled to define the rights, duties and privileges of Crown, Parliament and the individual in the political campaigns of the early and mid-seventeenth century. The learned compilations that were of particular service to Milton included Ussher's *Britannicarum Ecclesiarum Antiquitates* (1639), already mentioned, the most comprehensive and thorough investigation of the primitive church in Britain, its extent, organisation, doctrines and disputes from earliest times until the mission of St. Augustine at the end of the sixth century; Milton usually refers to this book as *De Primordiis* in his marginal notes. Also in 1639, the jurist and antiquary Henry Spelman had published his *Concilia, Decreta, Leges, Constitutiones in Re Ecclesiarum Orbis Britannici*, which furnished an immense and reliable collection of Saxon documents and a coherent account of church and society in the Saxon period. Spelman had established a chair at Cambridge for the study of Anglo-Saxon, first occupied by Abraham Wheelock, whose research led to the publication of an excellent edition of Bede's *Church History* in 1643, along with an edition of the *Anglo-Saxon Chronicle* in Old English, accompanied by a translation into Latin. In 1644, Wheelock reissued this volume together with William Lambarde's *Archaionomia*, a collection of Anglo-Saxon laws with Latin translations, first published in 1568. So, in terms of source material, Milton was better placed than any of his predecessors to write an informed history of the Saxon period. Even though Milton was not conversant with the Anglo-Saxon language, the texts were open to him.

Milton certainly thought of Book III as the critical section of his History. It runs from the departure of the Romans up to events just before the arrival of St. Augustine. In his introduction he insists that there are telling analogies to be drawn between the state of Britain in the mid-fifth century and the mid-seventeenth century. The common factor is the behaviour of a people when exceptional political liberty lies within their reach. The third book

> may deserve attention more than common, and repay it with like benefit to them that can judiciously read: considering especially that the late Civil Broils had cast us into a condition not much unlike to what the *Britans* then were in, when the Imperial Jurisdiction departing hence left them to the sway of thir own Councils; which times by comparing seriously with these later, and that confused Anarchy with this interreign, we may be able from two such remarkable turns of State, producing like events among us, to raise a knowledge of our selvs both great and weighty, by judging hence what kind of men the *Britans* generally are in matters of so high enterprise, how by nature, industry, or custom fitted to attempt or undergoe matters of so main consequence. (pp.117-18)

That hardly imaginable age, the middle of the fifth century, excites Milton because then, for the only time in recorded history, the British people had the chance of freedom and independence from an occupying power. The Romans withdrew, leaving the British to make what they would of their unsought liberty. What, Milton wishes to explore, was the temper of the British race then, how well prepared in spirit and ability for this sudden challenge of freedom? What could one infer about their character after centuries of Roman rule?

28

Was there an instinctive passion for liberty, a constructive genius in the people that would enable them to convert a historical opportunity into a permanent condition of independence? The questions were of pressing interest to Milton because he believed that once again, in the late 1640s, Britain confronted the challenge of freedom, this time achieved by force of arms in civil war. The King had been toppled, the whole structure of government associated with royal domination had been broken, the church hierarchy destroyed, and all the ecclesiastical and prerogative courts abolished. For the first time in twelve hundred years, the British people had gained a freedom from oppressive constraints, and had the chance to renovate their political state. What was the likelihood of success? Could the experience of the remote past furnish a lesson for the present? Milton evidently thought so. As a man of humanist education, he shared the common assumption that the history of the ancient world was a guide to the behaviour of men in the political circumstances of modern times. Human nature remained constant in certain respects. In the spheres of war and politics, for example, unity of purpose, enterprise in leadership, resolution sustained by faith, activism, dedication to values beyond those of personal power, these qualities would sustain a cause. Although the British then were no longer the British now, after all the admixture of successive invasions, some kind of characteristics must persist, and indeed the reformed and civilised British of the seventeenth century must be regarded as a more hopeful race than their rough ancestors.

Although not dealing here with readily comparable circumstances, Milton believes that the general situation, of a nation long oppressed and now given the responsibilities of liberty, justifies some analogies at least. When he looks at what is known of the state of Britain after the Roman exodus, his view is thoroughly pessimistic. No doubt the pessimism was charged with the despondency he felt at the failure of his fellow Englishmen and revolutionaries to utilise the advantage of their victories to create a more just and liberal society. The emotional dismay with which he recounts the confusion of the fifth century British is the displaced reaction to his contemporaries' behaviour. The burden of his complaint is that

> so soon as they felt by proof the weight of what it was to govern well themselves, and what was wanting within them, not stomach or the love of licence, but the Wisdom, the Virtue, the Labour, to use and maintain True Libertie, they soon remitted their heat, and shrunk more wretchedly under the burden of their own Libertie, than before under a Foren Yoke (p.118).

They soon found the strain of freedom intolerable, and before long sent embassies to request their masters the Romans to return, just as, after the painful experiment of the Commonwealth, the English would ask the Stuarts to return and rule. Milton does not make the last point, and almost certainly wrote Book III before the Restoration, but the parallel would not be lost on the first readers of the *History*. The Romans sent only temporary assistance, and thereafter the British, through 'sloth', factionalism and incompetence, as well as through religious division, disintegrated under the incursions of the Picts, Scots, and most formidably, the Saxons.

Milton finds his chief guide to these grim years totally in harmony with his own temperament at the time of writing. Gildas, writing in the mid-sixth century, was a chronicler of doom. His *De Excidio Britanniae*, which can be translated as 'The Ruin, or Destruction, of Britain', was the calamitous record of British collapse in the post-Roman era, a book of lamentation for the vices of the nation that were responsible for its overthrow. Gildas had been available in print ever since Polydore Vergil had first edited him in 1525. Milton was using the text provided by Jerome Commelin in *Rerum Britannicarum Scriptores*, published in Heidelberg in 1587. There had also been an English translation by Thomas Habington in 1638, so the work was well known to the historically minded. In utilising it for his own *History*, Milton exploited the mixture of lament and denunciation in Gildas to set the tone for his own discourse. The long section on the perversity of the British people and the corruption of the clergy on pp. 126-8 is derived closely from Gildas. History did repeat itself, with variations, and historians, taking a long view, pass similar judgements in diverse ages.

31

The misguided strategy of Vortigern in inviting the Saxons to defend England against the Picts interests Milton particularly as a specimen of short-sighted policy with dire long-term consequences, but he is equally engaged by the sexual politics of the Saxon leader Hengist, who baited Vortigern with his daughter to the great disadvantage of the Britons. The future author of *Samson* made a note to consider this episode for a possible tragedy.[2] Vortigern's successor as chief monarch, the Romano-British Ambrosius Aurelianus, commands Milton's respect as the last man of distinction in the expiring world of Britain. But as for Arthur, Arthur beloved of the poets, Milton has little time to spare or willingness to believe. The writer who had been so indulgent to Brutus and his line, 'in favour of our English Poets and Rhetoricians, who by their art will know how to use them judiciously', has grown more rigorous as he proceeded: '...who *Arthur* was, and whether ever any such reign'd in *Britan*, hath bin doubted heertofore, and may again with good reason' (p. 144). By Book III, Milton's trust in Geoffrey of Monmouth and William of Malmesbury as credible recorders has become exceedingly weak, and he has little respect either for 'Nennius', the eighth century Welsh monk whose *Historia Brittonum* chronicled events up to the mid-seventh century, and whom Milton dismissed as 'a very trivial

[2]   See Appendix II.

Writer yet extant' (p.145).'[3] Perhaps it was the growing seriousness of analysis in the politically charged Book III that caused Milton to distance himself from the Arthurian stories, which he had in easier days contemplated as a subject for an epic poem; now he hastens on, saying 'he who can accept of Legends for good story, may quickly swell a volume with trash' (p.145).

The third book ends with the establishment of the Saxons, and the surviving British driven 'out of a fair Country, into a Mountanous and Barren Corner'. By this time, Milton had developed a considerable distaste for the British, regarding them as 'a perverse nation' who have brought their destruction upon themselves by their divided condition, poor leadership, 'her princes and others given to vicious ease', and by their backsliding from the pure faith that had been so early established in the island.

---

[3] Nennius was first edited by Thomas Gale in 1691, though his work had been extensively quoted by Ussher in his volume of 1639. It has been argued that Milton might have used the Cambridge MSS of Nennius for his *History of Britain*. If this is the case, it is the only instance of Milton using manuscript material for his *History*. See Constance Nicholas, *Introduction and Notes to Milton's History of Britain* (Urbana, Illinois, 1957). Also Harry Glicksman, 'The Sources of Milton's *History of Britain*', in *Studies by Members of the Department of English, University of Wisconsin Studies in Language and Literature*, XI, Madison, Wisconsin, 1920.

There is an extra dimension of interest in the third book, for it is here that the notorious *Digression* belongs. (The *Digression* is here printed as an appendix.) The circumstances are as follows. In 1681, eleven years after the publication of the *History*, a pamphlet entitled 'Mr. John Milton's Character of the Long Parliament and Assembly of Divines in MDCXLI' appeared. This claimed to be a part of *The History of Britain* that had been omitted from its original publication, perhaps for being too offensive and harsh. The *Digression* rammed home with considerable force the analogies between the lost opportunities of the Britons in the mid-fifth century and the politics of Milton's own time, and it directed its attack particularly against the Long Parliament and the Westminster Assembly of Divines for their failure to secure for the nation the benefits of liberty gained from the conflicts of the Civil War. Having made some telling comparisons between ancient and modern times, Milton moves his narrative into the present, and angrily attacks Parliament for its betrayal of 'the Publick Faith'. Instead of reform there have been new taxation and new abuses. Men of no merit have filled high places, and have been able 'to huckster the Commonwealth'. Loans to Parliament have not been repaid, and there are 'innumerable thieves in office'. The clerics charged with reform have failed, perpetuating the abuses they were supposed to cure, such as pluralism, non-residency and the use of magistrates to enforce religion. Not only have the politicians and divines failed to advance the cause of reformation, but their misconduct has corrupted the people they were supposed to serve. 'For liberty hath a sharp and double edge, fit only to be handled by just and virtuous men; to bad and dissolute, it becomes a mischief in their own hands.' The intemperate rhetoric of Milton, familiar from the anti-episcopal pamphlets of the 1640s, flares out again in denunciation of the guardians of the public interest in church and Parliament. They are no better, he suggests, than the dismal post-Roman Britons before them, 'entangled and oppressed with things too hard and generous above their strain and temper'. One could object that liberty in the fifth century and in the seventeenth meant two plain different things, but Milton does not allow a pause for such cavils. He continues: the British are 'stout and courageous in war' but unable 'to govern justly and prudently in peace, trusting only to their mother-wit'. They are 'valiant indeed to win a field, but to know the end and reason of winning, injudicious and unwise'. The reasons for this failure may lie in climate (the old Aristotelian explanation), but most assuredly poor education and the lack of acquaintance with 'ancient and illustrious deeds' from the best ages mean that the British lack the spur to emulation of great models.

When restored to Book III, the *Digression* vitalises the narrative and gives a new interest to dark age events by enforced comparisons. It reveals something of Milton's temper when writing the *History*, and helps to explain his frequent scorn for the character and conduct of the British, and later the Saxons, as the frustrations of the present are displaced back into the remote past. It also serves to show how the unlikeliest episodes of history can be given a modern relevance, and should alert the reader to the probability that many other events of British and Saxon history contained covert references to contemporary affairs, a matter that will be raised again at the end of this introduction.

The *Digression* has attracted more critical attention in recent times than *The History of Britain* itself. Several issues have arisen, notably: when was the *Digression* composed, what people and what events does it attack under its general terms of denunciation, where should it be inserted, and why was it omitted from the first printing of the *History*? Its omission may be put down to the irrelevance of the passage in 1670. As for its position in Book III, Thomas Birch, who first included the *Digression* in his edition of the *History* in *Milton's Works* (1738), inserted it after the first paragraph of Book III, after the phrase 'great undertakings' on page 118, and there it remained in later editions. However, in 1926 a manuscript copy of the *Digression* came to light, slightly different in its content from the 1681 'Character'. This manuscript, now in the library of Harvard College, is prefaced by an instruction to insert the *Digression* on page 130, after the words 'from one misery to another'. This location is now preferred to the one chosen by Birch.[4]

The date of the *Digression* has been much argued over. The years 1647-48 have been the preferred date, when after the Civil War the benefits of victory were slipping away in the confusion of cross-purposes and when the disillusion with both Army and Parliament as leaders in reconstruction was intense. The wrangling and divisiveness that followed the Civil War, before the execution of King Charles imposed a new direction on events, could well have provided the occasion for Milton's outburst of frustration and despair.[5] Recently, a new approach

[4]   For a full discussion of the differences between the printed and manuscript versions of the *Digression*, and its placing, see French Fogle's introduction to the two pieces in the Yale Edition of the *Complete Prose Works of John Milton*, New Haven 1971, Vol. V, pp. 405-35. Fogle's introduction is the most substantial account of the *History* in print, but the unpublished Ph.D. thesis of Martin Michael Dzelzainis, 'The Ideological Context of John Milton's *History of Britain*' (Cambridge, 1983), has much to add to Fogle. The Yale edition provides detailed references for all of Milton's source material, as well as an extensive commentary on the text.

[5]   Sir Charles Firth seems to have been the first to assign the *Digression* to 1647-8 in 'Milton as an Historian' in *Proceedings of the British Academy*, III, 1907-8. He has been followed by most commentators, including French Fogle in the Yale edition, and Christopher Hill in *Milton and the Puritan Revolution* (London, 1977). Fogle is inclined to see the influence of the Leveller tracts of 1647 on the *Digression*.

by Austin Woolrych has argued persuasively for a later date, 1660, just after the Restoration of Charles II, when the cause of liberty was definitively lost.[6] Woolrych is inclined to believe that Milton composed the *Digression* after he had written Books III and IV, and sees similarities in tone and purpose with *A Ready and an Easy Way to Establish a Free Commonwealth* of early 1660. The finality of the collapse of 'The Good Old Cause' seems absolute in the *Digression*, a point of view which would suit 1660. In Woolrych's view, the true parallel intended with the fifth century was not the failure to seize liberty when offered, but 'between the Britons' self-imposed subjection to the Saxons and England's willing resubmission to the yoke of monarchy'.[7]

Book IV takes up the history of England under the Saxons. We assume that this book was written after 1652, for one of his sources for this period, the *Historia Regum Anglorum* of Simeon of Durham, was only published in this year. For the most part, Milton is dependent here on Bede, about whom he has mixed feelings: he regards him as a fairly reliable chronicler, but infuriatingly preoccupied with ecclesiastical history to the exclusion of civil

[6] See Austin Woolrych, 'The Date of the *Digression* in Milton's *History of Britain* in *For Veronica Wedgwood These*, ed. R. Ollard and P. Tudor-Craig (London, 1986), pp. 217-46.

[7] Ibid., p.221.

affairs. Moreover, Bede's fascination with miracles and the supernatural means that Milton has to read his history through a haze of superstition. But after Bede, there are only 'obscure and blockish Chronicles' (p.203). Milton announces that he has dutifully read them to sift out our ancient story from 'fables and impertinences', and to save others 'the like unpleasing labour'. There is evident here a Miltonic scorn for the antiquarians, those who are interested in the past for its own sake, and 'who take pleasure all their lifetime raking the foundations of old abbeys and cathedrals'. Presumably he has in mind here men like Roger Dodsworth and William Dugdale, who were collecting material for their *Monasticon Anglicanum* (1655), who had respect for the monastic system and were prepared to take the early medieval world at its own value. Milton wants his past to shed light on the present.

So, as he opens Book IV with the arrival of St. Augustine's mission to Ethelbert, the event that brought in a Roman domination in church affairs, he sees the origins of episcopal superiority and pride, and the imposition of Romish authority in matters of the spirit, a presumptuousness that was still retained by the order of bishops in Milton's own time. He notes how the new archbishops of Canterbury had themselves buried with kings, and pays special attention to Augustine's attempts to make the surviving British bishops conform to the Roman model. The British bishops, coming from their strongholds in Wales and the west, refused to submit, with the result that Augustine inspired a war against them and their people. In this conflict the thoughtful reader may see the first flickerings of an antagonism between the men of simple faith and the Rome-inclined clergy that would reach its height in the seventeenth century.

The conversion of the Saxons, and their frequent backslidings into paganism, take up much of the chapter. Earlier writers such as Camden had remarked on the wonderful readiness of the Saxons to receive Christianity as a sign of the natural disposition of the ancestors of the English to the gospel. Milton is sceptical of Saxon piety: it seems superficial, frequently distorted by barbarism, and easily shed. It also had a deplorable fondness for monasteries, with 'Kings one after another leaving thir Kingly Charge, to run thir heads fondly into a Monks Cowle' (p.202). This evasion of the responsibilities of state exposed the Saxon kingdom to the perils of chaotic succession. Milton has more sympathy with the faintly surviving Christianity of the British, who, he says, quoting Bede, held little communion with the Saxon Christians. One expects to hear this theme amplified as the *History* proceeds, with the British line becoming an underground link with the Reformation, but Milton fails or forgets to develop it.

The Saxons as a race he finds tiresome and exasperating. Their early valour declines, they prove endlessly fissile through their fighting and intrigues. Partly, Milton admits, the poverty of his source material is to blame for his impatience, for

40

there are many saints' lives and much church history, but only a fragmentary civil history. He is reduced to a bare outline of events enacted by the meagre shades of men. Milton's frustration with his subject matter is palpable. 'So many bare and reasonless actions, so many names of kings one after another' leave him cold. Far from writing a humanist history of his nation, he is reduced to a lean journal and threadbare lists. The real challenge of writing a detailed and interpretative history of Saxon England does not occur to him. He is working in a hurry, and depends entirely on printed sources. The barbarity of his subject alienates him: it is not the Tacitean task he had envisaged. His comment 'neither do I care to wrincle the smoothness of History with rugged names of places unknown, better harp'd at by *Camden* and the Chorographers' (p.209) betrays his sad recognition of the gulf between how he imagines history should be written, inspired by classical models, and what he finds himself doing, piecing together the patchy and incoherent accounts of primitive tribes. His well-known words that express his despair at trying to make sense of the 'bickerings' of Saxon war-lords, vaguely mentioned without time or place by monkish chroniclers, sum up his feelings of futility: 'what more worth is it than to Chronicle the Warrs of Kites, or Crows, flocking and fighting in the Air?' (p.216).

Given his complaints about Saxon barbarity, it is understandable that Milton should single out for praise the occasional example of what he calls 'civility' in Saxon times, a term that includes respect for classical learning and a desire to see society regulated by laws. Ethelbert, king of Kent, was an early figure of hope: 'a favourer of all Civility in that rude Age. He gave Laws and Statutes after the example of *Roman* Emperors, written with the advice of his sagest counsellors, but in the *English* Tongue' (p.171). Kent, with its nearness to the continent, was the favoured place for civility. Under King Egbert, Theodore, 'a learned *Greekish* monk of *Tarsus*', became Archbishop of Canterbury, under whom 'the *Greek* and *Latin* Tongue, with other Liberal Arts, Arithmetic, Music, Astronomie, and the like, began first to flourish among the *Saxons*' (p.191). Ina of the West Saxons 'made good laws' which remained extant in Milton's day, having been printed by Lambarde in his *Archaionomia* and by Spelman in his *Concilia*. Alcuin in York was a tower of learning, in communication with Charlemagne. So, by degrees, civility advanced. But the general condition of the Saxons, as the Danes began to make their attacks on England around 800, was morally abhorrent in Milton's eyes, with 'all the same Vices which Gildas alleg'd of old to have ruin'd the *Britans*' (p.221). Another age had ended in ruin.

Taking stock of events at the beginning of Book V, Milton introduces a new theme into his *History*: that of divine punishment. As the Saxon kingdoms fell under the rule of one king, Egbert, who could be regarded as the first true King of England, 'men might with som reason have expected from such Union, Peace and Plenty, Greatness, and the flourishing of all Estates and Degrees' (p.222). But no: instead of prosperity, the Danish raiders came. Milton interprets this development as a retribution on the Saxons for their many vices: 'brok'n with luxury and sloth, either secular or superstitious', neither valorous in arms nor rigorous in faith, they have incurred divine condemnation; 'when God hath decreed servitude on a sinful Nation, fitted by thir own Vices for no condition but servile, all Estates of Government are alike unable to avoid it' (p.223). One would have expected Milton to emphasise the role of divine providence in the history of his country from the very outset of his work. His whole outlook was attuned to the idea of the providential guidance of nations, and his pamphleteering of the 1640s frequently presented England as the theatre of God's judgements. Yet the *History* is restrained in this respect: whilst it is inevitably a moral record, it does not often call attention to the operations of divine justice. Even here, where Milton declares that the Danes were sent as a punishment on the Saxons, he may only be repeating the sentiments of his source, Henry of Huntingdon, who takes a similar view of these events.

Besides Henry of Huntingdon, Milton's main source for the period of Danish invasions was the thirteenth century chronicler called Matthew of

Westminster, exposed in the nineteenth century as a fictional author, whose work was a compilation based on the chronicle of Matthew Paris. Milton also made use of the *Life of Alfred* by the ninth century Welsh monk Asser that had been printed by Matthew Parker in 1574 and reprinted by Camden in 1603, and the *Anglo-Saxon Chronicle*, made available with the Anglo-Saxon text accompanied by a parallel Latin translation by Abraham Wheelock in 1643.

Once Egbert is reached, Milton can recount English history by reigns, and does so with increasing fullness as his source material improves. The fluctuation of Saxon fortunes against the Danes detains him for a while. Alfred holds the centre of attention here. For the first time in the *History*, we have a rounded and informed character of a king, one who commands Milton's admiration for his personal qualities, his love of learning and the arts, and his political skills in rallying the English in a dark time. Edgar too compels his admiration, but the occasional capable king does not shake Milton's conviction that Saxon England of the ninth and tenth centuries was politically unstable, and only marginally civilised. Good government seems an unattainable ideal.

The catalogue of humiliations and calamities continues throughout the last book. Ethelred's ignominious submission to the Danes is given a shameful prominence. The storm of devastation unleashed by the Danes over England is vividly remembered, with Milton's language reaching for an apocalyptic intensity as he describes the near 'destruction of mankind' by the remorseless Danes 'sallying out of their ships as out of savage dens', and 'like wild beasts glutted' retreating to their caves; 'like wild beasts, or rather sea-monsters to their water-stables' they return, only to make yet more sorties against a defenceless land. This is the racking of Britain, the punishing of a nation for its sins and infidelities as the Lord punished Israel with plagues and violent oppression. The eventual establishment of Danish kings in England is represented as a deserved subjection to foreign rulers. When Edward the Confessor attained the throne after the Danish line had faltered, he was strong enough to cease paying Danegeld, but by his close association with the Normans he opened the door to further troubles. Milton is impressed by Edward's capacity for survival, but not by his sanctity. He mentions in passing Edward's power of healing by touch, a power claimed by the Stuarts in Milton's time as evidence of the supernatural qualities of kingship, but refuses to offer an opinion on the matter: perhaps his indirect reporting carries its own sceptical message.

Finally Harold is elected king, makes his way to Hastings, and is overwhelmed by William. 'The yoke of an outlandish conqueror' is imposed. Here Milton breaks off his narrative, and does not stay to draw conclusions. There is little sense of a considered end to the book, only a certain sense of relief at finishing a survey of 'the misery and thraldom' of our ancestors. Blame for England's complete collapse before the Normans is harshly assigned: inadequate kings, a dissolute aristocracy, a clergy grown corrupt and illiterate. The common people were deprived of leadership and spiritual care.

The *History* ends with the brusque observation that the 'like Vices without amendment' might bring 'the Revolution of like Calamities'. Whether the last brief paragraph was added as a muted comment on the Restoration scene when the *History* was published in 1670 is not certainly known, but seems likely. It is unclear when Milton wrote the final two books of the work, as there is little evidence internally or externally to indicate the time of composition. The late 1650s would be a likely time, in view of his correspondence with the French scholar Henri de Brass in 1657 about the difficulties of writing history. In that correspondence Milton mentioned his admiration for Sallust as the exemplary historian, combining brevity, terseness and abundance of matter, narrated gravely 'in pure and chaste speech'. The contrast between Sallust's taut narrative of well defined and politically significant events with Milton's rough ordering of the chaotic bickerings of a semi-barbaric society, imperfectly transmitted by monkish chroniclers, is a painful one: it points up Milton's evident exasperation with his own *History* and helps to explain why he abandoned the attempt to carry it forward to his own age.

It is easy to see why the *History* was not published in the early years of the Restoration.

Milton was in great disfavour with the new regime, and came close to being executed as the apologist for the regicides. The vigorous censorship that clamped down on the press would ensure Milton's silence, and he published nothing between 1660 and 1667, when *Paradise Lost* was printed. Even when the *History* came out in 1670, we learn from John Toland, the editor of Milton's *Works* in 1698, that the censors 'expung'd several passages of it wherein he exposed the Superstition, Pride and Cunning of the Popish Monks in the Saxon Times, but apply'd by the sagacious Licencers to Charles the Second's Bishops'.[8] What else might have gone undetected by the censors? It was a common seventeenth century assumption that a history would bear in some way on the contemporary scene. A recent essay by Gary D. Hamilton has tried to identify a few instances where Milton's anecdotes of Saxon kings seem to reflect on Stuart politics, but they are of minor significance in themselves. More to the point is his observation that readers in 1670, knowing the author to be Milton, would expect something critical of monarchy and episcopacy, and would know how to read between the lines.[9] Bunyan, on the title-page of *Pilgrim's Progress*,

8   Life of Milton in *Works*, 1698, I.43.

9   See Gary D. Hamilton, '*The History of Britain* and its Restoration Audience', in *Politics, Poetics and Hermeneutics in Milton's Prose*, ed. D. Lowenstein and J.G. Turner (Cambridge, 1990), pp. 240-55.

quotes the verse 'I have used similitudes', and Milton his contemporary no doubt used historical similitudes in his long narrative of English events. Merely to end the book with the submission to the Norman yoke was suggestive in itself, for that concept was charged with associations of royal supremacy, an oppressive aristocratic and ecclesiastical establishment, a system of feudal tenure and the denial of popular rights.[10] As far as Milton and the supporters of the Good Old Cause were concerned, after 1660 the British had once again submitted to that yoke in the form of the restored monarchy and church.

In the last analysis, the questions that exercised Milton in *The History of Britain* were not to be resolved by historical enquiry. Why the British were unable to seize the opportunities for freedom that occurred at the critical juncture of their history, why good government was so difficult to achieve, and true Christian zeal so hard to sustain, why the leaders and the people fall prey to sloth and greed and kindred vices, and ultimately why the perfections of political life were and remain unattainable, these questions have to be referred back to first causes, to the transactions of Paradise, and man's first disobedience and the Fall. The *History of Britain* really needs to be read in the light of *Paradise Lost*.

Graham Parry, *University of York*

[10] See Christopher Hill's essay, 'The Norman Yoke' in *Puritanism and Revolution* (London, 1968), pp. 58-125.

THE
HISTORY
OF
BRITAIN,

That Part especially now call'd

ENGLAND.

From the first Traditional Beginning,
Continu'd to the

NORMAN CONQUEST.

Collected out of the Antientest and
Best Authours thereof by

JOHN MILTON.

LONDON,
Printed by *J. M.* for *John Martyn* at the
Sign of the *Bell* in St *Paul's Church-Yard,*
MDCLXXVII.

THE
HISTORY
OF
BRITAIN,

That Part especially now call'd
ENGLAND;

Continu'd to the
Norman Conquest.

BOOK I.

THe Beginning of Nations, thofe ex-
cepted of whom Sacred Books have
fpok'n, is to this day unknown.
Nor only the Beginning, but the
Deeds alfo of many fucceeding Ages, yea,
periods of Ages, either wholly unknown, or
obfcur'd and blemifht with Fables. Whether
it were that the ufe of Letters came in long
after, or were it the violence of Barbarous
A 3   Inundations,

Inundations, or they themselves at certain
Revolutions of Time, fatally decaying, and
degenerating into Sloth and Ignorance;
wherby the Monuments of more ancient civility have bin som destroy'd, som lost. Perhaps dif-esteem and contempt of the Public
Affairs then present, as not worth recording, might partly be in cause. Certainly oft-
times we see that wise Men, and of best Abi-
litie have forborn to Write the Acts of thir
own Daies, while they beheld with a just
loathing and disdain, not only how Unworthy, how Pervers, how Corrupt, but often
how Ignoble, how Petty, how below all History the persons and thir Actions were; who
either by Fortune, or som rude Election had
attain'd as a sore Judgment, and Ignominie
upon the Land, to have Cheif Sway in mana-
ging the Common-wealth. But that any Law,
or Superstition of our Old Philosophers the
Druids forbad the *Britans* to write thir Memorable Deeds, I know not why any out of
Cæsar should allege : He indeed saith, that
thir Doctrine they thought not lawful to
commit to Letters; but in most matters else,
both Privat, and Public, among which well
may History be reck'nd, they us'd the Greek
Tongue : And that the *British Druids*, who
taught those in *Gaule* would be ignorant of
any Language known and us'd by thir Disciples, or so frequently writing other things,
and so inquisitive into highest, would for
want of Recording be ever Children in the
Knowledge of Times and Ages, is not likely.
What

Cæf. l. 6.

What ever might be the reaſon, this we find, that of *Britiſh Affairs*, from the firſt peopling of the Iland to the coming of *Julius Cæſar*, nothing certain, either by Tradition, Hiſtory, or Ancient Fame hath hitherto bin left us. That which we have of oldeſt ſeeming, hath by the greater part of judicious Antiquaries bin long rejected for a Modern Fable.

Neverthelefs there being others beſides the firſt ſuppos'd Author, men not unread, nor unlearned in Antiquitie, who admitt that for approved Story, which the former explode for Fiction, and ſeeing that oft-times Relations heretofore accounted Fabulous, have bin after found to contain in them many foot-ſteps, and reliques of ſomthing true, as what we read in Poets of the Flood, and Giants little beleev'd, till undoubted witneſſes taught us, that all was not fain'd; I have therefore determin'd to beſtow the telling over ev'n of theſe reputed Tales; be it for nothing elſe but in favour of our Engliſh Poets, and Rhetoricians, who by thir Art will know, how to uſe them judiciouſly.

I might alſo produce Example, as *Diodorus* among the *Greeks*, *Livie* and others of the *Latines*, *Polydore* and *Virunnius* accounted among our own Writers.   But I intend not with Controverſies and Quotations to delay or interrupt the ſmooth courſe of Hiſtory; much leſs to argue and debate long who were the firſt Inhabitants, with what Probabilities, what Authorities each Opinion hath bin upheld, but ſhall endevor that which hitherto

hath bin needed moſt, with plain, and light-
ſom brevity, to relate well and orderly things
worth the Noting, ſo as may beſt inſtruct and
benefit them that read. Which imploring
Divine Aſſiſtance, that it may redound to his
Glory, and the good of the *Britiſh* Nation, *I
now begin.*

That the whole Earth was Inhabited before
the Flood, and to the utmoſt point of habi-
table Ground, from thoſe effectual words of
God in the Creation, may be more than conjectur'd. Hence that this Iland alſo had her
Dwellers, her Affairs, and perhaps her Stories, ev'n in that Old World thoſe many
hunderd years, with much reaſon we may inferr. After the Flood, and the diſperſing of
Nations, as they journey'd leaſurely from the
Eaſt, *Gomer* the eldeſt Son of *Japhet*, and his
Off-ſpring, as by Authorities, Arguments, and
Affinitie of divers names is generally beleev'd, were the firſt that peopl'd all theſe
Weſt and Northren Climes. But they of our
own Writers, who thought they had don nothing, unleſs with all circumſtance they tell
us when, and who firſt ſet foot upon this
Iland, preſume to name out of fabulous and
counterfet Authors a certain *Samothes* or *Dis*,
a fowrth or ſixt Son of *Japhet*, whom they
make about 200 years after the Flood, to
have planted with Colonies; firſt the Continent of *Celtica*, or *Gaule*, and next *this Iland*;
Thence to have nam'd it *Samothea*, to have
Reign'd heer, and after him Lineally fowr
Kings, *Magus*, *Saron*, *Druis*, and *Bardus*. But
the

the forg'd *Berosus*, whom only they have to cite, no where mentions that either hee, or any of those whom they bring, did ever pass into *Britan*, or send thir people hither.   So that this Outlandish figment may easily excuse our not allowing it the room heer so much as of a *British* Fable.

That which follows, perhaps as wide from truth, though seeming less impertinent, is, that these *Samotheans* under the Reign of *Bardus* were subdu'd by *Albion* a Giant, Son of *Neptune:* who call'd the Iland after his own name, and rul'd it 44 years. Till at length passing over into *Gaul*, in aid of his Brother *Lestrygon*, against whom *Hercules* was hasting out of *Spain* into *Italy*, he was there slain in fight, and *Bergion* also his Brother.

Sure anough we are, that *Britan* hath bin anciently term'd *Albion*, both by the *Greeks* and *Romans*. And *Mela* the Geographer makes mention of a stonie shoar in *Languedoc*, where by report such a Battel was fought. The rest, as his giving name to the Ile, or ever landing heer, depends altogether upon late surmises. But too absurd, and too unconscionably gross is that fond invention that wafted hither the fifty Daughters of a strange *Dioclesian King of Syria* ; brought in doubtless by some illiterate pretender to somthing mistak'n in the common Poetical Story of *Danaus King of Argos*, while his vanity, not pleas'd with the obscure beginning which truest Antiquity affords the Nation, labour'd to contrive us a Pedigree, as he thought, more noble.   These
                                                    Daughters

Daughters by appointment of *Danaus* on the Mariage-night having murder'd all thir Husbands, except *Linceus*, whom his Wives loialty sav'd, were by him at the suit of his Wife thir Sister, not put to death, but turn'd out to Sea in a Ship unmann'd; of which whole Sex they had incurr'd the hate : and as the Tale goes, were driv'n on *this Iland*. Where the Inhabitants, none but Devils, as som write, or as others, a lawless crew left heer by *Albion* without Head or Governour, both entertain'd them, and had issue by them a second breed of Giants, who tyranniz'd *the Ile*, till *Brutus* came.

The Eldest of these Dames in thir Legend they call *Albina*; and from thence, for which cause the whole Scene was fram'd, will have the name *Albion* deriv'd. Incredible it may seem so sluggish a conceit should prove so ancient, as to be authoriz'd by the Elder *Ninnius*, reputed to have liv'd above a thousand years agoe. This I find not in him; but that *Hi-* Holinſhed. *stion* sprung of *Japhet*, had four Sons; *Francus, Romanus, Alemannus*, and *Britto*, of whom the *Britans*; as true, I beleeve, as that those other Nations whose names are resembl'd, came of the other three; if these Dreams give not just occasion to call in doubt the Book it self, which bears that title.

Hitherto the things themselves have giv'n us a warrantable dispatch to run them soon over. But now of *Brutus* and his Line, with the whole Progeny of Kings, to the entrance of *Julius Cæſar*, we cannot so easily be discharg'd;

charg'd ; Defcents of Anceftry, long continu'd
Laws and Exploits not plainly feeming to be
borrow'd, or devis'd, which on the common
beleif have wrought no fmall impreffion : defended by many, deny'd utterly by few. For
what though *Brutus*, and the whole *Trojan* pretence were yeelded up, feeing they who firft
devis'd to bring us from fom noble Anceftor
were content at firft with *Brutus* the Conful ;
till better invention, although not willing to
forgoe the name, taught them to remove it
higher into a more fabulous Age, and by the
fame remove lighting on the *Trojan* Tales in
affectation to make the *Britan* of one Original
with the *Roman*, pitch'd there, yet thofe old
and inborn names of fucceffive Kings, never
any to have bin real perfons, or don in thir
lives at leaft fom part of what fo long hath
bin remember'd, cannot be thought without
too ftrict an incredulity.

For thefe, and thofe caufes above mention'd,
that which hath receav'd approbation from
fo many, I have chos'n not to omitt. Certain
or uncertain, be that upon the credit of thofe
whom I muft follow; fo far as keeps alooff
from impoffible and abfurd, attefted by ancient Writers from Books more ancient I re-
fufe not, as the due and proper fubject of Story. The principal Author is well know'n to
be *Geoffrey* of *Monmouth*; what he was, and *Henry* of
whence his Authority, who in his Age, or be- *Hunting-*
fore him have deliver'd the fame matter, and *don.*
fuch like general Difcourfes, will better ftand *Matthew*
in a Treatife by themfelvs. All of them agree *of Weftmin-*
fter.

in

in this, that *Brutus* was the Son of *Silvius*; he
of *Ascanius*; whose Father was *Æneas* a *Tro-*
jan Prince, who at the burning of that City,
with his Son *Ascanius*, and a collected number that escap'd, after long wandring on the
Sea, arriv'd in *Italy*. Where at length, by the
assistance of *Latinus King of Latium*, who had
giv'n him *his Daughter Lavinia*, he obtain'd to
succeed in that Kingdom, and left it to *Asca-*
nius, whose Son *Silvius* (though *Roman* Histories deny *Silvius* to be Son of *Ascanius*) had
maried secretly a Neece of *Lavinia*.

She being with Child, the matter became
known to *Ascanius*. Who commanding his
Magicians to enquire by Art, what sex the Maid
had conceiv'd, had answer, *that it was one who*
should be the death of both his Parents; and ba-
nish'd for the fact, should after all in a farr Coun-
try attain to highest honour. The prediction
fail'd not, for in travel the Mother di'd. And
Brutus (the Child was so call'd) at fifteen years
of Age, attending his Father to the Chace,
with an Arrow unfortunately kill'd him.

Banish'd therefore by his Kindred he retires
into *Greece*. Where meeting with the Race
of *Helenus King Priams Son*, held there in Servile condition by *Pandrasus then King*, with
them he abides. For *Pirrhus* in revenge of his
Father slain at *Troy* had brought thither with
him *Helenus*, and many others into servitude. There *Brutus* among his own Stock so
thrives in Vertue and in Arms, as renders him
belov'd to Kings, and great Captains above
all the Youth of that Land. Wherby the
Trojans

Trojans not only begin to hope, but secretly to move him, that he would lead them the way to liberty. They allege their numbers, and the promis'd help of *Assaracus* a Noble Greek-ish Youth, by the Mothers side a *Trojan*, whom for that cause his Brother went about to dispossess of certain Castles bequeath'd him by his Father. *Brutus* considering both the Forces offer'd him, and the strength of those Holds, not unwillingly consents.

First therefore having fortifi'd those Castles, he with *Assaracus* and the whole multitude betake them to the Woods and Hills ; as the safest place from whence to expostulate ; and in the name of all sends to *Pandrasus* this Message ; *That the* Trojans *holding it unworthy thir Ancestors to serve in a Foren Kingdom, had retreated to the Woods ; choosing rather a Savage life than a slavish ; If that displeas'd him, that then with his leave they might depart to some other soil.*

As this may pass with good allowance, that the *Trojans* might be many in these parts, for *Helenus* was by *Pirrhus* made King of the *Chaonians,* and the Sons of *Pirrhus* by *Andromache Hectors Wife* could not but be powerful through all *Epirus,* so much the more it may be doubted, how these *Trojans* could be thus in bondage, where they had Friends and Country-men so Potent. But to examin these things with diligence, were but to confute the Fables of *Britan* with the Fables of *Greece* or *Italy ;* for of this Age, what we have to say, as well concerning most other Countries, as this Iland, is equally under Queſtion. Be't how it will, *Pandraſus* not expecting ſo bold a Meſſage from the Sons of Captives, gathers an Army. And marching toward the Woods, *Brutus* who had notice of his approach nigh to a Town call'd *Sparatinum*, (I know not what Town, but certain of no Greek name) over night planting himſelf there with good part of his men, ſuddenly ſets upon him, and with ſlaughter of the *Greeks* purſues him to the paſſage of a River, which mine Author names *Akalon*, meaning perhaps *Achelous*, or *Acheron :* where at the Ford he overlaies them a-freſh. This victory obtain'd, and a ſufficient ſtrength left in *Sparatinum*, *Brutus* with *Antigonus*, the Kings Brother and his Freind *Anacletus*, whom he had tak'n in the fight, returns to the reſidue of his Freinds in the thick Woods. While *Pandraſus* with all ſpeed re-collecting, beſeiges the Town. *Brutus* to re-leive his men beſeig'd, who earneſtly call'd him, diſtruſting the ſufficiency of his Force, bethinks himſelf of this Policy. Calls to him *Anacletus*, and threatning inſtant death elſe, both to him and his freind *Antigonus*, enjoyns him, that he ſhould go at the ſecond howr of night to the Greekiſh Leagre, and tell the Guards he had brought *Antigonus* by ſtealth out of Priſon to a certain woody Vale ; un-able through the waight of his Fetters to move furder : entreating them to come ſpee-dily and fetch him in. *Anacletus* to ſave both himſelf and his freind *Antigonus*, ſwears this ; and at fit howr ſetts on alone toward the

Camp :

Camp : is mett, examin'd, and at laft unque-
ftionably known. To whom, great profeffion
of fidelity firft made, he frames his Tale, as
had bin taught him : and they now fully af-
fur'd, with a credulous rafhnefs leaving thir
Stations, far'd accordingly by the Ambufh
that there awaited them. Forthwith *Brutus*
dividing his men into three parts, leads on in
filence to the Camp; commanding firft each
part at a feveral place to enter, and forbear
Execution, till he with his Squadron poffefs'd
of the Kings Tent, gave Signal to them by
Trumpet.   The found whereof no fooner
heard, but huge havock begins upon the
fleeping, and unguarded Enemy; whom the
befeiged alfo now fallying forth, on the other
fide affaile. *Brutus* the while had fpecial care
to feife and fecure the *Kings Perfon*; whofe
Life ftill within his Cuftody, he knew was the
fureft pledge to obtain what he fhould demand. Day appearing, he enters the Town,
there diftributes the *Kings Treafury*, and leaving the place better fortify'd, returns with
the King his Prifner to the Woods. Strait the
ancient and grave Men he fummons to Coun-
fell, what they fhould now demand of the
King.

After long debate *Mempricius*, one of the
graveft, utterly diffuading them from thought
of longer ftay in *Greece*, unlefs they meant to
be deluded with a futtle peace, and the awaited revenge of thofe whofe freinds they had
flain, advifes them to demand firft the *Kings
Eldeſt Daughter Innogen* in mariage to thir
Leader

Leader *Brutus*, with a rich Dowry, next shipping, mony, and fitt provision for them all to
depart the Land.

This resolution pleasing best, the King now
brought in, and plac'd in a high Seat, is breisly
told, that on these conditions granted, he
might be free, not granted, he must prepare
to die.

Prest with fear of death the *King* readily
yeelds : especially to bestow his Daughter on
whom he confess'd so Noble and so Valiant :
offers them also the third part of his Kingdom, if they like to stay ; if not, to be thir Ho-
stage himself, till he had made good his word.

The Mariage therfore solemniz'd, and shipping from all parts got together, the *Trojans*
in a Fleet, no less writt'n then three hundred
fowr and twenty Sail, betake them to the wide
Sea ; where with a prosperous course two
daies and a night bring them on a certain Iland
long before dispeopl'd and left wast by Sea-
Roavers ; the name whereof was then *Leoge-
cia*, now unknow'n. They who were sent out
to discover, came at length to a ruin'd City ;
where was a Temple and Image of *Diana* that
gave Oracles : but not meeting first or last
save wild Beasts, they return with this notice
to thir Ships : Wishing thir General would
enquire of that Oracle what voiage to pur-
sue.

Consultation had, *Brutus* taking with him
Gerion his Diviner, and twelv of the ancient-
est, with wonted Ceremonies before the inward shrine of the Goddess, in Verse, as it
seems

seems the manner was, utters his request, *Diva potens nemorum*, &c.

Goddeß of Shades, and Huntreß, who at will
Walk'ft on the rowling fphear, and through the deep,
On thy third Reigne the Earth look now, and tell
What Land, what Seat of reft thou bidft me feek,
What certain Seat, where I may worfhip thee
For aye, with Temples vow'd, and Virgin quires.

To whom fleeping before the Altar, *Diana* in a Vifion that night thus anfwer'd, *Brute fub occafum Solis*, &c.

Brutus far to the Weft, in th' Ocean wide
Beyond the Realm of Gaul, *a Land there lies,*
Sea-girt it lies, where Giants dwelt of old,
Now void, it fits thy people ; thether bend
Thy courfe, there fhalt thou find a lafting feat,
There to thy Sons another Troy *fhall rife,*
And Kings *be born of thee, whofe dredded might*
Shall aw the World, and Conquer Nations bol .

Thefe Verfes Originally Greek, were put in Latin, faith *Virunnius*, by *Gildas* a Britifh Poet, and him to have liv'd under *Claudius*. Which granted true, adds much to the Anti- quitie of this Fable ; and indeed the Latin Verfes are much better, than for the Age of *Geoffrey* ap-*Arthur*, unlefs perhaps *Jofeph of Exeter*, the only fmooth Poet of thofe times, befreinded him ; in this *Diana* overfhot her Oracle thus ending, *Ipfis totius terræ fubditus orbis erit*, That to the race of *Brute* Kings of
B   this

this Iland, the whole Earth shall be subject.

But *Brutus* guided now, as he thought, by Divine Conduct , speeds him towards the West; and after som encounters on the *Afric* side , arrives at a place on the *Tyrrhen* Sea; where he happ'ns to find the Race of those *Trojans*, who with *Antenor* came into *Italy*; and *Corineus* a man much fam'd , was thir Chief : though by surer Authors it be reported, that those *Trojans* with *Antenor*, were seated on the other side of *Italie*, on the *Adriatic*, not the *Tyrrhen* shoar. But these joyning Company, and past the *Herculean Pillars*, at the mouth of *Ligeris in Aquitania* cast Anchor. Where after som discovery made of the place, *Corineus* Hunting nigh the shoar with his Men, is by Messengers of the King *Goffarius Pictus* mett, and question'd about his Errand there. Who not answering to thir mind, *Imbertus*, one of them, lets fly an Arrow at *Corineus*, which he avoiding, slaies him : and the *Pictavian* himself heerupon levying his whole Force, is overthrown by *Brutus*, and *Corineus*; who with the Battell Ax which he was wont to manage against the *Tyrrhen Giants* is said to have done marvells. But *Goffarius* having draw'n to his Aid the whole Country of *Gaul*, at that time govern'd by *Twelv Kings*, puts his Fortune to a second Trial , wherin the *Trojans* over-born by multitude, are driv'n back, and beseig'd in thir own Camp, which by good foresight was strongly situate. Whence *Brutus* unexpectedly issuing out, and *Corineus* in the mean while, whose device it was, assaulting

ing

ing them behind from a Wood, where he had
convay'd his men the night before, the *Tro-*
jans are again Victors, but with the lofs of *Tu-*
ron a Valiant Nefew of *Brutus*; whofe Afhes
left in that place, gave name to the City of
Tours, built there by the *Troians*. *Brutus* finding now his powers much lefsn'd, and this yet
not the place foretold him, leavs *Aquitain*,
and with an eafie courfe, arriving at *Totneß* in
Dev'nfhire, quickly perceivs heer to be the
promis'd end of his labours.

The Iland not yet *Britan* but *Albion*, was
in a manner defert and inhofpitable ; kept
only by a remnant of *Giants*; whofe exceffive
Force and Tyrannie had confum'd the reft.
Them *Brutus* deftroies, and to his People di-
vides the Land, which with fom reference to
his own name he thenceforth calls *Britan*. To
Corineus, Cornwal, as now we call it, fell by Lot;
the rather by him lik't, for that the hugeft
Giants, in Rocks and Caves were faid to lurk
ftill there ; which kind of Monfters to deal
with was his old exercife.

And heer, with leave befpok'n to recite a
grand Fable, though dignify'd by our beft
Poets ; While *Brutus* on a certain Feftival day
folemnly kept on that fhoar, where he firft
landed, was with the People in great jollity
and mirth, a crew of thefe Savages breaking
in upon them, began on the fuddain another
fort of Game than at fuch a meeting was expected. But at length by many hands overcome, *Goëmagog* the hugeft, in hight twelv
Cubits, is referv'd alive ; that with him *Cori-*

neus,

neus, who desir'd nothing more, might try his strength ; whom in a Wreſtle the Giant catching aloft, with a terrible hugg broke three of his Ribs : Nevertheleſs *Corineus* enrag'd, heaving him up by main force, and on his Shoulders bearing him to the next high Rock, threw him headlong all ſhatter'd into the Sea, and left his name on the Cliff, call'd ever ſince *Langoëmagog*, which is to ſay, the Giants leap.

After this, *Brutus* in a choſen place builds *Troia nova*, chang'd in time to *Trinovantum*, now *London* ; and began to enact Laws ; *Heli* beeing then high Preiſt in *Judæa* : and having govern'd the whole Ile 24 Years, dy'd, and was buried in his new *Troy*. His three Sons *Locrine*, *Albanact*, and *Camber* divide the Land by conſent. *Locrine* had the middle part *Loëgria* ; *Camber* poſſeſs'd *Cambria* or *Wales* ; *Albanact Albania*, now *Scotland*. But he in the end by *Humber* King of the *Hunns*, who with a Fleet invaded that Land, was ſlain in fight, and his People driv'n back into *Loëgria*. *Locrine* and his Brother goe out againſt *Humber* ; who now marching onward, was by them defeated, and in a River drown'd, which to this day retains his name. Among the ſpoils of his Camp and Navy, were found certain young Maids, and *Eſtrildis*, above the reſt, paſſing fair ; the Daughter of a *King in Germany* ; from whence *Humber*, as he went waſting the Sea-Coaſt, had led her Captive : whom *Locrine*, though before contracted to the Daughter of *Corineus*, reſolves to marry. But beeing forc'd and threatn'd by *Corineus*, whoſe Autority,

rity, and Power he fear'd, *Guendolen* the Daughter he yeelds to marry, but in secret loves the other : and oft-times retiring as to fom private Sacrifice, through Vaults and Passages made under ground; and seven years thus enjoying her, had by her a Daughter equally fair, whose name was *Sabra*. But when once his fear was off by the Death of *Corineus*, not content with secret enjoyment, divorcing *Guendolen*, he makes *Estrildis* now his Queen. *Guendolen* all in rage departs into *Cornwall*; where *Ma an*, the Son she had by *Locrine*, was hitherto brought up by *Corineus* his Grandfather. And gathering an Army of her Fathers Freinds and Subjects, gives Battail to her Husband by the River *Sture*; wherein *Locrine* shot with an Arrow ends his life. But not so ends the fury of *Guendolen*; for *Estrildis* and her Daughter *Sabra*, she throws into a River : and to leave a Monument of Revenge, proclaims, that the stream be thenceforth call'd after the Damsels name; which by length of time is chang'd now to *Sabrina*, or *Severn*.

Fifteen Years she governs in behalf of her Son; then resigning to him at Age, retires to her Fathers Dominion. This saith my Author, was in the daies of *Samuel*. *Madan* hath the praise to have well and peacefully rul'd the space of 40 years; leaving behind him two Sons, *Mempricius*, and *Malim*. *Mempricius* had first to doe with the ambition of his Brother, aspiring to share with him in the Kingdom; whom therefore at a meeting to

compose

compose matters, with a treachery which his cause needed not, he slew.

Nor was he better in the sole possession, whereof so ill he could endure a Partner, killing his Nobles, and those especially next to succeed him ; till lastly giv'n over to unnatural lust, in the twentieth of his Reigne, hunting in a Forest, he was devowr'd by Wolves.

His Son *Ebranc*, a man of mighty strength and stature, Reign'd 40 Years.   He first after *Brutus* wasted *Gaul* ; and returning rich and prosperous, builded *Caerebranc*, now *York* ; in *Albania Alclud, Mount Agned,* or *the Castle of Maydens, now Edinburgh*. He had 20 Sons and 30 Daughters by 20 Wives.   His Daughters he sent to *Silvius Alba* into *Italy*, who bestow'd them on his Peers of the *Trojan* Line. His Sons under the leading of *Assaracus* thir Brother, won them Lands and Signories in *Germany* ; thence call'd, from these Brethren, *Germania :* a derivation too hastily suppos'd, perhaps before the word *Germanus* or the Latin Tongue was in use. Som who have describ'd *Henault*, as *Jacobus Bergomas*, and *Lessabeus*, are cited to affirm that *Ebranc* in his Warre there, was by *Brunchildis Lord of Henault* put to the worse.

Brutus therefore surnamed *Greenshield* succeeding, to repair his Fathers losses, as the same *Lessabeus* reports, fought a second Battail in *Henault* with *Brunchild* at the mouth of *Scaldis*, and Encamp'd on the River *Hania*. Of which *our Spencer* also thus Sings.

Let Scaldis *tell, and let tell* Hania,
And let the Marsh of Esthambruges *tell*
                                        What

What colour were thir Waters that same day,
And all the Moar twixt Elversham *and* Dell,
With blood of Henalois *which therin fel* ;
How oft that day did sad Brunchildis *see*
The Greenshield *dy'd in dolorous Vermeil,* &c.

But *Henault*, and *Brunchild*, and *Greensheild*,
seeme newer names than for a Story pretended thus Antient.

Him succeeded *Leil*, a maintainer of Peace
and Equity; but slackn'd in his latter end,
whence arose some civil discord. He built in
the North *Cairleil*; and in the daies of *Solomon*.

Rudhuddibras, or *Hudibras* appeasing the
commotions which his Father could not,
fownded *Caerkeynt* or *Canturbury*, *Caerguent*, or
Winchester, and *Mount Paladur*, now *Septonia*
or *Shaftsbury* : but this by others is contradicted.

Bladud his Son built *Caerbadus* or *Bathe*, and
those medicinable waters he dedicated to *Minerva*, in whose Temple there he kept fire
continually burning. He was a man of great
Invention, and taught Necromancy : till having made him Wings to fly, he fell down upon the Temple of *Apollo* in *Trinovant*, and so
dy'd after twenty years Reigne.

Hitherto from Father to Son the direct
Line hath run on : but *Leir* who next Reign'd,
had only three Daughters, and no Male Issue :
govern'd laudably, and built *Caer-Leir*, now
Leicestre, on the Bank of *Sora*. But at last,
failing through Age, he determines to bestow
his Daughters, and so among them to divide
his Kingdom.   Yet first to try which of them

lov'd

lov'd him best (a Trial that might have made him, had he known as wisely how to try, as he seem'd to know how much the trying behoov'd him) *he resolves a simple resolution, to ask them solemnly in order ; and which of them should profess largest, her to beleev.* Gonoril th' Eldest apprehending too well her Fathers weakness, makes answer, invoking Heav'n, *That she lov'd him above her Soul. Therfore,* quoth the old man overjoy'd, *since thou so honourst my declin'd Age, to thee and the Husband whom thou shalt choose, I give the third part of my Realm.* So fair a speeding for a few words soon utter'd, was to *Regan* the second, ample instruction what to say. She on the same demand spares no protesting, and the Gods must witness, that otherwise to express her thoughts she knew not, but that *she lov'd him above all Creatures*; and so receavs an equal reward with her Sister. But *Cordelia* the youngest, though hitherto best belov'd, and now before her Eyes the rich and present hire of a little easie soothing, the danger also, and the loss likely to betide plain dealing, yet moves not from the solid purpose of a sincere and vertuous answer. *Father*, saith she, *my love towards you, is as my duty bids; what should a Father seek, what can a Child promise more? they who pretend beyond this, flatter.* When the old man, sorry to hear this, and wishing her to recall those words, persisted asking, with a loiall sadness at her Fathers infirmity, but somthing on the sudden, harsh, and glancing rather at her Sisters, than speaking her own mind,

mind, *Two waies only*, saith she, *I have to an-*
swer what you require mee; the former, Your
command is, I should recant; accept then this
other which is left mee; look how much you have,
so much is your value, and so much I love you.
Then hear thou, quoth *Leir* now all in passion,
what thy ingratitude hath gain'd thee; because
thou hast not reverenc'd thy aged Father equall
to thy Sisters, part in my Kingdom, or what else
is mine reck'n to have none.   And without delay gives in mariage his other Daughters, *Go-*
norill to *Maglaunus* Duke of *Albania*, *Regan* to
Henninus Duke of *Cornwall*; with them in present half his Kingdom; the rest to follow at
his Death.   In the mean while Fame was not
sparing to divulge the Wisdom, and other
Graces of *Cordeilla*, insomuch that *Aganippus*
a great King in Gaul (however he came by his
Greek name) seeks her to Wife, and nothing
alter'd at the loss of her Dowry, receavs her
gladly in such manner as she was sent him.
After this *King Leir*, more and more droop-
ing with Years, became an easy prey to his
Daughters and thir Husbands; who now by
dayly encroachment had seis'd the whole
Kingdom into thir hands: and the old King
is put to sojorn with his Eldest Daughter, attended only by threescore Knights.   But they
in a short while grudg'd at, as too numerous
and disorderly for continual Guests, are reduc'd to thirty.   Not brooking that affront,
the old King betakes him to his second Daughter: but there also discord soon arising between the Servants of differing Masters in one
Family,

Family, five only are suffer'd to attend him.
Then back again he returns to the other; hoping that fhe his Eldeft could not but have
more pity on his Gray Hairs: but fhe now re-
fufes to admitt him, unlefs he be content with
one only of his followers. At laft the remembrance of his youngeft *Cordeilla* comes to his
thoughts; and now acknowledging how true
her words had bin, though with little hope
from whom he had fo injur'd, be it but to
pay her the laft recompence fhe can have from
him, his confeffion of her wife forewarning,
that fo perhaps his mifery, the prooff and experiment of her Wifdom, might fomthing
foft'n her, he takes his Journey into *France*.
Now might be feen a difference between the
filent, or down-right fpok'n affection of fom
Children to thir Parents, and the talkative
obfequioufnefs of others; while the hope of Inheritance over-acts them, and on the tongues
end enlarges thir duty. *Cordeilla* out of meer
love, without the fufpicion of expected reward, at the meffage only of her Father in
diftrefs, powrs forth true filial tears. And not
enduring either that her own, or any other
Eye fhould fee him in fuch forlorn condition
as his Meffenger declar'd, difcreetly appoints
one of her trufted Servants, firft to convay
him privately toward fom good Sea Town,
there to array him, bathe him, cherifh him,
furnifh him with fuch Attendance and State,
as befeem'd his Dignity. That then, as from
his firft Landing, he might fend word of his
Arrival to her Husband *Aganippus*. Which
don

don with all mature, and requisite contrivance, *Cordelia* with the King her Husband, and all the Barony of his Realm, who then first had news of his passing the Sea, goe out to meet him ; and after all honourable and joyful entertainment, *Aganippus*, as to his Wives Father, and his Royal Guest, surrenders him, during his abode there, the Power and disposal of his whole Dominion : permitting his Wife *Cordeilla* to go with an Army, and set her Father upon his Throne. Wherin her piety so prosper'd, as that she vanquish'd her impious Sisters with those Dukes, and *Leir* again, as saith the story, three years obtain'd the Crown. To whom dying, *Cordeilla* with all Regal Solemnities gave Burial in the Town of *Leicestre*. And then as right Heir succeeding, and her Husband dead, Rul'd the Land five years in Peace. Untill *Marganus* and *Cunedagius* her two Sisters Sons, not bearing that a Kingdom should be govern'd by a Woman, in the unseasonablest time to raise that quarrel against a Woman so worthy, make War against her, depose her, and imprison her ; of which impatient, and now long unexercis'd to suffer, she there, as is related, kill'd her self. The Victors between them part the Land : but *Marganus* the Eldest Sisters Son, who held by agreement from the North-side of *Humber* to *Cathness*, incited by those about him, to invade all as his own right, warres on *Cunedagius* ; who soon met him, overcame, and overtook him in a Town of *Wales*, where he left his life, and ever since his name to the place. *Cune-*

Cunedagius was now sole King, and govern'd with much praise many years; about the time when *Rome* was built. Him succeeded *Rivallo* his Son, wise also and fortunat; save what they tell us of three daies raining blood, and swarmes of stinging Flies, whereof men dy'd. In order then *Gurgustius*, *Jago* or *Lago*, his Nefew; *Sisillius*, *Kinmarcus*. Then *Gorbogudo*, whom others name *Gorbodego*, and *Gorbodion*, who had two Sons, *Ferrex*, and *Porrex*. They in the old Age of thir Father failing to contend who should succeed, *Porrex* attempting by treachery his Brothers life, drives him into *France*; and in his return, though aided with the Force of that Country, defeats and slaies him. But by his Mother *Videna* who less lov'd him, is himself, with the assistance of her Women, soon after slain in his Bed: With whom ended, as is thought, the Line of *Brutus*. Wherupon, the whole Land with Civil Broils was rent into Five Kingdoms, long time waging Warr each on other; and som say 50 Years. At length *Dunwallo Molmutius* the Son of *Cloten King of Cornwall*, one of the foresaid five, excelling in valour, and goodliness of person, after his Fathers decease found means to reduce again the whole Iland into a Monarchy: subduing the rest at opportunities. First *Ymner King of Loegria* whom he flew; then *Rudaucus of Cambria*, *Staterius of Albania*, confederat together. In which fight *Dunwallo* is reported, while the Victory hung doubtfull, to have us'd this Art. He takes with him 600 stout men, bids them put on the
Armour

Armour of thir slain Enemies; and so unexpectedly approaching the Squadron, where
those two Kings had plac'd themselves in
fight, from that part which they thought se-
curest, assaults, and dispatches them.   Then
displaying his own Ensignes which before he
had conceal'd, and sending notice to the other
part of his Army what was don, adds to them
new courage, and gains a final Victory. This
Dunwallo was the first in Britan that wore a
Crown of Gold; and therfore by som reputed the
first King. He established the *Molmutine* Laws,
famous among the *English* to this day; writt'n
long after in Latine by *Gildas,* and in Saxon
by King *Alfred :* so saith *Geofrey,* but *Gildas*
denies to have known aught of the *Britans* before *Cæsar* ; much less knew *Alfred.*   These
Laws, whoever made them, bestow'd on Temples the privilege of Sanctuary; to Cities also,
and the waies thether leading, yea to Plows,
granted a kind of like refuge : and made such
riddance of Theeves and Robbers, that all
passages were safe. Forty Years he Govern'd
alone, and was buried nigh to *the Temple of*
Concord; which he, to the memory of peace
restor'd, had built in *Trinovant.*

His two Sons *Belinus* and *Brennus* contending about the Crown, by decision of Freinds
came at length to an accord ; *Brennus* to have
the North of *Humber, Belinus* the Sovrantie of
all. But the younger not long so contented,
that he, as they whisper'd to him, whose valour had so oft repell'd the Invasions of *Ceul-*
phus the Morine Duke, should now be subject to
his

his Brother, upon new Defigne fails into *Norway*; enters League and Affinitie with *Elfing* that King; which *Belinus* perceaving, in his abfence difpoffeffes him of all the North. *Brennus* with a Fleet of *Norwegians* makes toward *Britan*; but encounter'd by *Guithlac* the *Danish King*, who laying claim to his Bride, pur-fu'd him on the Sea, his haft was retarded, and he bereft of his Spoufe : who from the fight by a fudden Tempeft, was by the *Danish King* driv'n on *Northumberland*, and brought to *Belinus*. *Brennus* neverthelefs recollecting his Navy, lands in *Albania*, and gives Battel to his Brother in the Wood *Calaterium*; but lofing the day, efcapes with one fingle Ship into *Gaul*. Mean while the *Dane* upon his own offer to become tributary, fent home with his new prife, *Belinus* returns his thoughts to the adminiftring of Juftice, and the perfeting of his Fathers Laws; and to explain what High-waies might enjoy the forefaid privi-leges, he caus'd to be drawn out and pav'd four main Roades to the utmoft length and bredth of the Iland; and two others athwart; which are fince attributed to the *Romans*. *Brennus* on the other fide follicicing to his aid the Kings of *Gaul*, happ'ns at laft on *Seginus Duke of the Allobroges*; where his worth, and comlinefs of perfon wan him the Dukes Daughter and Heir. In whofe right he fhort-ly fucceeding, and by obtain'd leave paffing with a great Hoft through the length of *Gaul*, gets footing once again in *Britan*. Nor was *Belinus* unprepar'd, and now the Battel ready

to

to joyn, *Conuvenna* the Mother of them both all in a fright, throws her felf between; and calling earneftly to *Brennus* her Son, whofe abfence had fo long depriv'd her of his fight, after imbracements and tears, affails him with fuch a motherly power, and the mention of things fo dear and reverend, as irrefiftibly wrung from him all his enmity againft *Belinus*.

Then are hands joyn'd, reconciliation made firm, and Counfel held to turn thir united preparations on Foren parts. Thence that by thefe two all *Gallia* was overrun, the ftory tells; and what they did in *Italy*, and at *Rome*, if thefe be they, and not *Gauls*, who took that City, the Roman Authors can beft relate. So far from home I undertake not for the *Monmouth Chronicle*; which heer againft the ftream of Hiftory carries up and down thefe Brethren, now into *Germany*, then again to *Rome*, purfuing *Gabius* and *Porfena*, two unheard of Confuls. Thus much is more generally beleev'd, that both this *Brennus*, and another famous Captain, *Britomarus*, whom the Epitomift *Florus* and others mention, were not *Gauls* but *Britans*; the name of the firft in that Tongue fignifying a King, and of the other a Great *Britan*. However *Belinus* after a while returning home, the reft of his daies rul'd in Peace, Wealth, and Honour above all his Predeceffors; building fom Cities, of which one was *Caerofe* upon *Ofca*, fince *Caerlegion*; beautifying others, as *Trinovant* with a Gate, a Hav'n, and a Towr, on the Thames, retaining yet his name; on the top wherof his Afhes are

are said to have bin laid up in a Golden Urne.

After him *Gurguntius Barbirus* was King, mild and just, but yet inheriting his Fathers Courage , he subdu'd the *Dacian* or *Dane* , who refus'd to pay the Tribute Covnanted to *Belinus* for his enlargement. In his return finding about the *Orkneies* 30 ships of *Spain*, or *Bifcay*, fraught with Men and Women for a Plantation, whose Captain also *Bartholinus* wrongfully banish'd, as he pleaded, befaught him that some part of his Territory might be assign'd them to dwell in, he sent with them certain of his own men to *Ireland*, which then lay unpeopl'd ; and gave them that Iland to hold of him as in Homage. He was buried in *Caerlegion*, a City which he had wall'd about.

Guitheline his Son, is also remember'd, as a just and good Prince, and his Wife *Martia* to have excell'd so much in wisdom, as to venture upon a new Institution of Laws. Which *King Alfred* translating call'd *Marchen Leage*, but more truly therby is meant, the Mercian Law ; not translated by *Alfred*, but digested or incorporated with the West-Saxon. In the minority of her Son she had the rule , and then , as may be suppos'd, brought forth these Laws, not her self, for Laws are Masculin Births, but by the advice of her sagest Counselors ; and therin she might doe vertuously , since it befell her to supply the nonage of her Son : else nothing more awry from the Law of God and Nature, than that a Woman should give Laws to Men.

Hir Son *Sifilius* comming to Years receav'd
the

the Rule; then in order *Kimarus*, then *Danius* or *Elanius* his Brother.   Then *Morindus*, his Son by *Tanguestela* a Concubine, who is recorded a man of excessive Strength, Valiant, Liberal, and fair of Aspect, but immanely Cruell; not sparing in his Anger, Enemy, or Freind, if any Weapon were in his hand. A certain *King of the Morines*, or *Picards* invaded *Northumberland*; whose Army this King, though not wanting sufficient numbers, cheifly by his own prowefs overcame: But dishonour'd his Victory by the cruel usage of his Prisners, whom his own hands, or others in his presence put all to several Deaths: well fitted to such a bestial Cruelty was his end; for hearing of a huge Monster, that from the Irish Sea infested the Coast, and in the Pride of his Strength foolishly attempting to set manly valour against a Brute vastnefs, when his Weapons were all in vain, by that horrible mouth he was catch't up and devour'd.

Gorbonian the Eldest of his five Sons, than whom a Juster man liv'd not in his Age, was a great builder of Temples, and gave to all what was thir due; to his Gods devout Worship, to men of desert honour and preferment; to the Commons encouragement in thir Labours, and Trades, defence and protection from injuries and oppreffions, fo that the Land florish'd above her Neighbours, Violence and Wrong seldom was heard of: his Death was a general lofs: he was buried in *Trinovant*. *Archigallo* the second Brother follow'd not his Example; but deprefs'd the ancient Nobility,

C   and

and by peeling the wealthier fort, ftuff'd his
Treafury, and took the right way to be depos'd. *Elidure* the next Brother, furnam'd
the Pious, was fet up in his place; a mind fo
noble, and fo moderat, as almoft is incredible to have bin ever found. For having held
the Scepter five Years, hunting one day in the
Foreft of *Calater*, he chanc'd to meet his de-
pofed Brother, wandring in mean condition:
who had bin long in vain beyond the Seas,
importuning Foren aides to his Reftorement:
and was now in a poor Habit, with only ten
followers, privatly return'd to find fubfiftence
among his fecret freinds. At the unexpected fight of him, *Elidure* himfelf alfo then but
thinly accompanied, runns to him with open
Arms; and after many dear and fincere wel-
comings, convaies him to the Citty *Alclud*;
there hides him in his own Bed-Chamber. Afterwards faining himfelf fick, fummons all his
Peers as about greateft affairs; where admit-
ting them one by one, as if his weaknefs endur'd not the difturbance of more at once,
caufes them willing, or unwilling, once more
to fwear Allegiance to *Archigallo*. Whom
after reconciliation made on all fides, he leads
to *York*; and from his own Head, places the
Crown on the Head of his Brother. Who
thenceforth, Vice it felf diffolving in him, and
forgetting her firmeft hold with the admiration of a deed fo Heroic, became a true converted man; rul'd worthily 10 Years; dy'd,
and was Buried in *Caerleir*. Thus was a Brother fav'd by a Brother, to whom love of a
Crown,

Crown, the thing that fo often dazles, and
vitiats mortal men, for which, thoufands
of neereft blood have deftroy'd each other,
was in refpect of Brotherly dearnefs, a contemptible thing. *Elidure* now in his own behalf re-affumes the Government, and did as
was worthy fuch a man to doe.   When providence, that fo great vertue might want no
fort of tryal to make it more illuftrious, ftirs
up *Vigenius,* and *Peredure* his youngeft Brethren, againft him who had deferv'd fo nobly
of that relation, as leaft of all by a Brother to
be injur'd.   Yet him they defeat, him they
Imprifon in the Towr of *Trinovant,* and divide his Kingdom ; the North to *Peredure,* the
South to *Vigenius.*   After whofe Death *Peredure* obtaining all, fo much the better us'd his
power, by how much the worfe he got it.   So
that *Elidure* now is hardly mifs't.   But yet in
all right owing to his Elder the due place
whereof he had depriv'd him, Fate would that
he fhould die firft : and *Elidure* after many
years Imprifonment, is now the third time
feated on the Throne ; which at laft he enjoy'd
long in Peace ; finifhing the interrupted courfe
of his mild, and juft Reign, as full of vertuous
deeds, as daies to his end.   After thefe five
Sons of *Morindus,* fucceeded alfo thir Sons in
Order.   * *Regin of Gorbonian, Marganus of Ar-*   * *Matthew*
chigallo, both good Kings.   But *Enniaunus* his   of *Weftmin.*
Brother taking other courfes, was after fix
years depos'd.   Then *Idwallo* taught by a neer
Example, Govern'd foberly.   Then *Runno,*
then *Geruntius,* He of *Peredure,* this laft the
Son

Son of *Elidure*. From whose Loyns (for that likely is the durable, and surviving Race that springs of just Progenitors) issu'd a long descent of Kings, whose names only for many successions without other memory stand thus register'd, *Catellus, Coillus, Porrex, Cherin*, and his three Sons, *Fulgenius, Eldadus*, and *Andragius*, his Son *Urianus*; *Eliud, Eledaucus, Clotenus, Gurguntius, Merianus, Bleduno, Capis, Oenus, Sisillius*, twentie Kings in a continu'd row, that either did nothing, or liv'd in Ages that wrote nothing, at least a foul pretermission in the Author of this, whether Story or Fable; himself wearie, as seems, of his own tedious Tale.

But to make amends for this Silence, *Blegabredus* next succeeding, is recorded to have excell'd all before him in the Art of Music; opportunely, had he but left us one Song of his twentie Predecessors doings. Yet after him nine more succeeded in name; His Brother *Archimailus, Eldol, Redion, Rederchius, Samulius, Penissel, Pir, Capoirus*, but *Cliguellius*, with the addition of Modest, Wise, and Just. His Son *Heli* Reign'd 40 Years, and had three Sons, *Lud, Cassibelaun*, and *Nennius*. This *Heli* seems to be the same whom *Ninnius* in his fragment calls *Minocan*; for him he writes to be the Father of *Cassibelan*. *Lud* was that enlarg'd, and wall'd about *Trinovant*, there kept his Court, made it the prime City, and call'd it from his own name *Caer-lud*, or *Luds Town*, now *London*. Which, as is alledg'd out of *Gildas*, became matter of great

dissention

dissention betwixt him, and his Brother *Nen-nius* ; who took it hainously that the name of *Troy* thir ancient Country should be abolish'd for any new one. *Lud* was hardy, and bold in Warr, in Peace a jolly Feaster. He con-quer'd many Ilands of the Sea, saith *Hunting-don*, and was buried by the Gate which from thence wee call *Ludgate*. His two Sons *An-drogeus*, and *Tenuantius*, were left to the tui-tion of *Cassibelan* ; whose bounty, and high demeanor so wraught with the common peo-ple, as got him easily the Kingdom trans-ferr'd upon himself. He neverthelefs con-tinuing to favour and support his Nefews, conferres freely upon *Androgeus*, *London* with *Kent*, upon *Tenuantius*, *Cornwall* : reserving a superiority both over them, and all the o-ther Princes to himself ; till the *Romans* for a while circumscrib'd his power. Thus farr, though leaning only on the credit of *Geffrey Monmouth*, and his affertors, I yet for the specify'd caufes have thought it not beneath my purpofe, to relate what I found. Wherto I neither oblige the beleif of other perfon, nor over-haftily fubfcribe mine own. Nor have I ftood with others computing, or colla-ting Years and Chronologies, left I fhould be vainly curious about the time and circum-ftance of things wherof the fubftance is fo much in doubt. By this time, like one who had fet out on his way by night, and travail'd through a Region of fmooth or idle Dreams, our Hiftory now arrivs on the Confines, where day-light and truth meet us with a cleer dawn,

Huntingd.
L. 1.

C 3   reprefenting

reprefenting to our view, though at a farr diftance, true colours and fhapes. For albeit, *Cæfar*, whofe Autority we are now firft to follow, wanted not who tax'd him of mif-reporting in his Commentaries, yea in his Civil Warrs againft *Pompey*, much more, may wee think, in the *Britifh affairs*, of whofe little skill in writing he did not eafily hope to be contradicted, yet now in fuch variety of good Authors, we hardly can mifs from one hand or other to be fufficiently inform'd as of things paft fo long agoe. But this will better be referr'd to a fecond Difcourfe.

The End of the First Book.

T H E

THE

HISTORY

OF

BRITAIN.

BOOK II.

I Am now to write of what befell the *Britans* from *fifty and three years before the Birth of our Saviour*, when firſt the *Romans* came in, till the decay and cea-ſing of that Empire; a ſtory of much truth, and for the firſt hunderd years and ſomwhat more, Collected without much labour. So many and ſo prudent were the Writers, which thoſe two, the Civileſt, and the Wiſeſt of *European Nations*, both *Italy* and *Greece*, afford-ed to the Actions of that Puiſſant Citty. For Worthy Deeds are not often deſtitute of wor-thy Relaters : As by a certain Fate great Acts and great Eloquence have moſt commonly gon hand in hand, equalling and honouring each other in the ſame Ages. 'Tis true, that in obscureft times, by fhallow and unskilfull Writers; the indiftinct noife of many Battels, and Devaftations, of many Kingdoms over-run and loft, hath come to our Eares. For what wonder, if in all Ages, Ambition and the love of rapine hath ftirr'd up greedy and violent men to bold attempts in wafting and ruining Warrs, which to Pofterity have left the work of Wild Beafts and Deftroyers, rather than the Deeds and Monuments of Men and Conquerours? But he whofe juft and true valour ufes the neceffity of Warr and Dominion, not to deftroy but to prevent deftruction, to bring in Liberty againft Tyrants, Law and Civility among barbarous Nations, knowing that when he Conquers all things elfe, he cannot Conquer *Time*, or *Detraction*, wifely confcious of this his want as well as of his worth not to be forgott'n or conceal'd, honours and hath recourfe to the aid of Eloquence, his freindlieft and beft fupply; by whofe immortal Record his Noble Deeds, which elfe were tranfitory, becoming fixt and durable againft the force of Yeares and Generations, he fails not to continue through all Pofterity, over *Envy*, *Death*, and *Time*, alfo victorious. Therfore when the efteem of Science, and Liberal Study waxes low in the Common-wealth, wee may prefume that alfo there all Civil Vertue, and worthy Action is grown as low to a decline: and then Eloquence, as. it were conforted in the fame deftiny, with the decreafe and fall of Vertue corrupts alfo and fades; at leaft refignes her office of relating, to illiterat and frivolous Hiftorians;

storians ; such as the persons themselvs both
deserv, and are best pleas'd with; whilst they
want either the understanding to choose better, or the innocence to dare invite the examining, and searching stile of an intelligent
and faithfull Writer to the survay of thir un-
sound exploits, better befreinded by obscuri-
ty than Fame. As for these, the only Authors
wee have of *Brittish* matters, while the power
of *Rome* reach'd hither, (for *Gildas* affirms that
of the *Roman* times noe *Brittish* Writer was in
his daies extant, or if any ever were, either
burnt by Enemies, or transported with such as
fled the *Pictish* and *Saxon* Invasions) these therfore only *Roman* Authors there bee who in the
English Tongue have laid together, as much,
and perhaps more than was requisite to a History of *Britan*. So that were it not for leaving an unsightly gap so neer to the beginning,
I should have judg'd this labour, wherin so
little seems to be requir'd above transcription,
almost superfluous. Notwithstanding since I
must through it, if ought by diligence may
bee added, or omitted, or by other disposing
may be more explain'd, or more express'd, I
shall assay.

Julius Cæsar (of whom, and of the *Roman*
Free State, more than what appertains, is not
here to be discours'd) having subdu'd most
part of *Gallia*, which by a Potent Faction, he
had obtain'd of the Senat as his Province for
many years, stirr'd up with a desire of adding
still more glory to his name, and the whole *Suetonius*
Roman Empire to his ambition, som say, with *Vit. Cæs.*
a farr

a farr meaner and ignobler, the defire of *Brit-tifh* Pearls, whofe bignefs he delighted to bal-lance in his hand, determins, and that upon no unjuft pretended occafion, to trie his Force in the Conqueft alfo of *Britan*. For he under-ftood that the *Britans* in moft of his *Gallian* Warrs had fent Supplies againft him, had re-ceiv'd Fugitives of the *Bellovaci* his Enemies, and were call'd over to aid the Citties of *Ar-morica*, which had the year before confpir'd all in a new Rebellion. Therfore *Cæfar*, though now the Summer well nigh ending, and the feafon unagreeable to tranfport a Warr, yet judg'd it would be great advantage, only to get entrance into the *Ile*, knowledge of the men, the places, the ports, the acceffes ; which then, it feems, were eev'n to the *Gauls* thir Neighbours almoft unknown. For except Merchants and Traders, it is not oft, faith he, that any ufe to Travel thether ; and to thofe that doe, befides the Sea Coaft, and the Ports next to *Gallia*, nothing elfe is known. But heer I muft require, as *Pollio* did, the dili-gence, at leaft the memory of *Cæfar :* for if it were true, as they of *Rhemes* told him, that *Divitiacus*, not long before, a Puiffant King of the *Soiffons*, had *Britan* alfo under his Com-mand, befides the *Belgian Colonies* which he affirms to have nam'd and peopl'd many Pro-vinces there, if alfo the *Britans* had fo fre-quently giv'n them aid in all thir Warrs, if laftly the *Druid* learning honour'd fo much among them, were at firft taught them out of *Britan*, and they who fooneft would attain
　　　　　　　　　　　　　　　　that

Year be-
fore
Chrift, 53.

Suetonius.
Cæfar Com.
L. 1.

that Difcipline, fent hether to learn; it appears not how *Britan* at that time fhould be *Cæfar Com.*
L. 4.
fo utterly unknow'n in *Gallia,* or only know'n
to Merchants, yea to them fo little, that beeing call'd together from all parts, none could
be found to inform *Cæfar* of what bignefs the
Ile, what Nations, how great, what ufe of
Warr they had, what Laws, or fo much as
what commodious Havens for bigger Veffels.
Of all which things as it were then firft to
make difcovery, he fends *Caius Volufenus,* in a
long Galley, with Command to return affoon
as this could be effected. Hee in the mean
time with his whole power draws nigh to the
Morine Coaft, whence the fhorteft paffage was
into *Britan.* Hether his Navy which he us'd
againft the *Armoricans,* and what elfe of Shipping can be provided, he draws together.
This known in *Britan,* Embaffadors are fent
from many of the States there, who promife
Hoftages, and Obedience to the *Roman Empire.* Them, after Audience giv'n, *Cæfar* as
largely promifing, and exhorting to continue
in that mind, fends home, and with them *Comius of Arras,* whom he had made King of
that Country, and now fecretly employ'd to
gain a *Roman* party among the *Britans,* in as
many Citties as he found inclinable, and to
tell them, that he himfelf was fpeeding thether. *Volufenus* with what difcovery of the
Iland he could make from aboard his Ship, not
daring to venture on the fhoar, within five
daies returns to *Cæfar.* Who foon after, with
two Legions, ordinarily amounting, of *Ro-*
mans

mans and thir Allies, to about 25000 *Foot*, and 4500 *Horse*, the Foot in 80 Ships of burden, the Horse in 18, besides what Gallies were appointed for his Chief Commanders, setts off about the third watch of night with a good Gale to Sea ; leaving behind him *Sulpitius Rufus* to make good the Port with a sufficient strength. But the Horse whose appointed Shipping lay Wind-bound eight mile upward in another Hav'n, had much trouble to Imbark. *Cæsar* now within sight of *Britan* beholds on every Hill multitudes of armed men, ready to forbid his Landing ; and *Cicero* writes to his Freind *Atticus*, that the accesses of the Iland were wondrously fortify'd with strong Workes or Moles. Heer from the fowrth to the ninth hour of day he awaits at Anchor the coming up of his whole Fleet : Mean while with his Legatts and Tribuns consulting, and giving order to fitt all things for what might happ'n in such a various, and floating water-fight as was to be expected. This place, which was a narrow Bay, close environ'd with Hills, appearing no way Commodious, he removes to a plain and open shoar eight Mile distant ; commonly suppos'd about *Deal in Kent*. Which when the *Britans* perceav'd, thir Horse and Chariots, as then they us'd in fight, scowring before, thir main powr speeding after, som thick upon the shoar, others not tarrying to be assail'd, ride in among the Waves to encounter, and assault the *Romans* eev'n under their Ships ; with such a bold, and free hardihood, that *Cæsar* himself

Cic. Att. L. 4. Ep. 17.

Camden.

self between confessing and excusing that his
Souldiers were to com down from thir Ships,
to stand in water heavy arm'd, and to fight at
once, denies not but that the terrour of such
new and resolute opposition made them for-
get thir wonted valour.   To succour which,
he commands his Gallies, a sight unusual to
the *Britans*, and more apt for motion, drawn
from the bigger Vessels, to row against the
op'n side of the Enemy, and thence with
Slings, Engines, and Darts, to beat them back.
But neither yet, though amaz'd at the strangeness of those new Sea-Castles, bearing up so
neer, and so swiftly as almost to overwhelm
them, the hurtling of Oares, the battring of
feirce Engines against thir bodies barely expos'd, did the *Britans* give much ground, or
the *Romans* gain; till *he who bore the Eagle of
the Tenth Legion*, yet in the Gallies, first beseeching his Gods, said thus alowd, *Leap down
Souldiers, unless ye mean to betray your Ensigne; I
for my part will perform what I ow to the Common-
wealth and my General.* This utter'd, over-board
he leaps, and with his Eagle feircly advanc'd
runs upon the Enemy, the rest hartning one
another not to admit the dishonour of so nigh
losing thir Chief Standard, follow him resolutely. Now was fought eagerly on both sides. Ours
who well knew thir own advantages, and ex-
pertly us'd them, now in the shallows, now on
the Sand, still as the *Romans* went trooping to
thir Ensignes, receav'd them, dispatch'd them,
and with the help of thir Horse, put them
every where to great disorder.   But *Cæsar* causing

sing all his Boats and Shallops to be fill'd with
Souldiers, commanded to ply up and down
continually with releif where they saw need;
wherby at length all the Foot now dif-im-
bark't, and got together in som order on firm
ground, with a more steddy charge put the
Britans to flight: but wanting all thir Horse,
whom the winds yet with-held from Sailing,
they were not able to make poursuit. In this
confused fight *Scæva a Roman Souldier*, having
press'd too far among the *Britans*, and besett
round, after incredible valour shewn, single
against a multitude, swom back safe to his
General; and in the place that rung with his
praises, earnestly besought pardon for his rash
adventure against Discipline: which modest
confessing after no bad event, for such a deed
wherin valour, and ingenuity so much out-
weigh'd transgression, easily made amends,
and preferr'd him to be a Centurion. *Cæsar*
also is brought in by *Julian*, attributing to
himself the honour (if it were at all an honour to that person which he sustain'd) of being the first that left his Ship, and took Land:
but this were to make *Cæsar* less understand
what became him than *Scæva*. The *Britans*
finding themselvs maister'd in fight, forthwith
send Embassadors to treat of Peace; promi-
sing to give Hostages, and to be at Command.
With them *Comius of Arras* also return'd;
whom hitherto since his first coming from *Cæsar*, they had detain'd in Prison as a Spy: the
blame whereof they lay on the Common People; for whose violence, and thir own imprudence

Valer.
Max. Plu-
tarch.

In Cæsarib.

dence they crave pardon. *Cæsar* complaining they had first sought Peace, and then without cause had begun War, yet content to pardon them, commands Hostages : wherof part they bring in strait, others farr up in the Country to be sent for, they promise in a few daies. Mean while the people disbanded and sent home, many Princes, and Chief Men from all parts of the Ile submit themselves and thir Citties to the dispose of *Cæsar*, who lay then encamp'd, as is thought, on *Baram down*. Thus had the *Britans* made thir peace ; when suddenly an accident unlook'd for put new counsels into thir minds. Fowr daies after the coming of *Cæsar*, those 18 Ships of burden, which from the upper hav'n had tak'n in all the *Roman Horse*, born with a soft wind to the very Coast, in sight of the *Roman Camp*, were by a sudden tempest scatter'd, and driv'n back, some to the Port from whence they loos'd, others down into the West Country ; who finding there no safety either to Land, or to cast Anchor, chose rather to commit themselvs again to the troubl'd Sea ; and as *Orosius* reports, were most of them cast away. The same night, it being Full Moon, the Gallies left upon dry Land, were unaware to the *Romans*, cover'd with a Spring-tide, and the greater Ships that lay off at Anchor, torn and beat'n with Waves, to the great perplexity of *Cæsar*, and his whole Army ; who now had neither Shipping left to convay them back, nor any provision made to stay heer, intending to have winter'd in *Gallia*. All this the *Britans* well

well perceaving, and by the compaſs of his
Camp, which without baggage appear'd the
ſmaller, gueſſing at his numbers, conſult together, and one by one ſlily withdrawing from
the Camp, where they were waiting the con-
cluſion of a Peace, reſolve to ſtop all Proviſi-
ons, and to draw out the buſineſs till Winter.
Cæſar though ignorant of what they intended,
yet from the condition wherin he was, and thir
other Hoſtages not ſent, ſuſpecting what was
likely, begins to provide apace, all that might
be, againſt what might happ'n : laies in Corn,
and with materials fetch'd from the Continent,
and what was left of thoſe Ships which were
paſt help, he repairs the reſt. So that now by
the inceſſant labour of his Souldiers, all but
twelv were again made ſerviceable. While
theſe things are doing, one of the Legions being ſent out to forrage, as was accuſtom'd, and
no ſuſpicion of Warr, while ſom of the *Britans*
were remaining in the Country about, others
alſo going and coming freely to the *Roman
Quarters*, they who were in ſtation at the
Camp Gates ſent ſpeedy word to *Cæſar*, that
from that part of the Country, to which the
Legion went, a greater duſt than uſual was ſeen
to riſe. *Cæſar* gueſſing the matter, commands
the Cohorts of Guard to follow him thether,
two others to ſucceed in thir ſtead, the reſt all
to arm and follow. They had not march'd
long, when *Cæſar* diſcerns his Legion ſore o-
vercharg'd : for the *Britans* not doubting but
that thir Enemies on the morrow, would be in
that place which only they had left unreap'd
of

of all thir Harveſt, had plac'd an Ambuſh;
and while they were diſperſt and buſieſt at thir
labour, ſet upon them, kill'd ſom, and routed the reſt.   The manner of thir fight was
from a kind of Chariots; wherin riding about,
and throwing Darts, with the clutter of thir
Horſe, and of thir Wheels, they oft-times
broke the rank of thir Enemies; then retreating among the Horſe, and quitting their Chariots, they fought on Foot.   The Charioters,
in the mean while ſomwhat aſide from the Battel, ſet themſelvs in ſuch order, that thir Maiſters at any time oppreſs'd with odds, might
retire ſafely thether, having perform'd with
one perſon both the nimble ſervice of a Horſe-
man, and the ſtedfaſt duty of a Foot Souldier.
So much they could with thir Chariots by uſe,
and exerciſe, as riding on the ſpeed down a
ſteep Hill, to ſtop ſuddenly, and with a ſhort
rein turn ſwiftly, now running on the beam,
now on the Yoke, then in the Seat.   With this
ſort of new skirmiſhing, the *Romans* now o-
vermatch'd, and terrify'd, *Cæſar* with opportune aid appears; for then the *Britans* make
a ſtand :   But he conſidering that now was not
fitt time to offer Battel, while his men were
ſcarce recover'd of ſo late a fear, only keeps
his ground, and ſoon after leads back his Legions to the Camp.   Furder action for many
days following was hinder'd on both ſides by
foul weather; in which time the *Britans* diſ-
patching Meſſengers round about, to how few
the *Romans* were reduc'd, what hope of priſe
and booty, and now if ever of freeing them-

selvs from the fear of like invasions heerafter by making these an example, if they could but now uncamp thir Enemies; at this intimation multitudes of Horse and Foot coming down from all parts make towards the *Romans*. *Cæsar* foreseeing that the *Britans* though beat'n and put to flight would easily evade his Foot, yet with no more than 30 Horse, which *Comius* had brought over, draws out his men to Battel, puts again the *Britans* to flight, pursues with slaughter, and returning burns and laies waste all about. Wherupon Embassadors the same day being sent from the *Britans* to desire Peace, *Cæsar*, as his affairs at present stood, for so great a breach of Faith, only imposes on them double the former hostages, to be sent after him into *Gallia* : And because *September* was nigh half spent, a season not fit to tempt the Sea with his weather-beat'n Fleet, the same night with a fair wind he departs towards *Belgia*; whether two only of the *Britan* Citties sent Hostages, as they promis'd, the rest neglected. But at *Rome* when the news came of *Cæsars* Acts here, whether it were esteem'd a Conquest, or a fair Escape, supplication of 20 daies is decreed by the Senate, as either for an exploit done, or a discovery made, wherin both *Cæsar* and the *Romans* gloried not a little, though it brought no benefit either to him, or the Common-wealth.

Dion.

The Winter following, *Cæsar*, as his custom was, going into *Italy*, when as he saw that most *Cæsar Com.* of the *Britans* regarded not to send thir Ho-
5. stages, appoints his Legats whom he left in
Belgia,

Belgia, to provide what possible Shipping they could either build, or repair.   Low built they were to bee, as therby eafier both to fraught, and to hale afhoar ; nor needed to be higher, becaufe the Tyde fo often changing, was obferv'd to make the Billows lefs in our Sea than thofe in the *Mediterranean :* broader likewife they were made, for the better tranfporting of Horfes, and all other fraughtage, being intended cheifly to that end.   Thefe all about 600 in a readinefs, with 28 Ships of burden, and what with adventurers, and other hulks above 200, *Cotta* one of the Legates wrote them, as *Athenæus* affirms, in all 1600, *Cæfar* from Port *Iccius*, a paffage of fom 30 mile over, leaving behind him *Labienus* to guard the hav'n, and for other fupply at need, with five Legions, though but 2000 Horfe, about Sun fett hoyfing faile with a flack South-Weft, at midnight was becalm'd.   And finding when it was light, that the whole Navy lying on the current, had fal'n off from the Ile, which now they could defcry on thir left hand, by the unwearied labour of his Souldiers, who refus'd not to tugg the Oare, and kept courfe with Ships under fail, he bore up as neer as might bee, to the fame place where he had landed the year before ; where about noon arriving, no Enemy could be feen.   For the *Britans*, which in great number, as was after know'n, had bin there; at fight of fo huge a Fleet durft not abide. *Cæfar* forthwith landing his Army, and encamping to his beft advantage, fom notice being giv'n him by thofe he took, where

Before the Birth of Chrift, 52.

D 2   to

to find the Enemy, with his whole power, save only ten cohorts, and 300 Horse, left to *Quintus Atrius* for the guard of his Ships, about the third watch of the same night marches up twelv mile into the Country. And at length by a River commonly thought the *Stowre* in *Kent*, espies embattail'd *the Britifh Forces.* They with thir Horses and Chariots advancing to the higher Banks, oppofe the *Romans* in thir March, and begin the fight; but repuls't by the *Roman Cavalrie* give back into the Woods to a place notably made ftrong both by Art and Nature; which, it feems, had bin a Fort, or Hold of ftrength rays'd heertofore in time of Warrs among themfelvs. For entrance, and accefs on all fides, by the felling of huge Trees overthwart one another, was quite barr'd up; and within thefe the *Britans* did thir utmoft to keep out the Enemy. But the Souldiers of the feventh Legion locking all thir Sheilds together like a rooff clofe over head, and others rayfing a Mount, without much lofs of blood took the place, and drove them all to forfake the Woods. Purfuit they made not long, as beeing through ways unknow'n; and now ev'ning came on, which they more wifely fpent, in choofing out where to pitch and fortify thir Camp that night. The next Morning *Cæfar* had but newly fent out his Men in three Bodies to pourfue, and the laft no furder gon than yet in fight, when Horfemen all in Pofte from *Quintus Atrius* bring word to *Cæfar*, that almoft all his Ships in a Tempeft that night had fuffer'd wrack,

and

and lay brok'n upon the shoar. *Cæsar* at this news recalls his Legions, himself in all hast riding back to the Sea-side, beheld with his own Eyes the ruinous prospect. About forty Vessels were sunk and lost, the residue so torn, and shak'n as not to be new rigg'd without much labour. Strait he assembles what number of Ship-wrights either in his own Legions or from beyond Sea, could be summon'd; appoints *Labienus* on the *Belgian* side to build more; and with a dreadful industry of ten days, not respiting his Souldiers day or night, drew up all his Ships, and entrench'd them round within the circuit of his Camp. This don, and leaving to thir defence the same strength as before, he returns with his whole Forces to the same Wood, where he had defeated the *Britans:* who preventing him with greater powers than before, had now repossess'd themselvs of that place, under *Cassibelan* thir cheif Leader. Whose Territory from the States bordering on the Sea was divided by the *River Thames* about 80 mile inward. With him formerly other Citties had continual Warr; but now in the common danger had all made choise of him to be thir Generall. Heer the *British* Horse and Charioters meeting with the *Roman* Cavalrie fought stoutly; and at first, somthing overmatch'd they retreat to the neer advantage of thir Woods and Hills, but still follow'd by the *Romans*, make head again, cut off the forwardest among them, and after some pause, while *Cæsar*, who thought the days work had bin don,

D 3   was

was busied about the entrenching of his Camp, march out again, give feirce assault to the very Stations of his Guards and Senteries, and while the main cohorts of two Legions that were sent to the Alarme, stood within a small distance of each other terrify'd at the newness and the boldness of thir fight, charg'd back again through the midst, without loss of a man. Of the *Romans* that day was slain *Quintus Laberius Durus* a Tribune : the *Britans* having fought thir fill at the very entrance of *Cæsars* Camp, and sustain'd the resistance of his whole Army entrench'd, gave over the assault. *Cæsar* heer acknowledges that the *Roman* way both of arming, and of fighting, was not so well fitted against this kind of Enemy ; for that the Foot in heavy Armour could not follow thir cunning flight, and durst not by ancient Discipline stirr from thir Ensigne ; and the Horse alone, disjoyn'd from the Legions, against a Foe that turn'd suddenly upon them with a mixt encounter both of Horse and Foot, were in equall danger both following and retiring. Besides thir fashion was, not in great bodies, and close order, but in small divisions, and open distances to make thir onset ; appointing others at certain spaces, now to releev and bring off the weary, now to succeed and renew the conflict ; which argu'd no small experience, and use of Armes. Next day the *Britans* afarr off upon the Hills begin to shew themselves heer and there, and though less boldly than before, to skirmish with the *Roman* Horse. But at Noon *Cæsar* having sent

out

out three Legions, and all his Horse with *Tre-bonius* the Legat, to seek fodder, suddenly on all sides they set upon the Forragers, & charge up after them to the very Legions, and thir Standards. The *Romans* with great courage beat them back, and in the chace, beeing well seconded by the Legions, not giving them time either to rally, to stand, or to descend from thir Chariots as they were wont, slew many. From this overthrow, the *Britans*, that dwelt farder off, betook them home; and came no more after that time with so great a power against *Cæsar*. Wherof advertis'd he marches onward to the Frontiers of *Cassibelan*, which on this side were bounded by the *Thames*, not pas-sable except in one place and that difficult, a-bout *Coway stakes neer Oatlands*, as is conje-ctur'd. Hither coming he descries on the o-ther side great Forces of the Enemy, plac'd in good Array; the bank sett all with sharp stakes, others in the bottom, cover'd with wa-ter; whereof the marks in *Beda*'s time, were to be seene, as he relates. This having learnt by such as were tak'n, or had run to him, he first commands his Horse to pass over; then his Foot, who wadeing up to the neck went on so resolutely, and so fast, that they on the fur-der side not enduring the violence, retreated and fled. *Cassibelan* noe more now in hope to contend for Victorie, dismissing all but 4000 of those Charioters, through Woods, and in-tricate waies attends thir motion; where the *Romans* are to pass, drives all before him; and with continual sallies upon the Horse, where

Camden,

they

they leaft expected, cutting off fome and terrifying others, compells them foe clofe together, as gave them no leave to fetch in prey or bootie without ill fuccefs. Wherupon *Cæfar* ftrictly commanding all not to part from the Legions, had nothing left him in his way but empty Fields and Houfes, which he fpoil'd and burnt. Meane while the *Trinobantes* a State or Kingdome, and perhaps the greateft then among the *Britans*, lefs favouring *Caffibelan* fend Embaffadors, and yeild to *Cæfar* upon this reafon. *Immanuentius* had bin thir King: him *Caffibelan* had flaine, and purpos'd the like to *Mandubratius* his Son, whom *Orofius* calls *Androgorius*, *Beda Androgius*; but the youth efcaping by flight into *Gallia*, put himfelf under the protection of *Cæfar*. Thefe entreat that *Mandubratius* may be ftill defended; and fent home to fucceed in his Fathers right. *Cæfar* fends him, demands forty Hoftages and Provifion for his Armie, which they immediately bring in, and have thir Confines protected from the Souldier. By thir Example the *Cenimagni*, *Segontiaci*, *Ancalites*, *Bibroci*, *Caffi* (fo I write them for the modern names are but guefs'd) on like terms make thir peace. By them he learns that the Town of *Caffibelan*, fuppos'd to be *Verulam*, was not farr diftant; fenc't about with Woods and Marfhes, well ftuff't with men and much Cattel. For Towns then in *Britain* were only Wooddy places ditch't round, and with a Mud Wall encompafs'd againft the inrodes of Enemies. Thether goes *Cæfar* with his Legions, and though
a place

a place of great ſtrength both by Art and Nature, aſſaults it in two places. The *Britans* after ſom defence fled out all at another end of
the Town ; in the flight many were taken,
many ſlain, and great ſtore of Cattel found
there. *Caſſibelan* for all theſe loſſes yet deſerts
not himſelf ; nor was yet his Authoritie ſo
much impair'd, but that in *Kent*, though in
a manner poſſeſt by the Enemie, his Meſſengers and Commands finde obedience anough
to raiſe all the People.   By his direction *Cin-
getorix*, *Carvilius*, *Taximagulus* and *Segonax*,
fowr Kings Reigning in thoſe Countries which
ly upon the Sea, lead them on to aſſault that
Camp wherin the *Romans* had entrench'd thir
Shipping : but they whom *Cæſar* left there,
iſſuing out ſlew many, and took Priſners *Cin-
getorix* a noted Leader, without loſs of thir
own. *Caſſibelan* after ſo many defeats, mov'd
eſpecially by revolt of the Citties from him,
thir inconſtancie and falſhood one to another,
uſes mediation by *Comius of Arras* to ſend Embaſſadors about Treatie of Yeilding. *Cæſar*
who had determin'd to Winter in the Continent, by reaſon that *Gallia* was unſettl'd, and
not much of the Summer now behind, commands him only Hoſtages, and what yearly
Tribute the Iland ſhould pay to *Rome*, forbids
him to moleſt the *Trinobants*, or *Mandubratius* ; and with his Hoſtages, and great number of Captives he puts to Sea, having at twice
embark't his whole Armie. *At his return to* Pliny.
Rome, *as from a glorious enterpriſe, he offers to*
Venus *the Patroneß of his Family, a Corſlet of*
Britiſh

British Pearles. Howbeit other Ancient Writers have spok'n more doubtfully of *Cæsars* Victories heer; and that in plaine termes he fled from hence; for which the common Verse in *Lucan*, with divers passages heer and there in *Tacitus* is alleg'd. *Paulus Orosius*, who took what he wrote from a Historie of *Suetonius* now lost, writes that *Cæsar* in his first journey entertain'd with a sharp fight lost no small number of his Foot, and by tempest nigh all his Horse. *Dion* affirms that once in the second Expedition all his Foot were routed, *Orosius* that another time all his Horse. The *British* Author, whom I use only then when others are all silent, hath many trivial Discourses of *Cæsars* beeing heer, which are best omitted. Nor have wee more of *Cassibelan*, than what the same storie tells, how he warr'd soon after with *Androgeus*, about his Nefew slain by *Evelinus* Nefew to the other; which businefs at length compos'd, *Cassibelan* dies and was buried in *Yorke*, *if the Monmouth Book Fable not.* But at *Cæsars* coming hither, such likeliest were the *Britans*, as the Writers of those times, and thir own actions reprefent them; in courage and warlike readinefs to take advantage by ambush or sudden onset, not inferiour to the *Romans*, nor *Cassibelan* to *Cæsar*, in Weapons, Armes, and the skill of Encamping, Embattailing, Fortifying, overmatch't; thir Weapons were a short Speare and light Target, a Sword alfo by thir side, thir fight somtimes in Chariots phang'd at the Axle with Iron Sithes, thir bodies most part naked, only painted

Orof. Lib. 6. cap. 7. & 9.

Dion.
Mela.
Cæsar.

painted with woad in sundrie figures to seem
terrible as they thought, but poursu'd by Ene- *Herodian.*
mies, not nice of thir painting to run into
Bogs, worse than *wild Irish* up to the Neck,
and there to stay many daies holding a certain
morsel in thir mouths no bigger than a bean, *Dion.*
to suffice hunger; but that receit, and the
temperance it taught, is long since unknown
among us : thir Towns and strong Holds were
spaces of ground fenc't about with a Ditch *Cæsar.*
and great Trees fell'd overthwart each other,
thir buildings within were thatch't Houses for *Strabo.*
themselvs and thir Cattell : In peace the Up-
land Inhabitants besides hunting tended thir *Dion.*
flocks and heards, but with little skill of Countrie affaires; the making of Cheese they commonly knew not, Woole or Flax they spun not, *Strabo.*
gard'ning and planting many of them knew
not ; clothing they had none, but what the
skins of Beasts afforded them, and that not al- *Herodian.*
waies; yet gallantrie they had, painting thir
own skins with several Portratures of Beast, *Solinus.*
Bird, or Flower, *A Vanitie which hath not yet
left us, remov'd only from the skin to the skirt behung now with as many colour'd Ribands and Gewgawes*; towards the Sea side they till'd the *Cæsar.*
ground and liv'd much after the manner of
Gaules thir Neighbours, or first Planters : thir
money was brazen Pieces or iron Rings, thir *Tacitus,Di-*
best Merchandise Tin, the rest trifles of Glass, *odor. Strab.*
Ivorie and such like ; yet Gemms and Pearles
they had, saith *Mela*, in som Rivers : thir Ships *Lucan.*
of light timber wickerd with Oysier between,
and coverd over with Leather, serv'd not
                                        therefore

therefore to transport them far, and thir Commodities were fetch't away by Foren Merchants : thir dealing, faith *Diodorus*, plain and fimple without fraude ; thir Civil Government

Tacitus.

under many Princes and States, not confederate or confulting in common, but miftruftful,

Mela.

and oft-times warring one with the other, which gave them up one by one an eafie Conqueft to the *Romans :* thir Religion was govern'd by a fort of Priefts or Magicians call'd *Druides* from the Greek name of an *Oke*, which Tree they had in great reverence, and the *Misfleto* efpecially growing theron ; *Plinie* writes them skill'd in Magic no lefs than thofe of *Per-*

Dion.

fia : by thir abftaining from a Hen, a Hare, and a Goofe, from Fifh alfo, *faith Dion*, and thir Opinion of the Soules paffing after Death into

Cæfar.

other Bodies, they may be thought to have ftudied *Pythagoras* ; yet Philofophers I cannot call them, reported men factious and ambitious, contending fomtimes about the Arch-

Cæfar.

priefthood not without Civil Warr and flaughter ; nor reftrein'd they the People under them from a lew'd adulterous and inceftuous life, ten or twelv men abfurdly againft Nature, poffeffing one woman as thir common Wife, though of neereft Kin, Mother, Daughter, or Sifter ; Progenitors not to be glori'd in. But the Gofpel, not long after preach't heer abolifh'd fuch impurities, and of the *Romans* we have caufe not to fay much worfe, than that they beate us into fom civilitie ; likely elfe to have continu'd longer in a barbarous and favage manner of life. After *Julius* (for *Julius* before

before his Death tyrannously had made himself Emperor of the *Roman* Common-wealth,
and was slaine in the Senate for so doing) he
who next obtain'd the Empire, *Octavianus Cæ-*   Strabo *L.* 2.
sar Augustus, either contemning the *Iland*, as
Strabo would have us think, whose neither benefit was worth the having, nor enmitie worth
the fearing; or out of a wholsome State-ma-
xim, as som say, to moderate and bound the
Empire from growing vast and unweildie,
made no attempt against the *Britans*. But the
truer cause was partly civil Warr among the
Romans, partly other affairs more urging. For   Year be-
about 20 Years after, all which time the *Bri-*   fore the
tans had liv'd at thir own dispose, *Augustus* in   Birth of
imitation of his Uncle *Julius*, either intending   Christ, 32.
or seeming to intend an expedition hither, was   *Dion. L.* 49.
com into *Gallia*, when the news of a Revolt in   Year be-
Pannonia diverted him : About seven year af-   fore the
ter in the same Resolution, what with the un-   Birth of
settl'dness of *Gallia*, and what with Embassa-   Christ, 25.
dors from *Britain* which met him there, he   *Dion. L.* 53.
proceeded not. The next year, difference a-   24.
rising about Covnants, he was again prevented by other new Commotions in *Spaine*. Nevertheless some of the *British Potentates* omitted not to seek his freindship by guifts offer'd
in the Capitol, and other obsequious addresses.
Insomuch that the whole *Iland* became eev'n   Strabo *L.* 4.
in those daies well known to the *Romans*; too
well perhaps for them, who from the knowledge of us were so like to prove Enemies. But
as for Tribute, the *Britans* paid none to *Augu-*
stus, except what easie Customes were levied
                                            on

on the slight Commodities wherewith they
traded into *Gallia*. After *Cassibelan*, *Tenantius*
the younger Son of *Lud*, according to the *Monmouth* Storie was made King. For *Androgeus*
the Elder, conceaving himself generally hated,
for sideing with the *Romans*, forsook his claime
heer, and follow'd *Cæsars* Fortune. *This King
is recorded Just and Warlike.* His Son *Kymbeline* or *Cunobeline* succeeding, was brought up,
as is said, in the Court of *Augustus*, and with
him held freindly correspondencies to the end;
was a warlike Prince; his Chief Seat *Camalodunum*, or *Maldon*, as by certain of his Coines
yet to be seen, appears. *Tiberius* the next Emperor, adhering alwaies to the advice of *Augustus*, and of himself less careing to extend
the bounds of his Empire, sought not the *Britans*; and they as little to incite him, sent
home courteously the Souldiers of *Germanicus*, that by Shipwrack had bin cast on the *Britan shoar*. But *Caligula* his Successor, a wild
and dissolute Tyrant, haveing past the *Alpes*
with intent to rob and spoile those Provinces,
& stirr'd up by *Adminius* the Son of *Cunobeline*,
who by his Father banish'd, with a small number fled thether to him, made semblance of
marching toward *Britan*; but beeing come to
the Ocean, and there behaveing himself madly, and ridiculously, went back the same way:
yet sent before him boasting Letters to the Senate, as if all *Britan* had bin yeilded him. *Cunobeline* now dead, *Adminius* the Eldest by his
Father banish'd from his Country, and by his
own practice against it, from the Crown,
though

*Tacit. an. L.
2.*
Year after
the Birth
of Christ,
16.
*Dion. Sueton. Cal.
An. Dom.*
40.

though by an old Coine seeming to have also reign'd; *Togodumnus*, and *Caractacus* the two younger, uncertaine whether equal or subordinat in power, were advanc'd into his place. But through civil discord, *Bericus* (what he was furder, is not known) with others of his party flying to *Rome*, persuaded *Claudius* the Emperor to an Invasion. *Claudius* now Consul the third time, and desirous to do something, whence he might gain the honour of a Triumph, at the persuasion of these fugitives, whom the *Britans* demanding, he had deny'd to render, and they for that cause had deny'd furder amity with *Rome*, makes choise of *this Iland* for his Province : and sends before him *Aulus Plautius the Prætor*, with this command, if the business grew difficult to give him notice. *Plautius* with much ado persuaded the Legions to move out of *Gallia*, murmuring that now they must be put to make Warr beyond the Worlds End; for so they counted *Britan*; and what welcom *Julius* the Dictator found there, doubtless they had heard. At last prevail'd with, and hoyssing saile from three several Ports, lest thir Landing should in any one place be resisted, meeting cross winds, they were cast back and disheartn'd : till in the night a Meteor shooting flames from the East, and, as they fansi'd, directing thir course, they took heart again to try the Sea, and without opposition Landed. For the *Britans* haveing heard of thir unwillingness to come, had bin negligent to provide against them ; and retireing to the Woods and Moares, intended to frustrate,

Dion.

43.

Sueton.

ftrate, and wear them out with delaies, as they
had ferv'd *Cæfar* before. *Plautius* after much
trouble to find them out, encountring firft with
Caractacus, then with *Togodumnus*, overthrew
them; and receaving into conditions part of
the *Boduni*, who then were fubject to the *Ca-
tuellani*, and leaving there a Garrifon, went on
toward a River; where the *Britans* not imagining that *Plautius* without a bridge could
pafs, lay on the furder fide carelefs and fecure.
But he fending firft the *Germans*, whofe cu-
ftome was, arm'd as they were, to fwim with
eafe the ftrongeft current, commands them to
ftrike efpecially at the Horfes, whereby the
Chariots, wherein confifted thir chief art of
fight, became unferviceable. To fecond them
he fent *Vefpatian*, who in his later daies obtain'd the Empire, and *Sabinus* his Brother;
who unexpectedly affailing thofe who were
leaft aware, did much execution. Yet not for
this were the *Britans* difmaid; but reuniteing
the next day fought with fuch a courage, as
made it hard to decide which way hung the
Victorie : till *Caius Sidius Geta*, at point to
have bin tak'n, recover'd himfelf fo valiantly,
as brought the day on his fide; for which at
Rome he receav'd high honours. After this
the *Britans* drew back toward the mouth of
Thames, and acquainted with thofe places,
crofs'd over, where the *Romans* following them
through bogs and dangerous flats, hazarded
the lofs of all. Yet the *Germans* getting over,
and others by a bridge at fome place above,
fell on them again with fundry Alarmes and
                                                great

great flaughter; but in the heat of purfuit running themfelvs again into Bogs and Mires, loft as many of thir own. Upon which ill fuccefs, and feeing the *Britans* more enrag'd at the Death of *Togodumnus*, who in one of thefe Battels had bin flain, *Plautius* fearing the worft, and glad that he could hold what he held, as was enjoyn'd him, fends to *Claudius.* He who waited ready with a huge preparation, as if not fafe anough amidft the flowr of all his *Romans*, like a great Eaftern King, with armed Elephants marches through *Gallia.* So full of peril was this enterprife efteem'd, as not without all this Equipage, and ftranger terrors than *Roman* Armies to meet the Native and the naked *Britifh Valour* defending their Country. Joyn'd with *Plautius* who encamping on the Bank of *Thames* attended him, he paffes the River. The *Britans*, who had the courage, but not the wife conduct of old *Caffibelan*, laying all Stratagem afide, in down right Manhood fcrupl'd not to affront in op'n field almoft the whole Powr of the *Roman Empire.* But overcome and vanquifh'd, part by force, others by treatie com in and yeild. *Claudius* therfore who took *Camalodunum*, the Royal Seat of *Cunobeline*, was oft'n by his Armie faluted *Imperator* ; a Militarie Title which ufually they gave thir General after any notable exploit ; but to others not above once in the fame Warr ; as if *Claudius* by thefe Acts had defervd more than the Laws of *Rome* had provided honour to reward. Having therfore difarm'd the *Britans*, but remitted the confif-   *Dion. L.62.*

E   cation

cation of thir goods, for which they worship'd him with Sacrifice and Temple as a God, leaving *Plautius* to subdue what remain'd; he returns to *Rome*, from whence he had bin absent only six moneths, and in *Britan* but 16 daies; sending the news before him of his Victories, though in a small part of the *Iland*. To whom the Senate, as for atchievments of highest merit, decree'd excessive honours; *Arches, Triumphs, annual Solemnities, and the Sirname of Britannicus both to him and his Son.* *Suetonius* writes that *Claudius* found heer no resistance, and that all was done without stroke: but this seems not probable. The *Monmouth Writer* names these two Sons of *Cunobeline, Guiderius,* and *Arviragus*; that *Guiderius* beeing slain in fight, *Arviragus* to conceale it, put on his Brothers Habillements, and in his person held up the Battel to a Victorie; the rest, as of *Hamo* the *Roman Captaine*, *Genuissa* the Emperours Daughter, and such like stuff, is too palpably untrue to be worth reherfing in the midst of Truth. *Plautius* after this, employing his fresh Forces to Conquer on, and quiet the rebelling Countries, found work anough to deserve at his returne a kind of Tryumphant riding into the *Capitol* side by side with the Emperour. *Vespatian* also under *Plautius* had thirtie conflicts with the Enemie; in one of which encompass'd and in great danger, he was valiantly and piously rescu'd by his Son *Titus*: Two powerfull Nations he subdu'd heer, above 20 Townes and *the Ile of Wight*; for which he receaved at *Rome* Tryumphal Ornaments, and other

Tacit. an. 14. 44.

*Suetonius. Claud.*5.24

*Sueton. Vesp. Dion.L.*60. 47.

other great Dignities. *For that Cittie in reward of vertue was ever magnificent : and long after when true merit was ceas'd among them, lest any thing resembling vertue should want honour, the same rewards were yet allow'd to the very shadow and ostentation of merit.* Ostorius in the room of Plautius Vice-prætor, met with turbulent affaires; the *Britans* not ceasing to vex with inrodes all those Countries that were yeilded to the *Romans*; and now the more eagerly, supposing that the new General unacquainted with his Armie, and on the edge of Winter, would not hastily oppose them. But he waighing that first events were most available to breed fear or contempt, with such cohorts as were next at hand sets out against them: whom having routed, so close he follows, as one who meant not to be everie day molested with the cavils of a slight peace, or an emboldn'd Enemie. Lest they should make head again, he disarmes whom he suspects; and to surround them, places many Garrisons upon the Rivers of *Antona* and *Sabrina*. But the *Icenians*, a stout people untouch'd yet by these Warrs, as having before sought alliance with the *Romans*, were the first that brook'd not this. By thir example others rise; and in a chosen place, fenc't with high Banks of Earth, and narrow Lanes to prevent the Horse, warily Encampe. *Ostorius*, though yet not strengthn'd with his Legions, causes the Auxiliar Bands, his Troops also allighting, to assault the rampart. They within though pester'd with thir own number, stood to it like men resolv'd, and in a narrow

50. *Tacitus an.* 12.

compass

compass did remarkable deeds. But over-
powerd at laſt, and others by thir ſucceſs quieted, who till then waverd, *Oſtorius* next bends
his Force upon the *Cangians*, waſting all eeven
to the Sea of *Ireland*, without Foe in his way,
or them, who durſt, ill handl'd ; when the *Brigantes* attempting new matters, drew him back
to ſettle firſt what was unſecure behind him.
They, of whom the chief were puniſh'd, the
reſt forgiv'n, ſoon gave over, but the *Silures*
no way tractable were not to be repreſs'd
without a ſet Warr.   To furder this, *Camalodunum* was planted with a Colony of *Veteran
Souldiers* to be a firme and readie aid againſt
revolts, and a means to teach the Natives *Ro-*
Tacit. vit.   *man* Law and Civilitie.   *Cogidunus* alſo a *Bri-*
Agric.   *tiſh King*, thir faſt freind, had to the ſame intent certain Citties giv'n him : a haughtie
craft, which the *Romans* us'd, to make Kings
alſo the ſervile agents of enſlaving others. But
the *Silures* hardie of themſelvs, rely'd more on
the valour of *Caractacus* ; whom many doubtfull, many proſperous ſucceſſes had made eminent above all that rul'd in *Britan*. He adding
to his courage Policie, and knowing himſelf
to be of ſtrength inferiour, in other advantages the better ; makes the Seat of his Warr
among the *Ordovices* ; a Country wherein all
the odds were to his own Partie, all the difficulties to his Enemie. The Hills and every acceſs he fortifi'd with heaps of Stones, & guards
of men ; to come at whom a River of unſafe
paſſage muſt be firſt waded. The place, as *Camden conjectures*, had thence the name of *Caer-
Caradoc*

Caradoc on the *West* edge *of Shropshire*. He himself continually went up and down, animating
his Officers and Leaders, *that this was the day,*
this the field either to defend their Libertie, or to
die free; calling to mind the names of his glorious Anceſtors, who drove *Cæſar* the Dictator
out of *Britan*, whoſe valour hitherto had preſerv'd them from bondage, thir Wives and
Children from diſhonour. Inflam'd with theſe
words, they all vow thir utmoſt, with ſuch undaunted reſolution as amaz'd the *Roman Gene-*
ral; but the Souldier leſs waighing, becauſe
leſs knowing, clamourd to be led on againſt
any danger. *Oſtorius* after wary circumſpecti-
on bidds them paſs the River : the *Britans* no
ſooner had them within reach of thir Arrows,
Darts, and Stones, but ſlew and wounded
largly of the *Romans*. They on the other ſide
cloſing thir ranks, and over head cloſing thir
Targetts, threw down the looſe rampires of
the *Britans*, and perſue them up the Hills both
light arm'd and Legions; till what with gaul-
ing Darts and heavie ſtrokes, the *Britans* who
wore neither Helmet nor Cuiraſs to defend
them, were at laſt overcome. This the *Ro-*
mans thought a famous Victorie ; wherin the
Wife and Daughter of *Caractacus* were tak'n,
his Brothers alſo redüc'd to obedience ; himſelf eſcaping to *Cartiſmandua Queen of the Bri-*
gantes, againſt faith giv'n was to the Victors
deliverd bound : having held out againſt the
Romans nine years, *ſaith Tacitus*, but by truer
computation, *ſeaven*. Wherby his name was
up through all the adjoyning Provinces, eev'n

to

to *Italy* and *Rome :* many defiring to fee who
he was, that could withftand fo many years
the *Roman* Puiffance : and *Cæfar* to extoll his
own Victorie, extoll'd the man whom he had
vanquifh'd. Beeing brought to *Rome*, the people as to a Solemn fpectacle were call'd together, the Emperors Guard ftood in Armes. In
order came firft the Kings Servants, bearing
his Trophies won in other Warrs, next, his
Brothers, Wife, and Daughter, laft himfelf.
The behaviour of others through fear was low
and degenerate : he only neither in counte-
nance, word, or action, fubmiffive, ftanding at
the Tribunal of *Claudius*, breifly fpake to this
purpofe. *If my mind,* Cæfar, *had bin as mode-*
rate in the highth of Fortune, as my Birth and
Dignitie was eminent, I might have come a freind
rather than a captive into this Cittie. Nor couldft
thou have diflik'd him for a Confederate, fo Noble
of Defcent, and Ruling fo many Nations. My pre-
fent eftate to me difgracefull, to thee is glorious,
I had Riches, Horfes, Armes, and Men ; no won-
der then if I contended, not to lofe them. But if
by Fate, yours only muft be Empire, then of necef-
fitie ours among the reft muft be fubjection. If I
fooner had bin brought to yeild, my Misfortune had
bin leß notorious, your Conqueft had bin leß re-
nown' , and in your fevereft determining of me,
both will be foon forgott'n. But if you grant that
I fhall live, by me will live to you for ever that
praife which is fo neer divine , the clemency of a
Conquerour. Cæfar mov'd at fuch a fpectacle
of Fortune, but efpecially at the noblenefs of
his bearing it, gave him pardon, and to all the
reft,

rest. They all unbound, submissely thank him, and did like reverence to *Agrippina* the Emperors Wife, who sat by in State : a new and disdained sight to the manly eyes of *Romans,* a Woman sitting public in her Female pride among Ensignes and Armed Cohorts. To *Ostorius* Tryumph is decreed; and his Acts esteemed equall to theirs, that brought in Bonds to *Rome* famousest Kings. But the same prosperitie attended not his later Actions heer. For the *Silures,* whether to reveng thir loss of *Caractacus,* or that they saw *Ostorius,* as if now all were done, less earnest to restrain them, besett the Prefect of his Camp, left there with Legionarie Bands to appoint Garrisons : and had not speedie aid com in from the neighbouring Holds and Castles, had cutt them all off; notwithstanding which, the *Prafect with eight Centurions,* and many thir stoubtest men were slaine : and upon the neck of this, meeting first with *Roman* Forragers, then with other Troops hasting to thir releif, utterly foyl'd and broke them also. *Ostorius* sending more after, could hardly stay thir flight; till the waighty Legions coming on, at first poys'd the Battel, at length turn'd the Scale : to the *Britans* without much loss; for by that time it grew night. Then was the Warr shiverd as it were into small frayes and bickerings; not unlike sometimes to so many robberies, in Woods, at Waters, as chance or valour, advice or rashness led them on, commanded or without command. That which most exasperated the *Silures,* was a report of

certain

certain words cast out by the *Emperor*, *That he
would root them out to the verie name*. Therfore
two Cohots more of Auxiliars, by the avarice
of thir Leaders too securely pillageing, they
quite intercepted : and bestowing liberally the
Spoils and Captives, wherof they took plen-
tie ; drew other Countries to joyne with them.
These losses falling so thick upon the *Romans*,
Ostorius with the thought, and anguish therof
ended his daies : the *Britans* rejoycing, although no Battel, that yet adverse Warr had
worne out so great a Souldier. *Cæsar* in his
place ordains *Aulus Didius* : but ere his coming, though much hastn'd, that the Province
might not want a Governour ; the *Silures* had
giv'n an overthrow to *Manlius Valens* with his
Legion, rumor'd on both sides greater than
was true; by *the Silures* to amate the new General; by him in a double respect, of the more
praise if he queld them, or the more excuse if
he fail'd. Mean time the *Silures* forgett not to
infest the *Roman* pale with wide excursions ;
till *Didius* marching out, kept them somwhat
more within bounds. Nor were they long to
seek, who after *Caractacus* should lead them ;
for next to him in worth and skill of Warr,
Venutius a Prince of the Brigantes merited to be
thir chief. He at first faithfull to the *Romans*,
and by them protected, was the Husband of
Cartismandua Q. of the Brigantes, himself perhaps reigning elsewhere. She who had betray'd *Caractacus* and her Countrie to adorne
the Tryumph of *Claudius*, thereby grown powerfull and gratious with the *Romans*, presuming

ming on the hire of her treason, deserted her
Husband ; and marrying *Vellocatus* one of his
Squires, conferrs on him the Kingdom also.
This deed so odious and full of infamie, disturb'd the whole State : *Venutius* with other
Forces, and the help of her own Subjects, who
detested the example of so foule a fact, and
with all the uncomlines of thir Subjection to
the Monarchie of a Woman, a peece of manhood not every day to be found among *Britans*, though shee had got by suttle train his
Brother with many of his Kindred into her
hands, brought her soon below the confidence
of beeing able to resist longer.   When imploring the *Roman* aid, with much adoe, and after
many a hard encounter shee escap'd the punishment which was readie to have seis'd her. *Venutius* thus debar'd the autority of ruling his
own Houshold, justly turnes his anger against
the *Romans* themselvs ; whose magnanimitie
not wont to undertake dishonourable causes,
had arrogantly intermeddl'd in his domestic
affaires, to uphold the Rebellion of an adul-
tress against her Husband.   And the Kingdom
he retain'd against thir utmost opposition ; and
of Warr gave them thir fill : first in a sharpe
conflict of uncertain event, then against the
Legion of *Cæsius Nasica*. Insomuch that *Didius*
growing old and mannaging the Warr by Deputies, had work anough to stand on his defence, with the gaining now and then of a
small Castle.   And *Nero* (for in that part of *Tacit. vit.*
the *Ile* things continu'd in the same plight to *Agric.*
the Reigne of *Vespatian*) was minded but for
                                                  shame

Tacit. Hist.
3. *Sueton.* fhame to have withdrawn the *Roman* Forces
out of *Britan :* In other parts whereof, about
the fame time, other things befell. *Verannius,*
whom *Nero* fent hither to fucceed *Didius,* dying in his firft Year, fave a few inrodes upon
the *Silures,* left only a great boaft behind him,
That in two years, had he liv'd, he would have
Conquerd all. But *Suetonius Paulinus,* who next
was fent hither, efteem'd a Souldier equall to
the beft in that age, for two years together
went on profperoufly ; both confirming what
was got, and fubduing onward. At laft over-
confident of his prefent actions, and emula-
ting others, of whofe deeds he heard from a-
broad, marches up as farr as *Mona, the Ile of*
Anglefey, a populous place. For they it feems
had both entertain'd fugitives, and giv'n good
affiftance to the reft that withftood him. He
makes him Boates with flat bottoms, fitted to
the Shallows which he expected in that narrow Frith : His Foot fo pafs'd over, his Horfe
waded or fwom. Thick upon the fhoar ftood
feveral grofs bands of men well weapn'd, many women like furies running to and fro in dif-
mal habit with hair loofe about thir fhoulders,
held Torches in thir hands. The *Druids,* thofe
were thir Priefts, of whome more in another
place, with hands lift up to Heav'n uttering
direfull praiers, aftonifh'd the *Romans* ; who
at fo ftrange a fight ftood in a-maze though
wounded : at length awak'd and encourag'd
by thir General, not to fear a barbarous and
lunatic rout, fall on, and beat them down
fcorch't and rouling in thir own fire. Then
were

were they yoak'd with Garrisons, and the
places consecrate to thir bloodie superstitions destroi'd. For whom they took in Warr
they held it lawfull to Sacrifice; and by the
entrails of men us'd divination. While thus
Paulinus had his thought still fix'd before, to
goe on winning, his back lay broad op'n to occasion of losing more behind. For the *Britans* urg'd and opprefs'd with many unsuffer-
able injuries, had all banded themselvs to a
general revolt. The particular causes are not
all writt'n by one Author; *Tacitus* who liv'd
next those times of any to us extant, writes
that *Prasutagus King of the Icenians* abounding
in wealth had left *Cæsar* Coheir with his two
Daughters; thereby hoping to have secur'd
from all wrong both his Kingdome and his
House; which fell out far otherwise. For under colour to oversee and take possession of the
Emperours new Inheritance, his Kingdom became a prey to Centurions, his House to ra-
v'ning Officers, his Wife *Boadicea* violated
with Stripes, his Daughters with Rape, the
wealthiest of his Subjects, as it were by the
Will and Testament of thir King thrown out
of thir Estates, his Kindred made little better
than Slaves. The new Colony also at *Camalodunum* took House or Land from whome they
pleas'd, terming them Slaves and Vassals; the
Souldiers complying with the Colony, out of
hope hereafter to use the same licence themselvs. Moreover the Temple erected to *Claudius* as a badge of thir eternal slaverie, stood a
great Eye-fore; the Priests whereof under pre-
text

text of what was due to the Religious Service,
wasted and imbezl'd each mans substance up-

Dion.   on themselvs. And *Catus Decianus* the Procurator endeavour'd to bring all thir goods within the compass of a new Confiscation, by dif-
avowing the remittment of *Claudius.*   Lastly,
Seneca in his Books a Philosopher, having
drawn the *Britans* unwillingly to borrow of
him vast summs upon faire promises of easy
loan, and for repayment to take their own
time, on a sudden compells them to pay in all
at once with great extortion.   Thus provok't
by heaviest sufferings, and thus invited by opportunities in the absence of *Paulinus,* the *Icenians,* and by their Example the *Trinobantes,*
and as many else as hated servitude, rise up in
Armes. Of these ensuing troubles many foregoing signes appear'd : the image of Victorie
at *Camalodunum* fell down of it self with her
face turn'd as it were to the *Britans*; certaine
Women in a kind of ecstasie foretold of Calamities to come; in the Counsel-House were
heard by night barbarous noises, in the Thea-
ter hideous howlings, in the Creek horrid
fights betok'ning the destruction of that Colony ; heerto the Ocean seeming of a bloody
hew, and human shapes at a low ebb left im-
printed on the sand, wrought in the *Britans*
new courage, in the *Romans* unwonted fears.
Camalodunum where the *Romans* had seated
themselvs to dwell pleasantly, rather than de-
fensively, was not fortifi'd : against that therfore the *Britans* make first assault.   The Souldiers within were not very many.   *Decianus*
the

the Procurator could fend them but 200, thofe
ill arm'd : and through the treachery of fome
among them, who fecretly favour'd the infur-
rection, they had deferr'd both to entrench,
and to fend out fuch as bore not Armes ; fuch
as did, flying to the Temple, which on the fecond day was forcibly tak'n, were put all to
the Sword, the Temple made a heap, the reft
rifl'd and burnt. *Petilius Cerealis* coming to his
fuccour, is in his way met, and overthrown,
his whole Legion cut to peeces ; he with his
Horfe hardly efcaping to the *Roman Camp*. *Decianus*, whofe rapine was the caufe of all this,
fled into *Gallia*. But *Suetonius* at thefe tidings
not difmay'd, through the midft of his Enemies Countrie marches to *London* (though not
term'd a Colony, yet full of *Roman* Inhabitants, and for the frequency of trade and o-
ther commodities, a Town eev'n then of principal note) with purpofe to have made there
the feat of Warr. But confidering the fmall-
nefs of his numbers, and the late rafhnefs of
Petilius, he choofes rather with the lofs of one
Town to fave the reft. Nor was he flexible to
any prayers or weeping of them that befought
him to tarry there ; but taking with him fuch
as were willing, gave fignal to depart; they
who through weaknefs of Sex or Age, or love
of the place went not along, perifh'd by the E-
nemie ; fo did *Verulam a Roman free Town*. For
the *Britans* omitting Forts and Caftles, flew
thether firft where richeft bootie , and the
hope of pillageing toald them on. In this maf-
facre, about 70 thoufand *Romans* and thir affo-
ciats

ciats in the places above-mention'd, of a certaine, loſt thir lives. None might be ſpar'd, none ranſom'd, but taſted all either a preſent or a lingring Death; no crueltie that either outrage, or the inſolence of ſucceſs putt into thir heads, was left unacted. The *Roman*

Dion.L.62. Wives and Virgins hang'd up all naked, had thir Breaſts cut off, and ſow'd to thir mouths; that in the grimneſs of Death they might ſeem to eat thir own fleſh; while the *Britans* fell to feaſting and carouſing in the Temple of *Andate* thir Goddeſs of Victorie. *Suetonius* adding to his Legion other old Officers, and Souldiers therabout, which gatherd to him, were neer upon ten thouſand; and purpoſing with thoſe not to deferr Battel, had choſ'n a place narrow, and not to be overwing'd, on his rear a Wood; being well inform'd that his Enemies were all in Front on a plain unapt for ambuſh: the Legionaries ſtood thick in order, impal'd with light armed; the Horſe on either Wing. The *Britans* in Companies and Squadrons were every where ſhouting and ſwarming, ſuch a multitude as at other time never; no leſs reckon'd than 200 and 30 thouſand, ſo fierce and confident of Victorie, that thir Wives alſo came in Waggons to ſit and behold the ſport, as they made full account, of killing *Romans* : a folly doubtleſs for the ſerious *Romans* to ſmile at, as a ſure tok'n of proſpering that day : a Woeman alſo was thir Commander in Chief. For *Boadicea* and her Daughters ride about in a Chariot, telling the tall Champions as a great encouragement,

that

that with the *Britans* it was usual for Woemen
to be thir Leaders.   A deal of other fondness
they put into her mouth, not worth recital;
how she was lash'd, how her Daughters were
handl'd, things worthier silence, retirement,
and a Vail, than for a Woeman to repeat, as
don to hir own person, or to hear repeated
before an host of men.   *The Greek History* Dion.
setts her in the field on a high heap of Turves,
in a loose-bodied Gown declaming, a Spear in
her hand, a Hare in her bosome, which after
a long circumlocution she was to let slip a-
mong them for lucks sake, then praying to
Andate the British Goddeß, to talk again as
fondly as before.   And this they do out of a
vanity, hoping to embellish and set out thir
Historie with the strangeness of our manners,
not careing in the mean while to brand us
with the rankest note of Barbarism, as if in
Britain Woemen were Men, and Men Woemen.   I affect not set speeches in a Historie,
unless known for certain to have bin so spok'n
in effect as they are writ'n, nor then, unless
worth rehearsal; and to invent such, though
eloquently, as som Historians have done, is an
abuse of posteritie, raising, in them that read,
other conceptions of those times and persons
than were true.   Much less therfore do I purpose heer or elsewhere to Copie out tedious
Orations without decorum, though in thir
Authors compos'd ready to my hand.   Hitherto what we have heard of *Cassibelan, Togadum-
nus, Venusius,* and *Caractacus* hath bin full of
magnanimitie, soberness, and martial skill:
but

but the truth is, that in this Battel, and whole
bufinefs, the *Britans* never more plainly manifefted themfelves to be right *Barbarians*; no
rule, no forefight, no forecaft, experience or
eftimation, either of themfelves or of thir Enemies; fuch confufion, fuch impotence, as
feem'd likeft not to a Warr, but to the wild
hurrey of a diftracted Woeman, with as mad
a Crew at her heeles. Therfore *Suetonius* contemning thir unruly noifes, and fierce looks,
heart'ns his men but to ftand clofe a while,
and ftrike manfully this headlefs rabble that
ftood neereft, the reft would be a purchafe, rather than a toil. And fo it fell out; for the Legion, when they faw thir time, burfting out
like a violent wedge, quickly broke and diffi-
pated what oppos'd them; all elfe held only
out thir necks to the flayer, for thir own Carts
and Waggons were fo plac'd by themfelvs, as
left them but little room to efcape between.
The *Roman* flew all; Men, Woemen, and the
very drawing Horfes lay heap'd along the field
in a gory mixture of flaughter. About fowr-
fcore thoufand *Britans* are faid to have bin
flain on the place; of the Enemy fcarfe 400
and not many more wounded. *Boadicea* poyfon'd her felf, or, as others fay, fick'n'd and
dy'd. She was of Stature big and tall, of vi-
fage grim and ftern, harfh of voice, her hair
of bright colour flowing down to her hipps;
fhe wore a plighted Garment of divers colours, with a great gold'n Chain; button'd o-
ver all a thick robe. *Gildas* calls her the craf-
tie Lionefs, and leaves an ill fame upon her
doings.

Dion.

doings. *Dion* sets down otherwise the order of this fight, and that the field was not won without much difficultie, nor without inten- tion of the *Britans* to give another Battel, had not the Death of *Boadicea* come betweene. Howbeit *Suetonius* to preserve Discipline, and to dispatch the reliques of Warr, lodg'd with all his Armie in the op'n field; which was supply'd out of *Germany* with 1000 Horse, and 10000 Foot; thence dispers'd to Winter, and with Incursions to wast those Countries that stood out. But to the *Britans* Famine was a worse affliction; having left off during this uproar, to Till the ground, and made reck'n- ing to serve themselves on the Provisions of thir Enemie. Neverthelesse those Nations that were yet untaim'd, hearing of some discord ris'n between *Suetonius*, and the new Procura- tor *Classicianus*, were brought but slowly to terms of peace; and the rigor us'd by *Sueto- nius* on them that yeilded, taught them the better course to stand on thir defence. For it is *Tacit. vit* certaine, that *Suetonius*, though else a worthie *Agric.* man, over-proud of his Victorie, gave too much way to his anger against the *Britans*. *Classician* therfore sending such word to *Rome*, that these severe proceedings would beget an endlesse Warr, *Polycletus*, no *Roman* but a Cour- tier, was sent by *Nero* to examin how things went. He admonishing *Suetonius* to use more mildnesse, aw'd the Armie, and to the *Britans* gave matter of Laughter. Who so much eeven till then were nurs'd up in thir Native Liber- tie, as to wonder that so great a General with

F

his

his whole Armie should be at the rebuke and
ordering of a Court Servitor. But *Suetonius* a
while after having lost a few Gallies on the
shoar, was bid resigne his command to *Petro-
nius Turpilianus*, who not provoking the *Britans*, nor by them provok'd, was thought to
have pretended the love of peace to what indeed was his love of ease and sloth. *Trebellius
Maximus* follow'd his steps, usurping the name
of gentle Government to any remisness or
neglect of Discipline; which brought in first
licence, next disobedience into his Camp; incens'd against him partly for his covetousness,
partly by the incitement of *Roscius Cælius* Legat of a Legion; with whom formerly dis-
agreeing, now that Civil Warr began in the

Tacit. Hist. Empire, he fell to op'n discord; charging him
8.1. & vit. with disorder, and sedition, and him *Cælius*
Agric. with peeling and defrauding the Legions of
thir pay; insomuch that *Trebellius* hated, and
deserted of the Souldiers, was content a while
to govern by a base entreaty, and forc'd at
length to flie the Land. Which notwithstanding remain'd in good quiet, govern'd by *Cælius*
and the other Legat of a Legion, both faithful

69. to *Vitellius* then Emperour; who sent hither
Tacit. Hist. *Vettius Bolanus*; under whose lenity, though
2. & vit. not tainted with other fault, against the *Bri-*
Agric. *tans* nothing was done, nor in thir own Disci-
70. pline reform'd. *Petilius Cerealis* by appointment of *Vespasian* succeeding, had to doe with
the populous *Brigantes* in many Battails, and

74. som of those, not unbloodie. For as we heard
Calvis. before, it was *Venusius* who eeven to these
times

times held them tack, both himself remaining to the end unvanquish'd, and som part of his Countrie not so much as reach't. It appeares also by several passages in the Histories of *Tacitus*, that no small number of *British Forces* were commanded over Sea the year before to serve in those bloodie Warrs betweene *Otho* and *Vitellius*, *Vitellius* and *Vespasian* contending for the Empire. To *Cerealis* succeeded *Julius Frontinus* in the Government of *Britan*, who by tameing the *Silures*, a people warlike and strongly inhabiting, augmented much his reputation. But *Julius Agricola*, whom *Vespasian* in his last year sent hither, train'd up from his youth in the *British* Wars, extended with Victories the *Roman* Limit beyond all his Predecessors. His coming was in the midst of Summer ; and the *Ordovices* to welcome the new General, had hew'n in peeces a whole Squadron of Horse , which lay upon thir bounds, few escaping. *Agricola*, who perceav'd that the noise of this defeat had also in the Province desirous of novelty, stirr'd up new expectations, resolves to be before-hand with the danger : and drawing together the choice of his Legions with a competent number of Auxiliars, not beeing met by the *Ordovices*, who kept the Hills, himself in the head of his men hunts them up and down through difficult places, almost to the final extirpating of that whole Nation.   With the same current of success, what *Paulinus* had left unfinish'd he Conquers in the *Ile of Mona :* for the Ilanders altogether fearless of his approach, whom

Tacit. Hist.
3. & vit.
Agric.

79.

F 2   they

they knew to have no Shipping, when they saw themselvs invaded on a sudden by the Auxiliars, whose Countrie use had taught them to swimm over with Horse and Armes, were compel'd to yeild. This gain'd *Agricola* much opinion; who at his very entrance, a time which others bestow'd of course in hearing complements and gratulations, had made such early progress into laborious and hardest enterprises. But by farr not so famous was *Agricola* in bringing Warr to a speedie end, as in cutting off the causes from whence Warr arises. For he knowing that the end of Warr was not to make way for Injuries in Peace, began Reformation from his own House; permitted not his Attendants and Followers to sway, or have to doe at all in Public Affairs: laies on with equalitie the proportions of Corn and Tribute that were impos'd; takes off exactions, and the Fees of encroaching Officers, heavier than the tribute it self. For the Countries had bin compell'd before, to sitt and wait the op'ning of public Granaries, and both to sell and to buy thir Corn at what rate the Publicans thought fitt; the Pourveyers also commanding when they pleas'd to bring it in, not to the neerest, but still to the remotest places, either by the compounding of such as would be excus'd, or by causing a Dearth, where none was, made a particular gain. These greevances and the like, he in the time of peace removing, brought peace into som credit; which before, since the *Romans* coming, had as ill a name as Warr. The Summer following,

lowing, *Titus then Emperor*, he so continually
with inroads disquieted the Enemie over all
the Ile, and after terror so allur'd them with
his gentle demeanour, that many Citties which
till that time would not bend, gave Hostages,
admitted Garrisons, and came in voluntarily.
The Winter he spent all in worthie actions;
teaching and promoting like a public Father
the Institutes and Customes of civil Life. The
Inhabitants rude and scatter'd, and by that the
proner to Warr, he so perswaded as to build
Houses, Temples, and Seats of Justice; and
by praising the forward, quick'ning the flow,
assisting all, turn'd the name of necessitie into
an emulation. He caus'd moreover the No-
blemens Sons to be bred up in Liberal Arts;
and by preferring the Witts of *Britan*, before
the Studies of *Gallia*, brought them to affect
the Latine Eloquence, who before hated the
Language. Then were the *Roman* fashions imi-
tated, and the Gown; after a while the in-
citements also and materials of Vice, and vo-
luptuous life, proud Buildings, Baths, and the
elegance of Banqueting; which the foolisher
sort call'd Civilitie, but was indeed a secret
Art to prepare them for bondage. Spring appearing, he took the Field, and with a prosperous expedition wasted as farr Northward as
the Frith of *Taus* all that obey'd not; with
such a terror, as he went, that the *Roman* Armie, though much hinder'd by tempestuous
weather, had the leasure to build Forts and
Castles where they pleas'd, none daring to oppose them. Besides, *Agricola* had this excel-

lence

Ience in him, so providently to choose his places where to fortifie, as not another General
then alive. No Sconce, or Fortress of his raising was ever known either to have bin forc'd,
or yeilded up, or quitted. Out of these im-
pregnable by seige, or in that case duely releev'd, with continual irruptions he so prevail'd, that the Enemie, whose manner was in
Winter to regain, what in Summer he had
lost, was now alike in both seasons kept short,
and streit'n'd. For these exploits then e-
Dion. L.65. steem'd so great, and honourable, *Titus* in
whose Reign they were atcheev'd, was the fifteenth time saluted Imperator; and of him
Agricola receav'd triumphal honours. The
82. fourth Summer, *Domitian* then ruleing the
Empire, he spent in settling and confirming
what the year before he had travail'd over
with a running Conquest. And had the valour of his Souldiers bin answerable, he had
reach'd that year, as was thought, the utmost
bounds of *Britan.* For *Glota*, and *Bodotria*,
now *Dunbritton*, and the Frith of *Edinburrow*;
two opposite Armes of the Sea, divided only
by a neck of Land; and all the Creeks and In-
lets on this side, were held by the *Romans*, and
the Enemie driv'n as it were into another I-
83. land. In his fift year he pass'd over into the
Orcades, as we may probably guess, and other
Scotch Iles; discovering and subdueing Nations till then unknown. He gain'd also with
his Forces that part of *Britan* which faces *Ireland*, as aiming also to conquer that Iland;
where one of the Irish Kings driv'n out by Civil

vil Warrs, coming to him, he both gladly receav'd, and retain'd him as against a fitt time.
The Summer ensuing, on mistrust that the Nations beyond *Bodotria* would generally rise,
and forelay the passages by Land, he caus'd
his Fleet, making a great shew, to bear along
the Coast, and up the Friths and Harbours;
joyning most commonly at night on the same
shoar both Land and Sea Forces, with mutual
shouts and loud greetings.   At sight whereof
the *Britans*, not wont to see thir Sea so ridd'n,
were much daunted. Howbeit the *Caledonians*
with great preparation, and by rumor, as of
things unknown much greater, taking Armes,
and of thir own accord begining Warr by the
assault of sundry Castles, sent back some of
thir fear to the *Romans* themselves : and there
were of the Commanders, who cloaking thir
fear under shew of sage advice, counsel'd the
General to retreat back on this side *Bodotria*.
He in the mean while having intelligence, that
the Enemie would fall on in many Bodies, divided also his Armie into three parts. Which
advantage the *Britans* quickly spying, and on
a sudden uniting what before they had disjoyn'd, assaile by night with all thir Forces
that part of the *Roman* Armie, which they
knew to be the weakest; and breaking in upon the Camp surpris'd between sleep and fear,
had begun some Execution. When *Agricola*,
who had learnt what way the Enemies took,
and follow'd them with all speed, sending before him the lightest of his Horse and Foot to
charge them behind, the rest as they came on

to affright them with clamour, so ply'd them without respite, that by approach of day the *Roman* Ensigns glittering all about, had encompass'd the *Britans*: who now after a sharp fight in the very Ports of the Camp, betook them to thir wonted refuge, the Woods and Fens, poursu'd a while by the *Romans*, that day else in all appearance had ended the Warr. The Legions reincourag'd by this event, they also now boasting, who but lately trembl'd, cry all to be led on as farr as there was *British* ground. The *Britans* also not acknowledging the loss of that day to *Roman* Valour, but to the policy of thir Captain, abated nothing of thir stoutness; but arming thir Youth, conveying thir Wives and Children to places of safty, in frequent Assemblies, and by Solemn Covenants bound themselves to mutual assistance against the Common Enemy. About the same time a Cohort of *Germans* having slain thir Centurion with other *Roman* Officers in a mutiny, and for fear of punishment fled a Shipboard, launch'd forth in three light Gallies without Pilot: and by tide or weather carried round about the Coast, using Piracy where they landed, while thir Ships held out, and as thir skill serv'd them, with various fortune, were the first discoverers to the *Romans* that *Britan* was an Iland. The following Summer, *Agricola* having before sent his Navie to hover on the Coast, and with sundrie and uncertaine landings to divert and disunite the *Britans*, himself with a power best appointed for expedition, wherin also were many *Britans*,

Dion. L. 66.

85.

tans, whom he had long try'd both valiant and faithful, marches onward to the Mountaine *Grampius,* where the *British,* above 30000, were now lodg'd, and still encreasing : for neither would thir old men, so many as were yet vigorous and lusty, be left at home, long practis'd in Warr, and every one adorn'd with some badge, or cognisance of his warlike deeds long agoe. Of whom *Galgacus,* both by birth and merit the prime Leader, to thir courage, though of it self hot and violent, is by his rough Oratory, in detestation of servitude and the *Roman* yoke, said to have added much more eagerness of fight; testifi'd by thir shouts and barbarous applauses. As much did on the others side *Agricola* exhort his Souldiers to Victorie and Glorie ; as much the Souldiers by his firm and well grounded Exhortations were all on a fire to the onset. But first he orders them in this sort. Of 8000 Auxiliar Foot he makes his middle ward, on the wings 3000 Horse, the Legions as a reserve, stood in array before the Camp ; either to seise the Victorie won without thir own hazard, or to keep up the Battaile if it should need. The *British* Powers on the hill side, as might best serve for shew and terrour, stood in thir Battalions; the first on eeven ground, the next rising behind, as the hill ascended. The field between rung with the noise of Horsemen and Chariots ranging up and down. *Agricola* doubting to be over wing'd, stretches out his Front, though somwhat with the thinnest, insomuch that many advis'd to bring up the Legions : yet he not altering,

altering, alights from his Horſe, and ſtands on
foot before the Enſignes. The fight began a-
loof, and the *Britans* had a certain skill with
thir broad ſwaſhing Swords and ſhort Bucklers
either to ſtrike aſide, or to bear off the Darts
of their Enemies; and withall to ſend back
ſhowers of thir own. Until *Agricola* diſcern-
ing that thoſe little Targets and unweildie
Glaves ill pointed, would ſoon become ridiculous againſt the thruſt and cloſe, commanded
three *Batavian* Cohorts, and two of the *Tun-
grians* exercis'd and arm'd for cloſe fight, to
draw up, and come to handy ſtrokes. The *Batavians*, as they were commanded, running in
upon them, now with thir long Tucks thruſting at the face, now with thir piked Targets
bearing them down, had made good riddance
of them that ſtood below; and for haſt omitting furder Execution, began apace to advance
up hill, ſeconded now by all the other Cohorts.
Mean while the Horſe-men fly, the Charioters
mixe themſelves to fight among the Foot;
where many of thir Horſe alſo fall'n in diſor-
derly, were now more a miſchief to thir own,
than before a terrour to thir Enemies. The
Battaile was a confus'd heap; the ground un-
equal; Men, Horſes, Chariots crowded pel-
mel; ſomtimes in little room, by and by in
large, fighting, ruſhing, felling, over-bearing,
over-turning. They on the Hill, which were
not yet come to blows, perceaving the ſewneſs
of thir Enemies, came down amain; and had
enclos'd the *Romans* unawares behind, but that
Agricola with a ſtrong Body of Horſe, which he
                                          reſerv'd

referv'd for fuch a purpofe, repell'd them back
as faft : and others drawn off the front, were
commanded to wheel about and charge them
on the backs.   Then were the *Romans* clearly
Maifters; they follow, they wound, they take,
and to take more, kill whom they take : the
Britans in whole Troops with weapons in thir
hands, one while flying the purfuer, anon without weapons defperately running upon the
flayer.   But all of them, when once they got
the Woods to thir fhelter, with frefh boldnefs
made head again, and the forwardeft on a
fudden they turn'd and flew, the reft fo ham-
per'd, as had not *Agricola*, who was every
where at hand, fent out his readieft Cohorts,
with part of his Horfe to alight and fcowr the
Woods, they had receiv'd a foyle in the midft
of Victorie; but following with a clofe and
orderly pourfuit, the *Britans* fled again, and
were totally fcatter'd; till night and weari-
nefs ended the chafe.   And of them that day
10000 fell; of the *Romans* 340, among whom
Aulus Atticus the Leader of a Cohort, carried
with heat of youth and the fircenefs of his
Horfe too farr on.   The *Romans* jocond of this
Victorie, and the fpoile they got, fpent the
night; the vanquifhed wandring about the
field, both Men and Women, fom lamenting,
fom calling thir loft friends, or carrying off
thir wounded; others forfaking, fom burning
thir own Houfes; and it was certain anough,
that there were who with a ftern compaffion
laid violent hands on thir Wives and Children
to prevent the more violent hands of hoftile
injurie.

injurie. Next day appearing manifested more
plainly the greatnefs of thir lofs receav'd ; every where filence, defolation, houfes burning a-
far off, not a man feen, all fled, and doubtfull
whither : fuch word the Scouts bringing in
from all parts, and the Summer now fpent, no
fit feafon to difperfe a Warr, the *Roman* General leads his Armie among the *Horeftians* ; by
whom Hoftages being giv'n, he commands his
Admiral with a fufficient Navie to faile round
the Coaft of *Britan :* himfelf with flow marches, that his delay in paffing might ferve to
awe thofe new conquer'd Nations, beftows his
Armie in thir Winter-quarters. The Fleet
alfo having fetch't a profperous and fpeedy
compafs about the Ile, put in at the Haven
Camden. *Trutulenfis ,* now *Richborrow* neer *Sandwich ,*
Juvenal, from whence it firft fet out : and now likelieft,
Sat. 2. if not two years before, as was mention'd, the
Romans might difcover and fubdue the Iles of
Eutrop.L.7. *Orkney* ; which others with lefs reafon following *Eufebius* and *Orofius,* attribute to the deeds
of *Claudius.* Thefe perpetual exploits abroad
won him wide fame ; with *Domitian,* under
whom great virtue was as punifhable as op'n
Dion.L.66. crime, won him hatred. For he maligning the
renown of thefe his acts, in fhew decreed him
86. honours, in fecret devis'd his ruin. *Agricola*
therefore commanded home for doeing too
much, of what he was fent to doe, left the Province to his Succeffor quiet and fecure. Whether he, as is conjectured, were *Saluftius Lu-*
cullus, or before him fom other, for *Suetonius*
only names him Legat of *Britan* under *Domi-*
tian ;

tian; but furder of him, or ought elſe done
here until the time of *Hadrian*, is no where
plainly to be found. Some gather by a Preface
in *Tacitus* to the Book of his Hiſtories, that
what *Agricola* won here, was ſoon after by *Domitian* either through want of valour loſt, or
through envy neglected. And *Juvenal* the
Poet ſpeaks of *Arviragus* in theſe days, and
not before, King of *Britan:* who ſtood ſo well
in his reſiſtance, as not only to be talk'd of at
Rome, but to be held matter of a glorious Triumph, if *Domitian* could take him Captive, or
overcome him. Then alſo *Claudia Rufina* the
Daughter of a *Britan*, and ∢Wife of *Pudence* a
Roman Senator, liv'd at *Rome*; famous by the
Verſe of *Martial* for beauty, wit, and learning. The next we hear of *Britan*, is that when
Trajan was Emperor, it revolted, and was ſub-
dued. Under *Adrian*, *Julius Severus*, ſaith
Dion, govern'd the Iland, a prime Souldier of
that Age, but he being call'd away to ſuppreſs
the Jews then in tumult, left things at ſuch
paſs, as caus'd the Emperor in perſon to take
a journey hither; where many things he reform'd, and, as *Auguſtus* and *Tiberius* counſel'd to gird the Empire within moderate
bounds; he rais'd a Wall with great ſtakes
driv'n in deep, and faſtn'd together, in manner of a ſtrong mound, 80 mile in length, to
divide what was *Roman* from *Barbarian:* no
antient Author names the place, but old in-
ſcriptions, and ruin it ſelf yet teſtifies where
it went along between *Solway* Frith by *Carlile*,
and the mouth of *Tine*. *Hadrian* having quieted

*Spartianus
in vit. Ha-
drian.*

122.
*Spartianus
ibid.*

Camden.   ed the Iland, took it for honour to be titl'd on
his Coine, the Reſtorer of *Britan*. In his time
alſo *Priſcus Licinius,* as appears by an old in-
ſcription, was Lieutenant heer. *Antoninus*
Pauſan. ar- *Pius* reigning, the *Brigantes* ever leaſt patient
chad.   of Foren ſervitude, breaking in upon *Genou-*
nia (which *Camden* gueſſes to be *Guinethia* or
North-Wales) part of the *Roman* Province, were
with the loſs of much territory driv'n back by
Capitolin.   *Lollius Urbicus,* who drew another Wall of
vit. Anton. Turves; in likelihood much beyond the for-
144.   mer, and as *Camden* proves, between the Frith
Capitolin.
Marc. Ant. of *Dunbritton,* and of *Edinborrow*; to hedge
Philoſ.   out incurſions from the North. And *Seius Sa-*
162.   *turninus,* as is collected from the digeſts, had
Digeſt. L. charge heer of the *Roman* Navie. With like
36.   ſucceſs did *Marcus Aurelius* next Emperor by
his Legate *Calphurnius Agricola* finiſh heer a
new Warr : *Commodus* after him obteining the
Empire. In his time, as among ſo many different accounts may ſeem moſt probable, *Lu-*
Beda.   *cius* a ſuppos'd King in ſome part of *Britan,* the
firſt of any King in *Europe,* that we read of,
receav'd the Chriſtian Faith, and this Nation
the firſt by publick Authority profeſs'd it : a
high and ſingular Grace from above, if ſince-
ritie and perſeverance went along, otherwiſe
an empty boaſt, and to be fear'd the verifying
of that true ſentence, *the firſt ſhall be laſt.* And
indeed the praiſe of this action is more proper to King *Lucius* than common to the *Na-*
tion; whoſe firſt profeſſing by publick Authority was no real commendation of thir true
faith; which had appear'd more ſincere and
praiſe-

praiſe-worthy, whether in this or other Nation, firſt profeſs'd without publick Authority
or againſt it, might elſe have bin but outward
conformity. *Lucius* in our *Monmouth* Storie is
made the ſecond by deſcent from *Marius*. *Marius* the Son of *Arviragus* is there ſaid to have
overthrown the *Picts* then firſt coming out of
Scythia, ſlain *Roderic* thir King; and in ſign of
Victorie to have ſet up a Monument of Stone
in the Country ſince call'd *Weſtmaria*; but
theſe things have no foundation. *Coilus* the
Son of *Marius*, all his reign, which was juſt and
peaceable, holding great amity with the *Romans*, left it hereditary to *Lucius*. He (if *Beda*
err not, living neer 500 years after, yet our
antienteſt Author of this report) ſent to *Eleutherius* then Biſhop of *Rome*, an improbable
Letter, as ſome of the Contents diſcover, de-   181.
ſiring that by his appointment he and his people might receave Chriſtianitie. From whom
two Religious Doctors, nam'd in our Chronicles *Faganus* and *Deruvianus*, forthwith ſent,
are ſaid to have converted and baptiz'd well
nigh the whole Nation: thence *Lucius* to have   *Nennius.*
had the ſirname of *Levermaur*, that is to ſay,
great light. Nor yet then firſt was the Chriſtian Faith heer known, but eev'n from the later daies of *Tiberius*, as *Gildas* confidently affirms, taught and propagated, and that as ſom
ſay by *Simon Zelotes*, as others by *Joſeph* of *Ari-
mathæa*, *Barnabas*, *Paul*, *Peter*, and thir prime
Diſciples. But of theſe matters, variouſly written and believ'd, Eccleſiaſtic Hiſtorians can
beſt determin: as the beſt of them do, with
little

little credit giv'n to the particulars of such uncertain relations. As for *Lucius*, they write,
that after a long reigne he was buried at *Gloster* ; but dying without issue left the Kingdom in great commotion. By truer testimony
we find that the greatest Warr which in those
days busy'd *Commodus*, was in this Iland. For
the Nations Northward, notwithstanding the
Wall rais'd to keep them out, breaking in upon the *Roman* Province, wasted wide ; and
both the Army and the Leader that came a-
gainst them wholly routed, and destroy'd ;
which put the Emperor in such a fear, as to
dispatch hither one of his best Commanders,
Ulpius Marcellus. He a man endu'd with all
nobleness of mind, frugal, temperate, mild,
and magnanimous, in Warr bold and watch-
full, invincible against lucre, and the assault of
bribes, what with his valour, and these his o-
ther virtues, quickly ended this Warr that
look'd so dangerous, and had himself like to
have been ended by the peace which he
brought home, for presuming to be so worthy
and so good under the envy of so worthless
and so bad an Emperor. After whose departure the *Roman* Legions fell to sedition among
themselvs ; 1500 of them went to *Rome* in
name of the rest, and were so terrible to *Commodus* himself, as that to please them he put to
death *Perennis* the Captain of his Guard. Notwithstanding which compliance they endeavour'd heer to set up another Emperor against
him ; and *Helvius Pertinax* who succeeded
Governour, found it a work so difficult to ap-
peale

Geff. Mon.

Dion. L. 72.

183.

*Lamprid. in
comm.*

186.

peafe them, that once in a mutiny he was left
for dead among many flain; and was fain at   *Capitolin.*
length to feek a difmiffion from his charge.   *in Pert.*
After him *Clodius Albinus* took the Government; but he, for having to the Souldiers   *Capitolin.*
made an Oration againſt Monarchie, by the   *in Alb.*
appointment of *Commodus* was bid refign to
Junius Severus. But *Albinus* in thoſe trouble-   193.
fome times enſuing under the ſhort reign of   *Dion.*
Pertinax and *Didius Julianus*, found means to   *Did. Jul.*
keep in his hands the Government of *Britan*;   *Spartian.*
                                                 in Sever.
although *Septimius Severus* who next held the   *Herod. L.3.*
Empire, ſent hither *Heraclitus* to diſplace him;
but in vain, for *Albinus* with all the *Britiſh*
Powers and thoſe of *Gallia* met *Severus* about
Lyons in France, and fought a bloody Battail
with him for the Empire, though at laſt van-
quiſh'd and ſlain.   The Government of *Bri-*   *Herod. L.3.*
tan, *Severus* divided between two Deputies;
till then one Legat was thought ſufficient; the   *Digeſt. L.*
North he committed to *Virius Lupus.* Where   28. *tit.* 6.
the *Meatæ* rifing in Arms, and the *Caledonians*,
though they had promis'd the contrary to *Lu-*   *Dion.*
pus, preparing to defend them, ſo hard befet,
he was compell'd to buy his Peace, and a few
of Pris'ners with great Summs of money. But
hearing that *Severus* had now brought to an   *Herod. L.3.*
end his other Warrs, he writes him plainly
the ſtate of things heer, that the *Britans* of
the North made Warr upon him, broke into
the Province, and harraſs'd all the Countries
nigh them, that there needed ſuddenly either
more aid, or himſelf in perſon. *Severus*
though now much weak'nd with Age and the
                    G   Gout,

Gout, yet defirous to leav fom memorial of his warlike acheevements heer, as he had don in other places, and befides to withdraw by this means his two Sons from the pleafures of *Rome*, and his Souldiers from idlenefs, with a Mighty Power far fooner than could be ex-

208. pected, arrives in *Britan*. The Northern People much daunted with the report of fo great Forces brought over with him, and yet more preparing, fend Embaffadors to treat of Peace, and to excufe thir former doings. The Empe-ror now loth to returne home without fome memorable thing don, whereby he might af-fume to his other Titles the addition of *Bri-tannicus*, delays his anfwer, and quick'ns his preparations; till in the end, when all things were in readinefs to follow them, they are dif-mifs't without effect. His principal care was to have many Bridges laid over Bogs and rot-ten Moars, that his Souldiers might have to fight on fure footing. For it feems through lack of tillage, the Northern parts were then, as *Ireland* is at this day; and the Inhabitants in like manner wonted to retire, and defend themfelvs in fuch watrie places half naked.

209. He alfo being paft *Adrians* wall, cut down Woods, made way through Hills, faft'nd and fill'd up unfound and plafhy Fens. Notwith-ftanding all this induftrie us'd, the Enemie kept himfelf fo cunningly within his beft ad-vantages, and feldom appearing, fo oppor-tunely found his times to make irruption up-on the *Romans*, when they were moft in ftraits and difficulties, fomtimes training them on

with

with a few Cattel turn'd out, and drawn within ambush cruelly handling them, that many a time enclos'd in the midst of sloughs and quagmires, they chose rather themselvs to kill such as were faint and could not shift away, than leave them there a prey to the *Caledonians.* Thus lost *Severus;* and by sickness in those noisome places, no less than 50000 men: and yet desisted not, though for weakness carried in a Litter, till he had march't through with his Armie to the utmost Northern verge of the Ile : and the *Britans* offring Peace were compell'd to lose much of thir Country not before subject to the *Romans. Severus* on the Frontiers of what he had firmly conquer'd builds a Wall cross the Iland from Sea to Sea ; which one Author judges the most magnificent of all his other deeds ; and that he thence receav'd the stile of *Britannicus* ; in length 132 Miles. *Orosius* adds it fortify'd with a deep Trench, and between certain spaces many Towers, or Battlements. The place whereof som will have to be in *Scotland,* the same which *Lollius Urbicus* had wall'd before.   Others affirm it only *Hadrians* work re-edifi'd ; both plead Authorities and the ancient Tract yet visible : but this I leave among the studious of these Antiquities to be discus't more at large.   While Peace held, the Empress *Julia* meeting on a time certain *British* Ladies, and discoursing with the Wife of *Argentocoxus* a *Caledonian,* cast out a scoff against the loosenes of our Iland Women ; whose manner then was to use promiscuously the company of divers men.

Dion.

216.
Spartianus in Sever.

Eutropii Pean. Orosi l. 7. Cassidor. chro. Buchanan.

Whom

Whom ſtraight the *Britiſh* Woman boldly
thus anſwer'd : *Much better do we* Britans *fulfill
the work of Nature than you* Romans ; *we with
the beſt men accuſtom op'nly* ; *you with the baſeſt
commit private adulteries.* Whether ſhe thought
this anſwer might ſerve to juſtifie the practice
of her Countrie, as when Vices are compar'd,
the greater ſeems to juſtifie the leſs, or whether the Law and Cuſtome wherein ſhe was
bred, had wip't out of her conſcience the better dictate of Nature, and not convinc't her
of the ſhame ; certain it is that whereas other
Nations us'd a liberty not unnatural for one
man to have many Wives, the *Britans* altogether as licentious, but more abſurd and pre-
poſterous in thir licence, had one or many
Wives in common among ten or twelve Huſ-
bands ; and thoſe for the moſt part inceſtu-
ouſly. But no ſooner was *Severus* return'd into the Province, than the *Britans* take Arms
again. Againſt whom *Severus* worn out with
labours and infirmity, ſends *Antoninus* his eldeſt Son ; expreſly commanding him to ſpare
neither Sex nor Age. But *Antoninus* who had
his wicked thoughts tak'n up with the contriving of his Fathers death, a ſafer Enemie than
a Son, did the *Britans* not much detriment.
Whereat *Severus* more overcome with grief
than any other maladie, ended his life at *York*.
After whoſe deceaſe *Antoninus Caracalla* his
impious Son concluding Peace with the *Britans*, took Hoſtages and departed to *Rome*. The
Conductor of all this Northern Warr *Scottiſh*
Writers name *Donaldus*, he of *Monmouth Ful-*
genius,

Cæſar.

211.
Spartianus
in Sever.

genius, in the reft of his Relation nothing worth. From hence the *Roman* Empire declining apace, good Hiftorians growing fcarce, or loft, have left us little elfe but fragments for many years enfuing. Under *Gordian* the Emperour we find by the Infcription of an Altar ftone, that *Nonius Philippus* govern'd heer. Under *Galienus* we read there was a ftrong and general revolt from the *Roman* Legat. Of the thirty Tyrants which not long after took upon them the ftyle of Emperor, by many Coins found among us, *Lollianus*, *Victorinus*, *Pofthumus*, the *Tetrici* and *Marius* are conjectured to have ris'n or born great fway in this Iland. Whence *Porphyrius* a Philofopher then living, faid that *Britan* was a foil fruitful of Tyrants; and is noted to be the firft Author that makes mention of the *Scottish* Nation. While *Probus* was Emperor, *Bonofus* the Son of a Rhetorician, bred up a *Spanyard*, though by defcent a *Britan*, and a matchlefs drinker, nor much to be blamed, if, as they write, he were ftill wifeft in his cups, having attained in warfare to high honours, and laftly in his charge over the *German* fhipping, willingly, as was thought, mifcarried, trufting on his Power with the Weftern Armies, and join'd with *Proculus*, bore himfelf a while for Emperor; but after a long and bloodie fight at *Cullen*, vanquifh't by *Probus* he hang'd himfelf, and gave occafion of a ready jeft made on him for his much drinking; *Heer hangs a Tankard, not a man.* After this, *Probus* with much wifdom prevented a new Rifing heer in *Britan* by the fevere Loyaltie

242.
Camd. Cumber.

259.
Eumen. Paneg. Conft.
267.
Camden,

Gildas.

Hieronym.

282.
Vopifc. in Bonof,

Zozim. l. 1.

of *Victorinus* a *Moor*, at whoſe entreatie he
had plac't heer that Governour which rebel-
led. For the Emperor upbraiding him with
the diſloyaltie of whom he had commended,
Victorinus undertaking to ſet all right again,
haſtes hither, and finding indeed the Governour to intend Sedition, by ſome contrivance
not mention'd in the Storie, ſlew him, whoſe
name ſome imagine to be *Cornelius Lelianus.*

Camd.   They write alſo that *Probus* gave leave to the
Spanyards, Gauls, and *Britans* to plant Vines,
and to make Wine ; and having ſubdu'd the

Zozimus.   *Vandals,* and *Burgundians* in a great Battail,
ſent over many of them hither to inhabit,
where they did good ſervice to the *Romans*
when any Inſurrection happen'd in the Ile.

283.   After whom *Carus* Emperor going againſt the
Vopiſc. in   *Perſians,* left *Carinus* one of his Sons to Govern
Carin.   among other Weſtern Provinces this Iland
with Imperial Authority ; but him *Dioclefian*
ſaluted Emperor by the Eaſtern Armies over-

284.   came and ſlew. About which time *Carauſius*
Aurel.Vict.   a man of low Parentage, born in *Menapia,* a-
de Cæſar.   bout the parts of *Cleves* and *Juliers,* who
through all militarie degrees was made at
length Admiral of the *Belgic* and *Armoric* Seas,
then much infeſted by the *Franks* and *Saxons,*

285.   what he took from the Pirats, neither reſto-
Eutro. Oroſ.   ring to the owners, nor accounting to the Publick, but enriching himſelf, and yet not ſcowr-
ing the Seas, but conniving rather at thoſe Sea
Robbers, was grown at length too great a De-
linquent to be leſs than an Emperor : for fear
and guiltineſs in thoſe days made Emperors
ofter

ofter than merit : And understanding that
Maximianus Herculius, *Dioclesians* adopted
Son, was come against him into *Gallia*, pass'd   *Eumen. Pa-*
over with the Navie which he had made his   *neg.* 2.
own, into *Britan*, and possess'd the Iland.   286.
Where he built a new Fleet after the *Roman*
fashion, got into his Power the Legion that
was left heer in Garrison, other Outlandish
Cohorts detain'd, lifted the very Merchants
and Factors of *Gallia*, and with the allurement
of spoile invited great numbers of other barbarous Nations to his part, and train'd them
to Sea-service, wherin the *Romans* at that time
were grown so out of skill, that *Carausius* with
his Navie did at Sea what he listed, robbing on
every Coast ; whereby *Maximian*, able to com
no neerer than the shoar of *Boloigne*, was forc't
to conclude a Peace with *Carausius*, and yeild   *Victor. Eu-*
him *Britan* ; as one fittest to guard the Pro-   *trop.*
vince there against inroads from the North.   291.
But not long after having assum'd *Constantius*
Chlorus to the dignity of *Cæsar*, sent him against
Carausius ; who in the mean while had made
himself strong both within the Land and with-
out. *Galfred* of *Monmouth* writes that he made   *Buchanan.*
the *Picts* his Confederates ; to whom lately
com out of *Scythia* he gave *Albany* to dwell
in : and it is observ'd that before his time the
Picts are not known to have bin any where
mentioned, and then first by *Eumenius* a Rhetorician. He repair'd and fortifi'd the Wall   *Paneg.* 2,
of *Severus* with seven Castles, and a round
House of smooth stone on the Bank of *Carron*,
which River, saith *Ninnius*, was of his Name

fo call'd ; he built alfo a Triumphal Arch in
remembrance of fome Victory there obtain'd.
In *France* he held *Geffariacum*, or *Boloigne* ;
and all the *Franks* which had by his permiffion
feated themfelvs in *Belgia*, were at his Devo-

*Paneg. Si-
gonius.*
tion. But *Conftantius* hafting into *Gallia*, be-
fieges *Boloigne*, and with Stones and Timber
obftructing the Port, keeps out all relief that
could be fent in by *Caraufius*. Who ere *Conftantius* with the great Fleet which he had prepar'd, could arrive hither, was flain treacheroufly by *Alectus* one of his Friends,who long'd

292.
to ftep into his place ; when he feven years,
and worthily, as fome fay, as others, tyranni-
cally, had rul'd the Iland. So much the more

*Camd. ex
Nin. Eu-
men.
Pan. 3.*
did *Conftantius* profecute that opportunity, before *Alectus* could well ftrengthen his Affairs :
and though in ill weather, putting to Sea with
all urgency from feveral Hav'ns to fpread the
terror of his landing, and the doubt where to
expect him, in a Mift paffing the *Britifh* Fleet
unfeen, that lay fcouting neer the Ile of *Wight*,
no fooner got a fhoar, but fires his own Ships,
to leave no hope of refuge but in Victory. *A-
lectus* alfo, though now much difmaid, trans-
fers his Fortune to a Battel on the fhoar ; but
encountred by *Afclepiodotus* Captain of the
Prætorian Bands, and defperately rufhing on,
unmindful both of ordering his men, or bringing them all to fight, fave the acceffories of his
Treafon, and his outlandifh hirelings, is overthrown, and flain with little or no lofs to the
Romans, but great execution on the *Franks*.
His Body was found almoft naked in the field,
for

for his Purple Robe he had thrown aſide, left
it ſhould deſcry him, unwilling to be found,
The reſt taking flight to *London*, and purpoſing with the pillage of that City to eſcape by
Sea, are met by another part of the *Roman* Armie, whom the Miſt at Sea disjoining had by
chance brought thither, and with a new
ſlaughter chas'd through all the Streets. The
Britans, thir Wives alſo and Children, with
great joy go out to meet *Conſtantius*, as one
whom they acknowledge thir deliverer from
bondage and inſolence. All this ſeems by *Eumenius*, who then liv'd, and was of *Conſtantius*
houſhold, to have bin don in the courſe of one
continu'd action ; ſo alſo thinks *Sigonius* a
learned Writer : though all others allow three
years to the tyranny of *Alectus*. In theſe days *Eumen.*
were great ſtore of Workmen, and excellent
Builders in this Iland, whom after the alteration of things heer, the *Æduans* in *Burgundie*
entertain'd to build thir Temples and publick
Edifices. *Dioclefian* having hitherto ſuccefs-
fully us'd his valour againſt the Enemies of his
Empire, uſes now his rage in a bloodie perſe-
cution againſt his obedient and harmleſs Chriſtian Subjects : from the feeling whereof nei- *Gildas.*
ther was this Iland, though moſt remote, far
anough remov'd. Among them heer who ſuf-
fer'd gloriouſly, *Aron*, and *Julius* of *Caer leon*
upon *Uſk*, but chiefly *Alban* of *Verulam*, were
moſt renown'd : The Story of whoſe Martyr-
dom ſoil'd, and worſe martyr'd with the fabling zeal of ſome idle fancies, more fond of
Miracles, than apprehenſive of Truth, deſervs
not

not longer digreſſion. *Conſtantius* after *Diocle-ſian*, dividing the Empire with *Galerius*, had *Britan* among his other Provinces; where either preparing or returning with Victorie from an Expedition againſt the *Caledonians*, he di'd at *York*. His Son *Conſtantine*, who happily came Poſt from *Rome* to *Boloigne* juſt about the time, ſaith *Eumenius*, that his Father was ſetting ſail his laſt time hither, and not long before his death, was by him on his death-bed nam'd, and after his Funeral, by the whole Army ſaluted Emperor. There goes a fame, and that ſeconded by moſt of our own Hiſtorians, though not thoſe the ancienteſt, that *Conſtantine* was born in this Iland, his Mother *Helena* the Daughter of *Coilus* a *Britiſh* Prince, not ſure the Father of King *Lucius*, whoſe Siſter ſhe muſt then be, for that would detect her too old by an hundred years to be the Mother of *Conſtantine*. But to ſalve this incoherence, another *Coilus* is feign'd to be then Earl of *Colcheſter*. To this therfore the *Roman* Authors give no teſtimony, except a paſſage or two in the *Panegyrics*, about the ſenſe whereof much is argu'd : others neereſt to thoſe times clear the doubt, and write him certainly born of *Helena*, a mean Woeman at *Naiſus* in *Dardania*. Howbeit, ere his departure hence he ſeems to have had ſome bickerings in the North, which by reaſon of more urgent affairs compos'd, he paſſes into *Gallia* ; and after four years returns either to ſettle or to alter the ſtate of things heer; until a new War againſt *Maxentius* call'd him back, leaving *Pacatianus*

his

Author ignot. poſt Marcellin. Valeſii.
306.
Eutrop. Eumen. idem Auth. ignot.

Idem vit. Auth. ignot.
Euſeb. Conſt.

307.
Sigon.
311.
Camd.

his Vicegerent. He deceasing, *Constantine* his eldest Son enjoy'd for his part of the Empire, with all the Provinces that lay on this side the *Alpes*, this Iland also. But falling to Civil Warr with *Constans* his Brother, was by him slain; who with his third Brother *Constantius* coming into *Britan*, seis'd it as Victor. Against him rose *Magnentius*, one of his Chief Commanders, by som affirm'd the Son of a *Britan*, he having gain'd on his side great Forces, contested with *Constantius* in many Battails for the sole Empire; but vanquish'd, in the end slew himself. Somwhat before this time *Gratianus Funarius*, the Father of *Valentinian*, afterwards Emperor, had Chief Command of those Armies which the *Romans* kept heer. And the *Arrian* Doctrine which then divided Christendom, wrought also in this Iland no small disturbance : a Land, saith *Gildas*, greedy of every thing new, stedfast in nothing. At last *Constantius* appointed a *Synod* of more than 400 Bishops to Assemble at *Ariminum* on the Emperors charges, which the rest all refusing, three only of the *British*, poverty constreining them, accepted; though the other Bishops among them offer'd to have born thir charges : esteeming it more honourable to live on the Publick, than to be obnoxious to any private Purse. Doubtless an ingenuous mind, and far above the Presbyters of our Age; who like well to sit in Assembly on the Publick stipend, but like not the poverty that caus'd these to do so. After this *Martinus* was Deputy of the Province ; who being offended with the cruelty

Ammian.
L. 20. *&*
in eum Valesius.
340.
Libanius in Basilico.
343.
Camd. ex Firmico.
350.
Camden.
353.
Ammian.

359.

elty which *Paulus*, an Inquifitor fent from *Conftantius*, exercis'd in his enquiry after thofe Military Officers who had confpir'd with *Magnentius*, was himfelf laid hold on as an acceffory; at which enrag'd he runs at *Paulus* with his drawn Sword; but failing to kill him, turns it on himfelf. Next to whom, as may be guefs'd, *Alipius* was made Deputy. In the mean time *Julian*, whom *Conftantius* had made *Cæfar*, having recover'd much Territory about *Rhine*, where the *German* inrodes before had long infulted, to releeve thofe Countries almoft ruin'd, caufes 800 Pinaces to be built; and with them by frequent Voyages, plenty of Corn to be fetch'd in from *Britan*; which eeven then was the ufual bounty of this Soil to thofe parts, as oft as *French* and *Saxon* Pirats hinderd not the tranfportation. While *Conftantius* yet Reign'd, the *Scots* and *Picts* breaking in upon the Northern Confines, *Julian*, being at *Paris*, fends over *Lupicinus*, a well try'd Souldier, but a proud and covetous man; who with a Power of light arm'd *Herulians*, *Batavians*, and *Mæfians*, in the midft of Winter failing from *Boloigne*, arrives at *Rutupiæ* feated on the oppofite fhoar, and comes to *London*, to confult there about the Warr; but foon after was recall'd by *Julian* then chofen Emperor. Under whom we read not of ought happ'ning heer; only that *Palladius* one of his great Officers was hither banifh'd. This year *Valentinian* being Emperor, the *Attacots*, *Picts*, and *Scots* roaving up and down, and laft the *Saxons* with perpetual landings and invafions harryed

*Libon. Orat.*10. *Zozim. L.* 3. *Marcel. l.* 18.

*Amm. l.*23.

360.

Amm. L. 20.

364.
Amm. L 26, 27.

harryed the South Coast of *Britan*; flew *Ne-ctaridius* who govern'd the Sea Borders, and *Bulchobaudes* with his Forces by an ambush. With which news *Valentinian* not a little perplext, sends first *Severus* high Steward of his House, and soon recalls him, then *Jovinus*, who intimating the necessity of greater supplies, he sends at length *Theodosius*, a man of try'd Valour, and Experience, Father to the first Emperor of that Name. He with selected numbers out of the Legions, and Cohorts, crosses the Sea from *Boloigne* to *Rutupiæ*; from whence with the *Batavians*, *Herulians*, and other Legions that arriv'd soon after, he marches to *London*; and dividing his Forces into several Bodies, sets upon the dispers'd and plundring Enemie, lad'n with spoile; from whom recovering the booty which they led away, and were forc'd to leave there with thir lives, he restores all to the right owners, save a small portion to his wearied Souldiers, and enters *London* victoriously; which before in many straits and difficulties, was now reviv'd as with a great deliverance. The numerous Enemy with whom he had to deal, was of different Nations, and the Warr scatter'd: which *Theodosius*, getting daily som intelligence from fugitives and prisoners, resolves to carry on by sudden parties and surprisals rather than set Battails; nor omits he to proclaim Indemnity to such as would lay down Arms, and accept of Peace, which brought in many. Yet all this not ending the work, he requires that *Civilis*, a man of much uprightness, might be sent him,

to

367.

to be as Deputy of the Iland, and *Dulcitius* a famous Captain. Thus was *Theodosius* busy'd, besetting with ambushes the roaving Enemy, repressing his Roads, restoring Cities and Castles to thir former safety and defence, laying every where the firm foundation of a long Peace, when *Valentius* a *Pannonian* for some great offence banish'd into *Britan*, conspiring with certain Exiles and Souldiers against *Theodosius*, whose worth he dreaded as the only obstacle to his greater design of gaining the Ile into his Power, is discover'd, and with his chief accomplices deliver'd over to condign punishment : against the rest, *Theodosius* with a wise lenity suffer'd not inquisition to proceed too rigorously, lest the fear thereof appertaining to so many, occasion might arise of new trouble in a time so unsettl'd. This don, he applies himself to reform things out of order, raises on the Confines many Strong Holds; and in them appoints due and diligent watches; and so reduc'd all things out of danger, that the Province which but lately was under command of the Enemy, became now wholly *Roman*, new nam'd *Valentia* of *Valentinian*, and the City of *London Augusta*. Thus *Theodosius* nobly acquitting himself in all Affairs, with general applause of the whole Province, accompanied to the Sea-side, returns to *Valentinian*. Who about five years after sent hither *Fraomarius*, a King of the *Almans*, with authority of a Tribune over his own Country Forces, which then both for number and good service were in high esteem. Against *Gratian* who

368.
Amm. L.
28.
Zozim. L.4.

373.
Amm. L.
29.

who succeeded in the Western Empire, *Maximus* a *Spanyard*, and one who had serv'd in the *British* Warrs with younger *Theodosius* (for he also, either with his Father, or not long after him, seems to have don somthing in this Iland) and now General of the *Roman* Armies heer, either discontented that *Theodosius* was preferr'd before him to the Empire, or constrain'd by the Souldiers who hated *Gratian*, assumes the Imperial Purple, and having attain'd Victorie against the *Scots* and *Picts*, with the Flower and Strength of *Britan*, passes into *France*; there slays *Gratian*, and without much difficultie, the space of five years, obtains his part of the Empire, overthrown at length and slain by *Theodosius*. With whom perishing most of his followers, or not returning out of *Armorica*, which *Maximus* had giv'n them to possess, the South of *Britan* by this means exhausted of her youth, and what there was of *Roman* Souldiers on the Confines drawn off, became a prey to savage Invasions; of *Scots* from the *Irish* Seas, of *Saxons* from the *German*, of *Picts* from the North. Against them, first *Chrysanthus* the Son of *Marcian* a Bishop, made Deputy of *Britan* by *Theodosius*, demean'd himself worthily: then *Stilicho* a man of great Power, whom *Theodosius*, dying, left Protector of his Son *Honorius*, either came in person, or sending over sufficient aid, repress'd them, and as it seems new fortifi'd the Wall against them. But that Legion being call'd away, when the *Roman* Armies from all parts hasted to releive *Honorius* then besieg'd in *Asta* of *Piemont*, by

Alaric

Zozim. L.4.
Sigon.

Prosper. A-
quitanic.
Chron.
383.

Gildas.
388.
Beda.
Ninn.

389.

Socrat. L.7.

Claudian.
de laud,
Stil. l.2. &
de bel. Get.

402.

Alaric the *Goth*, *Britan* was left expos'd as before, to thofe Barbarous Robbers. Left any wonder how the *Scots* came to infeft *Britan* from the *Irifh* Sea, it muft be underftood, that the *Scots* not many years before had been driven all out of *Britan* by *Maximus*; and thir King *Eugenius* flain in fight; as thir own Annals report : whereby, it feems, wandring up and down, without certain feat, they liv'd by

Ethelwerd.
Sax. an.
Bede Epit.
in the year
565. and
Bede, L. 2.
c. 4.
405.

fcumming thofe Seas and fhoars as Pirats. But more Authentic Writers confirm us, that the *Scots*, whoever they be originally, came firft into *Ireland*, and dwelt there, and nam'd it *Scotia* long before the North of *Britan* took that name. About this time, though troublefom, *Pelagius* a *Britan* found the leafure to bring new and dangerous Opinions into the Church, and is largely writ againft by S⸴ *Auftin*. But the *Roman* Powers which were call'd into *Italy*, when once the fear of *Alaric* was over, made return into feveral Provinces: and perhaps *Victorinus* of *Tolofa*, whom *Rutilius* the Poet much commends, might be then Prefect of the Iland : if it were not he whom *Stilicho* fent hither. *Buchanan* writes, that endeavouring to reduce the *Picts* into a Province, he gave the occafion of thir calling back *Fergufius* and the *Scots*, whom *Maximus* with thir help had quite driv'n out of the Iland : and indeed the Verfes of that Poet fpeak him to have bin active in thofe parts. But the time which is affign'd him later by *Buchanan* after *Gratianus Municeps*, by *Camden*, after *Conftantine* the Tyrant, accords not with that which follows in the

the plain courſe of Hiſtorie.   For the *Vandals*
having broke in and waſted all *Belgia*, eev'n   407.
to thoſe places from whence eaſieſt paſſage is   *Zozim. L. 6.*
into *Britan*, the *Roman* Forces heer, doubting
to be ſuddenly invaded, were all in uproar,
and in tumultuous manner ſet up *Marcus*,
who it may ſeem was then Deputy. But him   *Sozom. L. 9.*
not found agreeable to thir heady courſes,
they as haſtily kill : for the giddy favour of a
mutining rout is as dangerous as thir furie.
The like they do by *Gratian* a *Britiſh Roman*, in   *Oroſ. L. 7.*
four Months advanc't, ador'd, and deſtroy'd.
There was among them a common Souldier
whoſe name was *Conſtantine*, with him on a
ſudden ſo taken they are, upon the conceit put
in them of a luckineſs in his name, as without
other viſible merit to create him Emperor. It
fortun'd that the man had not his name for
nought; ſo well he knew to lay hold, and
make good uſe of an unexpected offer.   He
therefore with a wak'n'd ſpirit, to the extent
of his Fortune dilating his mind, which in his
mean condition before lay contracted. and
ſhrunk up, orders with good advice his military affairs : and with the whole force of the
Province, and what of *Britiſh* was able to bear
Arms, he paſſes into *France*, aſpiring at leaſt
to an equal ſhare with *Honorius* in the Empire.
Where by the valour of *Edobecus* a *Frank*, and
Gerontius a *Britan*, and partly by perſwaſion
gaining all in his way, he comes to *Arles*.
With like felicity by his Son *Conſtans*, whom   408.
of a Monk he had made a *Cæſar*, and by the
conduct of *Gerontius* he reduces all *Spain* to
H   his

his obedience. But *Conſtans* after this diſpla-
cing *Gerontius*, the affairs of *Conſtantine* ſoon
went to wrack : for he by this means alienated, ſet up *Maximus* one of his friends againſt
him in *Spain* ; and paſſing into *France*, took
Vienna by aſſault, and having ſlain *Conſtans* in
that City, calls on the *Vandals* againſt *Conſtantine* ; who by him incited, as by him before
they had bin repreſs'd, breaking forward, o-
ver-run moſt part of *France*. But when *Conſtantius* comes, the Emperors General, with a
ſtrong power came out of *Italy*, *Gerontius* de-
ſerted by his own Forces, retires into *Spain* ;
where alſo growing into contempt with the
Souldiers, after his flight out of *France*, by
whom his Houſe in the night was beſet, having firſt with a few of his Servants defended
himſelf valiantly, and ſlain above 300, though
when his darts and other weapons were ſpent,
he might have ſcap'd at a private door, as all
his Servants did , not enduring to leave his
Wife *Nonnichia*, whom he lov'd, to the violence of an enraged crew, he firſt cuts off the
head of his friend *Alanus*, as was agreed ; next
his Wife, though loth and delaying, yet by
her entreated and importun'd, refuſing to out-
live her Husband, he diſpatches : for which
her reſolution *Sozomenus* an Eccleſiaſtic Writer
gives her high praiſe, both as a Wife, and as
a Chriſtian. Laſt of all againſt himſelf he turns
his Sword ; but miſſing the mortal place, with
his poinard finiſhes the work. Thus farr is
pourſu'd the Story of a famous *Britan*, related
negligently by our other Hiſtorians. As for
Conſtantine,

409.

Sozom. L. 9.

*Olympiod.
apud Pho-
tium.*

Constantine, his ending was not answerable to his setting out : for he with his other Son *Julian* beseig'd by *Constantius* in *Arles*, and mistrusting the change of his wonted success, to save his head, poorly turns Priest ; but that not availing him, is carried into *Italy*, and there put to death ; having four years acted the Emperor.   While these things were doing, the *Britans* at home destitute of *Roman* aid, and the chief strength of thir own youth, that went first with *Maximus*, then with *Constantine*, not returning home, vext, and harras'd by thir wonted Enemies, had sent messages to *Honorius* ; but he at that time not being able to defend *Rome* it self, which the same year was taken by *Alaric*, advises them by his Letter to consult how best they might for thir own safety, and acquits them of the *Roman* Jurisdiction.   They therefore thus relinquish't, and by all right the Government relapsing into thir own hands, thenceforth betook themselvs to live after thir own Laws, defending thir bounds as well as they were able, and the *Armoricans*, who not long after were call'd the *Britans* of *France*, follow'd thir Example. Thus expir'd this great Empire of the *Romans* ; first in *Britan*, soon after in *Italy* it self : having born chief sway in this Iland, though never throughly subdu'd, or all at once in subjection, if we reck'n from the coming in of *Julius* to the taking of *Rome* by *Alaric*, in which year *Honorius* wrote those Letters of discharge into *Britan*, the space of 462 years.   And with the Empire fell also what before in this We-

Gildas.
Beda.

Zozim. L.6.

Procopius Vandalic.

Calvis.
Sigon.

stern

stern World was chiefly *Roman*; Learning, Valour, Eloquence, History, Civility, and eev'n Language it self, all these together, as it were, with equal pace diminishing, and decaying. Henceforth we are to stear by another sort of Authors; neer anough to the things they write, as in thir own Countrie, if that would serve; in time not much belated, some of equal age; in expression barbarous; and to say how judicious, I suspend a while : this we must expect; in civil matters to find them dubious Relaters, and still to the best advantage of what they term Holy Church, meaning indeed themselvs : in most other matters of Religion, blind, astonish'd, and strook with Superstition as with a Planet; in one word, Monks. Yet these Guides, where can be had no better, must be follow'd; in grofs, it may be true anough; in circumstance each man as his judgment gives him, may reserve his Faith, or bestow it. But so different a state of things requires a several Relation.

The End of the Second Book.

THE

THE
HISTORY
OF
BRITAIN.

BOOK III.

THis Third Book having to tell of accidents as various and exemplary, as the intermiſſion or change of Government hath any where brought forth, may deſerve attention more than common, and repay it with like benefit to them who can judiciouſly read : conſidering eſpecially that the late Civil Broils had caſt us into a condition not much unlike to what the *Britans* then were in, when the Imperial Juriſdiction departing hence left them to the ſway of thir own Councils; which times by comparing ſeriouſly with theſe later, and that confuſed Anarchy with this interreign, we may be able from two ſuch remarkable turns of State, producing like events among us, to raiſe a

H 3   knowledge

knowledge of our ſelvs both great and weighty, by judging hence what kind of men the *Britans* generally are in matters of ſo high enterpriſe, how by nature, induſtry, or cuſtom fitted to attempt or undergoe matters of ſo main conſequence: for if it be a high point of wiſdom in every private man, much more is it in a Nation to know it ſelf; rather than puft up with vulgar flatteries, and encomiums, for want of ſelf-knowledge, to enterpriſe raſhly and come off miſerably in great undertakings. The *Britans* thus as we heard being left without Protection from the Empire, and the Land in a manner emptied of all her youth, conſumed in Warrs abroad, or not caring to return *Gild. Bede.* home, themſelvs through long ſubjection, ſer- *Malins.* vile in mind, ſloathful of body, and with the uſe of Arms unacquainted, ſuſtain'd but ill for many years the violence of thoſe barbarous Invaders, who now daily grew upon them. For *Zozim.L.6.* although at firſt greedy of Change, and to be thought the leading Nation to freedom from the Empire, they ſeem'd a while to beſtirr them with a ſhew of diligence in thir new affairs, ſom ſecretly aſpiring to Rule, others adoring the name of Liberty, yet ſo ſoon as they felt by proof the weight of what it was to govern well themſelvs, and what was wanting within them, not ſtomach or the love of licence, but the Wiſdom, the Virtue, the Labour, to uſe and maintain True Libertie, they ſoon remitted their heat, and ſhrunk more wretchedly under the burden of their own Libertie, than before under a Foren Yoke. Inſomuch

somuch that the residue of those *Romans* which
had planted themselvs heer, despairing of thir
ill deportment at home, and weak resistance
in the field by those few who had the courage,
or the strength to bear Arms, nine years after
the sacking of *Rome* remov'd out of *Britan* into *France*, hiding for haste great part of thir
Treasure, which was never after found. And
now again the *Britans*, no longer able to support themselvs against the prevailing Enemy,
sollicit *Honorius* to thir Aid, with mournfull
Letters, Embassages and Vows of Perpetual
Subjection to *Rome* if the Northern Foe were
but repuls't.   He at thir request spares them
one Legion, which with great slaughter of the
Scots and *Picts* drove them beyond the Borders, rescu'd the *Britans*, and advis'd them to
build a Wall cross the Iland, between Sea and
Sea, from the place where *Edinburg* now stands
to the Frith of *Dunbritton*, by the City *Alcluith*. But the material being only Turf, and
by the rude multitude unartificially built up
without better direction, avail'd them little.
For no sooner was the Legion departed, but
the greedy spoilers returning, land in great
numbers from thir Boats and Pinaces, wasting, slaying, and treading down all before
them.   Then are Messengers again posted to
Rome in lamentable sort, beseeching that they
would not suffer a whole Province to be destroy'd, and the *Roman* name, so honourable
yet among them, to become the subject of barbarian scorn and insolence. The Emperor, at
thir sad complaint, with what speed was pos-

418.
Ethelwerd.
annal. Sax.

Gildas.

422.
Diaconus,
L. 14.
Bede. L. 1.
C. 2.

Gildas.

423.

H 4   sible

fible fends to thir fuccour. Who coming fuddenly on thofe ravenous multitudes that minded only fpoil, furprife them with a terrible flaughter. They who efcap'd, fled back to thofe Seas, from whence yearly they were wont to arrive, and return lad'n with booties. But the *Romans* who came not now to Rule, but charitably to aid, declaring that it ftood not longer with the eafe of thir Affairs to make fuch laborious voyages in purfuit of fo bafe and vagabond robbers, of whom neither glory was to be got, nor gain, exhorted them to manage thir own warfare; and to defend like men thir Country, thir Wives, thir Children, and what was to be dearer than life, thir Liberty, againft an Enemy not ftronger than themfelves, if thir own floth and cowardife had not made them fo; if they would but only find hands to grafp defenfive Arms, rather than bafely ftretch them out to receave bonds.

Bede ibid. They gave them alfo thir help to build a new Wall, not of earth as the former, but of ftone

Gildas. (both at the public coft, and by particular contributions) traverfing the Ile in direct line from Eaft to Weft between certain Cities placed there as Frontiers to bear off the Enemy, where *Severus* had wall'd once before. They rais'd it twelve foot high, eight broad. Along the South fhoar, becaufe from thence alfo like hoftility was fear'd, they place Towers by the Sea fide at certain diftances, for fafety of the Coaft. Withall they inftruct them in the Art of Warr, leaving Patterns of thir Arms and Weapons behind them; and with animating words,

words, and many lessons of valour to a faint-
hearted audience, bid them finally farewell,
without purpose to return. And these two
friendly, Expeditions, the last of any hither by
the *Romans*, were perform'd, as may be gather'd out of *Beda*, and *Diaconus*, the two last
years of *Honorius*. Thir Leader, as som mo- *Blond.*
dernly write, was *Gallio* of *Ravenna*; *Buchanan*, who departs not much from the Fables of *Sabellic.*
his Predecessor *Boethius*, names him *Maximianus*, and brings against him to this Battel *Fergus* first King of *Scots* after thir second suppos'd
coming into *Scotland*, *Durstus* King of *Picts*,
both there slain, and *Dioneth* an imaginary
King of *Britan*, or Duke of *Cornwall*, who im-
probablie sided with them against his own
Countrie, hardlie escaping. With no less ex- *Buch. L. 5.*
actness of partitular circumstances, he takes
upon him to relate all those tumultuarie inrodes of the *Scots* and *Picts* into *Britan*, as if
they had but yesterday happen'd, thir order of
Battel, manner of Fight, number of Slain, Ar-
ticles of Peace, things whereof *Gildas* and *Beda*
are utterly silent, Authors to whom the *Scotch*
Writers have none to cite comparable in Antiquity; no more therefore to be beleev'd for
bare assertions, however quaintlie drest, than
our *Geofry* of *Monmouth* when he varies most
from authentick storie. But either the inbred
vanity of some, in that respect unworthily
call'd Historians, or the fond zeal of praising
thir Nations above truth hath so far transported them, that where they find nothing faithfully to relate, they fall confidently to invent
what

what they think may either best set off thir Historie, or magnifie thir Countrie. The *Scots*
and *Picts* in manners differing somwhat from
each other, but still unanimous to rob and
spoile, hearing that the *Romans* intended not
to return, from thir Gorroghs, or Leathern
Frigats pour out themselves in swarms upon
the Land, more confident than ever: and from
the North end of the Ile to the very Wall side,
then first took possession as Inhabitants; while
the *Britans* with idle Weapons in thir hands
stand trembling on the Battlements, till the
half-naked Barbarians with thir long and for-
midable Iron hooks pull them down headlong.
The rest not only quitting the Wall but Towns
and Cities, leave them to the bloody pursuer,
who follows killing, wasting, and destroying
all in his way. From these confusions arose a
Famin, and from thence Discord and Civil
Commotion among the *Britans*: each man living by what he rob'd or took violently from
his Neighbour. When all stores were consu-
med and spent where men inhabited, they betook them to the Woods, and liv'd by hunting, which was thir only sustainment. To the
heaps of these evils from without, were added
new divisions within the Church. For *Agricola* the Son of *Severianus* a *Pelagian* Bishop
had spread his Doctrine wide among the *Britans* not uninfected before. The sounder part
neither willing to embrace his Opinion to the
overthrow of Divine Grace, nor able to refute
him, crave assistance from the Churches of
France : who send them *Germanus* Bishop of
Auxerre,

Gildas.
Bede.

Bede.
Constant.

Auxerre, and *Lupus* of *Troyes*.   They by con- 429.
tinual preaching in Churches, in Streets, in *Prosp.*
Fields, and not without Miracles, as is writ- *Aquit.*
ten, confirm'd som, regain'd others, and at *Ve-*
rulam in a public Disputation put to silence *Math. West.*
thir Chief Adversaries.   This Reformation in *ad ann.*
the Church was beleev'd to be the cause of thir 446.
success a while after in the Field.   For the *Sa-* 430.
xons and *Picts* with joynt Force, which was no
new thing before the *Saxons* at least had any
dwelling in this Iland, during the abode of
Germanus heer, had made a strong impression
from the North.   The *Britans* marching out a- *Constant.*
gainst them, and mistrusting thir own Power, *vit. Germ.*
send to *Germanus* and his Collegue, reposing
more in the spiritual strength of those two
men, than in thir own thousands arm'd.   They
came, and thir presence in the Camp was not
less than if a whole Army had come to second
them.   It was then the time of *Lent*, and the
people instructed by the daily Sermons of these
two Pastors, came flocking to receave Baptism,   There was a place in the Camp set a-
part as a Church, and trick'd up with boughs
upon *Easter-day*.   The Enemy understanding
this, and that the *Britans* were tak'n up with
Religions more than with feats of Arms, advances, after the Paschal Feast, as to a certain
Victorie.   *German* who also had Intelligence
of thir approach, undertakes to be Captain
that day; and riding out with selected Troops
to discover what advantages the place might
offer, lights on a Valley compass't about with
Hills, by which the Enemy was to pass.   And
placing

placing there his ambush, warns them that what word they heard him pronounce aloud, the same they should repeat with universal shout. The Enemy passes on securely, and *German* thrice aloud cries *Halleluia*; which answered by the Souldiers with a sudd'n burst of clamour, is from the Hills and Valleys redoubled. The *Saxons* and *Picts* on a sudden supposing it the noise of a huge Hoast, throw themselvs into flight, casting down thir Arms, and great numbers of them are drown'd in the River which they had newly pass'd. This Victory, thus won without hands, left to the *Britans* plenty of spoile, and to the person and the preaching of *German* greater Authority and reverence than before. And the exploit might pass for current, if *Constantius*, the Writer of his Life in the next Age, had resolv'd us how the *British* Army came to want baptizing; for of any Paganism at that time, or long before, in the Land we read not, or that *Pelagianism* was re-baptiz'd. The place of this Victory, as is reported, was in *Flintshire* by a Town call'd *Guid-cruc*, and the River *Allen*, where a field retains the name of *Maes German* to this day. But so soon as *German* was return'd home, the *Scots* and *Picts*, though now so many of them Christians, that *Palladius* a Deacon was ordain'd and sent by *Celestine* the Pope to be a Bishop over them, were not so well reclaim'd, or not so many of them as to cease from doing mischief to thir Neighbours, where they found no impeachment to fall in yearly as they were wont. They therefore

Usse. Primord. p. 333.

431. Prosp. Aquit.

Ethelwerd. Florent. Gild. Bede.

fore of the *Britans* who perhaps were not yet
wholly ruin'd, in the strongest and South-west
parts of the Ile, send Letters to *Ætius*, then
third time Consul of *Rome*, with this super- *Malmsbury*
scription; *To Ætius thrice Consul, the groanes of* L.1.c.1.p.8.
the *Britans*. And after a few words thus, *The* 446.
Barbarians drive us to the Sea, the Sea drives us
back to the Barbarians ; thus bandied up and
down between two deaths we perish, either by the
Sword or by the Sea. But the Empire at that
time overspread with *Hunns* and *Vandals,* was
not in condition to lend them aid. Thus rejected and wearied out with continual flying
from place to place, but more afflicted with
Famine, which then grew outrageous among
them, many for hunger yielded to the Enemy, others either more resolute, or less expos'd to wants, keeping within Woods and
Mountainous places, not only defended themselves, but sallying out at length gave a stop
to the insulting Foe with many seasonable defeats ; led by some eminent person, as may be
thought, who exhorted them not to trust in
thir own strength, but in Divine assistance.
And perhaps no other heer is meant than the
foresaid deliverance by *German,* if computation would permit, which *Gildas* either not much
regarded, or might mistake ; but that he tar-
ried so long heer, the Writers of his Life assent
not. Finding therefore such opposition, the *Gildas.*
Scots or *Irish* Robbers, for so they are indiffe-
rently term'd, without delay get them home.
The *Picts,* as before was mentioned, then first
began to settle in the utmost parts of the Iland,
usíng

using now and then to make inrodes upon the *Britans*. But they in the mean while thus ridd of their Enemies, begin afresh to Till the Ground; which after cessation yields her fruit in such abundance, as had not formerly bin known for many Ages. But wantonness and luxury, the wonted companions of plenty, grow up as fast, and with them, if *Gildas* deserve belief, all other Vices incident to human corruption. That which he notes especially to be the chief perverting of all good in the Land, and so continued in his days, was the hatred of truth, and all such as durst appear to vindicate and maintain it. Against them, as against the only disturbers, all the malice of the Land was bent. Lies and falsities, and such as could best invent them, were only in request. Evil was embrac'd for good, wickedness honour'd and esteem'd as virtue. And this quality thir valour had, against a Foren Enemy to be ever backward and heartless; to Civil Broils eager and prompt. In matters of Government, and the search of Truth, weak and shallow, in falshood and wicked deeds pregnant and industrious. Pleasing to God, or not pleasing, with them weighed alike; and the worse most an end was the weightier. All things were don contrary to Public Welfare and Safety; nor only by Secular Men, for the Clergy also, whose Example should have guided others, were as vitious and corrupt. Many of them besotted with continual drunkenness; or swoln with pride and willfulness, full of contention, full of envy, indiscreet, incompetent

Judges

Judges to determine what in the practice of
life is good or evil, what lawful or unlawful.
Thus furnish'd with judgment, and for manners thus qualifi'd both Prieft and Lay, they
agree to chufe them feveral Kings of thir own;
as neer as might be, likeft themfelves; and
the words of my Author import as much.
Kings were anointed, faith he, not of Gods
anointing, but fuch as were cruelleft, and foon
after as inconfiderately, without examining
the truth, put to death by thir anointers, to
fet up others more fierce and proud.   As for
the Election of thir Kings (and that they had
not all one Monarch, appears both in Ages
paft and by the fequel) it began, as nigh as
may be guefs'd, either this Year or the following, when they faw the *Romans* had quite de-   447.
ferted thir claim.   About which time alfo *Pe-* *Conftant.*
lagianifm again prevailing by means of fome   *Bede.*
few, the *Britifh* Clergie too weak, it feems, at
difpute, entreat the fecond time *German* to
thir affiftance.   Who coming with *Severus* a
Difciple of *Lupus* that was his former affociate,
ftands not now to argue, for the people generally continu'd right; but enquiring thofe Authors of new difturbance, adjudges them to
banifhment.   They therefore by confent of all   448.
were deliver'd to *German*; who carrying them   *Sigon.*
over with him, difpos'd of them in fuch place *Gildas.*
where neither they could infect others, and
were themfelves under cure of better inftru-
ction.   But *Germanus* the fame year dy'd in
Italy; and the *Britans* not long after found
themfelves again in much perplexity, with no
                                                                    flight

flight rumour that thir old troublers the *Scots* and *Picts* had prepar'd a ftrong invafion, purpofing to kill all and dwell themfelves in the Land from end to end. But ere thir coming in, as if the inftruments of Divine Juftice had bin at ftrife, which of them firft fhould deftroy a wicked Nation, the Peftilence foreftalling the Sword left fcarce alive whom to bury the dead; and for that time, as one extremity keeps off another, preferv'd the Land from a worfe incumbrance of thofe barbarous difpof-

Malmf.L.1. feffors, whom the Contagion gave not leave now to enter farr. And yet the *Britans* nothing better'd by thefe heavy judgments, the one threatn'd, the other felt, inftead of acknowledging the hand of Heaven, run to the Palace of thir King *Vortigern* with complaints and cries of what they fuddenly fear'd, from the *Pictish* Invafion. *Vortigern*, who at that time was chief rather than fole King, unlefs the reft had perhaps left thir Dominions to the common Enemy, is faid by him of *Monmouth* to have procur'd the death firft of *Conftantine*, then of *Conftans* his Son, who of a Monk was made King, and by that means to have ufurp'd the Crown. But they who can remember how *Conftantine* with his Son *Conftans* the Monk, the one made Emperor, the other *Cæfar*, perifh'd in *France*, may difcern the fimple fraud of this Fable. But *Vortigern* however coming to Reign, is decipher'd by truer Stories a proud unfortunate Tyrant, and yet of the people much belov'd, becaufe his Vices forted fo well with theirs. For neither was wàs he skill'd in Warr, nor wife in Counfel, but covetous, luftful, luxurious, and prone to to all vice; wafting the publick Treafure in gluttony and riot, carelefs of the common danger, and through a haughty ignorance, unapprehenfive of his own.   Neverthelefs importun'd and awak'd at length by unufual clamours of the people, he fummons a general Council, to provide fome better means than heertofore had been us'd againft thefe continual annoyances from the North.   Wherein by advice of all it was determin'd, that the *Saxons* be invited into *Britan* againft the *Scots* and *Picts*; whofe breaking in they either fhortly expected, or already found they had not ftrength anough to oppofe.   The *Saxons* were a barbarous and heathen Nation, famous for nothing elfe but robberies and cruelties done to all thir Neighbours both by Sea and Land; in particular to this Iland, witnefs that military force which the *Roman* Emperors maintain'd heer purpofely againft them, under a fpecial Commander, whofe title, as is found, on good record, was Count of the *Saxon* fhoar in *Britan*; and the many mifchiefs done by thir landing heer, both alone and with the *Picts*, as above hath bin related, witnefs as much.   They were a people thought by good Writers, to be defcended of the *Sacæ*, a kind of *Scythian* in the North of *Afia*, thence call'd *Sacafons*, or Sons of *Sacæ*, who with a Flood of other Northern Nations came into *Europe*, toward the declining of the *Roman* Empire; and ufing Piracy from *Denmark* all along thefe

Notitiæ im-
perii.

Florent.
Wigorn. ad
an. 370.

I   Seas,

Seas, possess'd at length by intrusion all that
Ethelwerd. Coast of *Germany* and the *Nether-lands*, which
took thence the name of old *Saxony,* lying between the *Rhene* and *Elve,* and from thence
North as far as *Eidora,* the River bounding
Holsatia, though not so firmly, or so largely,
but that thir multitude wander'd yet uncertain of habitation. Such guests as these the
Britans resolve now to send for, and entreat
into thir houses and possessions, at whose very
name heertofore they trembl'd afar off. So
much do men through impatience count ever
that the heaviest which they bear at present,
and to remove the evil which they suffer, care
not to pull on a greater : as if variety and
change in evil also were acceptable. Or whether it be that men in the despair of better,
imagine fondly a kind of refuge from one mi-
Ethelwerd. sery to another. The *Britans* therefore, with
Malmsbur. *Vortigern,* who was then accounted King over
Witichind. them all, resolve in full Council to send Em-
gest. Sax. baſſadors to thir choicest men with great gifts,
L. 1. p. 3. and saith a *Saxon* Writer in these words, desiring thir aid. *Worthy* Saxons, *hearing the fame*
of your prowess, the distressed Britans *wearied out,*
and overprest by a continual invading Enemy, have
sent us to beseech your aid. They have a Land
fertile and spatious, which to your commands they
bid us surrender. Heertofore we have liv'd with
freedom, under the obedience and protection of the
Roman *Empire. Next to them we know none wor-*
thier than your selves; and therefore became sup-
pliants to your valour. Leave us not below our
present Enemies, and to ought by you impos'd, wil-
lingly

*l*ingly *we shall submit*. Yet *Ethelwerd* writes not
that they promis'd subjection, but only amity
and league.   They therefore who had chief *Malmf.*
rule among them, hearing themselves entreated by the *Britans*, to that which gladly they
would have wish't to obtain of them by entreating, to the *British* Embassy return this *Witichind.*
answer.   Be assur'd henceforth of the *Saxons*,
as of faithful friends to the *Britans*, no less
ready to stand by them in thir need, than in
thir best of fortune.   The Embassadors return
joyful, and with news as welcome to thir
Countrie, whose sinister fate had now blinded
them for destruction.   The *Saxons*, consult- *Gildas.*
ing first thir Gods (for they had answer, that
the Land whereto they went, they should hold
300 years, half that time conquering, and half
quietly possessing) furnish out three long Gallies, or Kyules, with a chos'n company of war- *Bede.*
like youth, under the conduct of two Brothers,
Hengist and *Horsa,* descended in the fourth degree from *Woden*; of whom, deify'd for the
fame of his acts, most Kings of those Nations
derive thir pedigree.   These, and either mixt
with these, or soon after by themselves, two
other Tribes, or neighbouring people, *Jutes*
and *Angles,* the one from *Jutland,* the other
from *Anglen* by the City of *Sleswich,* both Provinces of *Denmark,* arrive in the first year of *450.*
Martian the *Greek* Emperor, from the birth of *Nennius.*
Christ 450, receav'd with much good will of *Malmf.*
the People first, then of the King, who after
some assurances giv'n and tak'n, bestows on
them the Ile of *Tanet,* where they first land-
I 2   ed;

ed, hoping they might be made heerby more eager againſt the *Picts*, when they fought as for thir own Countrie, and more loyal to the *Britans*, from whom they had receav'd a place to dwell in, which before they wanted. The *Britiſh Nennius* writes, that theſe Brethren were driv'n into exile out of *Germany*, and to *Vortigern* who reigned in much fear, one while of the *Picts*, then of the *Romans*, and *Ambroſius*, came opportunely into the Hav'n. For it

Malmsb.   was the cuſtom in old *Saxony*, when thir numerous off-ſpring overflow'd the narrowneſs of thir bounds, to ſend them out by lot into new dwellings, wherever they found room, either vacant or to be forc't. But whether fought, or unfought, they dwelt not heer long

Henry Hun-   without employment. For the *Scots* and *Picts*
tingd.   were now come down, ſom ſay, as far as *Stam-*

Ethelwerd.   *ford* in *Lincoln ſhire*, whom, perhaps not imagining to meet new oppoſition, the *Saxons*, though not till after a ſharp encounter, put to

Bed. Nin.   flight ; and that more than once : ſlaying in fight, as ſom *Scotch* Writers affirm, thir King

Nenn.   *Eugenius* the Son of *Fergus*. *Hengiſt* perceaving the Iland to be rich and fruitful, but her Princes and other Inhabitants giv'n to vicious eaſe, ſends word home, inviting others to a ſhare of his good ſucceſs. Who returning with ſeventeen Ships, were grown up now to a ſufficient Army, and entertain'd without ſuſpicion on theſe terms, that they ſhould bear the brunt of War againſt the *Picts*, receaving ſtipend and ſom place to inhabit. With theſe was brought over the Daughter of *Hengiſt*, a Virgin

Virgin wondrous fair, as is reported, *Rowen*
the *Britiſh* call her : ſhe by commandment of
her Father, who had invited the King to a
Banquet, coming in preſence with a Bowle of
Wine to welcome him, and to attend on his
Cup till the Feaſt ended, won ſo much upon
his Fancy, though already wiv'd, as to demand her in mariage upon any conditions.
Hengiſt at firſt, though it fell out perhaps according to his drift, held off, excuſing his
meanneſs ; then obſcurely intimating a deſire
and almoſt a neceſſity, by reaſon of his augmented numbers, to have his narrow bounds
of *Tanet* enlarg'd to the Circuit of *Kent*, had
it ſtreit by donation : though *Guorangonus* till
then was King of that place : and ſo, as it were
overcome by the great munificence of *Vortigern*, gave his Daughter. And ſtill encroaching on the Kings favour, got furder leave to
call over *Octa* and *Ebiſſa*, his own and his Brothers Son ; pretending that they, if the North
were giv'n them, would ſit there as a continual defence againſt the *Scots*, while himſelf
guarded the Eaſt. They therfore ſayling with
forty Ships eev'n to the *Orcades*, and every
way curbing the *Scots* and *Picts*, poſſeſs'd that
part of the Ile which is now *Northumberland*.
Notwithſtanding this they complain that thir
monthly pay was grown much into arrear ;
which when the *Britans* found means to ſatis-
fie, though alleging withall that they to whom
promiſe was made of wages, were nothing ſo
many in number, quieted with this a while,
but ſtill ſeeking occaſion to fall off, they find

Gild. Bede.
Ninn.

I 3   fault

fault next, that thir pay is too small for the danger they undergo, threatning op'n Warr unless it be augmented. *Guortimer* the Kings Son perceaving his Father and the Kingdom thus betray'd, from that time bends his utmost endeavour to drive them out. They on the other side making League with the *Picts* and *Scots*, and issuing out of *Kent*, wasted without resistance almost the whole Land eev'n to the Western Sea, with such a horrid devastation, that Towns and Colonies overturn'd, Preists and People slain, Temples and Palaces, what with Fire and Sword lay altogether heaped in one mixt ruin. Of all which multitude, so great was the sinfullness that brought this upon them, *Gildas* adds that few or none were likely to be other than lew'd and wicked persons. The residue of these, part overtak'n in the Mountains were slain; others subdu'd with hunger preferr'd slavery before instant death; som getting to Rocks, Hills and Woods inaccessible, preferr'd the fear and danger of any Death before the shame of a secure slavery; many fled over Sea into other Countries; som into *Holland*, where yet remain the ruins of *Brittenburgh*, an old Castle on the Sea, to be seen at low water not far from *Leiden*; either built, as Writers of thir own affirm, or seis'd on by those *Britans* in thir escape from *Hengist* : Others into *Armorica*, peopl'd, as som think, with *Britans* long before; either by guift of *Constantine* the *Great*, or else of *Maximus* to those *British* Forces which had serv'd them in Forein Warrs; to whom those also that

Primord.
pag. 418.

Malmsb. L.
1. c. 1.
Huntingd.
L. 1.

that miscarried not with the latter *Constantine*
at *Arles*; and lastly, these exiles driv'n out by
Saxons, fled for refuge. But the antient Chronicles of those Provinces attest thir coming
thether to be then first when they fled the *Saxons*, and indeed the name of *Britan* in *France*
is not read till after that time. Yet how a sort
of Fugitives who had quitted without stroke
thir own Country, should so soon win another,
appears not; unless joyn'd to som party of thir
own settl'd there before. *Vortigern* nothing
better'd by these calamities, grew at last so
obdurat as to commit incest with his Daughter, tempted or tempting him out of an ambition to the Crown. For which beeing cen-
sur'd and condemn'd in a great Synod of *Clercs*,
and *Laics*, and partly for fear of the *Saxons*, according to the Counsel of his Peers he
retir'd into *Wales*, and built him there a strong
Castle in *Radnorshire* by the advice of *Ambrosius* a young Prophet, whom others call *Merlin*. Neverthelefs *Fauftus*, who was the Son
thus incestuously begott'n, under the instructi-
ons of *German*, or som of his Disciples, for
German was dead before, prov'd a Religious
man, and liv'd in devotion by the River *Rem-
nis* in *Glamorganshire*. But the *Saxons*, though
finding it so easie to subdue the Ile, with most
of thir Forces, uncertain for what cause, return'd home: when as the easiness of thir Conquest might seem rather likely to have call'd
in more. Which makes more probable that
which the *British* write of *Guortemir*. For he
coming to Reigne, instead of his Father de-

Ninn.
Malmsb.

Ninn.

Gildas.

Ninn.

I 4   pos'd

pos'd for Inceſt, is ſaid to have thrice driv'n and beſeig'd the *Saxons* in the Ile of *Taneth*; and when they iſſu'd out with powerful ſupplies ſent from *Saxony*, to have fought with them fowr other Battells, whereof three are nam'd; the firſt on the River *Darwent*, the ſecond at *Episford*, wherin *Horſa* the Brother of *Hengiſt* fell, and on the *Britiſh* part *Catigern* the other Son of *Vortigern*. The third in a Feild by *Stonar* then call'd *Lapis tituli* in *Tanet*, where he beat them into thir Ships that bore them home, glad to have ſo ſcap'd, and not venturing to Land again for five years after. In the ſpace whereof *Guortemir* dying, commanded they ſhould bury him in the Port of *Stonar*; perſwaded that his bones lying there would be terror anough to keep the *Saxons* from ever landing in that place : They, ſaith *Ninnius*, neglecting his command, buried him in *Lincoln*. But concerning theſe times, antienteſt Annals of the *Saxons* relate in this manner. In the year 455 *Hengiſt* and *Horſa* fought againſt *Vortigern*, in a place called *Egleſthrip*, now *Ailsford* in *Kent*; where *Horſa* loſt his life, of whom *Horſted*, the place of his burial, took name. After this firſt Battel and the death of his Brother, *Hengiſt* with his Son *Eſca* took on him Kingly Title, and peopl'd *Kent* with *Jutes*; who alſo then or not long after poſſeſs'd the Ile of *Wight*, and part of *Hamſhire* lying oppoſite. Two years after in a fight at *Creganford*, or *Craford*, *Hengiſt* and his Son ſlew of the *Britans* four Cheif Commanders, and as many thouſand men : the reſt in great diſorder

455.
Bede.
Ethelwerd.
Florent.
Annal. Sax.
The Kingdome of Kent.

457.

order flying to *London*, with the total lofs of   465.
Kent.   And eight years paffing between, he
made new Warr on the *Britans*; of whom in
a Battel at *Wippeds-fleot*, twelve Princes were
flain, and *Wipped* the *Saxon* Earl, who left his
name to that place, though not fufficient to
direct us where it now ftands.   His laft en-   473.
counter was at a place not mention'd, where
he gave them fuch an overthrow, that flying
in great fear they left the fpoil of all to thir
Enemies.   And thefe perhaps are the four Battels, according to *Nennius*, fought by *Guorte-*
mir, though by thefe Writers far differently
related; and happ'ning, befides many other
bickerings, in the fpace of twenty years, as
Malmsbury reck'ns.   Neverthelefs it plainly
appears that the *Saxons*, by whomfoever, were
put to hard fhifts, being all this while fought
withall in *Kent*, thir own allotted dwelling,
and fomtimes on the very edge of the Sea,
which the word *Wippeds-fleot* feems to intimat.   *Nennius.*
But *Guortemir* now dead, and none of courage
left to defend the Land, *Vortigern* either by
the power of his faction, or by confent of all,
reaffumes the Government : and *Hengift* thus
rid of his grand oppofer, hearing gladly the
reftorement of his old favourer, returns again
with great Forces; but to *Vortigern* whom he
well knew how to handle without warring, as
to his Son in Law, now that the only Author
of diffention between them was remov'd by
Death, offers nothing but all terms of new
league and amity.   The King both for his
Wives fake and his own fottifhnefs, confulting

ing also with his Peers not unlike himself, readily yields; and the place of parly is agree'd on; to which either side was to repair without Weapons. *Hengist*, whose meaning was not peace, but treachery, appointed his men to be secretly arm'd, and acquainted them to

Malmsb. what intent. The watch-word was *Nemet eour Saxes*, that is, *Draw your Daggers*; which they observing, when the *Britans* were throughly heated with Wine (for the Treaty it seems was not without Cups) and provok'd, as was plotted, by som affront, dispatch'd with those Poniards every one his next man, to the number of 300, the chief of those that could do ought against him either in Counsel or in Field. *Vortigern* they only bound and kept in Custody, until he granted them for his ransom three Provinces, which were called afterward *Essex*, *Sussex*, and *Middlesex*. Who thus dismist, retiring again to his solitary abode in the Country of *Guorthigirniaun*, so call'd by his name, from thence to the Castle of his own building in *North-Wales*, by the River *Tiebi*; and living there obscurely among his Wives, was at length burnt in his Towre by fire from Heav'n

Nin. ex le- at the Praier, as some say, of *German*, but that
gend. coheres not; as others, by *Ambrosius Aure-*
St. Ger. *lian*; of whom as we have heard at first, he
Galfrid. stood in great fear, and partly for that cause
Monmouth. invited in the *Saxons*. Who whether by constraint or of thir own accord after much mischeif don, most of them returning back into thir own Country, left a fair opportunity to the *Britans* of revenging themselves the easier

on

on thofe that ftaid behind. Repenting therefore, and with earneft fupplication imploring
divine help to prevent thir final rooting out,
they gather from all parts, and under the leading of *Ambrofius Aurelianus*, a vertuous and
modeft man, the laft heer of *Roman* ftock, advancing now onward againft the late Victors,
defeat them in a memorable Battel. Common
opinion, but grounded cheifly on the *Britifh*
Fables, makes this *Ambrofius* to be a younger
Son of that *Conftantine*, whofe eldeft, as we
heard, was *Conftance* the Monk: who both loft
thir lives abroad ufurping the Empire. But
the exprefs words both of *Gildas* and *Bede*, af-
fures us that the Parents of this *Ambrofius* having heer born regal dignity, were flain in thefe
Pictifh Wars and Commotions in the Iland.
And if the fear of *Ambrofe* induc'd *Vortigern*
to call in the *Saxons*, it feems *Vortigern* ufurp'd
his right. I perceave not that *Nennius* makes
any difference between him and *Merlin* : for
that Child without Father that propheci'd to
Vortigern, he names not *Merlin* but *Ambrofe*,
makes him the Son of a Roman Conful ; but
conceal'd by his Mother, as fearing that the
King therfore fought his life ; yet the youth
no fooner had confefs'd his parentage, but
Vortigern either in reward of his predictions,
or as his right, beftow'd upon him all the Weft
of *Britan* ; himfelf retiring to a folitary life.
Whofe ever Son he was, he was the firft, ac- *Gild. Bed.*
cording to fureft Authors, that led againft the
Saxons, and overthrew them ; but whether
before this time or after, none have writt'n.
This

This is certain, that in a time when most of the *Saxon* Forces were departed home, the *Britans* gather'd strength; and either against those who were left remaining, or against thir whole powers, the second time returning obtain'd this Victory. Thus *Ambrose* as Chief Monarch of the Ile succeeded *Vortigern*; to whose third Son *Pascentius* he permitted the rule of two Regions in *Wales, Buelth,* and *Guorthigirniaun.* In his daies, saith *Nennius,* the *Saxons* prevail'd not much: against whom *Arthur,* as beeing then Cheif General for the *British* Kings, made great War; but more renown'd in Songs and Romances, than in true stories. And the sequel it self declares as much. For in the year 477 *Ella* the *Saxon,* with his three Sons, *Cymen, Pleting,* and *Cissa,* at a place in *Sussex* call'd *Cymenshore,* arrive in three Ships, kill many of the *Britans,* chasing them that remain'd into the Wood *Andreds Leage.* Another Battel was fought at *Mercreds-Burnamsted,* wherin *Ella* had by far the Victory; but *Huntingdon* makes it so doubtful, that the *Saxons* were constrain'd to send home for supplies. Four year after dy'd *Hengist* the first *Saxon* King of *Kent*; noted to have attain'd that dignity by craft, as much as valour, and giving scope to his own cruel nature, rather than proceeding by mildness or civility. His Son *Oeric* surnam'd *Oisc,* of whom the *Kentish* Kings were call'd *Oiscings,* succeeded him, and sate content with his Fathers winnings; more desirous to settle and defend, than to enlarge his bounds: he reign'd twenty

four

Ninn.

477.
Sax. An.
Ethelw.
Florent.

485.
Florent.
Hunting.

489.

Malmsb.

Bed. L. 2.
c. 5.

four years. By this time *Ella* and his Son *Cissa*, beseiging *Andred-chester*, suppos'd now to be *Newenden* in *Kent*, take it by force, and all within it put to the Sword.　Thus *Ella* three years after the death of *Hengist*, began his Kingdom of the *South-Saxons*; peopling it with new Inhabitants, from the Country which was then old *Saxony*, at this day *Holstein* in *Denmark*, and had besides at his command all those Provinces which the *Saxons* had won on this side *Humber*.　Animated with these good successes, as if *Britan* were become now the field of *Fortune*, *Kerdic* another *Saxon* Prince, the tenth by Linage from *Woden*, an old and practis'd Souldier, who in many prosperous conflicts against the Enemy in those parts, had nurs'd up a Spirit too big to live at home with equals, coming to a certain place which from thence took the name of *Kerdic-shoar*, with five Ships, and *Kenric* his Son, the very same day overthrew the *Britans* that oppos'd him; and so effectually, that smaller skirmishes after that day were sufficient to drive them still furder off, leaving him a large territory.　After him *Porta* another *Saxon* with his two Sons *Bida* and *Megla*, in two Ships arrive at *Portsmouth* thence call'd, and at thir landing slew a young *British* Nobleman, with many others who unavisedly set upon them. The *Britans* to recover what they had lost, draw together all thir Forces led by *Natanleod*, or *Nazaleod*, a certain King in *Britan*, and the greatest saith one; but him with 5000 of his men *Kerdic* puts to rout and slaies. From whence the place

in

(marginal notes)
492.

Camden.

The Kingdome of South-Saxons.

Bed. L.1. c. 15. & L. 2. c. 5.

Sax. An. omn.

495.

501.

Sax. an. omn. Hunt.

508.

Ann. omn. Huntingd. Camden.

in *Hantshire*, as far as *Kerdicsford*, now *Chard-ford*, was call'd of old *Nazaleod*. Who this

Camd. Uss. primord.

King should be, hath bred much question; som think it to be the *British* name of *Ambrose*; others to be the right name of his Brother, who for the terror of his eagerness in fight, became more known by the Sirname of *Uther*, which in the *Welch* Tongue signifies Dreadful. And if ever such a King in *Britan* there were as *Uther Pendragon*, for so also the *Monmouth* Book surnames him, this in all likelihood must be he. *Kerdic* by so great a blow giv'n to the *Britans* had made large room about him; not only for the men he brought with him, but for such also of his friends, as he desir'd to make great; for which cause, and withall the more to strengthen himself, his two Nefews *Stuf*, and *Withgar*, in three Vessels bring him new

514.
An. omn.

levies to *Kerdic* shoar. Who that they might not come sluggishly to possess what others had won for them, either by thir own seeking, or by appointment, are set in place where they could not but at thir first coming give proof of themselves upon the Enemy: and so well they did it, that the *Britans* after a hard encounter left them Masters of the field. About

Huntingd.

the same time, *Ella* the first *South-Saxon* King dy'd; whom *Cissa* his youngest succeeded; the

The Kingdome of *East-Angl.*

other two failing before him. Nor can it be much more or less than about this time, for it was before the *West-Saxon* Kingdom, that *Uffa* the eighth from *Woden* made himself King of the *East-Angles*; who by thir name testifie the Country above mention'd; from whence they came

came in such multitudes, that thir native soil
is said to have remain'd in the daies of *Beda*
uninhabited. *Huntingdon* deserrs the time of
thir coming in, to the ninth year of *Kerdic*'s
Reigne : for saith he, at first many of them
strove for principality, seising every one his
Province, and for som while so continued making petty Warrs among themselves ; till in
the end *Uffa*, of whom those Kings were call'd
Uffings, overtop'd them all in the year 571,
then *Titilus* his Son, the Father of *Redwald*,
who became potent. And not much after the
East-Angles, began also the *East-Saxons* to e-
rect a Kingdom under *Sleda* the tenth from
Woden. But *Huntingdon*, as before, will have
it later by eleven years, and *Erchenwin* to be
the first King. *Kerdic* the same in Power,
though not so fond of Title, forbore the name
twenty four years after his arrival ; but then
founded so firmly the Kingdom of *West-Saxons*, that it subjected all the rest at length, and
became the sole Monarchie of *England*. The
same year he had a Victory against the *Britans*
at *Kerdics-Ford*, by the River *Aven* : and after
eight years, another great fight at *Kerdics
Leage*, but which won the day is not by any
set down. Hitherto hath bin collected what
there is of certainty with circumstance of time
and place to be found register'd, and no more
than barely register'd in Annals of best Note ;
without describing after *Huntingdon* the manner of those Battels and Encounters, which
they who compare, and can judge of Books,
may be confident he never found in any current

Malms. L.
1. c. 5.

Bed. L. 1.
c. 15.

Huntingd.
L. 2.p.313.
315.

Bede L. 2.
c. 15.

Malm. L.1.
c. 6.

The King-
dome of
East-Sax.

519.
The King-
dome of
West-Sax.

Sax. an.
omn.

527.

rent Author whom he had to follow. But this
difeafe hath bin incident to many more Hiftorians: and the Age wherof we now write, hath
had the ill hap, more than any fince the firft
fabulous times, to be furcharg'd with all the
idle fancies of Pofterity. Yet that we may not
rely altogether on *Saxon* Relaters, *Gildas*, in
Antiquity far before thefe, and every way
more credible, fpeaks of thefe Warrs in fuch
a manner, though nothing conceited of the
British Valour, as declares the *Saxons* in his
time and before to have bin foyl'd not feldom-
er than the *Britans*. For befides that firft Victory of *Ambrose*, and the interchangeable fuccefs long after, he tells that the laft overthrow
which they receav'd at *Badon* Hill, was not the
leaft; which they in thir oldeft Annals mention not at all. And becaufe the time of this
Battell, by any who could do more than guefs,
is not fet down, or any foundation giv'n from
whence to draw a folid compute, it cannot be
much wide to infert it in this place. For fuch
Authors as we have to follow, give the conduct and praife of this exploit to *Arthur*; and
that this was the laft of twelv great Battells
which he fought victorioufly againft the *Sax-*
ons. The feveral places writt'n by *Nennius* in
thir *Welch* names, were many hunder'd years
ago unknown, and fo heer omitted. But who
Arthur was, and whether ever any fuch reign'd
in *Britan*, hath bin doubted heertofore, and
may again with good reafon. For the Monk
of *Malmsbury*, and others whofe credit hath
fway'd moft with the learneder fort, we may
well

Ninn.

well perceave to have known no more of this *Arthur* 500 years paſt, nor of his doings, than we now living; And what they had to ſay, tranſcrib'd out of *Nennius,* a very trivial Writer yet extant, which hath already bin related. Or out of a *Britiſh* Book, the ſame which he of *Monmouth* ſet forth, utterly unknown to the world, till more than 600 years after the daies of *Arthur,* of whom (as *Sigebert* in his Chronicle confeſſes) all other Hiſtories were ſilent, both Forein and Domeſtic, except only that fabulous Book. Others of later time have ſought to aſſert him by old Legends and Cathedral regeſts. But he who can accept of Legends for good ſtory, may quickly ſwell a volume with traſh, and had need be furniſh'd with two only neceſſaries, leaſure and beleif, whether it be the writer, or he that ſhall read. As to *Artur,* no leſs is in doubt who was his Father; for if it be true as *Nennius* or his Notiſt avers, that *Artur* was call'd *Mab-Uther,* that is to ſay, a cruel Son, for the fierceneſs that men ſaw in him of a Child, and the intent of his name *Arturus* imports as much, it might well be that ſom in after Ages who ſought to turn him into a Fable, wreſted the word *Uther* into a proper name, and ſo fain'd him the Son of *Uther*; ſince we read not in any certain ſtory, that ever ſuch perſon liv'd, till *Geffry* of *Monmouth* ſet him off with the ſirname of *Pendragon.* And as we doubted of his parentage, ſo may we alſo of his puiſſance; for whether that Victory at *Badon* Hill were his or no, is uncertain; *Gildas* not naming him, as he did *Ambroſe* in

K   the

the former.   Next, if it be true as *Caradoc* re-

Caradoc.
Llancar-
von. vit.
Gildas.

lates, that *Melvas* King of that Country which
is now *Summerset*, kept from him *Gueniver* his
Wife a whole year in the Town of *Glaston*,
and restor'd her at the entreaty of *Gildas*, rather than for any enforcement, that *Artur*
with all his Chivalry could make against a
small Town defended only by a moory situation; had either his knowledge in War, or the
force he had to make, bin answerable to the
fame they bear, that petty King had neither
dar'd such an affront, nor he bin so long, and
at last without effect, in revenging it. Considering lastly how the *Saxons* gain'd upon him
every where all the time of his suppos'd reign,
which began, as som write, in the tenth year

Malmsb.
Antiquit.
Glaston.
529.

of *Kerdic*, who wrung from him by long warr
the Countries of *Summerset*, and *Hamshire*;
there will remain neither place nor circumstance in story, which may administer any

Primord.
pag. 468.
Polychro-
nic. L. 5.
c. 6.

likelihood of those great Acts that are ascri-
bed him.   This only is alleg'd by *Nennius* in
Arturs behalf, that the *Saxons*, though vanquish't never so oft, grew still more numerous
upon him by continual supplies out of *Germany*.   And the truth is, that valour may be o-
ver-toil'd, and overcom at last with endless
overcoming.   But as for this Battell of
Mount *Badon* where the *Saxons* were hemm'd
in, or beseig'd, whether by *Artur* won, or
whensoever, it seems indeed to have giv'n a
most undoubted and important blow to the
Saxons, and to have stop'd thir proceedings
for a good while after. *Gildas* himself witnes-
sing

sing that the *Britans* having thus compel'd
them to sit down with peace, fell thereupon to
civil discord among themselvs. Which words
may seem to let in some light toward the
searching out when this Battel was fought.
And we shall find no time since the first *Saxon*
Warr, from whence a longer peace ensu'd,
than from the fight of *Kerdics Leage* in the
year 527, which all the Chronicles mention,
without Victory to *Kerdic*; and give us argument from the custome they have of mag-
nifying thir own deeds upon all occasions, to
presume heer his ill speeding. And if we look
still onward, eev'n to the 44.th year after,
wherin *Gildas* wrote, if his obscure utterance
be understood, we shall meet with very little
Warr between the *Britans* and *Saxons*. This *Gildas.*
only remains difficult, that the Victory first
won by *Ambrose*, was not so long before this
at *Badon* Seige, but that the same men living
might be eye-witnesses of both; and by this
rate hardly can the latter be thought won by
Artur, unless we reck'n him a grown youth at
least in the daies of *Ambrose*, and much more
than a youth, if *Malmsbury* be heard, who affirms all the exploits of *Ambrose*, to have bin
don cheifly by *Artur* as his General, which
will add much unbeleif to the common assertion of his reigning after *Ambrose* and *Uther*,
especially the fight at *Badon* being the last of
his twelv Battels. But to prove by that which
follows, that the fight at *Kerdics Leage*, though
it differ in name from that of *Badon*, may be
thought the same by all effects; *Kerdic* three   530.

years after, not proceeding onward, as his manner was, on the continent, turns back his Forces on the Ile of *Wight*; which with the slaying of a few only in *Withgarburgh*, he soon maisters; and not long surviving, left it to

his Nefews by the Mothers side, *Stuff* and *Withgar*; the rest of what he had subdu'd, *Kenric* his Son held; and reign'd 26 years, in whose tenth year *Withgar* was buried in the Town of that Iland which bore his name. Notwithstanding all these unlikelihoods of *Artur*'s Reign and great acheivments, in a narration crept in I know not how among the Laws of *Edward* the *Confessor*, *Artur* the famous King of *Britans*, is said not only to have expell'd hence the *Saracens*, who were not then known in *Europe*, but to have conquer'd *Freesland*, and all the North East Iles as far as *Russia*, to have made *Lapland* the Eastern bound of his Empire, and *Norway* the Chamber of *Britan*. When should this be done? from the *Saxons*, till after twelve Battells, he had no rest at home; after those, the *Britans* contented with the quiet they had from thir *Saxon* Enemies, were so far from seeking Conquests abroad, that, by report of *Gildas* above cited, they fell to Civil Wars at home. Surely *Artur* much better had made War in old *Saxony*, to repress thir flowing hither, than to have won Kingdoms as far as *Russia*, scarce able heer to defend his own. *Buchanan* our Neighbour Historian reprehends him of *Monmouth* and others for fabling in the deeds of *Artur*, yet what he writes thereof himself, as of better credit,

shews

shews not whence he had but from those Fables; which he seems content to beleive in part, on condition that the *Scots* and *Picts* may be thought to have assisted *Arthur* in all his Wars and Atchievments, whereof appears as little ground by any credible story, as of that which he most counts Fabulous. But not furder to contest about such uncertainties. In the year 547, *Ida* the *Saxon*, sprung also from *Woden* in the tenth degree, began the Kingdome of *Bernicia* in *Northumberland*; built the Town *Bebbanburg*, which was after wall'd; and had twelv Sons, half by Wives, and half by Concubines. *Hengist* by leave of *Vortigern*, we may remember, had sent *Octa* and *Ebissa* to seek them seats in the North, and there by warring on the *Picts*, to secure the Southern parts. Which they so prudently effected, that what by force and fair proceeding, they well quieted those Countries; and though so far distant from *Kent*, nor without power in their hands, yet kept themselves nigh 180 years within moderation; and as Inferiour Governours, they and thir off-spring gave obedience to the Kings of *Kent*, as to the elder Family. Till at length following the example of that Age; when no less than Kingdoms were the prize of every fortunat Commander, they thought it but reason, as well as others of thir Nation, to assume Royalty. Of whom *Ida* was the first, a man in the prime of his years, and of Parentage as we heard; but how he came to wear the Crown, aspiring or by free choise, is not said. Certain enough it is, that his vertues

547.
The Kingdome of Northumberland.
An. omn.
Bed. Epit.
Malmsb.

Malms.

tues

tues made him not less Noble than his birth, in Warr undaunted, and unfoil'd ; in Peace tempring the aw of Magistracy, with a natural mildness:he raign'd about twelv years. In the

552.
Annal.omn.
556.
Camden.

mean while *Kenric* in a fight at *Searesbirig*, now *Salsbury*, kil'd and put to flight many of the *Britans* ; and the fourth year after at *Beranvirig*, now *Banbury*, as som think, with *Keaulin* his Son put them again to flight. *Keaulin* shortly after succeeded his Father in the *West-Saxons*. And *Alla* descended also of *Woden*,

560.
Annal.
Florent.

but by another Line, set up a second Kingdom in *Deira* the South part of *Northumberland*, and held it thirty years ; while *Adda* the Son of *Ida*, and five more after him reign'd without other memory in *Bernicia* : and in *Kent*,

561.

Ethelbert the next year began. For *Esca* the Son of *Hengist* had left *Otha*, and he *Emeric* to Rule after him ; both which without adding to thir bounds, kept what they had in peace fifty three years. But *Ethelbert* in length of Reign equal'd both his Progenitors, and as

Malmsb.

Beda counts, three years exceeded. Young at his first entrance, and unexperienc'd, he was the first raiser of Civil Warr among the *Saxons* ; claiming from the priority of time wherin *Hengist* took possession here, a kind of right over the later Kingdoms ; and thereupon was troublesome to thir Confines : but by them twise defeated, he who but now thought to seem dreadfull, became almost contemptible.

Ann. omn.,
568.

For *Keaulin* and *Cutha* his Son, persuing him into his own Territory, slew there in Battel, at *Wibbandun*, two of his Earls, *Oslac*, and *Cnebban,*

ban. By this means the *Britans,* but cheifly by
this Victory at *Badon,* for the space of fourty
four years ending in 571, receav'd no great
annoyance from the *Saxons :* but the peace
they enjoy'd, by ill using it, prov'd more de-
structive to them than War. For being rais'd
on a sudden by two such eminent successes,
from the lowest condition of thraldome, they
whose Eyes had beheld both those deliver-
ances, that by *Ambrose,* and this at *Badon,* were
taught by the experience of either Fortune,
both Kings, Magistrates, Priests, and privat
men, to live orderly. But when the next Age, *Gildas.*
unacquainted with past Evils, and only sensible of thir present ease and quiet, succeeded,
strait follow'd the apparent subversion of all
truth, and justice, in the minds of most men :
scarse the least footstep, or impression of good-
ness left remaining through all ranks and degrees in the Land ; except in som so very few,
as to be hardly visible in a general corruption :
which grew in short space not only manifest,
but odious to all the Neighbour Nations. And
first thir Kings, among whom also, the Sons
or Grand-Children of *Ambrose,* were fouly de-
generated to all Tyranny and Vitious Life.
Wherof to hear som particulars out of *Gildas*
will not be impertinent. They avenge, saith
he, and they protect ; not the innocent, but
the guilty : they swear oft, but perjure ; they
wage Warr, but civil and unjust Warr. They
punish rigorously them that rob by the high
way ; but those grand Robbers that sit with
them at Table, they honour and reward. They

give alms largely, but in the face of thir Alms-deeds, pile up wickednefs to a far higher heap. They fit in the feat of Judgment, but goe fel-dome by the rule of right ; neglecting and proudly overlooking the modeft and harm-lefs ; but countenancing the audacious, though guilty of abominableft crimes ; they ftuff thir Prifons, but with men committed rather by circumvention, than any juft caufe. Nothing better were the Clergy, but at the fame pafs or rather worfe, than when the *Saxons* came firft in ; Unlerned, Unapprehenfive, yet im-pudent ; futtle Prowlers, Paftors in Name, but indeed Wolves ; intent upon all occafi-ons, not to feed the Flock, but to pamper and well line themfelvs : not call'd, but feifing on the Miniftry as a Trade, not as a Spiritual Charge : teaching the People, not by found Doctrin, but by evil Example : ufurping the Chair of *Peter*, but through the blindnefs of thir own worldly lufts, they ftumble upon the Seat of *Judas* : deadly haters of truth, broach-ers of lies : looking on the poor Chriftian with Eyes of Pride and Contempt ; but fawning on the wickedeft rich men without fhame : great promoters of other mens Alms with thir fet Exhortations ; but themfelvs contributing ever leaft ; flightly touching the many Vices of the Age, but preaching without end thir own greivances, as don to Chrift ; feeking after preferments and degrees in the Church more than after Heav'n; and fo gain'd, make it thir whole ftudy how to keep them by any Tyran-ny. Yet left they fhould be thought things of

no

no ufe in thir eminent places, they have thir
niceties and trivial points to keep in awe the
fuperftitious multitude; but in true faving
knowledge leave them ftill as grofs and ftupid
as themfelves; bunglers at the Scripture, nay
forbidding and filencing them that know; but
in worldly matters, practis'd and cunning
Shifters; in that only Art and Symony, great
Clercs and Maifters, bearing thir heads high,
but thir thoughts abject and low. He taxes
them alfo as gluttonous, incontinent, and
daily Drunkards. And what fhouldft thou
expect from thefe, poor Laity, fo he goes
on, thefe beafts, all belly? fhall thefe amend
thee, who are themfelves laborious in evil
doings? fhalt thou fee with their Eyes, who
fee right forward nothing but gain? Leave
them rather, as bids our Saviour, left ye fall
both blind-fold into the fame perdition. Are
all thus? Perhaps not all, or not fo grofly.
But what avail'd it *Eli* to be himfelf blame-
lefs, while he conniv'd at others that were
abominable? who of them hath bin envi'd
for his better life? who of them hath hated
to confort with thefe, or withftood thir entring the Miniftry, or endeavour'd zealoufly
thir cafting out? Yet fom of thefe perhaps
by others are legended for great Saints. This
was the ftate of Government, this of Religion among the *Britans*, in that long calm of
Peace, which the fight at *Badon* Hill had
brought forth. Wherby it came to pafs, that
fo fair a Victory came to nothing. Towns
and Cittics were not reinhabited, but lay
ruin'd

ruin'd and waste; nor was it long e're dome-
stick Warr breaking out, wasted them more.
For *Britan*, as at other times, had then also
Primord.
p. 444.
several Kings. Five of whom *Gildas* living
then in *Armorica*, at a safe distance, boldly
reproves by name; First *Constantine* (fabl'd
the Son of *Cador*, Duke of *Cornwall*, *Artur's*
half Brother by the Mothers side) who then
Reign'd in *Cornwall* and *Devon*, a Tyrannical
and bloody King, polluted also with many
Adulteries: He got into his Power, two young
Princes of the Blood Royal, uncertain whether before him in Right, or otherwise suspected: And after Solemn Oath giv'n of thir
safety the year that *Gildas* wrote, slew them
with thir two Governours in the Church, and
in thir Mothers Arms, through the Abbots
Coap, which he had thrown over them, thinking by the Reverence of his Vesture to have
withheld the murderer. These are commonly suppos'd to be the Sons of *Mordred*, *Artur's*
Nefew, said to have revolted from his Uncle,
giv'n him in a Battel his deaths wound, and
by him after to have bin slain. Which things
were they true, would much diminish the
blame of cruelty in *Constantine*, revenging *Ar-*
tur on the Sons of so false a *Mordred*. In another part, but not expres'd where, *Aure-*
lius Conanus was King: him he charges also
with Adulteries, and Parricide; Cruelties
worse than the former; to be a hater of his
Countries Peace, thirsting after Civil War
and Prey. His condition it seems was not
very prosperous; for *Gildas* wishes him, being

ing now left alone, like a Tree withering in the midst of a barren field, to remember the vanity, and arrogance of his Father, and elder Brethren, who came all to untimely death in thir youth. The third reigning in *Demetia*, or *South Wales*, was *Vortipor*, the Son of a good Father; he was when *Gildas* wrote, grown old, not in years only, but in Adulteries, and in governing full of falshood, and cruel Actions. In his latter daies, putting away his Wife, who dy'd in divorce, he became, if we mistake not *Gildas*, incestuous with his Daughter. The fourth was *Cuneglas*, imbru'd in Civil Warr; he also had divorc'd his Wife, and tak'n her Sister, who had vow'd Widdowhood : he was a great Enemy to the Clergy, high-minded, and trusting to his wealth. The last, but greatest of all in power, was *Maglocune*, and greatest also in wickedness; he had driv'n out or slain many other Kings, or Tyrants; and was called the *Island Dragon*, perhaps having his seat in *Anglesey*; a profuse giver, a great Warrior, and of a goodly stature. While he was yet young, he overthrew his Uncle, though in the head of a compleat Army, and took from him the Kingdom : then touch't with remorse of his doings, not without deliberation took upon him the profession of a Monk; but soon forsook his Vow, and his Wife also, which for that Vow he had left, making Love to the Wife of his Brothers Son then living. Who not refusing the offer, if she were not rather the first that entic'd, found means both to dispatch her own Husband, and the former Wife of *Mag-locune*, to make her marriage with him the more unqueſtionable. Neither did he this for want of better inſtructions, having had the learnedeſt and wiſeſt man reputed of all *Britan*, the inſtituter of his youth. Thus much, the utmoſt that can be learnt by truer ſtory, of what paſt among the *Britans* from the time of thir uſeleſs Victory at *Badon*, to the time that *Gildas* wrote, that is to ſay, as may be gueſs't, from 527 to 571, is here ſet down all together; not to be reduc't under any certainty of years. But now the *Saxons*, who for the moſt part all this while had bin ſtill, unleſs among themſelvs, began afreſh to aſſault them, and e're long to drive them out of all which they yet maintain'd on this ſide *Wales*.

571.
Camden.
Ann. omn.

For *Cuthulf* the Brother of *Keaulin*, by a Victory obtain'd at *Bedanford*, now *Bedford*, took from them four good Towns, *Liganburgh*, *Eglesburh*, *Beſington*, now *Benſon* in *Oxfordſhire*, and *Igneſham*; but outliv'd not many months his good ſucceſs. And after ſix years

577.

more, *Keaulin*, and *Cuthwin* his Son, gave them a great overthrow at *Deorrham* in *Gloſterſhire*, ſlew three of thir Kings, *Comail*, *Condidan*, and *Farinmaile*, and took three of thir Cheif Citties; *Glocester*, *Cirencester*, and *Badencester*. The *Britans* notwithſtanding, after

584.

ſome ſpace of time, judging to have out-grown thir loſſes, gather to a head, and encounter *Keaulin* with *Cutha* his Son, at *Fethanleage*; whom valiantly fighting, they ſlew among the thickeſt, and as is ſaid, forc'd the *Saxons* to retire.

retire. But *Keaulin* reinforcing the fight, put them to a main rout, and following his advantage, took many Towns, and return'd laden with rich booty. The laſt of thoſe *Saxons* who rais'd thir own acheivments to a Monarchy, was *Crida*, much about this time, firſt founder of the *Mercian* Kingdom, drawing alſo his Pedigree from *Woden*. Of whom all to write the ſeveral Genealogies, though it might be done without long ſearch, were, in my opinion, to encumber the ſtory with a ſort of barbarous names, to little purpoſe. This may ſuffice, that of *Wodens* three Sons, from the Eldeſt iſſu'd *Hengiſt*, and his ſucceſſion; from the ſecond, the Kings of *Mercia*; from the third, all that Reign'd in *Weſt-Saxon*, and moſt of the *Northumbers*, of whom *Alla* was one, the firſt King of *Deira*; which, after his death, the Race of *Ida* ſeis'd, and made it one Kingdome with *Bernicia*, uſurping on the Childhood of *Edwin*, *Alla*'s Son, whom *Ethelric* the Son of *Ida* expel'd. Notwithſtanding others write of him; that from a poor life, and beyond hope in his old Age, coming to the Crown, he could hardly by the acceſs of a Kingdom, have overcome his former obſcurity, had not the fame of his Son preſerv'd him. Once more the *Britans*, e're they quitted all on this ſide the Mountains, forgot not to ſhew ſome manhood; for meeting *Keaulin* at *Wodens Beorth*, that is to ſay, *Wodens* Mount in *Wiltſhire*, whether it were by their owne Forces, or aſſiſted by the *Angles*, whoſe hatred *Keaulin* had incurr'd, they ruin'd his whole Army,

Huntingd.

The King-
dome of
Mercia.

Huntingd.
Mat.Weſtm.

Malms. L.
I. c. 3.

Florent.
ad ann.

559.

588.

Ann. omn.
592.
Florent.

Bed. L. 2.
c. 3.

Malmsb.
Florent.
Sax. An.

Army, and chas'd him out of his Kingdome, from whence flying, he dy'd the next year in poverty, who a little before was the moſt Potent and indeed Sole King of all the *Saxons* on this ſide *Humber.* But who was Chief among the *Britans* in this Exploit, had bin worth remembring, whether it were *Maglocune*, of whoſe proweſs hath bin ſpok'n, or *Teudric* King of *Glamorgan*, whom the Regeſt of *Landaff* recounts to have bin alwaies victorious in fight ; to have Reign'd about this time, and at length to have exchanged his Crown for a Hermitage ; till in the aid of his Son *Mouric*, whom the *Saxons* had reduc'd to extremes, taking Arms again, he defeated them at *Tinterne* by the River *Wye* ; but himſelf receav'd a mortal wound. The ſame year with *Keaulin*, whom *Keola* the Son

593.

of *Cuthulf*, *Keaulins* Brother ſucceeded, *Crida* alſo the *Mercian* King deceas'd, in whoſe room *Wibba* ſucceeded ; and in *Northumberland*, *Ethelfrid*, in the room of *Ethelric* ; Reigning twenty four years. Thus omitting Fables, we have the veiw of what with reaſon can be rely'd on for truth, don in *Britan*, ſince the *Romans* forſook it. Wherein we have heard the many Miſeries and Deſolations, brought by Divine Hand on a perverſe Nation ; driv'n, when nothing elſe would reform them, out of a fair Country, into a Mountanous and Barren Corner, by Strangers and Pagans. So much more tolerable in the Eye of Heav'n is Infidelity profeſs't,

feſs't, than Chriſtian Faith and Religion diſ-
honoured by unchriſtian works.   Yet they
alſo at length renounc'd thir Heatheniſm;
which how it came to paſs, will be the matter next related.

The End of the Third Book.

THE

THE
HISTORY
OF
BRITAIN.

BOOK IV.

THE *Saxons* grown up now to Seven Abſolute Kingdoms, and the lateſt of them eſtabliſh'd by ſucceſſion, finding thir Power arrive well nigh at the utmoſt of what was to be gain'd upon the *Britans*, and as little fearing to be diſplanted by them, had time now to ſurvey at leaſure one anothers greatneſs. Which quickly bred among them, either envy, or mutual jealouſies; till the Weſt Kingdom at length grown over Powerful, put an end to all the **Bed. Malm.** reſt. Mean while, above others, *Ethelbert* of *Kent*, who by this time had well rip'nd his young ambition, with more ability of years and experience in War, what before he attempted to his loſs, now ſucceſsfully attains; and

and by degrees brought all the other Monar-
chies between *Kent* and *Humber*, to be at his
devotion.   To which defign the Kingdom of
Weft-Saxons, being the firmeft of them all, at
that time fore fhak'n by thir over-throw at
Wodens-beorth, and the death of *Keaulin*, gave
him no doubt a main advantage ; the reft
yeilded not fubjection, but as he earn'd it by
continual Victories.   And to win him the *Bed. L. 1.*
more regard abroad, he marries *Bertha* the *c. 25.*
French Kings Daughter, though a Chriftian,
and with this condition, to have the free exercife of her Faith, under the care and inftru-
ction of *Letardus* a Bifhop, fent by her Parents
along with her ; the King notwithftanding
and his People retaining thir own Religion.
Beda out of *Gildas* laies it fadly to the *Bri-* *Bed. L. 1.*
tans charge, that they never would voutfafe *c. 22.*
their *Saxon* Neighbours the means of Conver-
fion : but how far to blame they were, and
what hope there was of converting in the
midft of fo much hoftility, at leaft falfhood *Bed. L. 2.*
from thir firft arrival, is not now eafie to de- *c. 1.*
termin.   Howbeit not long after, they had
the Chriftian Faith preach't to them by a Na- *Malmsb.*
tion more remote, and (as a report went, ac- *L. 1. c. 3.*
counted old in *Bedas* time) upon this occafion.
The *Northumbrians* had a Cuftom at that time,
and many hunderd years after not abolifh't,
to fell thir Children for a fmall value into any
Foren Land.   Of which number, two comly
Youths were brought to *Rome*, whofe fair and
honeft countnances invited *Gregory* Arch-Dea-
con of that Citty, among others that beheld
L   them,

them, pittying their condition, to demand
whence they were; it was answer'd by some
who stood by, that they were *Angli* of the
Province *Deira*, subjects to *Alla* King of *Northumberland*, and by Religion Pagans. Which
last *Gregory* deploring fram'd on a sudden this
allusion to the three names he heard; that
the *Angli* so like to Angels should be snatch'd
de ira, that is, from the wrath of God, to sing
Hallelujah : and forthwith obtaining licence
of *Benedict* the Pope, had come and preach't
heer among them, had not the *Roman* People,
whose love endur'd not the absence of so vigi-
lant a Pastor over them, recall'd him then on
his journey, though but deferr'd his pious intention.   For a while after, succeeding in the
Papal Seat, and now in his fourth year, ad-
monisht, saith *Beda*, by divine instinct, he sent
Augustine whom he had design'd for Bishop
of the *English* Nation, and other zealous
Monks with him, to preach to them the Gospel.   Who being now on thir way, discou-
raged by som reports, or thir own carnal fear,
sent back *Austin*, in the name of all, to beseech
Gregory they might return home, and not be
sent a journey so full of hazard, to a fierce and
infidel Nation, whose Tongue they understood
not. *Gregory* with Pious and Apostolic per-
swasions exhorts them not to shrink back from
so good a work, but cheerfully to go on in the
strength of Divine Assistance.   The Letter it
self yet extant among our Writers of Eccle-
siastic Story, I omit heer, as not professing to
relate of those Matters more than what mixes
aptly

596.

aptly with Civil Affairs. The Abbot *Austin*,
for so he was Ordain'd over the rest, reincourag'd by the Exhortations of *Gregory*, and his
Fellows by the Letter which he brought them,
came safe to the Ile of *Tanet*, in number about   597.
forty, besides som of the *French* Nation whom
they took along as Interpreters. *Ethelbert* the
King, to whom *Austin* at his landing had sent
a new and wondrous Message, that he came
from *Rome* to proffer Heav'n and Eternal Hap-
piness in the knowledge of another God than
the *Saxons* knew, appoints them to remain
where they landed, and necessaries to be provided them, consulting in the mean time what
was to be done. And after certain days coming into the Iland, chose a place to meet them
under the open Sky, possest with an old perswasion, that all Spells, if they should use any
to deceive him, so it were not within doors,
would be unavailable. They on the other side
call'd to his presence, advancing for thir Standard, a silver cross, and the painted Image of
our Saviour, came slowly forward singing thir
Solemn Litanies : which wrought in *Ethelbert*
more suspicion perhaps that they us'd enchant-
ments ; till sitting down as the King will'd
them, they there preach'd to him, and all
in that assembly, the tidings of Salvation.
Whom having heard attentively, the King
thus answer'd. Fair indeed and ample are the
promises which ye bring, and such things as
have the appearance in them of much good ;
yet such as being new and uncertain, I cannot
hastily assent to, quitting the Religion which
from

from my Ancestors, with all the *English* Nation, so many years I have retain'd. Nevertheless because ye are strangers, and have endured so long a journey, to impart us the knowledge of things, which I perswade me you believe to be the truest and the best, ye may be sure we shall not recompence you with any molestation, but shall provide rather how we may friendliest entertain ye ; nor do we forbid whom ye can by preaching gain to your belief. And accordingly thir residence he allotted them in *Doroverne* or *Canterbury* his chief Citty, and made provision for thir maintenance, with free leave to preach their Doctrine where they pleased. By which, and by the example of thir holy life, spent in prayer, fasting, and continual labour in the conversion of Souls, they won many ; on whose bounty and the Kings, receiving only what was necessary, they subsisted. There stood without the Citty, on the East-side, an ancient Church built in honour of St. *Martin*, while yet the *Romans* remain'd heer : in which *Bertha* the Queen went out usually to pray : Heer they also began first to preach, baptize, and openly to exercise Divine Worship. But when the King himself convinc't by thir good Life and Miracles, became Christian, and was Baptized, which came to pass in the very first year of thir arrival, then Multitudes daily, conforming to thir Prince, thought it honour to be reckon'd among those of his Faith. To whom *Ethelbert* indeed principally shewed his favour, but compell'd none. For so he had

598.

Bed. L. 2.
c. 5.

bin

bin taught by them who were both the Instru-
ctors and the Authors of his Faith, that Chri-
stian Religion ought to be voluntary, not compell'd.   About this time *Kelwulf* the Son of
Cutha Keaulins Brother reign'd over the *West-*
Saxons, after his Brother *Keola* or *Kelric,* and
had continual War either with *English, Welch,*
Picts, or *Scots.*   But *Austin,* whom with his
Fellows, *Ethelbert* now had endow'd with a
better place for thir abode in the Citty, and
other possessions necessary to livelihood, cros-
sing into *France,* was by the Arch-bishop of
Arles, at the appointment of Pope *Gregory,*
Ordain'd Arch-bishop of the *English :* and returning, sent to *Rome Laurence* and *Peter,* two
of his associates, to acquaint the Pope of his
good success in *England,* and to be resolv'd of
certain Theological, or rather Levitical questions : with answers to which, not proper in
this place, *Gregory* sends also to the great
work of converting, that went on so happily,
a supply of labourers, *Mellitus, Justus, Pauli-*
nus, Rufinian, and many others ; who what
they were, may be guess't by the stuff which
they brought with them, vessels and vestments
for the Altar, Coaps, Reliques, and for the
Arch-bishop *Austin* a Pall to say Mass in : to
such a rank superstition that Age was grown,
though some of them yet retaining an emulation of Apostolic Zeal : Lastly, to *Ethelbert*
they brought a Letter with many Presents.
Austin thus exalted to Archiepiscopal Authority, recover'd from the ruins and other profane uses, a Christian Church in *Canterbury*

Sax. An.
Malmsb.
601.
Bed. L. 1.
c. 27.

built

built of old by the *Romans* ; which he dedicated by the Name of *Chrifts Church*, and joyning to it built a feat for himfelf and his fucces-
fors ; a Monaftery alfo neer the Citty Eaft-
ward, where *Ethelbert* at his motion built
St. *Peters*, and enrich't it with great Endow-
ments, to be a place of burial for the Arch-
bifhops and Kings of *Kent :* fo quickly they

Bed. L. 2.
c. 34.
ftep't up into fellowfhip of pomp with Kings.
While thus *Ethelbert* and his People had thir
minds intent, *Ethelfrid* the *Northumbrian*
King, was not lefs bufied in far different Affairs : for being altogether warlike, and covetous of Fame, he more wafted the *Britans*
than any *Saxon* King before him ; winning
from them large Territories, which either he
made tributary, or planted with his own Sub-
603.
jects. Whence *Edan* King of thofe *Scots* that
dwelt in *Britan*, jealous of his fuccefses, came
againft him with a mighty Army, to a place
call'd *Degfaftan* ; but in the fight lofing moft
of his men, himfelf with a few efcap'd : only
Theobald the Kings Brother, and the whole
wing which he Commanded, unfortunately
cut off, made the Victory to *Ethelfrid* lefs in-
tire.   Yet from that time no King of *Scots* in
hoftile manner durft pafs into *Britan* for a
hunderd and more years after : and what fom
years before, *Kelwulf* the *Weft-Saxon* is annal'd
to have don againft the *Scots* and *Picts*, pafsing
through the Land of *Ethelfrid* a King fo Potent, unlefs in his Aid and Alliance, is not
likely. *Buchanan* writes as if *Ethelfrid*, affifted by *Keaulin* whom he miftitles King of
East-

Eaſt-Saxons, had before this time a battel with *Aidan*, wherein *Cutha Keaulins* Son was ſlain. But *Cutha*, as is above written from better Authority, was ſlain in fight againſt the *Welch* twenty years before. The number of Chriſtians began now to increaſe ſo faſt, that *Auguſtine* Ordaining Biſhops under him, two of his Aſſiſtants *Mellitus* and *Juſtus*, ſent them out both to the work of thir Miniſtry. And *Mellitus* by preaching converted the *Eaſt-Saxons*, over whom *Sebert* the Son of *Sleda*, by permiſſion of *Ethelbert*, being born of his Siſter *Ricula*, then reign'd. Whoſe Converſion *Ethelbert* to gratulate, built them the great Church of St. *Paul* in *London* to be thir Biſhops Cathedral ; as *Juſtus* alſo had his built at *Rocheſter*, and both gifted by the ſame King with fair Poſſeſſions. Hitherto *Auſtin* laboured well among Infidels, but not with like commendation ſoon after among Chriſtians. For by means of *Ethelbert* ſummoning the *Britan* Biſhops to a place on the edge of *Worceſterſhire*, call'd from that time *Auguſtines* Oke, he requires them to conform with him in the ſame day of Celebrating *Eaſter*, and many other points wherein they differ'd from the Rites of *Rome* : which when they refus'd to do, not prevailing by diſpute, he appeals to a Miracle, reſtoring to ſight a blind man whom the *Britans* could not cure. At this ſomething mov'd, though not minded to recede from their own Opinions without furder conſultation, they requeſt a ſecond meeting : to which came ſeven *Britan* Biſhops, with

604.
Bed. L. 2.
c. 3.

L 4   many

many other learned men, especially from the famous Monaſtery of *Bangor*, in which were ſaid to be ſo many Monks, living all by their own labour, that being divided under ſeven Rectors, none had fewer than three hundred. One man there was who ſtaid behind, a Hermit by the life he led, who by his wiſdom effected more than all the reſt who went : being demanded, for they held him as an Oracle, how they might know *Auſtin* to be a man from God, that they might follow him, he anſwer'd, that if they found him meek and humble, they ſhould be taught by him, for it was likelieſt to be the yoke of Chriſt, both what he bore himſelf, and would have them bear ; but if he bore himſelf proudly, that they ſhould not regard him, for he was then certainly not of God. They took his advice, and haſted to the place of meeting. Whom *Auſtin* being already there before them, neither aroſe to meet, nor receav'd in any brotherly ſort, but ſat all the while pontifically in his Chair. Whereat the *Britans*, as they were counſel'd by the Holy Man, neglected him, and neither harkned to his propoſals of Conformity, nor would acknowledge him for an Arch-Biſhop : And in name of the reſt, *Dmothus* then Abbot of *Bangor*, is ſaid, thus ſagely to have anſwer'd him. As to the ſubjection which you require, be thus perſwaded of us, that in the Bond of Love and Charity we are all Subjects and Servants to the Church of God, yea to the Pope of *Rome*, and every good Chriſtian to help them forward, both by word

Spelman.
*Concil.*pag.
108.

word and deed, to be the Childern of God :
other obedience than this we know not to be
due to him whom you term the Pope ; and
this obedience we are ready to give both to
him and to every Christian continually.   Besides, we are govern'd under God by the Bishop of *Caerleon*, who is to oversee us in spiritual matters.   To which *Austin* thus presa-
ging, som say menacing, replies, Since ye re-
fuse to accept of Peace with your brethren,
ye shall have Warr from your enemies ; and
since ye will not with us preach the Word of
Life, to whom ye ought, from thir hands ye
shall receive death.   This, though Writers a-
gree not whether *Austin* spake it as his pro-
phecy, or as his plot against the *Britans*, fell
out accordingly.   For many years were not
past, when *Ethelfrid*, whether of his own accord, or at the request of *Ethelbert* incens't by
Austin, with a powerful Host came to *Westche-
ster*, then *Caer-legion*.   Where being met by
the *British* Forces, and both sides in readines
to give the onset, he discerns·a company of
men, not habited for Warr, standing together
in a place of som safety ; and by them a Squadron arm'd.   Whom having lernt upon some
enquiry to be Priests and Monks, assembl'd
thither after three dayes fasting, to pray for
the good success of thir Forces against him,
therefore they first, saith he, shall feel our
Swords ; for they who pray against us, fight
heaviest against us by thir prayers, and are our
dangerousest enemies.   And with that turns
his first charge upon the Monks : *Brocmail* the

Sax. An.
Huntingd.
607.

Captain

Captain set to guard them, quickly turns his
back, and leaves above 1200 Monks to a sudden massacher, whereof scarse fifty scap'd, but
not so easie work found *Ethelfrid* against another part of *Britans* that stood in arms,
whom though at last he overthrew, yet with
slaughter nigh as great to his own souldiers.
To excuse *Austin* of this bloodshed, lest some
might think it his revengeful policy, *Beda*
writes that he was dead long before, although
if the time of his sitting Arch-bishop be right
computed sixteen years, he must survive this

Malmsb.
gest. Pont.
l. 1.

action. Other just ground of charging him
with this imputation appears not, save what
evidently we have from *Geffry Monmouth*,

Sax. An.

whose weight we know. The same year *Kelwulf* made Warr on the *South-Saxons*, bloody,
saith *Huntingdon*, to both sides, but most to

611.

them of the *South :* and four years after dying

Sax. an.
Malmsb.

left the Government of *West-Saxons* to *Kinegils* and *Cuichelm* the Sons of his Brother *Keola.*
Others, as *Florent* of *Worster* and *Mathew* of

614.

Westminster, will have *Cuichelm* Son of *Kinegils,* but admitted to reign with his Father, in
whose third year they are recorded with joynt
Forces or conduct to have fought against

Camden.
616.
Sax. an.

Britans in *Beandune,* now *Bindon* in *Dorsetshire,*
and to have slain of them above two thousand.
More memorable was the second year following, by the death of *Ethelbert* the first Christian King of *Saxons,* and no less a favourer of
all Civility in that rude Age. He gave Laws
and Statutes after the example of *Roman* Emperors, written with the advice of his sagest
Counsellors,

Counsellors, but in the *English* Tongue, and
obferv'd long after. Wherein his fpecial care
was to punifh thofe who had ftoln ought from
Church or Churchman, thereby fhewing how
gratefully he receav'd at thir hands the Chriftian Faith. Which, he no fooner dead, but
his Son *Eadbald* took the courfe as faft to ex-
tinguifh; not only falling back to Heathenifm,
but that which Heathenifm was wont to ab-
hor, marrying his Fathers fecond Wife. Then
foon was perceav'd what multitudes for fear
or countenance of the King had profefs't
Chriftianity, returning now as eagerly to thir
old Religion. Nor ftaid the Apoftafie within
one Province, but quickly fpread over to the
Eaft-Saxons; occafion'd there likewife, or fet
forward by the death of thir Chriftian King
Sebert : whofe three Sons, of whom two are
nam'd, *Sexted* and *Seward,* neither in his life *Malmsb.*
time would be brought to baptifm, and after
his deceafe re-eftablifh'd the free exercife of
Idolatry; nor fo content, they fet themfelves
in defpight to do fom op'n profanation againft
the other Sacrament. Coming therfore into
the Church, where *Mellitus* the Bifhop was
miniftring, they requir'd him in abufe and
fcorn to deliver to them unbaptiz'd the Con-
fecrated Bread; and him refufing, drove dif-
gracefully out of thir dominion. Who crofs'd
forthwith into *Kent,* where things were in the
fame plight, and thence into *France,* with *Ju-
ftus* Bifhop of *Rochefter.* But Divine venge-
ance deferr'd not long the punifhment of men
fo impious; for *Eadbald,* vext with an evil
Spirit,

Spirir, fell oft'n into foul fits of distraction;
and the Sons of *Sebert*, in a fight against the
West-Saxons perish'd, with thir whole Army.
But *Eadbald*, within the year, by an extraordinary means became penitent. For when
Laurence the Arch-bishop and Successor of *Austin* was preparing to ship for *France*, after
Justus and *Mellitus*, the Story goes, if it be
worth beleeving, that Saint *Peter*, in whose
Church he spent the night before in watching
and praying, appear'd to him, and to make
the Vision more sensible, gave him many stripes
for offering to desert his flock; at sight wherof the King (to whom next morning he shewed the marks of what he had suffer'd, by whom
and for what cause) relenting and in great fear
dissolv'd his incestuous marriage, and appli'd
himself to the Christian Faith more sincerely
than before, with all his people. But the *Londoners* addicted still to Paganism, would not
be perswaded to receave again *Mellitus* thir
Bishop, and to compell them was not in his
power. Thus much through all the South was
troubl'd in Religion, as much were the North
parts disquieted through Ambition. For *Ethelfrid* of *Bernicia*, as was touch't before, having
thrown *Edwin* out of *Deira*, and joyn'd that
Kingdome to his own, not content to have
bereav'd him of his right, whose known vertues and high parts gave cause of suspicion to
his Enemies, sends Messengers to demand him
of *Redwald* King of *East-Angles*; under whose
protection, after many years wandring obscurely through all the Iland, he had plac'd
his

617.

his safety. *Redwald*, though having promis'd all defence to *Edwin* as to his suppliant, yet tempted with continual and large offers of gold, and not contemning the puissance of *Ethelfrid*, yeilded at length, either to dispatch him, or to give him into thir hands : but earnestly exhorted by his Wife, not to betray the Faith and inviolable Law of Hospitality and refuge giv'n, preferrs his first promise as the more Religious, nor only refuses to deliver him; but since War was therupon denounc't, determins to be beforehand with the danger; and with a sudden Army rais'd, surprises *Ethelfrid*, little dreaming an Invasion, and in a fight neer to the East-side of the River *Idle*, on the *Mercian* border, now *Nottinghamshire*, slays him, dissipating easily those few Forces which he had got to march out over-hastily with him; who yet as a testimony of his Fortune, not his Valour to be blam'd, slew first with his own hands, *Reiner* the Kings Son.   His two Sons *Oswald*, and *Oswi*, by *Acca*, *Edwins* Sister, escap'd into *Scotland*. By this Victory, *Redwald* became so far Superiour to the other *Saxon* Kings, that *Beda* reck'ns him the next after *Ella* and *Ethelbert* ; who besides this Conquest of the North, had likewise all on the hither-side *Humber* at his obedience.   He had formerly in *Kent* receav'd Baptism, but coming home and perswaded by his Wife, who still it seems, was his Chief Counseller to good or bad alike, relaps'd into his old Religion; yet not willing to forgoe his new, thought it not the worst way, lest perhaps he might err in
either,

Malmsb. L 1. C. 3.

Camden.

Bed. L. 2. c. 15.

either, for more assurance to keep them both ;
and in the same Temple erected one Altar to
Christ, another to his Idols. But *Edwin*, as
with more deliberation he undertook, and
with more sincerity retain'd the Christian profession, so also in power and extent of dominion far exceeded all before him ; subdueing
all, saith *Beda*, *English* or *British*, eev'n to the
Iles, then call'd *Mevanian*, *Anglesey*, and *Man* ;
setl'd in his Kingdom by *Redwald*, he sought in
mariage *Edelburga*, whom others call *Tate*,
the Daughter of *Ethelbert*. To whose Embassadors, *Eadbald* her Brother made answer,
that to wed thir Daughter to a Pagan, was
not the Christian Law. *Edwin* repli'd, that
to her Religion he would be no hindrance,
which with her whole Houshold she might
freely exercise. And moreover, that if examin'd it were found the better, he would imbrace it. These ingenuous offers, op'ning so
fair a way to the advancement of truth, are
accepted, and *Paulinus* as a spiritual Guardian
sent along with the Virgin. He being to that
purpose made Bishop by *Justus*, omitted no
occasion to plant the Gospel in those parts,
but with small success, till the next year, *Cuichelm*, at that time one of the two *West-Saxon*
Kings, envious of the greatness which he saw
Edwin growing up to, sent privily *Eumerus* a
hir'd Sword-man to assassin him ; who under
pretence of doing a message from his Master,
with a poison'd Weapon, stabs at *Edwin*, con-
ferring with him in his House, by the River
Derwent in *York-shire*, on an Easter-day; which
Lilla

625.

626.

Lilla one of the Kings Attendants, at the in-
ftant perceaving, with a loyalty that ftood
not then to deliberate, abandon'd his whole
body to the blow; which notwithftanding
made paffage through to the Kings Perfon,
with a wound not to be flighted.   The murderer encompafs'd now with Swords, and de-
fperate, fore-revenges his own fall with the
death of another, whom his Poinard reach'd
home.   *Paulinus* omitting no opportunity to
win the King from misbeleif, obtain'd at
length this promife from him; that if Chrift,
whom he fo magnifi'd, would give him to recover of his wound, and victory of his Enemies who had thus affaulted him, he would
then become Chriftian, in pledge whereof he
gave his young Daughter *Eanfled* to be bred
up in Religion; who with twelv others of his
Family, on the day of *Pentecoft* was baptiz'd.
And by that time well recover'd of his wound;
to punifh the Authors of fo foul a fact, he
went with an Army againft the *Weft-Saxons:*
whom having quell'd by War, and of fuch as
had confpir'd againft him, put fom to death,
others pardon'd, he return'd home victorious,
and from that time worfhip'd no more his
Idols, yet ventur'd not rafhly into Baptifm,
but firft took care to be inftructed rightly,
what he learnt, examining and ftill confidering with himfelf and others, whom he held
wifeft; though *Boniface* the Pope, by large
Letters of Exhortation, both to him and his
Queen, was not wanting to quicken his beleif.   But while he ftill deferr'd, and his de-
ferring

ferring might feem now to have paft the ma-
turity of wifdom to a faulty lingring, *Pauli-*
nus by Revelation, as was beleev'd, coming
to the knowledge of a fecret, which befell him
ftrangely in the time of his troubles, on a certain day went in boldly to him, and laying his
right hand on the head of the King, ask'd
him if he rememberd what that fign meant ;
the King trembling, and in a maze rifing up,
ftraight fell at his Feet. Behold, faith *Paulinus*,
raifing him from the ground ; God hath deliver'd you from your Enemies, and giv'n you
the Kingdom, as you defir'd : perform now
what long fince you promis'd him, to receave
his Doctrine which I now bring you, and the
Faith, which if you accept, fhall to your tem-
poral felicity , add Eternal. The promife
claim'd of him by *Paulinus*, how and wherefore made, though favouring much of Legend,
is thus related. *Redwald*, as we heard before,
dazl'd with the gold of *Ethelfrid*, or by his
threatning over-aw'd, having promis'd to
yeild up *Edwin*, one of his faithfull Companions, of which he had fome few with him in
the Court of *Redwald*, that never fhrunk from
his adverfity, about the firft howr of night
comes in haft to his Chamber, and calling him
forth for better fecrecy, reveles to him his
danger, offers him his aid to make efcape ;
but that courfe not approv'd, as feeming dif-
honourable without more manifeft caufe to
begin diftruft towards one who had fo long
bin his only refuge, the friend departs. *Ed-*
win left alone without the Palace Gate, full of
fadnefs

sadnefs and perplext thoughts, difcerns about the dead of night, a man neither by counte-nance nor by habit to him known, approach-ing towards him. Who after falutation, ask'd him why at this howr, when all others were at reft, he alone fo fadly fat waking on a cold Stone? *Edwin* not a little mifdoubting who he might be, ask'd him again, what his fitting within doors, or without, concern'd him to know? To whom he again, Think not that who thou art, or why fitting heer, or what danger hangs over thee, is to me unknown: But what would you promife to that man, who ever would befriend you out of all thefe trou-bles, and perfwade *Redwald* to the like? All that I am able, anfwer'd *Edwin.* And he, What if the fame man fhould promife to make you greater than any *Englifh* King hath bin before you? I fhould not doubt, quoth *Edwin,* to be anfwerably grateful. And what if to all this he would inform you, faid the other, in a way to happinefs, beyond what any of your Ance-ftors hath known? would you hark'n to his Counfel? *Edwin* without ftopping promis'd he would. And the other laying his right hand on *Edwins* head, When this fign, faith he, fhall next befall thee, remember this time of night, and this difcourfe, to perform what thou haft promis'd; and with thefe words dif-appearing, left *Edwin* much reviv'd, but not lefs fill'd with wonder, who this unknown fhould be. When fuddenly the friend who had bin gon all this while to lift'n furder what was like to be decree'd of *Edwin,* comes back and

M   joyfully

joyfully bids him rife to his repofe, for that
the Kings mind, though for a while drawn a-
fide, was now fully refolv'd not only not to
betray him, but to defend him againft all Enemies, as he had promis'd. This was faid to
be the caufe why *Edwin* admonifh't by the Bifhop of a fign which had befaln him fo ftrangely, and as he thought fo fecretly, arofe to him
with that reverence and amazement, as to one
fent from Heav'n, to claim that promife of
him which he perceav'd well was due to a Divine Power, that had affifted him in his troubles. To *Paulinus* therfore he makes anfwer,
that the Chriftian Beleef he himfelf ought by
promife, and intended to receave; but would
conferr firft with his Cheif Peers and Counfellers, that if they likewife could be won, all at
once might be baptiz'd. They therfore being
ask'd in Counfel what thir Opinion was concerning this New Doctrine, and well perceaving which way the King enclin'd, every one
thereafter fhap'd his reply. The Chief Prieft
fpeaking firft, difcover'd an old grudge he had
againft his Gods, for advancing others in the
Kings Favour above him thir Chief Prieft:
another hiding his Court-compliance with a
grave fentence, commended the choife of certain before uncertain, upon due examination;
to like purpofe anfwer'd all the reft of his Sa-
ges, none op'nly diffenting from what was
likely to be the Kings Creed: whereas the
preaching of *Paulinus* could work no fuch effect upon them, toiling till that time without fuccefs. Whereupon *Edwin* renouncing
Heathenifm,

Heathenifm, became Chriftian: and the Pagan Prieft, offring himfelf freely to demolifh the Altars of his former Gods, made fome amends for his teaching to adore them. With *Edwin*, his two Sons *Osfrid* and *Eanfrid*, born to him by *Quenburga*, Daughter, as faith *Beda*, of *Kearle* King of *Mercia*, in the time of his banifhment, and with them moft of the People, both Nobles and Commons, eafily Converted, were Baptiz'd; he with his whole Family at *York*, in a Church haftily built up of Wood, the multitude moft part in Rivers. *Northumberland* thus chrift'nd, *Paulinus* croffing *Humber*, converted alfo the Province of *Lindfey*, and *Blecca* the Governour of *Lincoln*, with his Houfhold and moft of that Citty; wherein he built a Church of Stone, curioufly wrought, but of fmall continuance; for the Roof in *Bedas* time, uncertain whether by neglect or Enemies, was down; the Walls only ftanding. Mean while in *Mercia*, *Kearle* a Kinfman of *Wibba*, faith *Huntingdon*, not a Son, having long withheld the Kingdom from *Penda Wibba*'s Son, left it now at length to the fiftieth year of his Age: with whom *Kinegils* and *Cuichelm*, the *Weft-Saxon* Kings, two year after, having by that time it feems recover'd ftrength, fince the Inrode made upon them by *Edwin*, fought at *Cirencefter*, then made Truce. But *Edwin* feeking every way to propagate the Faith, which with fo much deliberation he had receav'd, perfuaded *Eorpwald* the Son of *Redwald*, King of *Eaft-Angles*, to imbrace the fame beleef; willingly or in

aw,

627.

629.
Sax. An.

632.

aw, is not known, retaining under *Edwin* the name only of a King. But *Eorpwald* not long surviv'd his Conversion, slain in fight by *Ricbert* a Pagan : whereby the People having lightly follow'd the Religion of thir King, as lightly fell back to thir old superstitions for above three years after : *Edwin* in the mean while, to his Faith adding Vertue, by the due administration of Justice wrought such peace over all his Territories, that from Sea to Sea, Man or Woman might have travail'd in safety. His care also was of Fountains by the way side, to make them fittest for the use of Travellers. And not unmindful of Regal State, whether in Warr or Peace, he had a Royal Banner carried before him. But having Reign'd with much Honour seventeen years, he was at length by *Kedwalla*, or *Cadwallon*, King of the *Britans*, who with aid of the *Mercian Penda*, had rebell'd against him, slain in a Battel with his Son *Osfrid*, at a place call'd *Hethfeild*, and his whole Army over-thrown or disperst in the year 633, and the 47th of his Age, in the Eye of man worthy a more peacefull end. His Head brought to *York*, was there buried in the Church by him begun. Sad was this overthrow, both to Church and State of the *Northumbrians* : for *Penda* being a Heathen, and the *British* King, though in name a Christian, yet in deeds more bloody than the Pagan, nothing was omitted of barbarous cruelty in the slaughter of Sex or Age; *Kedwalla* threatning to root out the whole Nation, though then newly Christian.

For

For the *Britans*, and, as *Beda* faith, eev'n to his daies, accounted *Saxon* Christianity no better than Paganism, and with them held as little Communion. From these calamities no refuge being left but flight, *Paulinus* taking with him *Ethilburga* the Queen and her Children, aided by *Baßus*, one of *Edwins* Captains, made escape by Sea to *Eadbald* King of *Kent :* who receaving his Sister with all kindness, made *Paulinus* Bishop of *Rochester*, where he ended his days. After *Edwin,* the Kingdome of *Northumberland* became divided as before, each rightfull Heir seising his part; in *Deira Ofric*, the Son of *Elfric*, *Edwins* Uncle, by profession a Christian, and baptiz'd by *Paulinus*; in *Bernicia, Eanfrid*, the Son of *Ethelfrid*; who all the time of *Edwin*, with his Brother *Oswald*, and many of the young Nobility, liv'd in *Scotland* exil'd, and had bin there taught and baptiz'd. No sooner had they gott'n each a Kingdom, but both turn'd recreant, sliding back into thir old Religion; and both were the same year slain; *Ofric* by a sudden eruption of *Kedwalla*, whom he in a strong Town had unadvisedly beseig'd ; *Eanfrid* seeking Peace, and inconsideratly with a few surrendring himself. *Kedwalla* now rang'd at will through both those Provinces, using cruelly his Conquest; when *Ofwald* the Brother of *Eanfrid* with a smgll but Christian Army, unexpectedly coming on, defeated and destroy'd both him and his huge Forces, which he boasted to be invincible, by a little River running into *Tine*, neer the antient *Roman* Wall then

634.

call'd

call'd *Denisburn*, the place afterwards *Heav'n field*, from the Cross reported miraculous for Cures, which *Oswald* there erected before the Battail, in tok'n of his Faith against the great number of his Enemies. Obtaining the Kingdom, he took care to instruct again the People in Christianity. Sending therefore to the Scotish Elders, *Beda* so terms them, among whom he had receav'd Baptism, requested of them som faithful Teacher, who might again settle Religion in his Realm, which the late troubles had impar'd; they as readily hearkning to his request, send *Aidan* a Scotch Monk and Bishop, but of singular zeal and meeknefs, with others to assist him, whom at thir own desire he seated in *Lindisfarne*, as the Episcopal Seat, now *Holy Iland*: and being the Son of *Ethilfrid*, by the Sister of *Edwin*, as right Heir, others failing, easily reduc'd both Kingdoms of *Northumberland* as before into one; nor of *Edwins* Dominion lost any part, but enlarg'd it rather; over all the fowr *British* Nations, *Angles*, *Britans*, *Picts* and *Scots*, exerciseing Regal Authority. Of his Devotion, Humility, and Almes-deeds, much is spok'n; that he disdain'd not to be the interpreter of *Aidan*, preaching in *Scotch* or bad *English*, to his Nobles and Houshold Servants; and had the poor continually serv'd at his Gate, after the promiscuous manner of those times: his meaning might be upright, but the manner more antient of privat or of Church contribution, is doubtless more Evangelical. About this time, the *West-Saxons*, antiently call'd *Gevissi*,

Geviſſi, by the preaching of *Berinus*, a Biſhop, whom Pope *Honorius* had ſent, were converted to the Faith with *Kinegils* thir King : him *Oſwald* receav'd out of the Font, and his Daughter in mariage. The next year *Cuichelm* was baptiz'd in *Dorcheſter*, but liv'd not to the years end. The *Eaſt-Angles* alſo this year were reclaim'd to the Faith of Chriſt, which for ſom years paſt they had thrown off. But *Sigbert* the Brother of *Eorpwald* now ſucceeded in that Kingdom, prais'd for a moſt Chriſtian and Learned Man : who while his Brother yet Reign'd, living in *France* an exile, for ſome diſpleaſure conceav'd againſt him by *Redwald* his Father, lern'd there the Chriſtian Faith ; and reigning ſoon after, in the ſame inſtructed his People, by the preaching of *Felix* a *Burgundian* Biſhop. In the year 640 *Eadbald* deceaſing, left to *Ercombert* his Son by *Emma* the *French* Kings Daughter, the Kingdom of *Kent* ; Recorded the firſt of *Engliſh* Kings, who commanded through his limits the deſtroying of Idols ; laudably, if all Idols without exception ; and the firſt to have eſtabliſht *Lent* among us, under ſtrict penalty, not worth remembring, but only to inform us, that no *Lent* was obſerv'd heer till his time by compulſion : eſpecially being noted by ſom to have fraudulently uſurp'd upon his Elder Brother *Ermenred*, whoſe right was precedent to the Crown. *Oſwald* having Reign'd eight years, worthy alſo as might ſeem of longer life, fell into the ſame fate with *Edwin*, and from the ſame hand, in a great Battel overcom and ſlain by

636.

640.

Mat.Weſtm.

642.

M 4 *Penda*,

Penda, at a place call'd *Maferfield*, now *Ofwe-ftre*, in *Shropfhire*, miraculous, as faith *Beda*, after his Death. His Brother *Ofwi* fucceeded him; reigning, though in much trouble, twenty eight years; oppos'd either by *Penda*, or his own Son *Alfred*, or his Brothers Son *Ethilwald*. Next year *Kinegils* the *Weft-Saxon* dying, left his Son *Kenwalk* in his ftead, though as yet unconverted. About this time *Sigebert*, King of *Eaft-Angles*, having lernt in *France*, e're his coming to Reign, the manner of thir Schools, with the affiftance of fom Teachers out of *Kent*, inftituted a School heer after the fame Difcipline, thought to be the Univerfity of *Cambridge* then firft Founded : and at length weary of his Kingly Office, betook him to a Monaftical Life; commending the care of Government to his Kinfman *Egric*, who had fuftain'd with him part of that burden before. It happen'd fom years after, that *Penda* made Warr on the *Eaft-Angles* : they expecting a fharp encounter, befought *Sigebert*, whom they efteem'd an expert Leader, with his prefence to confirm the Souldiery : and him refufing carried by force out of the Monaftery into the Camp; where acting the Monk rather than the Captain, with a fingle wand in his hand, he was flain with *Egric*, and his whole Army put to flight. *Anna* of the Royal Stock, as next in right, fucceeded; and hath the praife of a vertuous and moft Chriftian Prince. But *Kenwalk* the *Weft-Saxon* having maried the Sifter of *Penda*, and divorc't her, was by him with more appearance of a juft çaufe

Camden.

Bed. L. 3.
c. 14.

643.
Sax. An.

645.
Sax. An.

caufe vanquifht in fight, and depriv'd of his Crown: whence retiring to *Anna* King of the *Eaft-Angles*, after three years abode in his Court, he there became Chriftian, and afterwards regain'd his Kingdom. *Ofwi* in the former years of his Reign, had fharer with him, *Ofwin* Nephew of *Edwin*, who rul'd in *Deira* feven years, commended much for his zeal in Religion, and for comlinefs of perfon, with other princely qualities, belov'd of all. Notwithftanding which, diffentions growing between them, it came to Arms. *Ofwin* feeing himfelf much exceeded in numbers, thought it more prudence, difmiffing his Army, to referve himfelf for fome better occafion. But committing his perfon with one faithful attendant to the Loyalty of *Hunwald* an Earl, his imagin'd friend, he was by him treacheroufly difcover'd, and by command of *Ofwi* flain. After whom within twelv days, and for grief of him whofe death he foretold, dy'd Bifhop *Aidan*, famous for his Charity, Meeknefs, and labour in the Gofpel. The fact of *Ofwi* was deteftable to all ; which therefore to expiate, a Monaftery was built in the place where it was don, and Prayers there daily offer'd up for the Souls of both Kings, the flain and the flayer. *Kenwalk* by this time reinftall'd in his Kingdom, kept it long, but with various Fortune ; for *Beda* relates him oft-times afflicted by his Enemies with great loffes : and in 652 by the Annals, fought a Battel (Civil War *Ethelwerd* calls it) at *Bradanford* by the River *Afene*; againft whom, and for what caufe,

648.

651.
Bede.

Bed. L. 3.
c. 7.
652.

cause, or who had the Victory, they write not.
Camden names the place *Bradford* in *Wiltshire*,
by the *River Avon*, and *Cuthred* his neer Kinfman, against whom he fought, but cites no
Autority; certain it is, that *Kenwalk* fowr
years before had giv'n large poffeffions to his
Nephew *Cuthred*, the more unlikely therefore

653.   now to have rebell'd.   The next year *Peada*,
whom his Father *Penda*, though a Heathen,
had for his Princely Vertues made Prince of
Middle-Angles, belonging to the *Mercians*, was
with that people converted to the Faith.   For
coming to *Ofwi* with requeft to have in mariage *Alfleda* his Daughter, he was deni'd her
but on condition, that he with all his People
fhould receave Chriftianity.   Hearing therefore not unwillingly what was preach't to him
of Refurrection and Eternal Life, much perfuaded alfo by *Alfrid* the Kings Son, who had
his Sifter *Kyniburg* to Wife, he eafily affented,
for the truths fake only as he profefs'd, whether he obtain'd the Virgin or no, and was baptiz'd with all his followers.   Returning, he
took with him fowr Presbyters to teach the
people of his Province; who by their daily
preaching won many.   Neither did *Penda*,
though himfelf no Beleever, prohibit any in
his Kingdom to hear or beleeve the Gofpel,
but rather hated and defpis'd thofe, who pro-
feffing to beleeve, atefted not thir Faith by
good works; condemning them for miferable
and juftly to be defpis'd, who obey not that
God in whom they choofe to beleeve.   How
well might *Penda* this Heathen rife up in judgment

ment againſt many pretending Chriſtians,
both of his own and theſe daies! yet being a
man bred up to War (as no leſs were others
then reigning, and oft-times one againſt another, though both Chriſtians) he warr'd on
Anna, King of the *Eaſt-Angles*, perhaps without cauſe, for *Anna* was eſteem'd a juſt man,
and at length ſlew him. About this time the
Eaſt-Saxons, who as above hath bin ſaid, had
expell'd thir Biſhop *Mellitus*, and renounc'd
the Faith, were by the means of *Oſwi* thus re-
converted. *Sigebert* ſurnam'd the *Small*, being the Son of *Seward*, without other memory
of his Reign, left his Son King of that Province, after him *Sigebert* the Second, who coming oft'n to viſit *Oſwi* his great friend, was by
him at ſeveral times fervently diſſuaded from
Idolatry, and convinc't at length to forſake
it, was there baptiz'd ; on his return home
taking with him *Kedda* a laborious Preacher,
afterwards made Biſhop ; by whoſe teaching
with ſome help of others, the people were a-
gain recover'd from misbeleef. But *Sigebert*
ſome years after, though ſtanding faſt in Religion, was by the Conſpiracy of two Brethren
in place neer about him, wickedly murder'd ;
who being ask'd what mov'd them to do a
deed ſo hainous, gave no other than this barbarous anſwer ; that they were angry with
him for being ſo gentle to his Enemies, as to
forgive them thir injuries whenever they be-
ſought him. Yet his death ſeems to have happen'd not without ſome cauſe by him giv'n of
Divine diſpleaſure. For one of thoſe Earls
who

654.
Sax. An.

who flew him, living in unlawfull wedlock, and therfore excommunicated fo feverely by the Bifhop, that no man might prefume to enter into his Houfe, much lefs to fit at meat with him, the King not regarding this Church cenfure, went to feaft with him at his invitation. Whom the Bifhop meeting in his return, though penitent for what he had don, and faln at his feet, touch'd with the rod in his hand, and angerly thus foretold : Becaufe thou haft neglected to abftain from the Houfe of that Excommunicate, in that Houfe thou fhalt die; and fo it fell out, perhaps from that prediction, God bearing witnefs to his Minifter in the power of Church Difcipline, fpiritually executed, not juridically on the contemner therof. This year 655 prov'd fortunate to *Ofwi*, and fatal to *Penda*, for *Ofwi* by the continual inrodes of *Penda*, having long endur'd much devaftation, to the endangering once by affault and fire *Bebbanburg*, his ftrongeft City, now *Bamborrow* Caftle, unable to refift him, with many rich prefents offerd to buy his Peace. Which not accepted by the Pagan, who intended nothing but deftruction to that King, though more than once in affinity with him, turning guifts into vows, he implores Divine Affiftance, devoting, if he were deliverd from his Enemy, a Child of one year old, his Daughter to be a Nun, and twelv portions of land whereon to build Monafteries. His vows, as may be thought, found better fuccefs than his profferd guifts; for heerupon with his Son *Alfrid*, gathering a fmall power,

he

655.

Bed. L. 3.
c. 16.
Camd.

he encounterd and difcomfited the *Mercians*, Camden.
thirty times exceeding his in number, and led
on by expert Captains : at a place call'd *Loy-*
des, now *Leeds* in *York-fhire*. Befides this *Ethel-*
wald, the Son of *Ofwald*, who Rul'd in *Deira*,
took part with the *Mercians*, but in the fight
withdrew his Forces, and in a fafe place expected the event : with which unfeafonable
retreat,the *Mercians* perhaps terrifi'd and mifdoubting more danger, fled ; thir Commanders, with *Penda* himfelf, moft being flain, a-
mong whom *Edelhere* the Brother of *Anna*,
who rul'd after him the *Eaft-Angles*, and was
the Author of this War ; many more flying
were drown'd in the River, which *Beda* calls
Winved, then fwoln above his Banks. The Mat. *Weft*.
death of *Penda*, who had bin the death of fo
many good Kings, made general rejoicing, as
the Song witnefs'd. At the River *Winwed*,
Anna was aveng'd. To *Edelhere* fucceeded
Ethelwald his Brother, in the *Eaft-Angles* ; to
Sigebert in the *Eaft-Saxons*, *Suidhelm* the Son of
Sexbald, faith *Bede*, the Brother of *Sigebert*, Bed. L. 3.
faith *Malmsbury*; he was baptiz'd by *Kedda*, c. 22.
then refiding in the *Eaft-Angles*, and by *Ethel-*
wald the King, receav'd out of the Font. But
Ofwi in the ftrength of his late Victory, with- 658.
in three years after fubdu'd all *Mercia*, and of Sax. *An*.
the *Pictifh* Nation greateft part, at which time
he gave to *Peada* his Son in Law the Kingdom
of *South-Mercia*, divided from the Northern
by *Trent*. But *Peada* the Spring following, as 659.
was faid , by the Treafon of his Wife the Sax. *An*.
Daughter of *Ofwi*, married by him for a fpecial

cial Christian, on the Feast of *Easter*, not protected by the holy time, was slain. The *Mercian* Nobles, *Immin*, *Eaba*, and *Eadbert*, throwing off the Government of *Oswi*, set up *Wulfer* the other Son of *Penda* to be thir King,
whom till then they had kept hid, and with
him adhered to the Christian Faith. *Kenwalk*
the *West-Saxon*, now settl'd at home, and desirous to enlarge his Dominion, prepares a-
gainst the *Britans*, joins Battel with them at
Pen in *Somersetshire*, and overcoming persues
them to *Pedridan*. Another fight he had with
them before, at a place call'd *Witgeornesbrug*,
barely mention'd by the Monk of *Malmsbury*.

661.
Sax. An.

Nor was it long e're he fell at variance with
Wulfer the Son of *Penda*, his old Enemy, scarce
yet warm in his Throne, fought with him at
Possentesburg, on the *Easter* Holy-days, and as
Ethelwerd saith, took him Prisner; but the
Saxon Annals, quite otherwise, that *Wulfer*
winning the field, wasted the *West-Saxon*
Country as far as *Eskesdun*; nor staying there,
took and wasted the Ile of *Wight*, but causing
the Inhabitants to be baptiz'd, till then un-
beleevers, gave the Iland to *Ethelwald* King of
South-Saxons, whom he had receav'd out of

664.
Bede.

the Font. The year 664 a Synod of *Scotch*
and *English* Bishops, in the presence of *Oswi*
and *Alfred* his Son, was held at a Monastery
in those parts, to debate on what Day *Easter*
should be kept; a Controversie which long
before had disturb'd the *Greek* and *Latin*
Churches : wherein the *Scots* not agreeing
with the way of *Rome*, nor yeilding to the
Disputants

Disputants on that side, to whom the King
most enclin'd, such as were Bishops heer, resign'd, and return'd home with thir Disciples.
Another clerical question was there also much
controverted, not so superstitious in my opinion as ridiculous, about the right shaving of
Crowns. The same year was seen an Eclips of
the Sun in *May*, followed by a sore Pestilence
beginning in the South, but spreading to the
North, and over all *Ireland* with great mor-
tality. In which time the *East-Saxons* after *Malmsb.*
Swithelms decease, being govern'd by *Siger* the
Son of *Sigebert* the *Small*, and *Sebbi* of *Seward*,
though both subject to the *Mercians*. *Siger*
and his People unstedie of Faith, supposing
that this Plague was come upon them for renouncing thir old Religion, fell off the second
time to Infidelity. Which the *Mercian* King
Wulfer understanding, sent *Jerumannus* a faithfull Bishop, who with other his fellow Labourers, by sound Doctrin and gentle dealing,
soon recur'd them of thir second relaps. In
Kent, *Ercombert* expiring, was succeeded by
his Son *Ecbert*. In whose fowrth year, by   668.
means of *Theodore*, a learned *Greekish* Monk   *Sax. Ann.*
of *Tarsus*, whom Pope *Vitalian* had Ordain'd
Arch-bishop of *Canterbury*, the *Greek* and *La-*
tin Tongue, with other Liberal Arts, Arithmetic, Music, Astronomie, and the like; began first to flourish among the *Saxons*; as did
also the whole Land, under Potent and Religious Kings, more than ever before, as *Bede*
affirms, till his own days. Two years after,   670.
in *Northumberland* dy'd *Oswi*, much addicted *Sax. Ann.*

to

to *Romish* Rites, and resolv'd, had his Disease releas'd him, to have ended his days at *Rome* :

Ecfrid the eldest of his Sons begot in Wedlock, succeeded him. After other three years, *Ecbert* in *Kent* deceasing, left nothing memorable behind him, but the general suspicion to have slain or conniv'd at the slaughter of his

Uncles two Sons, *Elbert*, and *Egelbright*. In recompence wherof, he gave to the Mother of them part of *Tanet*, wherein to build an Abbey ; the Kingdom fell to his Brother *Lothair*. And much about this time, by best account it should be, however plac'd in *Beda*,

that *Ecfrid* of *Northumberland*, having Warr with the *Mercian Wulfer*, won from him *Lindsey*, and the Country thereabout. *Sebbi* having Reign'd over the *East-Saxons* thirty years, not long before his death, though long before desiring, took on him the Habit of a Monk ; and drew his Wife at length, though unwilling, to the same Devotion. *Kenwalk* also dying, left the Government to *Sexburga* his Wife, who out-liv'd him in it but one year, driv'n out, saith *Mat. West.* by the Nobles,

disdaining Female Government. After whom several petty Kings, as *Beda* calls them, for

ten years space divided the *West-Saxons* ; others name two, *Escwin* the Nephew of *Kinigils*, and *Kentwin* the Son, not petty by thir deeds : for *Escwin* fought a Battel with *Wulfer*, at *Bedanhafde*, and about a year after both deceas'd ; but *Wulfer* not without a stain left behind him, of selling the Bishoprick of *London*, to *Wini* the first *Simonist* we read of in this Story ;

ry ; *Kenwalk* had before expell'd him from his
Chair at *Winchester* ; *Ethelred* the Brother of
Wulfer obtaining next the Kingdom of *Mercia*, not only recoverd *Lindsey*, and what besides in those parts *Wulfer* had lost to *Ecfrid*
some years before, but found himself strong
anough to extend his Arms another way, as
far as *Kent*, wasting that Country without respect to Church or Monastery, much also endamaging the Citty of *Rochester* : Notwithstanding what resistance *Lothair* could make
against him. In *August* 678 was seen a Morning Comet for three Months following, in
manner of a fiery Pillar.   And the *South-Saxons* about this time were Converted to the
Christian Faith, upon this occasion. *Wilfrid*
Bishop of the *Northumbrians* entring into contention with *Ecfrid* the King, was by him depriv'd of his Bishoprick, and long wandring
up and down as far as *Rome*, return'd at length
into *England*, but not dareing to approach the
North, whence he was banish'd, bethought
him where he might to best purpose elsewhere
exercise his Ministery. The South of all other
Saxons remain'd yet Heathen ; but *Edelwalk*
thir King not long before had bin baptiz'd in
Mercia, persuaded by *Wulfer*, and by him, as
hath bin said, receav'd out of the Font. For
which Relations sake he had the Ile of *Wight*,
and a Province of the *Meannari* adjoining,
giv'n him on the Continent about *Meanesborow* in *Hantshire*, which *Wulfer* had a little before gott'n from *Kenwalk*. Thether *Wilfrid*
takes his journey, and with the help of other

Bed. L. 4.
c. 12.

678.

679.

Bed. L. 4.
c. 13.
Camden.

N   Spiritual

Spiritual Labourers about him, in short time
planted there the Gospel. It had not rain'd,
as is said, of three years before in that Country, whence many of the people daily perish'd
by Famin; till on the first day of thir public
Baptism, soft and plentifull showers descend-
ing, restor'd all abundance to the Summer following. Two years after this, *Kentwin* the o-
ther *West-Saxon* King above-nam'd, chac'd the
Welch-Britans, as is Chronicl'd without circumstance, to the very Sea shoar. But in the year,
by *Beda's* reck'ning, 683, *Kedwalla* a *West-
Saxon* of the Royal Line (whom the *Welch* will
have to be *Cadwallader*, last King of the *Britans*) thrown out by faction, return'd from banishment, and invaded both *Kentwin*, if then
living, or whoever else had divided the succession of *Kenwalk*, slaying in fight *Edelwalk*
the *South-Saxon*, who oppos'd him in thir aid;
but soon after was repuls'd by two of his Captains, *Bertune*, and *Andune*, who for a while
held the Province in thir power. But *Kedwalla* gathering new Force, with the slaughter
of *Bertune*, and also of *Edric* the successor of
Edelwalk, won the Kingdom : But reduc'd
the People to heavy thraldome. Then addres-
sing to Conquer the Ile of *Wight*, till that time
Pagan, saith *Beda* (others otherwise, as above
hath bin related) made a vow, though himself yet unbaptiz'd, to devote the fowrth part
of that Iland, and the spoils thereof, to holy
uses. Conquest obtain'd, paying his vow as
then was the beleef, he gave his fowrth to Bishop *Wilfrid*, by chance there present ; and he
to

681.
Sax. Ann.

683.
Sax. an.

Bed. L. 4.
c. 15.

Malmsb.

684.

Bed. L. 4.
c. 16.

to *Bertwin* a Prieſt, his Siſters Son, with com-
miſſion to baptiſe all the vanquiſht, who meant
to ſave thir lives. But the two young Sons of
Arwald, King of that Iland, met with much
more hoſtility; for they at the Enemies approach flying out of the Ile, and betray'd
where they were hid not far from thence, were
led to *Kedwalla*, who lay then under Cure of
ſome wounds receav'd, and by his appointment, after inſtruction and Baptiſm firſt giv'n
them, harſhly put to death, which the Youths
are ſaid above thir Age to have Chriſtianly
ſufferd. In *Kent*, *Lothair* dy'd this year of his
wounds receav'd in fight again the *South-Saxons*, led on by *Edric*, who deſcending from
Ermenred, it ſeems challeng'd the Crown; and
wore it, though not commendably, one year
and a half : but coming to a violent Death,   *685.*
left the Land expos'd a prey either to home-   *Malmsb.*
bred Uſurpers, or neighbouring Invaders. A-
mong whom *Kedwalla*, taking advantage from
thir Civil Diſtempers, and marching eaſily
through the *South-Saxons*, whom he had ſubdu'd, ſorely harraſs'd the Country, untouch'd
of a long time by any hoſtile incurſion. But
the *Kentiſh* men, all parties uniteing againſt a
Common Enemy, with joint power ſo oppos'd
him, that he was conſtrained to retire back;
his Brother *Mollo* in the fight with twelv men   *Sax. An.*
of his Company, ſeeking ſhelter in a Houſe,   *Malmsb.*
was beſet and therin burnt by the perſuers :
Kedwalla much troubl'd at ſo great a loſs, re-
calling and ſoon rallying his diſorderd Forces,
return'd fiercely upon the chaſeing Enemy;   *686.*

nor could be got out of the Province, till both
by Fire and Sword, he had aveng'd the Death
of his Brother. At length *Victred* the Son of
Ecbert, attaining the Kingdom, both settl'd
at home all things in peace, and secur'd his
Borders from all outward Hostility. While
thus *Kedwalla* disquieted both West and East,
after his winning the Crown, *Ecfrid* the *Nor-*
thumbrian, and *Ethelred* the *Mercian*, fought a
sore Battel by the River *Trent*; wherin *Elfwin*
Brother to *Ecfrid*, a Youth of eighteen years,
much belov'd, was slain; and the accident
likely to occasion much more sheding of blood,
Peace was happily made by the grave exhortation of Arch-bishop *Theodore*, a pecuniary
fine only paid to *Ecfrid*, as som satisfaction for
the loss of his Brothers life. Another adver-
sity befell *Ecfrid* in his Family, by means of
Ethildrith his Wife, King *Anna*'s Daughter,
who having tak'n him for hir Husband, and
professing to love him above all other men,
persisted twelv years in the obstinat refusal of
his bed, therby thinking to live the purer life.
So perversly then was chastity instructed a-
gainst the Apostles Rule. At length obtaining of him with much importunity her departure, she veild her self a Nun, then made Abbess of *Ely*, dy'd seven years after the Pestilence; and might with better warrant have
kept faithfully her undertak'n Wedlock,
though now canoniz'd St. *Audrey* of *Ely*. In
the mean while *Ecfrid* had sent *Bertus* with a
Power to subdue *Ireland*, a harmless Nation,
saith *Beda*, and ever friendly to the *English*;
in

687.

Bede.

in both which they seem to have left a Posterity much unlike them at this day : miserably
wasted, without regard had to places hallow-
ed or profane, they betook them partly to
thir Weapons, partly to implore Divine Aid;
and, as was thought, obtain'd it in thir full a-
vengement upon *Ecfrid*. For he the next year,
against the mind and perswasion of his sagest
freinds, and especially of *Cudbert* a famous Bishop of that Age, marching unadvisedly a-
gainst the *Picts*, who long before had bin subject to *Northumberland*, was by them feigning
flight, drawn unawares into narrow streights
overtopt with Hills, and cut off with most of
his Army. From which time, saith *Bede*, military valour began among the *Saxons* to decay, nor only the *Picts* till then peaceable, but
some part of the *Britans* also recover'd by
Arms thir Liberty for many years after. Yet
Aldfrid elder, but base Brother to *Ecfrid*, a
man said to be learned in the Scriptures, recall'd from *Ireland*, to which place in his Brothers Reign he had retir'd, and now succeeding, upheld with much honour, though in nar-
rower bounds, the residue of his Kindome.
Kedwalla having now with great disturbance
of his Neighbours Reign'd over the *West-Saxons* two years, besides what time he spent
in gaining it, wearied perhaps with his own
turbulence, went to *Rome*, desirous there to
receave Baptism, which till then his worldly
affairs had deferr'd, and accordingly, on *Easter* Day, 689, he was baptiz'd by *Sergius* the
Pope, and his name chang'd to *Peter*. All
which

which notwithstanding, surpris'd with a Disease, he outliv'd not the Ceremony so far sought, much above the space of five weeks, in the thirtieth year of his Age, and in the Church of St. *Peter* was there buried, with a large Epitaph upon his Tomb. Him succeeded *Ina* of the Royal Family, and from the time of his coming in, for many years oppress'd the Land with like greevances, as *Kedwalla* had done before him, insomuch that in those times there was no Bishop among them. His first Expedition was into *Kent*, to demand satisfaction for the burning of *Mollo : Victred* loth to hazard all for the rash act of a few, deliver'd up thirty of those that could be found accessory, or as others say, pacifi'd *Ina* with a

Malm. Sax. great sum of money. Mean while, at the in-
an. Ethel- citement of *Ecbert*, a devout Monk, *Wilbrod* a
werd. Priest eminent for Learning, past over Sea, having twelv others in Company, with intent
694. to preach the Gospel in *Germany*. And coming to *Pepin* Cheif Regent of the *Franks*, who a little before had conquer'd the hither *Frisia*, by his countnance and protection, promise also of many benefits to them who should beleeve, they found the work of Conversion much the easier, and *Wilbrod* the first Bishoprick in that Nation. But two Priests, each of them *Hewald* by name, and for distinction surnam'd from the colour of thir Hair, the Black and the White, by his example, piously affected to the Souls of thir Country-men the old *Saxons*, at thir coming thether to convert them met with much worse entertainment.

For

For in the House of a Farmer who had promis'd to convey them, as they desir'd, to the Governour of that Country, discoverd by thir daily Ceremonies to be Christian Priests, and the cause of thir coming suspected, they were by him and his Heathen Neighbours cruelly butcherd; yet not unaveng'd, for the Governour enrag'd at such violence offerd to his Strangers, sending armed Men, slew all those Inhabitants, and burnt thir Village. After three years in *Mercia, Ostrid* the Queen, Wife to *Ethelred,* was kill'd by her own Nobles, as *Beda*'s Epitome Records; *Florence* calls them *Southimbrians,* negligently omitting the cause of so strange a fact. And the year following, *Bertred* a *Northumbrian* General was slain by the *Picts. Ethelred* seven years after the violent Death of his Queen, put on the Monk, and resign'd his Kingdom to *Kenred* the Son of *Wulfer* his Brother. The next year, *Aldfrid* in *Northumberland* dy'd, leaving *Osred* a Child of eight years to succeed him. Fowr years after which, *Kenred* having a while with praise govern'd the *Mercian* Kingdom, went to *Rome* in the time of Pope *Constantine,* and shorn a Monk spent there the residue of his daies. *Kelred* succeeded him, the Son of *Ethelred,* who had reign'd the next before. With *Kenred* went *Offa* the Son of *Siger,* King of *East-Saxons,* and betook him to the same habit, leaving his Wife and Native Country; a comely Person in the prime of his Youth, much desir'd of the People; and such his Vertue by report, as might have otherwise bin worthy to have
N 4   Reign'd.

697.

698.
704.

705.

709.

710.
Sax. An.
Hunting.
711.
Bede Epit.
715.
Sax. An.
Sax. an.
Hunting.
716.
718.
L. 5. c. 9.
725.
728.

Reign'd. *Ina* the *West-Saxon* one year after fought a Battel, at first doubtfull, at last successfull, against *Gerent* King of *Wales*. The next year *Bertfrid*, another *Northumbrian* Captain, fought with the *Picts*, and slaughter'd them, saith *Huntingdon*, to the full avengement of *Ecfrids* Death. The fowrth year after, *Ina* had another doubtfull and cruell Battel at *Wodnesburg* in *Wiltshire*, with *Kelred* the *Mercian*, who dy'd the year following a lamentable death: for as he sat one day feasting with his Nobles, suddenly possess'd with an Evil Spirit, he expir'd in despair, as *Boniface* Arch-bishop of *Ments*, an *English* man, who taxes him for a defiler of Nuns, writes by way of caution to *Ethelbald*, his next of Kin, who succeeded him. *Ofred* also the young *Northumbrian* King, slain by his Kindred in the eleventh of his Reign, for his vitious life and incest committed with Nuns; was by *Kenred* succeeded and aveng'd. He reigning two years left *Ofric* in his room. In whose seventh year, if *Beda* calculate right, *Victred* King of *Kent* deceas'd, having reign'd thirty four years, and some part of them with *Suebhard*, as *Beda* testifies. He left behind him three Sons, *Ethelbert, Eadbert,* and *Alric* his Heirs. Three years after which, appear'd two Comets about the Sun, terrible to behold, the one before him in the Morning, the other after him in the Evening, for the space of two weeks in *January*, bending thir blaze toward the North, at which time the *Saracens* furiously invaded *France*, but were expell'd soon after with great overthrow.

throw. The same year in *Northumberland*,
Osric dying or slain, adopted *Kelwulf* the Bro- *Bed. L.* 5,
ther of *Kenred* his Succeſſor, to whom *Beda* de- *c.* 24.
dicates his ſtory; but writes this only of him,
that the beginning, and the proceſs of his
Reign met with many adverſe commotions,
whereof the event was then doubtfully expected. Mean while *Ina* ſeven years before,
having ſlain *Kenwulf*, to whom *Florent* gives
the addition of *Clito*, giv'n uſually to none
but of the Blood Royal, and the fourth year
after overthrown and ſlain *Albright* another
Clito, driv'n from *Taunton* to the *South-Saxons*
for aid, vanquiſh't alſo the *Eaſt-Angles* in more
than one Battel, as *Malmsbury* writes, but not
the year, whether to expiate ſo much blood,
or infected with the contagious humour of
thoſe times, *Malmsbury* ſaith, at the perſuaſion
of *Ethelburga* his Wife, went to *Rome*, and
there ended his days; yet this praiſe left behind him, to have made good Laws, the firſt
of *Saxon* that remain extant to this day, and
to his Kinſman *Edelard*, bequeath'd the Crown;
No leſs than the whole Monarchy of *England*
and *Wales*. For *Ina*, if we beleeve a digreſſion
in the Laws of *Edward* Confeſſor, was the firſt
King Crown'd of *Engliſh* and *Britiſh*, ſince the
Saxons entrance; of the *Britiſh* by means of
his ſecond Wife, ſome way related to *Cad-*
wallader laſt King of *Wales*, which I had not
noted being unlikely, but for the place where
I found it. After *Ina*, by a ſurer Author, *E-* *Bede.*
thelbald King of *Mercia* commanded all the 731.
Provinces on this ſide *Humber*, with thir Kings:
the

the *Picts* were in League with the *English*, the *Scots* peaceable within thir bounds, and the *Britans* part were in thir own Government, part subject to the *English*. In which peacefull state of the Land, many in *Northumberland*, both Nobles and Commons, laying aside the exercise of Arms, betook them to the Cloister: and not content so to do at home, many in the dayes of *Ina*, Clerks and Laics, Men and Women, hasting to *Rome* in Herds, thought themselves no where sure of Eternal Life, till they were Cloisterd there. Thus representing the state of things in this Iland, *Beda* surceas'd to write. Out of whom cheifly hath bin gatherd, since the *Saxons* arrival, such as hath bin deliverd, a scatterd story pickt out here and there, with some trouble and tedious work from among his many Legends of Visions and Miracles; toward the latter end so bare of Civil matters, as what can be thence collected may seem a Calendar rather, than a History, tak'n up for the most part with succession of Kings, and computation of years, yet those hard to be reconcil'd with the *Saxon Annals*. Thir actions we read of, were most commonly Wars, but for what cause wag'd, or by what Counsells carried on, no care was had to let us know: wherby thir strength and violence we understand, of thir wisdom, reason, or justice little or nothing, the rest superstition and monastical affectation; Kings one after another leaving thir Kingly Charge, to run thir heads fondly into a Monks Cowle: which leaves us uncertain, whether *Beda* was

wanting

wanting to his matter, or his matter to him. Yet from hence to the *Danish* Invasion it will be worse with us, destitute of *Beda*. Left only to obscure and blockish Chronicles; whom *Malmsbury*, and *Huntingdon*, (for neither they than we had better Authors of those times) ambitious to adorn the History, make no scruple oft-times, I doubt, to interline with conjectures and surmises of thir own : them rather than imitate, I shall choose to represent the truth naked, though as lean as a plain Journal. Yet *William* of *Malmsbury* must be acknowledg'd, both for stile and judgement, to be by far the best Writer of them all : but what labour is to be endur'd, turning over Volumes of Rubbish in the rest, *Florence* of *Worster, Huntingdon, Simeon* of *Durham, Hoveden, Mathew* of *Westminster*, and many others of obscurer note, with all thir Monachisms, is a penance to think. Yet these are our only Registers, transcribers one after another for the most part, and somtimes worthy enough for the things they Register. This travail rather than not know at once what may be known of our Ancient Story, sifted from Fables and Impertinences, I voluntarily undergo; and to save others, if they please, the like unpleasing labour ; except those who take pleasure to be all thir life time, rakeing in the Foundations of old Abbies and Cathedrals : But to my Task now as it befalls. In the year 733, on the 18th Kalends of *September*, was an Eclipse of the Sun about the third howr of day, obscureing almost his whole Orb, as with

a black

733.

Sax. An.

Ethelwerd.

a black sheild. *Ethelbald* of *Mercia*, beseig'd
and took the Castle or Town of *Somerton :* and
two years after, *Beda* our Historian dy'd, som
say the year before. *Kelwulf* in *Northumberland* three years after became Monk in *Lindisfarne*, yet none of the severest, for he brought
those Monks from Milk and Water, to Wine
and Ale ; in which Doctrine no doubt but
they were soon docil, and well might, for *Kelwulf* brought with him good provision, great
treasure and revenues of Land, recited by *Simeon*, yet all under pretense of following (I
use the Authors words) poor *Christ*, by voluntary poverty : no marvel then if such applause
were giv'n by Monkish Writers to Kings turning Monks, and much cunning perhaps us'd to
allure them. To *Eadbert* his Uncle's Son he
left the Kingdome, whose Brother *Ecbert*,
Arch-bishop of *York* built a Library there.
But two years after, while *Eadbert* was busied
in War against the *Picts*, *Ethelbald* the *Mercian*, by foul fraud, assaulted part of *Northumberland* in his absence, as the supplement of
Beda's Epitomy records. In the *West-Saxons*,
Edelard who succeeded *Ina*, having bin much
molested in the beginning of his Reign, with
the Rebellion of *Oswald* his Kinsman, who
contended with him for the right of succession, overcoming at last those Troubles, dy'd
in Peace 741, leaving *Cuthred* one of the same
Linage to succeed him : who at first had much
War with *Ethelbald* the *Mercian*, and various
success, but joyning with him in League two
years after, made War on the *Welch* : *Huntingdon*

735.
738.
Malmsb.

740.

741.
Malmsb.
Sax. Ann.
743.
Sim. Dun.

tingdon doubts not to give them a great Victory. And *Simeon* reports, another Battel fought   744.
between *Britans* and *Picts* the year enfueing.   *Hoved.*
Now was the Kingdom of *East-Saxons* draw-   *Malmsb.*
ing to a period, for *Sigeard* and *Senfred* the
Sons of *Sebbi* having reign'd a while, and after them young *Offa*, who foon quitted his
Kingdom to go to *Rome* with *Kenred*, as hath   *Sax. Ann.*
bin faid, the Government was conferr'd on
Selred Son of *Sigebert* the good, who having
Rul'd thirty eight years, came to a violent   746.
death ; how or wherefore, is not fet down.
After whom *Swithred* was the laft King, driven out by *Ecbert* the *Weft-Saxon :* but *London*, with the Countries adjacent, obey'd the
Mercians till they alfo were diffolv'd.   *Cuth-*   748.
red had now reign'd about nine years, when
Kinric his Son a valiant young Prince, was in a   *Sax. An.*
military tumult flain by his own Souldiers.
The fame year *Eadbert* dying in *Kent*, his Bro-   *Hunting.*
ther *Edilbert* reign'd in his ftead.   But after   750.
two years, the other *Eadbert* in *Northumber-
land*, whofe War with the *Picts* hath bin a-
bove- mention'd , made now fuch Progrefs
there, as to fubdue *Kyle*, fo faith the Auctarie
of *Bede*, and other Countries thereabouts, to
his dominion ; while *Cuthred* the *Weft-Saxon*
had a fight with *Ethelhun*, one of his Nobles,
a ftout Warrier, envi'd by him in fome matter of the Common-wealth, as far as by the
Latin of *Ethelwerd* can be underftood (others   *Hunting.*
interpret it Sedition) and with much adoe o-   752.
vercoming, took *Ethelhun* for his valour into   *Camden.*
favour, by whom faithfully ferv'd in the twelf
or

or thirteenth of his Reign, he encounter'd in a set Battel with *Ethelbald* the *Mercian* at *Beorford*, now *Burford* in *Oxfordshire*; one year

753.

after against the *Welch*, which was the last but one of his life. *Huntingdon*, as his manner is to comment upon the annal Text, makes a terrible description of that fight between *Cuthred* and *Ethelbald*, and the Prowess of *Ethelhun*, at *Beorford*, but so affectedly, and therfore suspiciously, that I hold it not worth rehersal; and both in that and the latter con-

Sax. Ann.

flict, gives Victory to *Cuthred*; after whom

754.
Malmsb.

Sigebert, uncertain by what right, his Kinsman, saith *Florent*, step'd into the Throne, whom hated for his cruelty and other evil doings, *Kinwulf* joining with most of the Nobility, dispossess'd of all but *Hamshire*, that Pro-

755.

vince he lost also within a year, together with the love of all those who till then remain'd his adherents, by slaying *Cumbran*, one of his Chief Captains, who for a long time had faithfully serv'd, and now dissuaded him from in-

Hunting.
Hunting.

censing the People by such Tyrannical practices. Thence flying for safety into *Andreds* Wood, forsak'n of all, he was at length slain by the Swineheard of *Cumbran* in revenge of his Maister, and *Kinwulf* who had undoubted right to the Crown, joyfully saluted King.

756.
Camden.

The next year *Eadbert* the *Northumbrian* joining forces with *Unust* King of the *Picts*, as *Simeon* writes, beseig'd and took by surrender the City *Alcluith*, now *Dunbritton* in *Lennox*, from the *Britans* of *Cumberland*; and ten days after, the whole Army perished about *Niwanbirig,*

birig, but to tell us how, he forgetts. In *Mer-* Camden.
cia, *Ethelbald* was flain, at a place call'd *Secan-* 757.
dune, now *Seckinton* in *Warwick-shire*, the year Sax. Ann.
following, in a bloody fight against *Cuthred*,
as *Huntingdon* furmifes, but *Cuthred* was dead Epit. Bed.
two or three years before; others write him Sim. Dun.
murder'd in the night by his own Guard, and
the Treafon, as fom fay, of *Beornred*, who fucceeded him; but ere many Months, was defeated and flain by *Offa*. Yet *Ethelbald* feems
not without caufe, after a long and profperous Reign, to have fall'n by a violent death;
not fhameing on the vain confidence of his
many Alms, to commit uncleannefs with con-
fecrated Nuns, befides Laic Adulteries, as the
Arch-bifhop of *Ments* in a letter taxes him and
his Predeceffor, and that by his Example moft
of his Peers did the like; which adulterous
doings he foretold him were likely to produce
a flothfull off-fpring, good for nothing but to
be the ruin of that Kingdom, as it fell out not
long after. The next year *Ofmund*, according 758.
to *Florence*, ruleing the *South-Saxons*, and *Swi-*
thred the *Eaft*, *Eadbert* in *Northumberland*, following the fteps of his Predeceffor, got him
into a Monks Hood; the more to be won- Sim. Dun.
der'd, that having reign'd worthily twenty Eccles. L. 2.
one years, with the love and high eftimation
of all, both at home and abroad, able ftill to
Govern, and much entreated by the Kings his
Neighbours, not to lay down his charge; with
offer on that condition to yield up to him part
of thir own Dominion, he could not be mov'd
from his refolution, but relinquifh'd his Regal
Office

759.

Office to *Oswulf* his Son; who at the years end, though without juſt cauſe, was ſlain by his own Servants. And the year after dy'd *Ethelbert*, Son of *Victred*, the ſecond of that name in *Kent*. After *Oswulf*, *Ethelwald*, otherwiſe call'd *Mollo*, was ſet up King; who in his third year had a great Battel at *Eldune*, by *Melros*, ſlew *Oswin* a great Lord, rebelling, and gain'd the Victory. But the third year after, fell by the treachery of *Alcred*, who aſſum'd his place. The fowrth year after which, *Cataracta* an antient and fair Citty in *York-ſhire*, was burnt by *Arnred* a certain Tyrant, who the ſame year came to like end. And after five years more, *Alcred* the King depos'd and forſak'n of all his People, fled with a few, firſt to *Bebba*, a ſtrong Citty of thoſe parts, thence to *Kinot* King of the *Picts*. *Ethelred* the Son of *Mollo*, was crown'd in his ſtead. Mean while *Offa* the *Mercian*, growing powerfull, had ſubdu'd a Neighbouring People by *Simeon*, call'd *Heſtings*; and fought ſuccesfully this year with *Alric* King of *Kent*, at a place call'd *Ottanford:* the Annals alſo ſpeak of wondrous Serpents then ſeen in *Suſſex*. Nor had *Kinwulf* the *Weſt-Saxon* giv'n ſmall proof of his valour in ſeveral Battles againſt the *Welch* heretofore; but this year 775 meeting with *Offa*, at a place call'd *Beſington*, was put to the worſe, and *Offa* won the Town for which they contended. In *Northumberland*, *Ethelred* having caus'd three of his Nobles, *Aldwulf*, *Kinwulf*, and *Ecca*, treacherouſly to be ſlain by two other Peers, was himſelf the next year driv'n into baniſhment,

762.

Sim. Dun.
Mat.Weſtm.

765.

Sim. Dun.

769.

774.

Sim. Dun.

775.

Sax. Ann.

778.

Sim. Dun.

ment, *Elfwald* the Son of *Oswalf* succeeding in
his place, yet not without Civil Broils; for in
his second year *Osbald* and *Ethelheard*, two Noblemen, raising Forces against him, routed
Bearne his General, and persueing, burnt him
at a place call'd *Seletune*.   I am sensible how
wearisom it may likely be to read of so many
bare and reasonless Actions, so many names of
Kings one after another, acting little more
than mute persons in a Scene : what would it
be to have inserted the long Bead-roll of Arch-
bishops, Bishops, Abbots, Abbesses, and thir
doeings, neither to Religion profitable, nor
to Morality, swelling my Authors each to a
voluminous body, by me studiously omitted ;
and left as thir propriety, who have a mind to
write the Ecclesiastical matters of those Ages ;
neither do I care to wrincle the smoothness of
History with rugged names of places unknown, better harp'd at in *Camden*, and other
Chorographers.   Six years therefore pass'd o-
ver in silence, as wholely of such Argument,
bring us to relate next the unfortunate end of
Kinwulf the *West-Saxon* ; who having laudably
reign'd about thirty one years, yet suspecting
that *Kineard* Brother of *Sigebert* the former
King, intended to usurp the Crown after his
Decease, or revenge his Brothers expulsion,
had commanded him into banishment ; but
he lurking here and there on the borders with
a small Company, having had intelligence that
Kenwulf was in the Country thereabout, at
Merantun, or *Merton* in *Surrey*, at the House of
a Woman whom he lov'd, went by night & be-

780.
Sim. Dun.

786.
Ethelwerd.
Malmsb.

Sax. Ann.

Camden.

O   set

set the place. *Kenwulf* over-confident either of his Royal presence, or personal valour, issuing forth with the few about him, runs feirfly at *Kineard*, and wounds him sore, but by his followers hem'd in, is kill'd among them. The report of so great an accident soon running to a place not far off, where many more attendants awaited the Kings return, *Osric* and *Wivert*, two Earles hasted with a great number to the House, where *Kineard* and his fellows yet remain'd. He seeing himself surrounded, with fair words and promise of great guifts, attempted to appease them; but those rejected with disdain, fights it out to the last, and is slain with all but one or two of his Retinue, which were nigh a hunderd. *Kinwulf* was succeeded by *Birthric*, being both descended of *Kerdic* the Founder of that Kingdome. Not better was the end of *Elfwald* in *Northumberland*, two years after slain miserably by the Conspiracy of *Siggan*, one of his Nobles, others say of the whole People at *Scilcester* by the *Roman* Wall; yet undeservedly, as his Sepulchre at *Hagustald*, now *Hexham* upon *Tine*, and some Miracles there said to be done, are alleg'd to witness; and *Siggan* five years after laid violent hands on himself. *Ofred* Son of *Alcred* advanc't into the room of *Elfwald*; and within one year driv'n out, left his Seat vacant to *Ethelred* Son of *Mollo*, who after ten years of banishment (impris'nment, saith *Alcuin*) had the Scepter put again into his hand. The third year of *Birthric* King of *West-Saxons*, gave beginning from abroad to a new

788.

Sim. Dun.
Malmsb.

Camden.

Malmsb.

Sim. Dun.
789.

new and fatal revolution of Calamity on this
Land. For three *Danish* Ships, the first that
had bin seen heer of that Nation arriving in
the West, to visit these, as was suppos'd, Foren Merchants, the Kings gatherer of Customes taking Horse from *Dorchester*, found
them Spies and Enemies. For being commanded to come and give account of thir la-
ding at the Kings Custome-House, they slew
him and all who came with him; as an earnest of the many slaughters, rapines, and hosti-
lities, which they return'd not long after to
commit over all the Iland. Of this *Danish*   *Pontan.*
first arrival, and on a sudden worse than ho-   *L.* 3.
stile Aggression, the *Danish* History far otherwise relates, as if thir landing had bin at the
mouth of *Humber*, and thir spoilfull march
far into the Countrey; though soon repell'd
by the Inhabitants, they hasted back as fast to
thir Ships : But from what cause, what reason of State, what Authority or Public Coun-
sell the Invasion proceeded, makes not mention, and our wonder yet the more, by telling
us that *Sigefrid* then King in *Denmarke*, and
long after, was a man studious more of Peace
and Quiet than of Warlike matters. These   *Pontan.*
therefore seem rather to have bin some wan-   *L.* 4.
derers at Sea, who with publick Commission,
or without, through love of spoil, or hatred
of Christianity, seeking booties on any Land
of Christians, came by chance or weather on
this shore. The next year *Ofred* in *Northum-*   790.
berland, who driv'n out by his Nobles had gi-   *Sim. Dun.*
ven place to *Ethelred*, was tak'n and forcibly
shav'n

791.
Sim. Dun. shav'n a Monk at *York*. And the year after, *Oelf*, and *Oelfwin*, Sons of *Elfwald*, formerly King, were drawn by fair promises from the Principal Church of *York*, and after by command of *Ethelred*, cruelly put to death at *Wonwaldremere*, a Village by the great Pool in

Camden. *Lancashire*, now call'd *Winandermere*. Nor
792.
Sim. Dun.
Sim. Dun.
Eccles. L.2. was the third year less bloody; for *Osred*, who not likeing a shav'n Crown, had desir'd banishment and obtain'd it, returning from the Ile of *Man* with small Forces, at the secret but deceitfull Call of certain Nobles, who by Oath had promis'd to assist him, was also tak'n, and by *Ethelred* dealt with in the same manner; who the better to avouch his Cruelties, thereupon married *Elfled* the Daughter of *Offa*: for in *Offa* was found as little Faith or Mercy. He the same year having drawn to his Palace *Ethelbrite* King of *East-Angles*, with fair invitations to marry his Daughter, caus'd him to be there inhospitably beheaded, and his Kingdome wrongfully seis'd, by the wicked counsel of his Wife, saith *Mat. West.* annexing thereto a long unlikely Tale. For which violence and bloodshed to make attonement, with Fryers at least, he bestows the reliques of S*t* *Alban*, in a shrine of Pearl and Gold. Far worse it far'd the next year with

793.
Sim. Dun. the reliques in *Lindisfarne*; where the *Danes* landing, pillag'd that Monastery, and of Fryers kill'd some, carried away others Captive, sparing neither Priest nor Lay: which many strange thunders and fiery Dragons, with other impressions in the Air seen frequently before,

fore, were judg'd to foresignifie. This year
Alric third Son of *Victred* ended in *Kent* his
long Reign of thirty four years : with him
ended the Race of *Hengist :* thenceforth whomsoever Wealth or Faction advanc'd, took on
him the Name and State of a King. The *Sax-*
on Annals of 784 name *Ealmund* then Reigning in *Kent* ; but that consists not with the
time of *Alric,* and I find him no where else
mention'd. The year following was remarkable for the Death of *Offa* the *Mercian,* a stre-
nuous and suttle King ; he had much inter-
course with *Charles* the Great, at first enmity,
to the interdicting of Commerce on either
side, at length much amity and firm League,
as appears by the Letter of *Charles* himself yet
extant, procur'd by *Alcuin* a learned and prudent man, though a Monk, whom the Kings
of *England* in those dayes had sent Orator into *France,* to maintain good correspondence
between them and *Charles* the Great. He
granted, saith *Huntingdon,* a perpetual tribute
to the Pope out of every House in his Kingdome ; for yielding perhaps to translate the
Primacy of *Canterbury* to *Lichfield* in his own
Dominion. He drew a trench of wondrous
length between *Mercia* and the *British* Confines, from Sea to Sea. *Ecferth* the Son of *Offa,*
a Prince of great hope, who also had bin
Crown'd nine years before his Fathers Decease, restoring to the Church what his Father
had seis'd on : yet within fowr Months by a
sickness ended his Reign. And to *Kenulf* next
in right of the same Progeny bequeath'd his
O 3   Kingdome.

794.
Malmsb.

Asser. Mer.,
Sim. Dun.

Kingdome. Mean while the *Danish* Pirats who still wasted *Northumberland*, ventring on shoar to spoil another Monastery at the mouth of the River *Don*, were assail'd by the *English*, thir Chief Captain slain on the place ; then returning to Sea, were most of them Ship-wracked ; others driv'n again on shoar, were put all to the Sword. *Simeon* attributes this thir punishment to the power of St *Cudbert*, offended with them for the rifling of his Covent.

796.
Sim. Dun. Two years after this, dy'd *Ethelred* twice King, but not exempted at last from the fate of many his predecessors, miserably slain by his People, some say deservedly, as not inconscious with them who train'd *Osred* to his ruin. *Osbald* a Nobleman exalted to the Throne, and in less than a month, deserted and expelled, was forc'd to fly at last from *Lindisfarne* by Sea to the *Pictish* King, and dy'd an Abbot. *Eardulf* whom *Ethelred* six years before had commanded to be put to death at *Ripun*, before the Abbey-Gate, dead as was suppos'd, and with solemn Dirge carried into the Church, after midnight found there alive, I read not how, then banish'd, now recall'd, was in *York* Created King. In *Kent*, *Ethelbert* or *Pren*, whom the Annals call *Eadbright* (so different they often are one from another, both in timing and in naming) by som means having usurp'd Regal Power, after two years Reign contending with *Kenulf* the *Mercian*, was by him tak'n Pris'ner, and soon after, out of pious commiseration let go : but not receav'd of his own, what became of him,
Malmsbury

Malmsbury leaves in doubt. *Simeon* writes, that *Kenulf* commanded to put out his Eyes, and lop off his hands; but whether the sentence were executed or not, is left as much in doubt by his want of expression. The second year after this, they in *Northumberland* who had conspir'd against *Ethelred*, now also raising Warr against *Eardulf*, under *Wada* thir Chief Captain, after much havock on either side at *Langho*, by *Whaley* in *Lancashire*, the Conspirators at last flying, *Eardulf* return'd with Victory. The same year *London*, with a great multitude of her Inhabitants, by a sudden fire was consum'd. The year 800 made way for great alteration in *England*, uniting her seven Kingdoms into one, by *Ecbert* the famous *West-Saxon*; him *Birthric* dying Childless left next to Reign, the only surviver of that Linage, descended from *Inegild* the Brother of King *Ina*. And according to his Birth liberally bred, he began early from his youth to give signal hopes of more than ordinary worth growing up in him; which *Birthric* fearing, and withall his juster Title to the Crown, secretly sought his life, and *Ecbert* perceaving, fled to *Offa* the *Mercian*: but he having married *Eadburg* his Daughter to *Birthric*, easily gave ear to his Embassadors coming to require *Ecbert*: He again put to his shifts, escap'd thence into *France*; but after three years banishment there, which perhaps contributed much to his Education, *Charles* the great then Reigning, he was call'd over by the Public Voice (for *Birthric* was newly dead)

O 4   and

and with general applause Created King of
West-Saxons. The same day *Ethelmund* at *Kin-
neresford,* passing over with the *Worcestershire*
men, was met by *Weolstan* another Nobleman
with those of *Wiltshire,* between whom happen'd a great fray, wherin the *Wiltshire* men
overcame, but both Dukes were slain, no reason of thir quarrel writ'n; such bickerings to
recount, met oft'n in these our Writers, what
more worth is it than to Chronicle the Warrs
of Kites, or Crows, flocking and fighting in
the Air? The year following, *Eardulf* the *Northumbrian,* leading forth an Army against *Kenulf* the *Mercian,* for harboring certain of his
Enemies, by the diligent mediation of other
Princes and Prelats, Arms were laid aside, and
amity soon sworn between them. But *Eadburga* the Wife of *Birthric,* a Woeman every
way wick'd, in malice especially cruel, could
not or car'd not to appease the general hatred
justly conceiv'd against her; accustom'd in her
Husbands days to accuse any whom she spight-
ed; and not prevailing to his ruine, her practice was by poison secretly to contrive his
death. It fortun'd that the King her Husband,
lighting on a Cup which she had temperd, not
for him, but for one of his great Favourites,
whom she could not harm by accusing, sip'd
therof only, and in a while after still pineing
away, ended his days; the favourite drinking
deeper found speedier the Operation. She
fearing to be question'd for these facts, with
what treasure she had, pass'd over-sea to *Charles*
the Great, whom with rich guifts coming to
his

801.
Sim. Dun.

Malmsb.
L. 2.
Asser.

802.
Sim. Dun.

his presence, the Emperour courtly receav'd with this pleasant proposal: Choose *Eadburga*, which of us two thou wilt, me or my Son (for his Son stood by him) to be thy Husband: She no dissembler of what she lik'd best, made easie answer. Were it in my choice, I should choose of the two your Son rather, as the younger man. To whom the Emperour between jest and earnest, Hadst thou chosen me, I had bestow'd on thee my Son; but since thou hast chos'n him, thou shalt have neither him nor me. Nevertheless he assign'd her a rich Monastery to dwell in as Abbess; for that life it may seem, she chose next to profess; but being a while after detected of unchastity, with one of her followers, she was commanded to depart thence; from that time wandring poorly up and down with one Servant, in *Pavia* a City of *Italy*, she finish'd at last in beggery her shamefull life. In the year 805 *Cuthred*, whom *Kenulf* the *Mercian* had, instead of *Pren*, made King in *Kent*, having obscurely Reign'd eight years, deceas'd. In *Northumberland*, *Eardulf* the year following was driv'n out of his Realm by *Alfwold*, who Reign'd two years in his room; after whom *Eandred* Son of *Eardulf* 33 years; but I see not how this can stand with the sequel of story out of better Authors: Much less that which *Buchanan* relates, the year following, of *Acaius* King of *Scots*, who having Reign'd 32 years, and dying in 809, had formerly aided (but in what year of his Reign tells not) *Hungus* King of *Picts* with 10000 *Scots*, against *Athelstan* a *Saxon*

805.
Malmsb.
Sax. An.
806.
Hunting.
Sim. Dun.
808.
Mat. Westm.
809.

on or *English man*, then wasting the *Pictish* Borders; that *Hungus* by the aid of those *Scots* and the help of St *Andrew* thir Patron, in a Vision by night, and the appearance of his Cross by day, routed the astonisht *English*, and slew *Athelstan* in fight. Who this *Athelstan* was, I believe no man knows; *Buchanan* supposes him to have bin som *Danish* Commander, on whom King *Alured*, or *Alfred*, had bestow'd *Northumberland*; but of this I find no footstep in our Ancient Writers; and if any such thing were done in the time of *Alfred*, it must be little less than 100 years after; this *Athelstan* therfore, and this great overthrow, seems rather to have bin the fancy of som Legend than any warrantable Record. Mean while *Ecbert*,

Sim. Dun.
813.
Sax. Ann.

having with much Prudence, Justice, and Clemency, a work of more than one year, establisht his Kingdom and himself in the affections of his People, turns his first enterprise against the *Britans*, both them of *Cornwal*, and those beyond *Seavern*, subduing both. In *Mercia*, *Kenulf* the 6th year after, having reign'd with great praise of his Religious mind and Vertues, both in Peace and War, deceas'd.

819.
Sax. an.
Malmsb.

His Son *Kenelm*, a Child of seven years, was committed to the care of his Elder Sister *Quendred*; who with a female ambition aspiring to the Crown, hir'd one who had the charge of his Nurture, to murder him, led into a woody place upon pretence of hunting. The murder, as is reported, was miraculously reveal'd; but to tell how, by a Dove dropping a writt'n Note on the Altar at *Rome*, is a long story, told,

told, though out of order, by *Malmsbury* ; and under the year 821 by *Mat. Weſt.* where I leave it to be ſought by ſuch as are more credulous than I wiſh my Readers. Only the Note was to this purpoſe.

Low in a Mead of Kine under a Thorn,
Of head bereft li'th poor Kenelm *King-born.*

Keolwulf the Brother of *Kenulf*, after one years Reign was driv'n out by one *Bernulf* an Uſurper : who in his third year, uncertain whether invading or invaded , was by *Ecbert*, though with great loſs on both ſides, overthrown and put to flight at *Ellandune* or *Wilton* : yet *Malmsbury* accounts this Battel ſought in 806 a wide difference, but frequently found in thir computations. *Bernulf* thence retireing to the *Eaſt-Angles*, as part of his Dominion by the late ſeiſure of *Offa*, was by them met in the field and ſlain : but they doubting what the *Mercians* might do in revenge hereof, forthwith yeilded themſelves both King and People to the Sovranty of *Ecbert*. As for the Kings of *Eaſt-Angles* our *Annals* mention them not ſince *Ethelwald* ; him ſucceeded his Brothers Sons, as we find in *Malmsbury*, **Aldulf** (a good King, well acquainted with *Bede*) and *Elwold* who left the Kingdom to *Beorn*, he to *Ethelred* the Father of this *Ethelbrite*, whom *Offa* perfidiouſly put to death. *Simeon* and *Hoveden*, in the year 749 write that *Elfwald* King of *Eaſt-Angles* dying, *Humbeanna* and *Albert* ſhar'd the Kingdome between them ; but
where

820.
Ingulf.
823.
Sax. Ann.

Florent.
Genealog.
Bed. L. 2.
c. 15.

where to inſert this among the former ſucceſ-
ſions is not eaſie, nor much material : after
Ethelbrite, none is nam'd of that Kingdom till
thir ſubmitting now to *Ecbert* : he from this
Victory againſt *Bernulf* ſent part of his Army
under *Ethelwulf* his Son, with *Alſtan* Biſhop of
Shirburn, and *Wulferd* a Chief Commander,
into *Kent*. Who finding *Baldred* there reigning in his 18th year, overcame and drove him
over the *Thames*; whereupon all *Kent*, *Surrey*,
Suſſex, and laſtly *Eſſex*, with her King *Swithred*, became ſubject to the Dominion of *Ecbert*.
Neither were theſe all his exploits of this year,
the firſt in order ſet down in *Saxon Annals*, being his fight againſt the *Devonſhire Welch*, at a
place call'd *Gafulford*, now *Camelford* in *Corn-*

Camden.
825.
Ingulf.

wall. *Ludiken* the *Mercian*, after two years
preparing to avenge *Bernulf* his Kinſman on
the *Eaſt-Angles*, was by them with his five
Conſuls, as the Annals call them, ſurpris'd and
put to the Sword : and *Withlaf* his Succeſſor
firſt vanquiſht, then upon ſubmiſſion with all
Mercia, made tributary to *Ecbert*. Mean
while the *Northumbrian* Kingdom of it ſelf
was fall'n to ſhivers; thir Kings one after another ſo oft'n ſlain by the People, no man daring, though never ſo ambitious, to take up
the Scepter which many had found ſo hot, (the
only effectual cure of ambition that I have
read) for the ſpace of 33 years, after the death
of *Ethelred* Son of *Mollo*, as *Malmsbury* writes,
there was no King : many Noblemen and Prelats were fled the Country. Which miſ-rule
among them, the *Danes* having underſtood,
oſt-

oft-times from thir Ships entring far into the Land, infested those parts with wide depopulation, wasting Towns, Churches, and Monasteries, for they were yet Heathen : The *Lent* before whose coming, on the North-side of St *Peter*'s Church in *York*, was seen from the roof to rain blood. The causes of these Calamities, and the ruin of that Kingdom, *Alcuin*, a learned Monk living in those dayes, attributes in several Epistles, and well may, to the general ignorance and decay of lerning, which crept in among them after the death of *Beda*, and of *Ecbert* the Arch-bishop; thir neglect of breeding up youth in the Scriptures, the spruce and gay apparel of thir Priests and Nuns, discovering thir vain and wanton minds, examples are also read, eev'n in *Beda*'s days, of thir wanton deeds : thence Altars defil'd with Perjuries, Cloisters violated with Adulteries, the Land polluted with blood of thir Princes, Civil Dissentions among the People, and finally all the same Vices which *Gildas* alleg'd of old to have ruin'd the *Britans*. In this estate *Ecbert*, who had now Conquer'd all the South, finding them in the year 827 (for he was march'd thether with an Army to compleat his Conquest of the whole Iland) no wonder if they submitted themselves to the yoke without resistance, *Eandred* thir King becoming Tributary. Thence turning his Forces the year following, he subdu'd more throughly what remain'd of *North-Wales*.

827.

828.
Mat. West.

The End of the Fourth Book.

THE

HISTORY

OF

BRITAIN.

BOOK V.

THE summe of things in this Iland, or the best part therof, reduc't now under the Power of one Man; and him one of the worthiest, which, as far as can be found in good Authors, was by none attain'd at any time heer before unless in Fables; men might with som reason have expected from such Union, Peace and Plenty, Greatness, and the flourishing of all Estates and Degrees: but far the contrary fell out soon after, Invasion, Spoil, Desolation, slaughter of many, slavery of the rest, by the forcible landing of a fierce Nation; *Danes* commonly called, and somtimes *Dacians*, by others, the same with *Normans*; as barbarous as the *Saxons* themselves were at first reputed, and much more;

more; for the *Saxons* firſt invited came hither
to dwell; theſe unſent for, unprovok'd, came
only to deſtroy. But if the *Saxons*, as is above   *Calviſius.*
related, came moſt of them from *Jutland* and
Anglen, a part of *Denmarke*, as *Daniſh* Writers affirm, and that *Danes* and *Normans* are
the ſame; then in this Invaſion, *Danes* drove
out *Danes*, thir own Poſterity. And *Normans*
afterwards, none but Ancienter *Normans*.
Which Invaſion perhaps, had the Heptarchie   *Pontan.*
ſtood divided as it was, had either not bin attempted, or not uneaſily reſiſted; while each
Prince and People, excited by thir neereſt con-
cernments, had more induſtriouſly defended
thir own bounds, than depending on the neglect of a deputed Governour, ſent oft-times
from the remote reſidence of a ſecure Monarch. Though as it fell out in thoſe troubles,
the leſſer Kingdoms revolting from the *Weſt-
Saxon* yoke, and not aiding each other, too
much concern'd with thir own ſafety, it came
to no better paſs; while ſeverally they ſought
to repell the danger nigh at hand, rather than
jointly to prevent it far off. But when God
hath decreed ſervitude on a ſinful Nation, fitted by thir own Vices for no condition but
ſervile, all Eſtates of Government are alike
unable to avoid it. God had purpos'd to puniſh our inſtrumental puniſhers, though now
Chriſtians, by other Heathen, according to his
Divine retaliation; Invaſion for invaſion,
ſpoil for ſpoil, deſtruction for deſtruction.
The *Saxons* were now full as wicked as the
Britans were at thir arrival, brok'n with luxury

xury and floth, either fecular or fuperftitious; for laying afide the exercife of Arms, and the ftudy of all vertuous Knowledge, fom betook them to over-worldly or vicious Practice, others to Religious Idlenefs and Solitude, which brought forth nothing but vain and delufive Vifions; eafily perceav'd fuch, by thir commanding of things, either not belonging to the Gofpel, or utterly forbidden, Ceremonies, Reliques, Monafteries, Maffes, Idols, add to thefe oftentation of Alms, got oft-times by rapine and oppreffion, or intermixt with violent and luftfull deeds, fomtimes prodigally beftow'd as the expiation of cruelty and bloodfhed. What longer fuffering could there be, when Religion it felf grew fo void of fincerity, and the greateft fhews of purity were impur'd?

Ecbert.

E*Cbert* in full highth of Glory, having now enjoy'd his Conqueft feven peaceful years, his victorious Army long fince disbanded, and the exercife of Armes perhaps laid afide, the more was found unprovided againft a fudden ftorm of *Danes* from the Sea, who landing in the 32 of his Reign, wafted *Shepey* in *Kent*. *Ecbert* the next year, gathering an Army, for he had heard of thir arrival in 35 Ships, gave them Battail by the River *Carr* in *Dorfetfhire*; the event whereof was, that the *Danes* kept thir

832.
Sax. Ann.
833.
Sax. Ann.

thir ground, and encampt where the field was fought; two *Saxon* Leaders, *Dudda* and *Osmund*, and two Bishops, as som say, were there slain. This was the only check of Fortune we read of, that *Ecbert* in all his time receav'd. For the *Danes* returning two years after with a great Navy, and joining Forces with the *Cornish*, who had enter'd League with them, were overthrown and put to flight. Of these Invasions against *Ecbert*, the *Danish* History is not silent; whether out of thir own Records or ours, may be justly doubted; for of these times at home, I find them in much uncertainty, and beholding rather to Out-landish Chronicles than any Records of thir own. The Victor *Ecbert*, as one who had done enough, seasonably now, after prosperous success, the next year with glory ended his days, and was buried at *Winchester*.

835.
Sax. Ann.
Pontan.
Hist. Dan.
L. 4.

836.
Sax. Anni

Ethelwolf.

ETHELWOLF the Son of *Ecbert* succeeded, by *Malmsbury* describ'd a man of mild nature, not inclin'd to War, or delighted with much Dominion; that therfore contented with the ancient *West-Saxon* bounds, he gave to *Ethelstan* his Brother, or Son, as som write, the Kingdom of *Kent* and *Essex*. But the *Saxon* Annalist, whose Autority is Elder, saith plainly, that both these Countries and *Sussex*, were bequeath'd to *Ethelstan* by *Ecbert* his Father. The unwarlike disposition of *Ethelwolf*, Mat. West.

P   gave

gave encouragement no doubt, and easier entrance to the *Danes*, who came again the next year with thirty three Ships; but *Wulfheard*, one of the Kings Chief Captains, drove them back at *Southamton* with great slaughter; himself dying the same year, of Age, as I suppose, for he seems to have bin one of *Ecberts* old Commanders, who was sent with *Ethelwolf* to subdue *Kent*. *Ethelhelm* another of the Kings Captains with the *Dorsetshire* men, had at first like success against the *Danes* at *Portsmouth*; but they reinforcing stood thir ground, and put the *English* to rout. Worse was the success of Earl *Herebert* at a place call'd *Mereswar*, slain with the most part of his Army. The year following in *Lindsey* also, *East-Angles,* and *Kent*, much mischief was don by thir landing; where the next year, embold'nd by success, they came on as far as *Canterbury, Rochester,* and *London* it self, with no less cruel hostility: and giving no respit to the peaceable mind of *Ethelwolf*, they yet return'd with the next year in thirty five Ships, fought with him, as before with his Father, at the River *Carr*, and made good thir ground. In *Northumberland*, *Eandred* the Tributary King deceasing, left the same tenure to his Son *Ethelred* driv'n out in his fowrth year, and succeeded by *Readwulf*, who soon after his Coronation hasting forth to Battel against the *Danes* at *Alvetheli*, fell with the most part of his Army; and *Ethelred* like in fortune to the former *Ethelred*, was re-exalted to his Seat. And to be yet further like him in Fate, was slain the fowrth year after.

837.
Sax. an.

838.
Sax. An.
839.
Sax. An.

840.
Sax. An.
Sim. Dun.
Mat. West.
844.

ter. *Osbert* succeeded in his room. But more
southerly, the *Danes* next year after met with
som stop in the full course of thir outragious
insolences. For *Earnulf* with the men of *So-*
merset, *Alstan* the Bishop, and *Osric* with those
of *Dorsetshire*, setting upon them at the Rivers
mouth of *Pedridan*, slaughter'd them in great
numbers, and obtain'd a just Victory. This
repulse queld them, for ought we hear, the
space of six years; Then also renewing thir
Invasion, with little better success. For *Ke-*
orle an Earl, aided with the Forces of *Devon-*
shire, assaulted and over-threw them at *Wig-*
ganbeorch with great destruction; as prosperously were they fought with the same year at
Sandwich, by King *Ethelstan*, and *Ealker* his
General, thir great Army defeated, and nine
of thir Ships tak'n, the rest driv'n off, however to ride out the Winter on that shoar, *As-*
fer saith, they then first winter'd in *Shepey Ile*.
Hard it is, through the bad expression of these
Writers, to define this fight, whether by Sea
or Land; *Hoveden* terms it a Sea fight. Nevertheless with fifty Ships (*Asser* and others
add three hundred) they enter'd the mouth
of *Thames*, and made excursions as far as *Can-*
terbury and *London*, and as *Ethelwerd* writes,
destroy'd both; of *London*, *Asser* signifies only
that they pillag'd it. *Bertulf* also the *Mercian*,
successor of *Withlaf*, with all his Army they
forc'd to fly, and him beyond the Sea.   Then
passing over *Thames* with thir Powers into *Sur-*
rey, and the *West-Saxons*, and meeting there
with King *Ethelwolf* and *Ethelbald* his Son, at a

845.
Sax. An.

851.
Sax. An.
Asser.

Hunting.
Mat. West.

P 2   place

place call'd *Ak-Lea*, or *Oak-Lea*, they receav'd
a total defeat with memorable flaughter. This
was counted a lucky year to *England*, and

brought to *Ethelwolf* great reputation. *Burhed*
therfore, who after *Bertulf* held of him the
Mercian Kingdom, two years after this, imploring his Aid againft the *North-Welch*, as
then troublefom to his Confines, obtain'd it of
him in perfon, and therby reduc'd them to
obedience. This done, *Ethelwolf* fent his Son
Alfrid a Child of five years, well accompanied
to *Rome*, whom *Leo* the Pope both Confecra-
ted to be King afterward, and adopted to be
his Son; at home *Ealker* with the Forces of
Kent, and *Huda* with thofe of *Surrey*, fell on
the *Danes* at thir landing in *Tanet*, and at firft
put them back; but the flain and drown'd
were at length fo many on either fide, as left
the lofs equal on both : which yet hinder'd
not the folemnity of a Marriage at the Feaft

of *Eafter*, between *Burhed* the *Mercian*, and
Ethelfwida King *Ethelwolf*'s Daughter. Howbeit the *Danes* next year winter'd again
in *Shepey*. Whom *Ethelwolf* not finding humane health fufficient to refift, growing daily
upon him, in hope of Divine Aid, regifterd in
a Book, and dedicated to God the tenth part
of his own Lands, and of his whole Kingdom,
eas'd of all impofitions, but converted to the
maintenance of Maffes and Pfalms weekly to
be fung for the profpering of *Ethelwolf* and his
Captains, as appears at large by the Patent it
felf, in *William* of *Malmsbury*. *Affer* faith, he
did it for the redemption of his Soul, and the
Soul

Soul of his Ancestors.   After which, as having done som great matter, to shew himself at
Rome, and be applauded of the Pope; he takes
a long and cumbersome journey thether with
young *Alfrid* again, and there stayes a year,
when his place requir'd him rather heer in the
field against Pagan Enemies left wintring in
his Land.   Yet so much manhood he had, as
to return thence no Monk; and in his way
home took to Wife *Judith* Daughter of *Charles*
the Bald, King of *France*.   But ere his return,
Ethelbald his Eldest Son, *Alstan* his trusty Bishop, and *Enulf* Earl of *Somerset* conspir'd a-
gainst him; thir complaints were, that he had
tak'n with him *Alfrid* his youngest Son to be
there inaugurated King, and brought home
with him an Out-landish Wife; for which
they endeavour'd to deprive him of his Kingdome.   The disturbance was expected to bring
forth nothing less than Warr: but the King
abhorring Civil Discord, after many confe-
rences tending to Peace, condescended to divide the Kingdom with his Son; division was
made, but the matter so carried, that the
Eastern and worst part was malignly afforded
to the Father: The Western and best giv'n to
the Son, at which many of the Nobles had
great indignation, offring to the King thir utmost assistance for the recovery of all; whom
he peacefully dissuading, sat down contented
with his portion assign'd.   In the *East-Angles*,
Edmund Lineal from the Ancient Stock of
those Kings, a Youth of fourteen years only,
but of great hopes, was with consent of all

855.
Asser.

Asser.

but

857.

but his own Crown'd at *Burie*. About this time, as *Buchanan* relates, the *Picts*, who not long before had by the *Scots* bin driv'n out of thir Countrey, part of them coming to *Osbert* and *Ella*, then Kings of *Northumberland*, obtain'd Aid against *Donaldus* the *Scotish* King, to recover thir Ancient Possession. *Osbert* who in person undertook the Expedition, marching into *Scotland*, was at first put to a retreat; but returning soon after on the *Scots*, over-secure of thir suppos'd Victory, put them to flight with great slaughter, took Pris'ner thir King, and persu'd his Victory beyond *Sterlinbridge*. The *Scots* unable to resist longer, and by Embassadors entreating Peace, had it granted them on these Conditions: the *Scots* were to quit all they had possess'd within the Wall of *Severus*: The Limits of *Scotland* were beneath *Sterlinbridge* to be the River *Forth*, and on the other side, *Dunbritton Frith*; from that time so call'd of the *British* then seated in *Cumberland*, who had joind with *Osbert* in this Action, and so far extended on that side the *Brittish* Limits. If this be true, as the *Scotch* Writers themselv's witness (and who would think them fabulous to the disparagement of thir own Country?) how much wanting have bin our Historians to thir Countries Honour, in letting pass unmention'd an exploit so memorable, by them remember'd and attested, who are wont ofter to extenuate than to amplifie aught done in *Scotland* by the *English?* *Donaldus* on these conditions releas't, soon after dyes; according to *Buchanan*, in 858.

Ethelwolf

Ethelwolf Chief King in *England*, had the year before ended his life, and was buried as his Father at *Winchester*.   He was from his youth *Mat. West.* much addicted to devotion; so that in his Fathers time he was ordain'd Bishop of *Winchester*; and unwillingly, for want of other Legitimate Issue, succeeded him in the Throne; mannaging therfore his greatest Affairs by the Activity of two Bishops, *Alstan* of *Sherburne*, and *Swithine* of *Winchester*.   But *Alstan* is no- *Malmsb.* ted of Covetousness and Oppression, by *William* of *Malmsbury*; the more vehemently no doubt for doing som notable damage to that Monastery.   The same Author writes, that *Sigon. de Ethelwolf* at *Rome*, paid a Tribute to the Pope, *regn. Ital.* continu'd to his days.   However he were fa- *L. 5.* cil to his Son, and seditious Nobles, in yeilding up part of his Kingdome, yet his Queen he treated not the less honourably, for whomsoever it displeas'd.   The *West-Saxons* had de- *Asser.* creed ever since the time of *Eadburga*, the infamous Wife of *Birthric*, that no Queen should sit in State with the King, or be dignifi'd with the Title of Queen.   But *Ethelwolf* permitted not that *Judith* his Queen should lose any point of Regal State by that Law.   At his death, he divided the Kingdome between his two Sons, *Ethelbald*, and *Ethelbert*; to the younger *Kent*, *Essex*, *Surrey*, *Sussex*, to the Elder all the rest; to *Peter* and *Paul* certain Revenues yearly, for what uses let others relate, who write also his Pedigree, from Son to Father, up to *Adam*.

P 4   *Ethelbald*,

Ethelbald, and *Ethelbert*.

Asser.
Malmsb.
Sim. Dun.

E*Thelbald*, unnatural and disloyal to his Father, fell justly into another, though contrary sin, of too much love to his Fathers Wife; and whom at first he oppos'd coming into the Land, her now unlawfully marrying, he takes into his Bed; but not long enjoying, dy'd at three years end, without doing aught more worthy to be rememberd; having reigned two years with his Father, impiously usurping, and three after him, as unworthily inheriting. And his hap was all that while to be unmolested by the *Danes*; not of Divine favour doubtless, but to his greater condemnation, living the more securely his incestuous life. *Huntingdon* on the other side much praises *Ethelbald*, and writes him buried at *Sherburn*, with great sorrow of the People, who miss'd him long after. *Mat. West.* saith, that he repented of his Incest with *Judith*, and dismiss'd her: but *Asser* an Eye witness of those times, mentions no such thing.

860.
Sax. Ann.

Ethelbert alone.

E*Thelbald* by death remov'd, the whole Kingdom came rightfully to *Ethelbert* his next Brother. Who though a Prince of great Vertue and no blame, had as short a Reign allotted him as his faulty Brother; nor that so peaceful;

peaceful; once or twice Invaded by the *Danes*.
But they having landed in the West with a
great Army, and fackt *Winchester*, were met
by *Osric* Earl of *Southampton*, and *Ethelwolf* of
Bark-shire, beat'n to thir Ships, and forc't to
leave thir booty.   Five years after, about the   855.
time of his death, they set foot again in *Ta*-   *Sax. Ann.*
net ; the *Kentish* men wearied out with so frequent Alarms, came to agreement with them
for a certain summe of money ; but ere the
Peace could be ratifi'd, and the money gather'd, the *Danes* impatient of delay by a sudden eruption in the night, soon wasted all the
East of *Kent*.   Mean while or something before, *Ethelbert* deceasing was buried as his Brother at *Sherburne*.

Ethelred.

EThelred the third Son of *Ethelwolf*, at his   866.
first coming to the Crown was entertain-   *Sax. ann.*
ed with a fresh Invasion of *Danes*, led by *Hin*-   *Hunting.*
guar and *Hubba*, two Brothers, who now had
got footing among the *East-Angles* ; there
they winter'd, and coming to terms of Peace
with the Inhabitants, furnish'd themselves of
Horses, forming by that means many Troops
with Riders of thir own : These Pagans, *Asser*
saith, came from the River *Danubius*.   Fitted   867.
thus for a long expedition, they ventur'd the   *Sax. ann.*
next year to make thir way over Land and
over *Humber*, as far as *York*, them they found
to thir hands imbroil'd in Civil Dissentions;
thir

thir King *Osbert* they had thrown out, and
Ella Leader of another Faction chosen in his
room; who both, though late, admonish'd
by thir Common Danger, towards the years
end with United Powers made Head against
the *Danes* and prevail'd; but persueing them

Asser. over-eagerly into *York*, then but slenderly
wall'd, the *Northumbrians* were every where
slaughter'd, both within and without; thir
Kings also both slain, thir City burnt, saith
Malmsbury, the rest as they could, made thir
Peace, over-run and vanquisht as far as the
River *Tine*, and *Egbert* of *English* Race appointed King over them. *Bromton* no Ancient
Author (for he wrote since *Mat. West.*) nor
of much Credit, writes a particular Cause of
the *Danes* coming to *York*: that *Bruern* a Nobleman, whose Wife King *Osbert* had ravisht,
call'd in *Hinguar* and *Hubba* to revenge him.
The example is remarkable if the truth were

868. as evident. Thence victorious, the *Danes* next
year enter'd into *Mercia* towards *Nottingham*,
where they spent the winter. *Burhed* then King
of that Country, unable to resist, implores the
Aid of *Ethelred* and young *Alfred* his brother,
they assembling thir Forces and joyning with
the *Mercians* about *Nottingham*, offer Battel:

Asser. the *Danes* not daring to come forth, kept
themselves within that Town and Castle, so
that no great fight was hazarded there; at
length the *Mercians* weary of long suspence,
enter'd into conditions of Peace with thir E-
nemies. After which the *Danes* returning
back to *York*, made thir abode there the space
of

of one year, committing, som say, many Cruelties.   Thence imbarking to *Lindsey*, and all
the Summer destroying that Country, about
September they came with like fury into *Kesteven*, another part of *Lincolnshire*, where *Algar* the Earle of *Howland* now *Holland*, with
his Forces, and two hunder'd stout Souldiers
belonging to the Abbey of *Croiland*, three
hunder'd from about *Boston*, *Morcar* Lord of
Brunne, with his numerous Family, well train-
ed and armed, *Osgot* Governour of *Lincoln*
with 500 of that City, all joyning together,
gave Battel to the *Danes*, slew of them a great
multitude, with three of thir Kings, and per-
sued the rest to thir Tents; but the night following, *Gothrun*, *Baseg*, *Osketil*, *Halfden*, and
Hamond, five Kings, and as many Earls, *Fre-
na*, *Hinguar*, *Hubba*, *Sidroc* the Elder and
Younger, coming in from several parts with
great Forces and Spoils, great part of the *English* began to slink home.   Neverthelefs *Algar* with such as forsook him not, all next day
in order of Battel facing the *Danes*, and sustain-
ing unmov'd the brunt of thir assaults, could
not with-hold his Men at last from persueing
thir counterfitted flight; whereby op'n'd and
disorder'd, they fell into the snare of thir E-
nemies, rushing back upon them.   *Algar* and
those Captains fore-nam'd with him, all resolute men, retreating to a hill side, and slaying of such as follow'd them, manifold thir
own number, dy'd at length upon heaps of
dead which they had made round about them.
The *Danes* thence passing on into the Country
of

869.
Sim. Dun.
870.
Ingulf.

of *East-Angles*, rifl'd and burnt the Monaſtery of *Elie*, overthrew Earl *Wulketul* with his whole Army, and lodg'd out the Winter at *Thetford*; where King *Edmund* aſſailing them, was with his whole Army put to flight, himſelf tak'n, bound to a ſtake, and ſhot to death with Arrows, his whole Country ſubdu'd. The next year with great Supplies, ſaith *Huntingdon*, bending thir march toward the *Weſt-Saxons*, the only People now left, in whom might ſeem yet to remain ſtrength or courage likely to oppoſe them, they came to *Reading*, fortifi'd there between the two Rivers of *Thames*, and *Kenet*, and about three dayes after, ſent out wings of Horſe under two Earls to forage the Country; but *Ethelwulf* Earl of *Bark-ſhire*, at *Englefeild* a Village nigh, encounter'd them, ſlew one of thir Earls, and obtain'd a great Victory. Four dayes after came the King himſelf and his Brother *Alfred* with the main Battail; and the *Danes* iſſuing forth, a bloody fight began, on either ſide great ſlaughter, in which Earl *Ethelwulf* loſt his life; but the *Danes* loſing no ground, kept thir place of ſtanding to the end. Neither did the *Engliſh* for this make leſs haſt to another Conflict at *Eſceſdune*, or *Aſhdown*, four days after, where both Armies with thir whole Force on either ſide met. The *Danes* were imbattail'd in two great Bodies, the one led by *Baſcai* and *Half-den*, thir two Kings, the other by ſuch Earls as were appointed; in like manner the *Engliſh* divided thir Powers, *Ethelred* the King ſtood againſt thir Kings; and though on the lower ground,

ground, and coming later into the Battail from his Orisons, gave a fierce onset, wherin *Bascai*, (the *Danish* History names him *Ivarus* the Son of *Regnerus*) was slain. *Alfred* was plac'd against the Earls, and beginning the Battail ere his Brother came into the Field, with such resolution charg'd them, that in the shock most of them were slain; they are nam'd *Sidroc* Elder and Younger, *Osbern*, *Frean*, *Harald*; at length in both Divisions, the *Danes* turn thir backs; many thousands of them cut off, the rest persu'd till night. So much the more it may be wonder'd to hear next in the Annals, that the *Danes* fourteen days after such an Overthrow, fighting again with *Ethelred* and his Brother *Alfred* at *Basing*, under Conduct, saith the *Danish* History, of *Agnerus* and *Hubbo*, Brothers of the slain *Ivarus*, should obtain the Victory; especially since the new supply of *Danes* mention'd by *Asser*, arriv'd after this Action. But after two Months, the King and his Brother fought with them again at *Mertun*, in two Squadrons as before, in which fight hard it is to understand who had the better; so darkly do the *Saxon Annals* deliver thir meaning with more than wonted infancy. Yet these I take (for *Asser* is heer silent) to be the Chief Fountain of our Story, the Ground and Basis upon which the Monks later in time Gloss and Comment at thir pleasure. Nevertheless it appears, that on the *Saxon* part, not *Heamund* the Bishop only, but many valiant men lost thir lives. This fight was follow'd by a heavy Summer Plague; whereof, as is

thought,

Pontan. Hist. Dan. L. 4.

Camd.   thought, King *Ethelred* dy'd in the fifth of his
Reign, and was buried at *Winburne*, where
his Epitaph inscribes that he had his deaths
wound by the *Danes*, according to the *Danish*
History 872. Of all these terrible Landings
and Devastations by the *Danes*, from the days
of *Ethelwolf* till thir two last Battels with *E-
thelred*, or of thir Leaders, whether Kings,
Dukes, or Earls, the *Danish* History of best
Credit saith nothing; so little Wit or Conscience it seems they had to leave any memory of thir brutish, rather than manly actions;
unless we shall suppose them to have come, as
above was cited out of *Asser*, from *Danubius*,
rather than from *Denmark*, more probably
some barbarous Nations of *Prussia*, or *Livo-
nia*, not long before seated more Northward
on the *Baltic* Sea.

Alfred.

A Lfred the fourth Son of *Ethelwolf*, had
scarce perform'd his Brothers Obse-
quies, and the Solemnity of his own Crown-
ing, when at the months end in hast with a
small Power he encounter'd the whole Army
of *Danes* at *Wilton*, and most part of the day
foyl'd them; but unwarily following the chase,
gave others of them the advantage to rally;
who returning upon him now weary, remained Masters of the field. This year, as is affirm'd in the Annals, nine Battels had bin
fought against the *Danes* on the South-side of
Thames,

Thames, besides innumerable excursions made
by *Alfred* and other Leaders; one King, nine
Earls were fall'n in fight, so that weary on
both sides at the years end, League or Truce
was concluded. Yet next year the *Danes* 872.
took thir march to *London*, now expos'd thir *Sax. ann.*
prey, there they winter'd, and thether came
the *Mercians* to renue Peace with them. The
year following they rov'd back to the parts
beyond *Humber*, but winter'd at *Torksey* in
Lincolnshire, where the *Mercians* now the third 873.
time made Peace with them. Notwithstand- *Sax. ann.*
ing which, removing thir Camp to *Rependune* *Camden.*
in *Mercia*, now *Repton* upon *Trent* in *Darbi-* 874.
shire, and there wintring, they constrein'd *Sax. ann.*
Burhed the King to fly into Forein Parts, making seisure of his Kingdom, he running the
direct way to *Rome*, with better reason than
his Ancestors, dy'd there, and was buried in
a Church by the *English* School. His Kingdom the *Danes* farm'd out to *Kelwulf*, one of
his Houshold Servants or Officers, with condition to be resign'd them when they commanded. From *Rependune* they dislodg'd, *Haf-* 875.
den thir King leading part of his Army North- *Sax. ann.*
ward, winter'd by the River *Tine*, and sub-
jecting all those Quarters, wasted also the
Picts and *British* beyond: but *Cuthrun*, *Oski-*
tell, and *Anwynd*, other three of thir Kings
moving from *Rependune*, came with a great
Army to *Grantbrig*, and remain'd there a
whole year. *Alfred* that Summer purposing
to try his Fortune with a Fleet at Sea (for he
had found that the want of Shipping and neglect

lect of Navigation, had expos'd the Land to these Piracies) met with seven *Danish* Rovers, took one, the rest escaping; an acceptable success from so small a beginning : for the *English* at that time were but little experienc't
876.
Sax. ann.
in Sea affairs. The next years first motion of the *Danes* was towards *Warham* Castle : where *Alfred* meeting them, either by Policy, or thir doubt of his Power; *Ethelwerd* faith, by Money brought them to such terms of Peace, as that they swore to him upon a hallow'd
Florent.
Bracelet, others say upon certain Reliques (a Solemn Oath it seems which they never voutfafed before to any other Nation) forthwith to depart the Land : but falsifying that Oath, by night with all the Horse they had
Florent.
(*Asser* faith, slaying all the Horsemen he had) stole to *Exeter*, and there winter'd. In *Northumberland*, *Hafden* thir King began to settle, to divide the Land, to Till, and to Inhabit. Mean while they in the West who were marched to *Exeter*, enter'd the City, coursing now
877.
Sax. ann.
and then to *Warham*; but thir Fleet the next year sailing or rowing about the West, met with such a tempest neer to *Swanswich*, or *Gnavewic*, as wrack'd 120 of thir Ships, and left the rest easie to be maister'd by those Gallies which *Alfred* had set there to guard the Seas,
Asser.
and streit'n *Exeter* of provision. He the while beleagering them in the City; now humbl'd with the loss of thir Navy (two Navies, faith *Asser*, the one at *Gnavewic*, the other at *Swanwine*) distrefs'd them so, as that they gave him as many hostages as he requir'd, and as many

Oaths,

Oaths, to keep thir Covnanted Peace, and kept it. For the Summer comming on, they departed into *Mercia*, wherof part they divided amongſt themſelves, part left to *Kelwulf* thir ſubſtituted King. The Twelftide following, all Oaths forgott'n, they came to *Chippenham* in *Wiltſhire*, diſpeopling the Countries round, diſpoſſeſſing ſome, driving others beyond the Sea; *Alfred* himſelf with a ſmall Company was forc'd to keep within Woods and Fenny places, and for ſome time all alone, as *Florent* ſaith, ſojourn'd with *Dunwulf* a Swine-heard, made afterwards for his devotion, and aptneſs to Learning, Biſhop of *Wincheſter*. *Hafden* and the Brother of *Hinguar*, coming with twenty three Ships from *North-Wales*, where they had made great ſpoil, landed in *Devonſhire*, nigh to a ſtrong Caſtle nam'd *Kinwith*; where by the Garriſon iſſuing forth unexpectedly, they were ſlain with twelv hunder'd of thir men. Mean while the King about *Eaſter*, not deſpairing of his Affairs, built a Fortreſs at a place call'd *Athelney* in *Somerſetſhire*, therin valiantly defending Himſelf and his Followers, frequently ſallying forth. The ſeventh week after, he rode out to a place call'd *Ecbryt-ſtone* in the Eaſt part of *Selwood*: thether reſorted to him with much gratulation the *Somerſet* and *Wiltſhire* men, with many out of *Hamſhire*, ſome of whom a little before had fled thir Countrey; with theſe marching to *Ethandune* now *Ediſndon* in *Wiltſhire*, he gave Battel to the whole *Daniſh* Power, and put them to flight: Then beſeiging thir Caſtle,

878.
Sax. An.

Sim. Dun.

Aſſer.

Camden.

Q   within

within fourteen dayes took it. *Malmsbury* writes, that in this time of his receſs, to go a ſpy into the *Daniſh* Camp, he took upon him with one Servant the habit of a Fidler; by this means gaining acceſs to the Kings Table, and ſomtimes to his Bed-Chamber, got knowledge of thir ſecrets, thir careleſs encamping, and therby this opportunity of aſſailing them on a ſudden. The *Danes* by this misfortune brok'n, gave him more hoſtages, and renu'd thir Oaths to depart out of his Kingdom. Thir King *Gytro*, or *Gothrun*, offer'd willingly to receave Baptiſm, and accordingly came with thirty of his Friends, to a place call'd *Aldra*,

Camd.

or *Aulre*, neer to *Athelney*, and were baptiz'd at *Wedmore*; where *Alfred* receav'd him out of the Font, and nam'd him *Athelſtan*. After which, they abode with him twelv daies,

879.

Sax. An.

and were diſmiſs't with rich preſents. Whereupon the *Danes* remov'd next year to *Cirenceſter*, thence peaceably to the *Eaſt-Angles*; which *Alfred*, as ſome write, had beſtow'd on *Gothrun* to hold of him; the bounds wherof may be read among the Laws of *Alfred*. Others of them went to *Fulham* on the *Thames*, and joyning there with a great Fleet newly come into the River, thence paſs'd over into *France* and *Flanders*, both which they enter'd ſo far conquering or waſting, as witneſs'd ſufficiently, that the *French* and *Flemiſh* were no more able than the *Engliſh*, by Policy or proweſs to keep off that *Daniſh* Inundation from thir Land. *Alfred* thus rid of them, and intending for the future to prevent thir landing;

ing; three years after (quiet the mean while)   882.
with more Ships and better provided, puts to *Sax. ann.*
Sea, and at first met with four of theirs, wherof two he took, throwing the men over-board,
then with two others, wherein were two of
their Princes, and took them also, but not
without some loss of his own.   After three   885.
years another Fleet of them appear'd on these *Sax. ann.*
Seas, so huge that one part thought themselvs
sufficient to enter upon *East-France*, the other
came to *Rochester*, and beleaguer'd it, they
within stoutly defending themselves, till *Alfred* with great Forces, coming down upon
the *Danes*, drove them to thir Ships, leaving
for hast all thir Horses behind them.   The
same year *Alfred* sent a Fleet toward the
East-Angles, then inhabited by the *Danes*, *Sim. Dun.*
which at the mouth of *Stour*, meeting with
sixteen *Danish* Ships, after some flight took
them all, and slew the Souldiers aboard; but
in thir way home lying careless, were overtak'n by another part of that Fleet, and came
off with loss, whereupon perhaps those *Danes*
who were settl'd among the *East-Angles*, erected with new hopes, violated the Peace which
they had sworn to *Alfred*, who spent the next   886.
year in repairing *London*, (beseiging, saith *Sax. ann.*
Huntingdon) much ruin'd and unpeopl'd by
the *Danes*; the *Londoners*, all but those who
had bin led away Captive, soon return'd to
thir dwellings, and *Ethred* Duke of *Mercia*, *Sim. Dun.*
was by the King appointed thir Governour.   893.
But after thirteen years respite of Peace, an- *Sax. ann.*
other *Danish* Fleet of 250 Sail, from the *East*

part of *France* arriv'd at the mouth of a River in *East Kent*, call'd *Limen*, nigh to the
great Wood *Andred*, famous for length and
bredth; into that Wood they drew up thir
Ships four mile from the Rivers mouth, and
built a Fortrefs.　After whom *Haeften* with
another *Danifh* Fleet of Eighty Ships, entring
the mouth of *Thames*, built a Fort at *Middle-
ton*, the former Army remaining at a place
call'd *Apeltre*. *Alfred* perceaving this, took
of those *Danes* who dwelt in *Northumberland*,
a new Oath of Fidelity, and of those in *Effex*,
hoftages, left they fhould joyn, as they were
wont, with thir Countrey-men newly arriv'd.

894.
Sax. ann.

And by the next year, having got together his
Forces, between either Army of the *Danes*
encamp'd fo, as to be ready for either of them,
who firft fhould happ'n to ftir forth; Troops
of Horfe alfo he fent continually abroad, affifted by fuch as could be fpar'd from ftrong
places, wherever the Countries wanted them,
to encounter forageing parties of the Enemy.
The King alfo divided fometimes his whole
Army, marching out with one part by turns,
the other keeping intrencht. In conclufion,
rowling up and down, both fides met at *Farn-
ham* in *Surrey*; where the *Danes* by *Alfreds*
Horfe Troops were put to flight, and croffing
the *Thames* to a certain Iland neer *Coln* in *Effex*, or as *Camden* thinks, by *Colebrooke*, were
befeig'd there by *Alfred* till provifion fail'd
the befeigers, another part ftaid behind with
thir King wounded. Mean while *Alfred* preparing to reinforce the feige in *Colney*, the
Danes

Danes of *Northumberland* breaking Faith, came by Sea to the *East-Angles*, and with a hunderd Ships Coasting Southward, landed in *Devonshire*, and beseig'd *Exeter*; thether *Alfred* hasted with his Powers, except a Squadron of *Welch* that came to *London* : with whom the Citizens marching forth to *Beamflet*, where *Haesten* the *Dane* had built a strong Fort, and left a Garrison, while he himself with the main of his Army was enter'd far into the Countrey, luckily surprise the Fort, maister the Garrison, make prey of all they find there ; thir Ships also they burnt or brought away with good booty; and many Prisners, among whom, the Wife and two Sons of *Heasten* were sent to the King, who forthwith set them at liberty. Whereupon *Heasten* gave Oath of Amitie and Hostages to the King ; he in requital, whether freely, or by agreement, a summe of money. Nevertheless without regard of Faith giv'n, while *Alfred* was busied about *Exeter*, joyning with the other *Danish* Army, he built another Castle in *Essex* at *Shoberie*, thence marching Westward by the *Thames*, aided with *Northumbrian* and *East-Anglish Danes*, they came at length to *Severn*, pillaging all in thir way. But, *Ethred, Ethelm,* and *Ethelnoth,* the Kings Captains, with united Forces pitch'd nigh to them at *Buttingtun,* on the *Severn* Bank in *Montgomery-shire,* the River running between, and there many weeks attended ; the King mean while blocking up the *Danes* who beseig'd *Exeter*, having eat'n part of thir Horses, the

Camden,

rest

rest urg'd with hunger broke forth to thir fellows, who lay encamp't on the East-side of the River, and were all there difcomfitted, with fome lofs of valiant men on the Kings party; the reft fled back to *Effex* and thir Fortrefs there. Then *Laf*, one of thir Leaders, gather'd before Winter a great Army of *Northumbrian* and *Eaft-Anglifh Danes*, who leaving thir Money, Ships, and Wives with the *Eaft-Angles*, and marching day and night, fat down before a City in the Weft call'd *Wirheal* neer to *Chefter*, and took it ere they could be overtak'n. The *Englifh* after two daies feige hopelefs to diflodge them, wafted the Countrey round to cut off from them all Provifion, and departed. Soon after which, next year the *Danes* no longer able to hold *Wirheal*, deftitute of Vittles, enter'd *North Wales*; thence lad'n with fpoils, part return'd into *Northumberland*, others to the *Eaft-Angles* as far as *Effex*, where they feis'd on a fmall Iland call'd *Merefig*. And heer again the Annals Record them to befeige *Exeter*, but without coherence of fence or ftory. Others relate to this purpofe, that returning by Sea from the Seige of *Exeter*, and in thir way landing on the Coaft of *Suffex*, they of *Cichefter* fallied out, and flew of them many hunderds, taking alfo fome of thir Ships. The fame year they who poffefs'd *Merefig*, intending to winter thereabout, drew up thir Ships, fome into the *Thames*, others into the River *Lee*, and on the Bank therof built a Caftle twenty miles from *London*; to affault which the *Londoners* aided

895.
Sax. An.

Sim. Dun.
Florent.

ed with other Forces march'd out the Summer following, but were soon put to flight, losing four of the Kings Captains. *Hunting-don* writes quite the contrary, that these four were *Danish* Captains, and the overthrow theirs: but little credit is to be plac'd in *Huntingdon* single. For the King therupon with his Forces, lay encamp't neerer the City, that the *Danes* might not infest them in time of Harvest; in the mean time, suttlely devising to turn *Lee* stream several wayes; wherby the *Danish* Bottoms were left on dry ground: which they soon perceaving, march'd over Land to *Quatbrig* on the *Severn*, built a Fortress and winter'd there; while thir Ships left in *Lee*, were either brok'n or brought away by the *Londoners*; but thir Wives and Children they had left in safety with the *East-Angles*. The next year was Pestilent, and besides the common sort took away many great Earls, *Kelmond* in *Kent*, *Brithulf* in *Essex*, *Wulfred* in *Hampshire*, with many others; and to this Evil, the *Danes* of *Northumberland* and *East-Angles* ceas'd not to endamage the *West-Saxons*, especially by stealth, robbing on the South-shoar in certain long Gallies. But the King causing to be built others twice as long as usually were built, and some of sixty or seventy Oars higher, swifter and steddier than such as were in use before either with *Danes* or *Frisons*, his own invention, some of these he sent out against six *Danish* Pirats, who had done much harm in the Ile of *Wight* and parts adjoyning. The bickering was doubtfull and intricate,

896.
Sax. An.

897.
Sax. an.

Q 4

intricate, part on the water, part on the fands;
not without lofs of fome Eminent Men on the
Englifh fide. The Pirats at length were either
flain or tak'n, two of them ftranded; the
men brought to *Winchefter*, where the King
then was, were executed by his Command;
one of them efcap'd to the *Eaft-Angles*, her
men much wounded: the fame year not fewer
than twenty of thir Ships perifh'd on the
South Coaft with all thir Men. And *Rollo* the
Dane or *Norman* Landing heer, as *Mat. Weft.*
writes, though not in what part of the Iland,
after an unfuccefsful fight againft thofe Forces
which firft oppos'd him, fail'd into *France*,
and conquer'd the Country, fince that time
called *Normandy*. This is the fumme of what
pafs'd in three years againft the *Danes*, returning out of *France*, fet down fo perplexly by
the *Saxon* Annalift, ill-guifted with utterance,
as with much ado can be underftood fomtimes
what is fpok'n, whether meant of the *Danes*,
or of the *Saxons*. After which troublefome
time, *Alfred* enjoying three years of Peace,
by him fpent, as his manner was, not idlely
or voluptuoufly, but in all vertuous employments both of mind and body, becoming a
Prince of his Renown, ended his daies in the
year 900, the 51 of his Age, the 30th of his
Reign, and was buried Regally at *Winchefter*;
he was born at a place call'd *Wanading* in *Bark-
fhire*, his Mother *Osburga* the Daughter of
Oflac the Kings Cup-bearer, a *Goth* by Nation, and of Noble defcent. He was of perfon comlier than all his Brethren, of pleafing
tongue

900.
After.

tongue and gracefull behaviour, ready wit and memory; yet through the fondnefs of his Parents towards him, had not bin taught to read till the twelfth year of his Age; but the great defire of learning which was in him, foon appear'd, by his conning of *Saxon* Poems day and night, which with great attention he heard by others repeated. He was befides, excellent at Hunting, and the new Art then of Hawking, but more exemplary in devotion, having collected into a Book certain Prayers and Pfalms, which he carried ever with him in his bofome to ufe on all occafions. He thirfted after all liberal knowledge, and oft complain'd that in his Youth he had no Teachers, in his middle Age fo little vacancy from Wars, and the cares of his Kingdom, yet leafure he found fometimes, not only to learn much himfelf, but to communicate therof what he could to his People, by tranflating Books out of Latin into Englifh, *Orofius*, *Boethius*, *Beda*'s Hiftory and others, permitted none unlern'd to bear Office, either in Court or Common-wealth; at twenty years of Age not yet Reigning, he took to Wife *Egelswitha* the Daughter of *Ethelred* a *Mercian* Earl. The Extremities which befell him in the fixt of his Reign, *Neothan* Abbot told him, were juftly come upon him for neglecting in his younger dayes the complaints of fuch as injur'd and opprefs'd repair'd to him, as then fecond perfon in the Kingdome for redrefs; which neglect were it fuch indeed, were yet excufable in a Youth, through jollity of mind unwilling

perhaps

perhaps to be detain'd long with sad and sorrowful Narrations; but from the time of his undertaking Regal Charge, no man more patient in hearing Causes, more inquisitive in Examining, more exact in doing Justice, and providing good Laws, which are yet extant; more severe in punishing unjust Judges or obstinate Offenders. Theeves especially and Robbers, to the terrour of whom in cross wayes were hung upon a high Post certain Chains of Gold, as it were daring any one to take them thence; so that Justice seem'd in his dayes not to flourish only, but to triumph: no man than hee more frugal of two precious things in Mans life, his Time and his Revenue; no man wiser in the disposal of both. His Time, the day, and night, he distributed by the burning of certain Tapours into three equall portions: the one was for Devotion, the other for Publick or private Affairs, the third for bodily refreshment: how each hour past, he was put in mind by one who had that Office. His whole Annual Revenue, which his first care was should be justly his own, he divided into two equall parts; the first he imploy'd to Secular Uses, and subdivided those into three, the first to pay his Souldiers, Houshold-Servants and Guard, of which divided into three Bands, one attended monthly by turn; the second was to pay his Architects and Workmen, whom he had got together of several Nations; for he was also an Elegant Builder; above the custome and conceit of *Englishmen* in those days: the third he had in
readiness

readiness to releive or honour Strangers according to thir worth, who came from all parts to see him, and to live under him. The other equal part of his yearly wealth he dedicated to Religious uses, those of four sorts; the first to releive the poor, the second to the building and maintenance of two Monasteries, the third of a School, where he had perswaded the Sons of many Noblemen to study Sacred Knowledge and Liberal Arts, some say at *Oxford*; the fourth was for the releif of *Foreign* Churches, as far as *India* to the shrine of St *Thomas*, sending thether *Sigelm* Bishop of *Sherburn*, who both return'd safe, and brought with him many rich Gems and Spices; guifts also and a Letter he receav'd from the Patriarch of *Jerusalem*, sent many to *Rome*, and for them receav'd Reliques. Thus far, and much more might be said of his Noble Mind, which render'd him the Miror of Princes; His Body was diseas'd in his youth with a great soreness in the Seige, and that ceasing of it self, with another inward pain of unknown cause, which held him by frequent fits to his dying day; yet not disinabl'd to sustain those many glorious labours of his Life both in Peace and War.

Malmsb.

Edward the Elder.

EDward the Son of *Alfred* succeeded, in Learning not equal, in Power and Extent of Dominion, surpassing his Father. The beginning

Malmsb.

Hunting.

ginning of his Reign had much disturbance by *Ethelwald* an ambitious young man, Son of the Kings Uncle, or Cosin German, or Brother, for his Genealogy is variously deliver'd. He vainly avouching to have equal right with *Edward* of Succession to the Crown, possess'd himself of *Winburne* in *Dorset*, and another Town diversly nam'd, giving out that there he would live or dye; but encompass'd with the Kings Forces at *Badburie* a place nigh, his heart failing him, he stole out by night, and fled to the *Danish* Army beyond *Humber*. The King sent after him, but not overtaking, found his Wife in the Town, whom he had married out of a Nunnery, and commanded her to be sent back thether. About this time the *Kentish* men, against a multitude of *Danish* Pirats, fought prosperously at a place call'd *Holme*, as *Hoveden* records. *Ethelwald* aided by the *Northumbrians* with Shipping, three years after, sailing to the *East-Angles*, perswaded the *Danes* there to fall into the Kings Territory, who marching with him as far as *Crecklad*, and passing the *Thames* there, wasted as far beyond as they durst venture, and lad'n with spoils return'd home. The King with his Powers making speed after them, between the *Dike* and *Ouse*, suppos'd to be *Suffolk* and *Cambridge-shire*, as far as the Fenns Northward, laid wast all before him. Thence intending to return, he commanded that all his Army should follow him close without delay; but the *Kentish* men, though oft'n call'd upon, lagging behind, the *Danish* Army prevented them, and joyn'd

901.
Sax. An.

902.

905.
Sax. Ann.

joyn'd Battel with the King : where Duke
Sigulf and Earle *Sigelm*, with many other
of the Nobles were slain ; on the *Danes* part,
Eoric thir King, and *Ethelwald* the Author of
this War, with others of high note, and of
them greater number, but with great ruin on
both sides ; yet the *Danes* kept in thir Power
the burying of thir slain.   What ever followed upon this conflict, which we read not, the
King two years after with the *Danes*, both of   907.
East-Angles, and *Northumberland* concluded *Sax. Ann.*
Peace, which continu'd three years, by whom- 910.
soever brok'n : for at the end thereof King *Sax. ann.*
Edward raising great Forces out of *West-Sex*,
and *Mercia*, sent them against the *Danes* beyond *Humber* ; where staying five weeks, they
made great spoil and slaughter.   The King
offer'd them terms of Peace, but they reject-
ing all, enter'd with the next year into *Mer-* 911.
cia, rendring no less hostility than they had *Sax. ann.*
suffer'd ; but at *Tetnal* in *Staffordshire*, saith
Florent, were by the *English* in a set Battel o-
verthrown.   King *Edward* then in *Kent*, had
got together of Ships about a hunderd Sail,
others gon Southward, came back and met
him. The *Danes* now supposing that his main
Forces were upon the Sea, took liberty to
rove and plunder up and down, as hope of
prey led them, beyond *Severn*. The King *Ethelwerd.*
guessing what might imbold'n them, sent before him the lightest of his Army to entertain
them ; then following with the rest, set upon
them in thir return over *Cantbrig* in *Gloster-*
shire, and slew many thousands, among whom
Ecwils,

Ecwils, Hafden, and Hinguar thir Kings, and many other harfh names in Huntingdon; the place alfo of this fight is varioufly writt'n by Ethelwerd and Florent, call'd Wodensfield. The

912.
Sax. Ann.

year following Ethred Duke of Mercia, to whom Alfred had giv'n London, with his Daughter in Marriage; now dying, King Edward refum'd that City, and Oxford, with the Countries adjoyning, into his own hands, and

913.
Sax. An.

the year after, built, or much repair'd by his Souldiers, the Town of Hertford on either fide Lee, and leaving a fufficient number at the work, march'd about middle Summer, with the other part of his Forces into Essex, and encamp'd at Maldon, while his Souldiers built Witham; where a good part of the Countrey, fubject formerly to the Danes, yielded them-felves to his Protection. Four years after

917.
Sax. Ann.

(Florent allows but one year) the Danes from Leifter and Northampton, falling into Oxford-fhire, committed much rapine, and in fome Towns thereof great flaughter; while ano-ther party wafting Hertfordfhire, met with o-ther Fortune; for the Countrey-people inur'd now to fuch kind of Incurfions, joyning ftout-ly together, fell upon the fpoilers, recover'd thir own goods, with fome booty from thir Enemies. About the fame time Elfled the Kings Sifter fent her Army of Mercians into

Hunting.
Camden.

Wales, who routed the Welch, took the Caftle of Bricnam-mere by Brecknock, and brought away the Kings Wife of that Country, with other Prifners. Not long after fhe took Derby from the Danes, and the Caftle by a fharp affault.

assault.   But the year ensueing brought a new
Fleet of *Danes* to *Lidwic* in *Devonshire*, under
two Leaders, *Otter* and *Roald*; who sailing
thence Westward about the Lands end, came
up to the mouth of *Severn*; there landing wasted the *Welch* Coast, and *Irchenfield* part of *Herefordshire*; where they took *Kuneleac* a *Brittish* Bishop, for whose Ransome King *Edward*
gave forty pound, but the men of *Hereford*
and *Glostershire* assembling, put them to flight;
slaying *Roald* and the Brother of *Otter*, with
many more, persu'd them to a Wood, and
there beset, compel'd them to give hostages
of present departure.   The King with his
Army sat not far off, securing from the South
of *Severn* to *Avon*; so that openly they durst
not, by night they twice ventur'd to Land;
but found such welcome, that few of them
came back; the rest anchord by a small Iland
where many of them famish'd; then sailing
to a place call'd *Deomed*, they cross'd into *Ireland*.   The King with his Army went to *Buckingham*, staid there a month, and built two
Castles or Forts on either Bank of *Ouse* ere his
departing, and *Turkitel* a *Danish* Leader, with
those of *Bedford* and *Northampton*, yeilded him
subjection.   Wherupon the next year he came
with his Army to the Town of *Bedford*, took
possession thereof, staid there a month, and
gave order to build another part of the Town,
on the South-side of *Ouse*.   Thence the year
following went again to *Maldon*, repair'd and
fortifi'd the Town.   *Turkitel* the *Dane* having
small hope to thrive heer, where things with
such

such prudence were mannag'd against his interess, got leave of the King, with as many Voluntaries as would follow him, to pass into France. Early the next year King *Eaward* re-edifi'd *Tovechester*, now *Torchester*; and another City in the Annals call'd *Wigingmere*. Mean while the *Danes* of *Leister* and *Northampton-shire*; not liking perhaps to be neighboured with Strong Towns, laid Seige to *Torchester* [but they within repelling the assault one whole day till supplies came] quitted the seige by night; and persu'd close by the beseig'd, between *Birnwud* and *Ailsbury* were surpris'd, many of them made Prisners, and much of thir baggage lost. Other of the *Danes* at *Huntingdon,* aided from the *East-Angles,* finding that Castle not commodious, left it, and built another at *Temsford,* judging that place more opportune from whence to make thir excursions; and soon after went forth with design to assail *Bedford :* but the Garrison issuing out, slew a great part of them, the rest fled. After this a great Army of them gather'd out of *Mercia* and the *East-Angles,* came and beseig'd the City call'd *Wigingmere* a whole day; but finding it defended stoutly by them within, thence also departed, driving away much of thir Cattel : wherupon the *English* from Towns and Citties round about joyning Forces, laid Seige to the Town and Castle of *Temsford,* and by assault took both; slew thir King with *Toglea* a Duke, and *Mannan* his Son an Earl, with all the rest there found; who chose to die rather than yield. Encourag'd by this, the men
of

of *Kent*, *Surrey*, and part of *Essex*, enterprise
the Seige of *Colchester*, nor gave over till they
won it, sacking the Town, and putting to
Sword all the *Danes* therein, except som who
escap'd over the Wall. To the succour of
these, a great number of *Danes* inhabiting
Ports and other Towns in the *East-Angles*, united thir Force; but coming too late, as in revenge beleaguer'd *Maldon*; but that Town
also timely releiv'd, they departed, not only
frustrate of thir design, but so hotly persu'd,
that many thousands of them lost thir lives in
the flight. Forthwith King *Edward* with his
West-Saxons went to *Paßham* upon *Ouse*, there
to guard the passage, while others were building a stone Wall about *Torchester*; to him
there Earl *Thurfert*, and other Lord *Danes*,
with thir Army thereabout as far as *Weolud*,
came and submitted. Wherat the Kings Sol-
diers joyfully cry'd out to be dismiss't home:
therfore with another part of them he enter-
ed *Huntingdon*, and repair'd it, where breaches
had bin made; all the people thereabout returning to obedience. The like was done at
Colnchester by the next remove of his Army,
after which both *East* and *West-Angles*, and
the *Danish* Forces among them, yeilded to the
King, swearing Allegiance to him both by Sea
and Land: the Army also of *Danes* at *Grantbrig*, surrendring themselves took the same
Oath. The summer following he came with
his Army to *Stamford*, built a Castle there
on the South-side of the River, where all the
People of those quarters acknowledg'd him

922.
Sax. Ann

R   Supream.

Supream. During his abode there, *Elfled* his Sister a martial Woeman, who after her Husbands death would no more marry, but gave her self to Publick Affairs, repairing and fortifying many Towns, warring somtimes, dy'd at *Tamworth* the Cheif Seat of *Mercia*, wherof by guift of *Alfred* her Father, she was Lady or Queen; whereby that whole Nation became obedient to King *Edward*, as did also *North Wales*, with *Howel, Cledaucus,* and *Jeothwell* thir Kings. Thence passing to *Nottingham,* he enter'd and repair'd the Town, plac'd there part *English*, part *Danes*, and receav'd fealty from all in *Mercia* of either Nation. The next Autumn, coming with his Army into *Cheshire*, he built and fortifi'd *Thelwel*; and while he staid there, call'd another Army out of *Mercia*, which he sent to repair and fortifie *Manchester*. About Midsummer following he march'd again to *Nottingham,* built a Town over against it on the South-side of that River, and with a Bridge joyn'd them both; thence journied to a place call'd *Bedecanwillan* in *Pictland*; there also built and fenc'd a City on the Borders, where the King of *Scots* did him Honour as to his Sovran, together with the whole *Scotish* Nation; the like did *Reginald* and the Son of *Eadulf, Danish* Princes, with all the *Northumbrians,* both *English,* and *Danes.* The King also of a People thereabout call'd *Streatgledwalls* (the *North Welch,* as *Camden* thinks, of *Strat-Cluid* in *Denbigh-shire,* perhaps rather the *British* of *Cumberland*) did him homage, and

923.
Sax. ann.

924.
Sax. ann.

and not undeserv'd.   For *Buchanan* himself
confesses, that this King *Edward* with a small
number of men compar'd to his Enemies, o- *Buch. L. 6.*
verthrew in a great Battel, the whole United
Power both of *Scots* and *Danes,* slew most of
the *Scotish* Nobility, and forc'd *Malcolmb,*
whom *Constantine* the *Scotch* King had made
General, and design'd Heir of his Crown, to
save himself by flight sore wounded.   Of the
English, he makes *Athelstan* the Son of *Edward* Chief Leader; and so far seems to con-
found Times and Actions, as to make this
Battel the same with that fought by *Athelstan,* about twenty four years after at *Bruneford,* against *Anlaf* and *Constantine,* whereof
hereafter.   But here *Buchanan* takes occasion
to inveigh against the *English* Writers, upbraiding them with ignorance, who affirm *A- Buch. L. 6.
thelstan* to have bin Supream King of *Britan,*
Constantine the *Scotish* King with others to
have held of him : and denies that in the Annals of *Marianus Scotus,* any mention is to be
found therof; which I shall not stand much
to contradict, for in *Marianus,* whether by
Surname or by Nation *Scotus,* will be found as
little mention of any other *Scotish* affairs, till
the time of King *Dunchad* slain by *Machetad,*
or *Mackbeth,* in the year 1040 which gives
cause of suspicion, that the Affairs of *Scotland*
before that time were so obscure as to be unknown to thir own Countrey-man, who liv'd
and wrote his Chronicle not long after.   But
King *Edward* thus nobly doing, and thus ho-   925.
nour'd, the year following dy'd at *Farendon*; *Sax. and.*
R 2   a builder

Hunting.
Mat. West.

a builder and restorer eev'n in War, not a destroyer of his Land. He had by several Wives many Children; his Eldest Daughter *Edgith* he gave in marriage to *Charles* King of *France*, Grand-Child of *Charles* the *Bald* above-mention'd; of the rest in place convenient. His Laws are yet to be seen. He was buried at *Winchester*, in the Monastery by *Alfred* his Father. And a few days after him dy'd *Ethelwerd* his Eldest Son, the Heir of his Crown. He had the whole Iland in subjection, yet so

Sim. Dun.

as petty Kings Reign'd under him. In *Northumberland*, after *Ecbert* whom the *Danes* had set up, and the *Northumbrians* yet unruly under thir Yoke, at the end of six years had expell'd, one *Ricsig* was set up King, and bore the name three years; then another *Ecbert*, and *Guthred*; the latter, if we beleeve Legends, of a Servant made King by command of St *Cudbert*, in a Vision; and enjoyn'd by another Vision of the same Saint, to pay well for his Royalty many Lands and Privileges to his Church and Monastery. But now to the Story.

Athelstan.

A Thelstan next in Age to *Ethelward* his Brother, who deceas'd untimely few dayes before, though born of a Concubine, yet for the great appearance of many Vertues in him, and his Brethren being yet under Age, was

926.

exalted to the Throne, at *Kingstone* upon
Thames,

Thames, and by his Fathers laſt Will, ſaith
Malmsbury, yet not without ſome oppoſition
of one *Alfred* and his Accomplices; who not
liking he ſhould Reign, had conſpir'd to ſeiſe
on him after his Fathers death, and to put
out his Eyes. But the Conſpiratours diſco-
ver'd, and *Alfred* denying the Plot, was ſent *Malmsb.*
to *Rome,* to aſſert his innocence before the
Pope; where taking his Oath on the Altar,
he fell down immediatly, and carried out by
his Servants, three daies after dy'd. Mean
while beyond *Humber,* the *Danes,* though
much aw'd were not idle. *Inguald* one of thir *Sim. Dun.*
Kings took poſſeſſion of *York. Sitric* who ſom
years before had ſlain *Niel* his Brother, by
force took *Davenport* in *Cheſhire;* and however he defended theſe doings, grew ſo con-
ſiderable, that *Athelſtan* with great Solemnity *Malmsb.*
gave him his Siſter *Edgith* to Wife: but he *Mat. Weſt.*
enjoy'd her not long, dying ere the years end,
nor his Sons *Anlaf* and *Guthfert* the King- *927.*
dome, driv'n out the next year by *Athelſtan;* *Sax. ann.*
not unjuſtly ſaith *Huntingdon,* as being firſt
raiſers of the War. *Simeon* calls him *Gudfrid* a
Britiſh King, whom *Athelſtan* this year drove
out of his Kingdome; and perhaps they were
both one, the name and time not much differing, the place only miſtak'n. *Malmsbury* dif-
fers in the name alſo, calling him *Aldulf* a certain Rebel. Them alſo I wiſh as much miſtak'n, who write that *Athelſtan,* jealous of
his younger Brother *Edwin's* towardly Vertues, leſt added to the right of Birth, they
might ſome time or other call in queſtion his
R 3   illegitimate

933.
Sim. Dun.

illegitimate precedence, caus'd him to be drown'd in the Sea; expos'd, some say, with one Servant in a rott'n Bark, without Sail or Oar; where the youth far off Land, and in rough weather despairing, threw himself over-board; the Servant more patient, got to Land and reported the success. But this *Malmsbury* confesses to be sung in old Songs, not read in warrantable Authors : and *Huntingdon* speaks as of a sad accident to *Athelstan*, that he lost his Brother *Edwin* by Sea; far the more credible, in that *Athelstan*, as is writ'n by all, tenderly lov'd and bred up the rest of his Brethren, of whom he had no less cause to be jealous. And the year following he pro-

934.
Sax. An.
Sim. Dun.

sper'd better than from so foul a Fact, passing into *Scotland* with great Puissance, both by Sea and Land, and chaceing his Enemies before him, by Land as far as *Dunfeoder*, and *Wertermore*, by Sea as far as *Cathneß*. The cause of this Expedition, saith *Malmsbury*, was to demand *Gudfert* the Son of *Sitric*, thether fled, though not deny'd at length by *Constantine*, who with *Eugenius* King of *Cumberland*, at a place call'd *Dacor* or *Dacre* in that Shire, surrender'd himself and each his Kingdom to *Athelstan*, who brought back with him for ho-

Florent.

stage the Son of *Constantine*. But *Gudfert* escaping in the mean while out of *Scotland*, and *Constantine* exasperated by this Invasion, perswaded *Anlaf* the other Son of *Sitric* then fled

Florent.
Sim. Dun.

into *Ireland*, others write *Anlaf* King of *Ireland* and the *Iles*, his Son in Law, with 615 Ships, and the King of *Cumberland* with other Forces,

Forces, to his aid. This within four years effected, they enter'd *England* by *Humber*, and
fought with *Athelstan* at a place call'd *Wen-*
dune, others term it *Brunanburg*, others *Brune-*
ford, which *Ingulf* places beyond *Humber*, *Cam-*
den in *Glendale* of *Northumberland* on the *Scotch*
Borders; the bloodiest fight, say Authors, that
ever this Island saw, to describe which, the
Saxon Annalist wont to be sober and succinct,
whether the same or another writer, now labouring under the weight of his Argument,
and over-charg'd, runs on a sudden into such
extravagant Fansies and Metaphors, as bear
him quite beside the scope of being understood.
Huntingdon, though himself peccant enough in
this kind, transcribes him word for word as a
pastime to his Readers. I shall only summe up
what of him I can attain, in usual Language.
The Battel was fought eagerly from morning
till night; some fell of King *Edwards* old Army, try'd in many a Battel before; but on the
other side great multitudes, the rest fled to
thir Ships. Five Kings, and seven of *Anlaf*'s
Chief Captains were slain on the place, with
Froda a *Norman* Leader; *Constantine* escap'd
home, but lost his Son in the fight, if I understand my Author; *Anlaf* by Sea to *Dublin*,
with a small remainder of his great Hoast.
Malmsbury relates this War, adding many circumstances after this manner. That *Anlaf*
joyning with *Constantine* and the whole Power
of *Scotland*, besides those which he brought
with him out of *Ireland*, came on far South-
wards, till *Athelstan* who had retir'd on set
purpose

purpose to be the surer of his Enemies, enclosed from all succour and retreat, met him at *Bruneford*. *Anlaf* perceaving the valour and resolution of *Athelstan*, and mistrusting his own Forces though numerous, resolv'd first to spie in what posture his Enemies lay : and imitating perhaps what he heard attempted by King *Alfred* the Age before, in the habit of a Musician, got access by his Lute and Voice to the Kings Tent, there playing both the Minstrel and the Spie : then towards Evening dismis't, he was observ'd by one who had bin his Souldier and well knew him, viewing earnestly the Kings Tent, and what approaches lay about it, then in the twilight to depart. The Souldier forthwith acquaints the King, and by him blamed for letting go his Enemy, answer'd, that he had giv'n first his military Oath to *Anlaf*, whom if he had betray'd, the King might suspect him of like treasonous mind towards himself; which to disprove, he advis'd him to remove his Tent a good distance off; and so don, it happ'nd that a Bishop with his Retinue coming that night to the Army, pitch'd his Tent in the same place, from whence the King had remov'd. *Anlaf* coming by night as he had design'd, to assault the Camp, and especially the Kings Tent, finding there the Bishop in stead, slew him with all his Followers. *Athelstan* took the Alarm, and as it seems, was not found so unprovided, but that the day now appearing, he put his men in order, and maintain'd the fight till Evening ; wherin *Constantine* himself was slain with five other King, and twelv Earls,

Earls, the Annals were content with feav'n, in
the reſt not diſagreeing. *Ingulf* Abbot of *Croyland* from the autority of *Turketul* a principal
Leader in this Battel, relates it more at large
to this effect : that *Athelſtan* above a mile di-
ſtant from the place where execution was don
upon the Biſhop and his Supplies, allarm'd at
the noiſe, came down by break of day, upon
Anlaf and his Army, overwatch't and wearied
now with the ſlaughter they had made, and
ſomthing out of order, yet in two main Battels. The King therefore in like manner dividing, led the one part, conſiſting moſt of
Weſt-Saxons, againſt *Anlaf* with his *Danes* and
Iriſh, committing the other to his Chancellor
Turketul, with the *Mercians* and *Londoners* a-
gainſt *Conſtantine* and his *Scots*. The ſhowr of
Arrows and Darts over-paſs't, both Battels
attack'd each other with a cloſe and terrible
ingagement, for a long ſpace neither ſide giving ground. Till the Chancellor *Turketul*, a
man of great ſtature and ſtrength, taking with
him a few *Londoners* of ſelect valour, and *Sin-
gin* who led the *Worſterſhire* men, a Captain of
undaunted courage, broke into the thickeſt,
making his way firſt through the *Picts* and *Or-
keners*, then through the *Cumbrians* and *Scots*,
and came at length where *Conſtantine* himſelf
fought, unhors'd him, and us'd all means to
take him alive ; but the *Scots* valiantly defending thir King, and laying load upon *Turketul*,
which the goodneſs of his Armour well endured, he had yet bin beat'n down, had not *Sin-
gin* his faithfull ſecond at the ſame time ſlain

Con-

Conftantine; which once known, *Anlaf* and the whole Army bètook them to flight, wherof a huge multitude fell by the Sword. This *Turke-tul* not long after leaving worldly Affairs, became Abbot of *Croyland*, which at his own coft he had repair'd, from *Danifh* ruins, and left there this memorial of his former actions. *Athelftan* with his Brother *Edmund* victorious, thence turning into *Wales*, with much more eafe vanquifh'd *Ludwal* the King, and poffeft his Land. But *Malmsbury* writes, that commiferating human chance, as he difplac'd, fo he reftor'd both him and *Conftantine* to their Regal State; for the furrender of King *Conftantine* hath bin above fpok'n of. However the *Welch* did him homage at the City of *Hereford*, and covnanted yearly payment of Gold 20 pound, of Silver 300, of *Oxen* 25 thoufand, befides Hunting Dogs and Hawks. He alfo took *Exeter* from the *Cornifh Britans*, who till that time had equal right there with the *Englifh*, and bounded them with the River *Tamar*, as the other *Brittifh* with *Wey*. Thus dreaded of his Enemies, and renown'd far and neer, three years after he dy'd at *Glofter*, and was buried with many Trophies at *Malmsbury*, where he had caus'd to be laid his two Cofin Germans, *Elwin* and *Ethelftan*, both flain in the Battel againft *Anlaf*. He was thirty years old at his coming to the Crown, mature in wifdom from his Childhood, comly of perfon and behaviour; fo that *Alfred* his Grandfather in bleffing him was wont to pray he might live to have the Kingdom, and put him yet a Child

941.
Sax. Ann.
Malmsb.
Ingulf.

Child into Souldiers habit. He had his breeding in the Court of *Elfled* his Aunt, of whose
Vertues more than female we have related,
sufficient to evince that his Mother, though
said to be no wedded Wife, was yet such of
parentage and worth, as the Royal Line disdain'd not, though the Song went in *Malms-*
buries daies (for it seems he refus'd not the autority of Ballats for want of better) that his
Mother was a Farmers Daughter, but of excellent feature ; who dreamt one night she
brought forth a Moon that should enlight'n
the whole Land : which the Kings Nurse hearing of, took her home and bred up Courtly ;
that the King coming one day to visit his
Nurse, saw there this Damsel, lik'd her, and
by earnest suit prevailing, had by her this famous *Athelstan*, a bounteous, just and affable
King, as *Malmsbury* sets him forth ; nor less
honour'd abroad by Foren Kings, who sought
his Friendship by great guifts or affinity ; that
Harold King of *Noricum* sent him a Ship, whose
Prow was of Gold, Sails Purple, and other
golden things, the more to be wonder'd at,
sent from *Noricum*, whether meant *Norway* or
Bavaria, the one place so far from such super-
fluity of wealth, the other from all Sea : the
Embassadors were *Helgrim* and *Offrid*, who
found the King at *York*. His Sisters he gave
in marriage to greatest Princes, *Elgif* to *Otho*
Son of *Henry* the Emperour, *Egdith* to a certain Duke about the *Alpes*, *Edgiv* to *Ludwic*
King of *Aquitain*, sprung of *Charles* the Great,
Ethilda to *Hugo* King of *France*, who sent *Al-*
dulf

dulf Son of *Baldwin*, Earl of *Flanders*, to obtain her. From all these great Suitors, especially from the Emperour and King of *France* came rich presents, Horses of excellent breed, gorgeous Trappings and Armour, Reliques, Jewels, Odors, Vessels of Onyx, and other precious things, which I leave poetically describ'd in *Malmsbury*, tak'n, as he confesses, out of an old versifier, some of whose Verses he recites. The only blemish left upon him, was the exposing of his Brother *Edwin*, who disavow'd by Oath the treason wherof he was accus'd, and implor'd an equal hearing. But these were Songs, as before hath bin said, which add also that *Athelstan*, his anger over, soon repented of the Fact, and put to death his Cup-bearer, who had induc't him to suspect and expose his Brother, put in mind by a word falling from the Cup-bearers own mouth, who slipping one day as he bore the Kings Cup, and recovring himself on the other leg, said aloud, fatally as to him it proved, One Brother helps the other. Which words the King laying to heart, and pondring how ill he had done to make away his Brother, aveng'd himself first on the adviser of that Fact, took on him seav'n years penance, and as *Mat. West.* saith, built two Monasteries for the Soul of his Brother. His Laws are extant among the Laws of other *Saxon* Kings to this day.

Edmund.

Edmund.

Edmund not above eighteen years old suc-
ceeded his Brother *Athelstan*, in courage
not inferiour. For in the second of his Reign
he free'd *Mercia* of the *Danes* that remain'd
there, and took from them the Citties of *Lincoln*, *Nottingham*, *Stamford*, *Darby*, and *Leister*, where they were plac'd by King *Edward*,
but it seems gave not good proof of thir fidelity. *Simeon* writes that *Anlaf* setting forth
from *York*, and having wasted Southward as
far as *Northampton*, was met by *Edmund* at
Leister; but that e're the Battails joyn'd,
Peace was made between them by *Odo* and
Wulstan the two Arch-bishops, with conversion of *Anlaf*; for the same year *Edmund* receav'd at the Font-stone this or another *Anlaf*, as saith *Huntingdon*, not him spok'n of before, who dy'd this year (so uncertain they
are in the Story of these times also) and held
Reginald another King of the *Northumbers*,
while the Bishop confirm'd him : thir limits
were divided North and South by *Watling-
street*. But spiritual kindred little avail'd to
keep peace between them, whoever gave the
cause; for we read him two years after driving *Anlaf* (whom the Annals now first call
the Son of *Sitric*) and *Suthfrid* Son of *Reginald* out of *Northumberland*, taking the whole
Country into subjection. *Edmund* the next
year harras'd *Cumberland*, then gave it to
Malcolm

942.
Sax. Ann.

944.
Sax. ann.

945.
Sax. Ann.

946.
Sax. An.
Camd.

Malcolm King of *Scots*, thereby bound to affift him in his Wars, both by Sea and Land ; *Mat. Weft.* adds that in this action *Edmund* had the aid of *Leolin* Prince of *Northwales*, againft *Dummail* the *Cumbrian* King, him depriving of his Kingdome, and his two Sons of their fight. But the year after he himfelf by ftrange accident came to an untimely death, feafting with his Nobles on St *Auftin*'s Day at *Pucle-kerke* in *Glofterfhire*, to celebrate the memory of his firft converting the *Saxons*. He fpi'd *Leof* a noted Theef, whom he had banifh'd, fitting among his Guefts ; whereat tranfported with too much vehemence of Spirit, though in a juft caufe, rifeing from the Table he ran upon the Theef, and catching his hair, pull'd him to the ground. The Theef who doubted from fuch handling no lefs than his death intended, thought to die not unreveng'd ; and with a fhort Dagger ftrook the King, who ftill laid at him, and little expected fuch affaffination, mortally into the breft. The matter was done in a moment, ere men fet at Table could turn them, or imagine at firft what the ftir meant, till perceiving the King deadly wounded, they flew upon the murderer and hew'd him to peeces ; who like a wild Beaft at abbay, feeing himfelf furrounded, defperately laid about him, wounding fome in his fall. The King was buried at *Glafton*, wherof *Dunftan* was then Abbot, his Laws yet remain to be feen among the Laws of other *Saxon* Kings.

Edred.

Edred.

EDred the third Brother of *Athelstan*, the Sons of *Edmund* being yet but Children, next Reign'd, not degenerating from his worthy predeceſſors, and Crown'd at *Kingſton*. *Northumberland* he throughly ſubdu'd, the *Scots* without refuſal ſwore him Allegiance; yet the *Northumbrians*, ever of doubtful Faith, ſoon after choſe to themſelvs one *Eric a Dane*. *Huntingdon* ſtill haunts us with this *Anlaf* (of whom we gladly would have bin ridd) and will have him before *Eric* recall'd once more and Reign four years, then again put to his ſhifts. But *Edred* entring into *Northumberland*, and with ſpoils returning, *Eric* the King fell upon his rear. *Edred* turning about, both ſhook off the Enemy, and prepar'd to make a ſecond inroad : which the *Northumbrians* dreading rejected *Eric*, ſlew *Amancus* the Son of *Anlaf*, and with many preſents appeaſing *Edred*, ſubmitted again to his Government; nor from that time had Kings, but were govern'd by Earls, of whom *Oſulf* was the firſt. About this time *Wulſtan* Arch-biſhop of *York*, accus'd to have ſlain certain men of *Thetford* in revenge of thir Abbot whom the Townſmen had ſlain, was committed by the King to cloſe Cuſtody; but ſoon after enlarg'd, was reſtor'd to his place. *Malmsbury* writes that his Crime was to have conniv'd at the revolt of his Countreymen : But King *Edred* two

950.

Sim. Dun.

Hoved.

953.

Sim. Dun.

years

955.
Sim. Dun.

years after fick'ning in the flowr of his youth, dy'd much lamented, and was buried at *Winchester.*

Edwi.

Ethelwerd.

EDwi the Son of *Edmund* now come to Age, after his Uncle *Eared*'s death took on him the Government, and was Crown'd at *Kingston.* His lovely person firnamed him the Fair, his actions are diverfly reported, by *Huntingdon* not thought illaudable. But *Malmsbury* and fuch as follow him write far otherwife, that he married or kept as Concubine, his

Mat. West.

neer Kinfwoman, fome fay both her and her Daughter; fo inordinatly giv'n to his pleafure, that on the very day of his Coronation, he abruptly withdrew himfelf from the Company of his Peers, whether in Banquet or Confultation, to fit wantoning in the Chamber with this *Algiva*, fo was her name, who had fuch power over him. Whereat his Barons offended, fent Bifhop *Dunftan*, the boldeft among them, to requeft his return: he going to the Chamber, not only interrupted his dalliance and rebuk'd the Lady, but taking him by the hand, between force and perfuafion

956.

brought him back to his Nobles. The King highly difpleas'd, and inftigated perhaps by her who was fo prevalent with him, not long after fent *Dunftan* into banifhment, caus'd his Monaftery to be rifl'd, and became an Enemy to all Monks. Whereupon *Odo* Archbifhop bishop of *Canterbury* pronounc't a separation or divorce of the King from *Algiva*. But that which most incited *William* of *Malmsbury* against him, he gave that Monastery to be dwelt in by Secular Priests, or, to use his own phrase, made it a Stable of Clerks; at length these affronts done to the Church were so resented by the People, that the *Mercians* and *Northumbrians* revolted from him, and set up *Edgar* his Brother, leaving to *Edwi* the *West-Saxons* only, bounded by the River *Thames*; with grief whereof, as is thought, he soon after ended his dayes, and was buried at *Winchester*. Mean while *Elfsin* Bishop of that place after the death of *Odo*, ascending by Simony to the Chair of *Canterbury*, and going to *Rome* the same year for his Pall, was frozen to death in the *Alps*.

Hoved.

957.

Sax. Ann.

958.

Mat. West.

Edgar.

EDgar by his Brothers death now King of all *England* at sixteen years of Age, called home *Dunstan* out of *Flanders*, where he liv'd in Exile. This King had no Warr all his Reign; yet alwayes well prepar'd for Warr, govern'd the Kingdom in great Peace, Honour, and Prosperity, gaining thence the Sirname of Peaceable, much extoll'd for Justice, Clemency, and all Kingly Vertues, the more, ye may be sure, by Monks, for his building so many Monasteries; as some write, every year one : for he much favour'd the

959.

Malmsb.

Mat. West.

　　　Monks

Monks againſt Secular Prieſts, who in the
time of *Edwi* had got poſſeſſion in moſt of thir
Covents. His care and wiſdome was great
in guarding the Coaſt round with ſtout ſhips,
to the number of three thouſand ſix hundred,
Mat. Weſt. reck'ns them four thouſand eight
hundred, divided into four Squadrons, to ſail
to and fro about the four quarters of the Land,
meeting each other ; the firſt of one thouſand
two hundred ſail from Eaſt to Weſt, the ſecond of as many from Weſt to Eaſt, the third
and fourth between North and South, himſelf
in the Summer time with his Fleet. Thus he
kept out wiſely the force of Strangers, and
prevented Forein War ; but by thir too frequent reſort hither in time of Peace, and his
too much favouring them, he let in thir Vices
unaware. Thence the People, ſaith *Malms-*
bury, learnt of the Out-landiſh *Saxons* rude-
neſs, of the *Flemiſh* daintineſs and ſoftneſs;
of the *Danes* drunk'neſs ; though I doubt theſe
Vices are as naturally home-bred heer as in
any of thoſe Countries. Yet in the Winter
and Spring time he uſually rode the Circuit
as a Judge Itinerant through all his Provinces, to ſee Juſtice well adminiſterd, and
the poor not oppreſs'd. Theeves and Robbers he routed almoſt out of the Land, and
wild Beaſts of prey altogether ; enjoining *Lud-*
wal King of *Wales* to pay the yearly Tribute
of three hundred Wolves, which he did for
two years together, till the third year no more
were to be found, nor ever after ; but his
Laws may be read yet extant. Whatever was
the

the caufe he was not Crown'd till the 30th of
his Age, but then with great fplendour and
magnificence at the City of *Bath*, in the Feaft
of *Pentecoft*. This year dy'd *Swarling* a Monk
of *Croyland*, in the 142 year of his Age, and another foon after him in the 115th in that Fenny and watrifh Air, the more remarkable.
King *Edgar* the next year went to *Chefter*, and
fummoning to his Court there all the Kings
that held of him, took Homage of them : thir
names are *Kened* King of *Scots*, *Malcolm* of
Cumberland, *Maccufe* of the Iles, five of *Wales*,
Dufwal, *Huwal*, *Grifith*, *Jacob*, *Judethil*, thefe
he had in fuch aw, that going one day into a
Gally, he caus'd them to take each man his
Oar, and row him down the River *Dee*, while
he himfelf fat at the Stern : which might be
done in meriment and eafily obey'd ; if with
a ferious brow, difcover'd rather vain glory,
and infulting haughtinefs, than moderation of
mind.   And that he did it ferioufly tryumph-
ing, appears by his words then utter'd, That
his Succeffors might then glory to be Kings of
England, when they had fuch Honour done
them.   And perhaps the Divine Power was
difpleas'd with him for taking too much Honour to himfelf ; fince we read that the year
following he was tak'n out of this life by fick-
nefs in the heighth of his Glory and the prime
of his Age, buried at *Glafton* Abby. The fame
year, as *Mat. Weft*. relates, he gave to *Kened*
the *Scottifh* King, many rich prefents, and the
whole Countrey of *Laudian*, or *Lothien*, to
hold of him on condition that he and his Suc-

973.
Sax. ann.
Ingulf.

974.
Sax. ann.

979.

ceffors fhould repair to the *Englifh* Court at high Feftivals when the King fat Crown'd; gave him alfo many lodging places by the way, which till the days of *Henry* the Second were ftill held by the Kings of *Scotland.* He was of Stature not tall, of body flender, yet fo well made, that in ftrength he chofe to contend with fuch as were thought ftrongeft, and diflik'd nothing more than that they fhould fpare him for refpect or fear to hurt him. *Kened* King of *Scots* then in the Court of *Edgar*, fitting one day at Table was heard to fay jeftingly among his Servants, he wonder'd how fo many Provinces could be held in fubjection by fuch a little dapper man : His words were brought to the Kings Ear; he fends for *Kened* as about fome private bufinefs, and in talk drawing him forth to a fecret place, takes from under his garment two Swords which he had brought with him, gave one of them to *Kened*; and now faith he, it fhall be try'd which ought to be the fubject; for it is fhamefull for a King to boaft at Table, and fhrink in fight. *Kened* much abafh'd fell prefently at his Feet, and befought him to pardon what he had fimply fpok'n, no way intended to his difhonour or difparagement : wherewith the King was fatisfi'd. *Camden* in his defcription of *Ireland*, cites a Charter of King *Edgar*, wherein it appears, he had in fubjection all the Kingdomes of the Iles as far as *Norway*, and had fubdu'd the greateft part of *Ireland*, with the City of *Dublin :* but of this other Writers make no mention. In his youth having

ing heard of *Elfrida*, Daughter to *Ordgar* Duke of *Devonshire*, much commended for her Beauty, he sent Earl *Athelwold*, whose loyalty he trusted most, to see her; intending, if she were found such as answer'd report, to demand her in marriage. He at the first view tak'n with her presence, disloyally, as it often happ'ns in such employments, began to sue for himself; and with consent of her Parents obtain'd her. Returning therefore with scarse an ordinary commendation of her Feature, he easily took off the Kings mind, soon diverted another way. But the matter coming to light how *Athelwold* had forestall'd the King, and *Elfrida*'s Beauty more and more spok'n of, the King now heated not only with a relapse of Love, but with a deep sense of the abuse, yet dissembling his disturbance, pleasantly told the Earl, what day he meant to come and visit him and his fair Wife. The Earl seemingly assur'd his welcome, but in the mean while acquainting his Wife, earnestly advis'd her to deform her self, what she might, either in dress or otherwise, left the King, whose amorous inclination was not unknown, should chance to be attracted. She who by this time was not ignorant, how *Athelwold* had step'd between her and the King, against his coming arraies her self richly, useing whatever Art she could devise might render her the more amiable; and it took effect. For the King inflam'd with her love, the more for that he had bin so long defrauded and robbed of her, resolv'd not only to recover his

intercepted

intercepted right, but to punish the interloper of his destin'd Spouse, and appointing with him as was usual, a day of hunting, drawn aside in a Forest, now call'd *Harewood*, smote him through with a Dart. Some censure this Act as cruel and tyrannical, but consider'd well, it may be judg'd more favourably, and that no man of sensible Spirit, but in his place, without extraordinary perfection, would have done the like : for next to Life what worse Treason could have bin committed against him ? It chanc'd that the Earls base Son coming by upon the Fact, the King sternly ask'd him how he lik'd this Game ; he submisly answering, that whatsoever pleas'd the King, must not displease him ; the King return'd to his wonted temper, took an affection to the Youth, and ever after highly favour'd him, making amends in the Son for what he had done to the Father. *Elfrida* forthwith he took to Wife, who to expiate her former Husbands death, though therin she had no hand, cover'd the place of his bloodshed with a Monastery of Nuns to sing over him. Another fault is laid to his charge, no way excusable, that he took a Virgin *Wilfrida* by force out of the Nunnery, where she was plac'd by her friends to avoid his persuit, and kept her as his Concubine ; but liv'd not obstinatly in the offence ; for sharply reprov'd by *Dunstan* he submitted to seven years penance, and for that time to want his Coronation : But why he had it not before, is left unwritt'n. Another story there goes of *Edgar*, fitter for a Novel than a History ;

ry; but as I find it in *Malmsbury*, so I relate
it. While he was yet unmarried, in his youth
he abstain'd not from Woemen, and coming
on a day to *Andover*, caus'd a Dukes Daughter
there dwelling, reported rare of Beauty, to
be brought to him. The Mother not dareing
flatly to deny, yet abhorring that her Daughter should be so deflour'd, at fit time of night
sent in her attire, one of her waiting Maids;
a Maid it seems not unhansom nor unwitty;
who supply'd the place of her young Lady.
Night pass'd, the Maid going to rise, but day-
light scarce yet appearing, was by the King
askt why she made such hast, she answer'd, to
do the work which her Lady had set her; at
which the King wondring, and with much ado
staying her to unfold the riddle, for he took
her to be the Dukes Daughter, she falling at
his Feet besought him, that since at the command of her Lady she came to his Bed, and
was enjoy'd by him, he would be pleas'd in recompence to set her free from the hard service
of her Mistress. The King a while standing
in a study whether he had best be angry or not,
at length turning all to a jest, took the Maid
away with him, advanc'd her above her Lady,
lov'd her and accompanied with her only, till
he married *Elfrida*. These only are his faults
upon Record, rather to be wonder'd how they
were so few, and so soon left, he coming at
sixteen to the Licence of a Scepter; and that
his Vertues were so many and so mature, he
dying before the Age wherein Wisdom can in
others attain to any ripeness: however with
him

him dy'd all the *Saxon* Glory. From hence-forth nothing is to be heard of but thir decline and ruin under a double Conquest, and the causes foregoing ; which, not to blur or taint the praises of thir former Actions and Liberty well defended , shall stand severally related, and will be more than long enough for ano-other Book.

The End of the Fifth Book.

THE

THE
HISTORY
OF
BRITAIN.

BOOK VI.

Edward the Younger.

EDward the Eldeſt Son of *Edgar* by *E-gelfleda* his firſt Wife, the Daughter of Duke *Ordmer*, was according to Right and his Fathers Will, plac'd in the Throne; *Elfrida* his ſecond Wife, and her Faction only repineing, who labour'd to have had her Son *Ethelred* a Child of ſeven years, preferr'd before him; that ſhe under that pretence might have rul'd all. Mean while Comets were ſeen in Heav'n, portending not Famin only, which follow'd the next year, but the troubl'd State of the whole Realm not long after to enſue. The Troubles begun

in

in *Edwi*'s dayes, between Monks and Secular
Priests, now reviv'd and drew on either side
many of the Nobles into parties. For *Elfere*
Duke of the *Mercians*, with many other Peers,
corrupted as is said with guifts, drove the
Monks out of those Monasteries where *Edgar*
had plac'd them, and in thir stead put Secular
Priests with thir Wives. But *Ethelwin* Duke
of *East-Angles*, with his Brother *Elfwold*, and
Earl *Britnoth* oppos'd them, and gathering an
Army defended the Abbies of *East-Angles*
from such intruders. To appease these Tu-
mults, a Synod was call'd at *Winchester*, and
nothing there concluded, a General Council
both of Nobles and Prelates, was held at *Caln*
in *Wiltshire*, where while the dispute was hot,
but chiefly against *Dunstan*, the room wherein they sat fell upon thir heads, killing some,
maiming others, *Dunstan* only escaping upon a
beam that fell not, and the King absent by
reason of his tender Age. This accident quieted the Controversie, and brought both parts
to hold with *Dunstan* and the Monks. Mean
while the King addicted to a Religious Life,
and of a mild Spirit, simply permitted all
things to the ambitious will of his Step-mo-
ther and her Son *Ethelred* : to whom she displeas'd that the name only of King was wanting, practis'd thenceforth to remove King
Edward out of the way; which in this manner
she brought about. *Edward* on a day wearied
with hunting, thirsty and alone, while his attendance follow'd the Dogs, hearing that *E-
thelred* and his mother lodg'd at *Corvesgate*
(*Corse*

Florent.
Sim. Dun.

(*Corfe* Castle, saith *Camden*, in the Ile of *Purbeck*) innocently went thether. She with all shew of kindness welcoming him, commanded drink to be brought forth, for it seems he lighted not from his Horse; and while he was drinking, caus'd one of her Servants, privately before instructed, to stab him with a poignard. The poor Youth who little expected such unkindness there, turning speedily the Reins, fled bleeding; till through loss of blood falling from his Horse, and expiring, yet held with one foot in the Stirrop, he was dragg'd along the way, trac'd by his blood, and buried without honour at *Werham*, having reigned about three years: but the place of his burial not long after grew famous for Miracles. After which by Duke *Elfer* (who, as *Malmsbury* saith, had a hand in his death) he was Royally enterr'd at *Skepton*, or *Shaftsbury*. The murdress *Elfrida* at length repenting spent the residue of her dayes in sorrow and great penance.

978.
Malmsb.

Ethelred.

EThelred second Son of *Edgar* by *Elfrida* (for *Edmund* dy'd a Child) his Brother *Edward* wickedly remov'd, was now next in right to succeed, and accordingly Crown'd at *Kingston*: reported by some, fair of visage, comly of person, elegant of behaviour; but the event will shew, that with many sluggish and ignoble Vices he quickly sham'd his outside;

979.
Malmsб.

Florent.
Sim. Dun.

side; born and prolong'd a fatal mischief of the People, and the ruine of his Countrey; wherof he gave early signs from his first infancy, bewraying the Font and Water while the Bishop was baptizing him. Whereat *Dunstan* much troubl'd, for he stood by and saw it, to them next him broke into these words, By God and Gods Mother this Boy will prove a Sluggard. Another thing is writt'n of him in his Childhood, which argu'd no bad nature, that hearing of his Brother *Edward*'s cruel death, he made loud lamentation; but his furious Mother offended therewith, and having no rod at hand, beat him so with great Wax Candles, that he hated the sight of them ever after. *Dunstan* though unwilling set the Crown upon his head; but at the same time foretold op'nly, as is reported, the great Evils that were to come upon him and the Land, in avengment of his Brothers innocent blood.

Sim. Dun. And about the same time, one midnight, a Cloud somtimes bloody, somtimes fiery, was

982.

Malmsb. seen over all *England*; and within three years the *Danish* Tempest, which had long surceast, revolv'd again upon this Iland. To the more ample relating whereof, the *Danish* History, at least thir latest and diligentest Historian, as neither from the first landing of *Danes*, in the Reign of *West-Saxon Brithric*, so now again from first to last, contributes nothing; busied more than enough to make out the bare names and successions of thir uncertain Kings, and thir small actions at home: unless out of him I should transcribe what he takes, and I better may,

may, from our own Annals ; the furer, and
the fadder witneffes of thir doings here, not
Glorious, as they vainly boaft, but moft inhu-
manly Barbarous. For the *Danes* well under- *Eadmer.*
ftanding, that *England* had now a flothfull *Florent.*
King to thir wifh, firft landing at *Southampton*
from feven great Ships, took the Town, fpoil-
ed the Country, and carried away with them
great pillage ; nor was *Devonfhire* and *Corn-* *Hoved.*
wall uninfefted on the fhore ; Pirats of *Nor-*
way alfo harried the Coaft of *Weft Chefter :*
and to add a worfe Calamity, the City of *Lon-* *Sim. Dun.*
don was burnt, cafually or not, is not writt'n. *Hoved.*
It chanc'd four years after, that *Ethelred* be- 986.
feig'd *Rochefter*, fome way or other offended *Malmsb.*
by the Bifhop therof. *Dunftan* not approving *Ingulf.*
the caufe, fent to warn him that he provoke
not St *Andrew* the Patron of that City, nor
waft his Lands ; an old craft of the Clergy to
fecure thir Church Lands, by entailing them
on fome Saint ; the King not hark'ning, *Dun-*
ftan on this condition that the feige might be
rais'd, fent him a hunderd pound, the money
was accepted and the feige diffolv'd. *Dunftan*
reprehending his avarice, fent him again this
word, Becaufe thou haft refpected money more
than Religion, the evils which I foretold fhall
the fooner come upon thee ; but not in my
dayes, for fo God hath fpok'n. The next year 987.
was Calamitous, bringing ftrange fluxes upon *Malmsb.*
men, and murren upon Cattel. *Dunftan* the 988.
year following dy'd, a ftrenuous Bifhop, zea- *Malmsb.*
lous without dread of perfon, and for ought
appears, the beft of many Ages, if he bufied
not

not himself too much in secular Affairs. He was Chaplain at first to King *Athelstan*, and *Edmund* who succeeded, much imploy'd in Court Affairs, till envi'd by some who laid many things to his charge, he was by *Edmund* forbidd'n the Court, but by the earnest mediation, saith *Ingulf*, of *Turkitul* the Chancellour, receav'd at length to favour, and made Abbot of *Glaston*, lastly by *Edgar* and the general Vote, Arch-bishop of *Canterbury*. Not long after his death, the *Danes* arriving in *Devonshire* were met by *Goda* Lieutenant of that Country, and *Strenwold* a valiant Leader, who put back the *Danes*, but with loss of thir own lives. The third year following, under the Conduct of *Justin* and *Guthmund* the Son of *Steytan*, they landed and spoil'd *Ipswich*, fought with *Brithnoth* Duke of the *East-Angles* about *Maldon*, where they slew him; the slaughter else had bin equal on both sides. These and the like depredations on every side the *English* not able to resist, by counsel of *Siric* then Arch-bishop of *Canterbury*, and two Dukes, *Ethelward* and *Alfric*; it was thought best for the present to buy that with Silver which they could not gain with thir Iron; and ten thousand pound was paid to the *Danes* for Peace. Which for a while contented; but taught them the ready way how easiest to come by more. The next year but one they took by storm and rifl'd *Bebbanburg* an ancient City nigh *Durham* : sailing thence into the mouth of *Humber*, they wasted both sides thereof, *Yorkshire* and *Lindsey*, burning and destroying all

991.
Sim. Dun.

993.
Sim. Dun.

all before them.   Against these went out three
Noblemen, *Fræna*, *Frithegist*, and *Godwin*, but
being all *Danes* by the Fathers side, willingly
began flight, and forsook thir own Forces betray'd to the Enemy.   No less treachery was *Florent.*
at Sea; for *Alfric* the Son of *Elfer* Duke of *Hunting.*
Mercia, whom the King for some offence had
banish'd but now recall'd, sent from *London*
with a Fleet to surprise the *Danes*, in some
place of disadvantage, gave them over night
intelligence thereof, then fled to them himself; which his Fleet, saith *Florent*, perceave-
ing, persu'd, took the Ship, but miss'd of his
person ; the *Londoners* by chance grapling
with the *East-Angles* made them fewer, saith
my Author, by many thousands. Others say,   994.
that by this notice of *Alfric*, the *Danes* not *Sim. Dun.*
only escap'd, but with a greater Fleet set up-
on the *English*, took many of thir Ships, and
in tryumph brought them up the *Thames*, intending to beseige *London* : for *Anlaf* King
of *Norway*, and *Swane* of *Denmark*, at the
head of these, came with ninety four Gallies.
The King for this treason of *Alfric*, put out
his Sons Eyes; but the *Londoners* both by Land
and Water, so valiantly resisted thir beseigers,
that they were forc't in one day with great
loss to give over.   But what they could not on
the City, they wreck'd themselves on the
Countries round about, wasting with Sword
and Fire all *Essex*, *Kent*, and *Sussex*.   Thence
horsing thir Foot, diffus'd far wider thir outragious incursions, without mercy either to
Sex or Age. The slothful King instead of War- *Malmsb.*
                                        like

like oppofition in the Field, fends Embaffadors to treat about another payment; the Summe promis'd was now 16000^l; till which paid, the *Danes* winter'd at *Southampton*; *Ethelred* inviteing *Anlaf* to come and vifit him at *Andover* : where he was royally entertain'd, fome fay baptiz'd, or confirm'd, adopted Son by the King, and difmis't with great Prefents, promifing by Oath to depart and moleft the Kingdome no more; which he perform'd, but the Calamity ended not fo, for after fome intermiffion of thir rage for three years, the other Navy of *Danes* failing about to the Weft, enter'd *Severn*, and wafted one while *South-Wales*, then *Cornwall* and *Devonfhire*, till at length they winter'd about *Taviftoc.* For it were an endlefs work to relate how they wallow'd up and down to every particular place, and to repeat as oft what devaftations they wrought, what defolations left behind them, eafie to be imagin'd. In fumm, the next year they afflicted *Dorfetfhire*, *Hamfhire*, and the Ile of *Wight*; by the *Englifh* many refolutions were tak'n, many Armies rais'd, but either betray'd by the falfhood, or difcourag'd by the weaknefs of thir Leaders, they were put to rout, or disbanded themfelves. For Souldiers moft commonly are as thir Commanders, without much odds of valour in one Nation or other, only as they are more or lefs wifely difciplin'd and conducted. The following year brought them back upon *Kent*, where they enter'd *Medway*, and befeig'd *Rochefter*; but the *Kentifh* men affembling, gave them

Malmsb.

Hunting.

997.
Sim. Dun.

998.
Sim. Dun.

999.
Sim. Dun.

them a sharp encounter, yet that suffic'd not to hinder them from doing as they had done in other places. Against these depopulations, the King leavied an Army; but the unskilful Leaders not knowing what to do with it when they had it, did but drive out time, burdening and impoverishing the people, consuming the publick treasure, and more imboldning the Enemy, than if they had sat quiet at home. What cause mov'd the *Danes* next year to pass into *Normandy*, is not recorded; but that they return'd thence more outragious than before. Mean while the King, to make some diversion, undertakes an Expedition both by Land and Sea into *Cumberland*, where the *Danes* were most planted; there and in the Ile of *Man*, or as *Camden* saith, *Anglesey*, imitating his Enemies in spoiling and unpeopling; the *Danes* from *Normandy* arriving in the River *Ex*, laid seige to *Exeter*; but the Cittizens, as those of *London*, valourously defending themselves, they wreck'd thir anger, as before, on the Villages round about. The Countrey People of *Somerset* and *Devonshire* assembling themselves at *Penho*, shew'd their readiness, but wanted a head; and besides, being then but few in number, were easily put to flight; the Enemy plundring all at will, with loaded spoils pass'd into the Ile of *Wight*; from whence all *Dorsetshire*, and *Hamshire*, felt again thir fury. The *Saxon* Annals write, that before thir coming to *Exeter*, the *Hamshire* men had a bickering with them, wherin *Ethelward* the Kings General was slain, adding

other

Margin notes:

1000.
Sim. Dun.

1001.
Sim. Dun.

T

1002.
Sim. Dun.

other things hardly to be underſtood, and in one ancient Copy; ſo end. *Ethelred*, whom no adverſity could awake from his ſoft and ſluggiſh life, ſtill coming by the worſe at fighting, by the advice of his Peers not unlike himſelf, ſends one of his gay Courtiers, though looking loftily, to ſtoop baſely and propoſe a third tribute to the *Danes :* they willingly hark'n, but the ſumm is enhaunc't now to twenty four thouſand pound, and paid; the *Danes* therupon abſtaining from hoſtility. But the King to ſtrengthen his Houſe by ſome Potent Affinity, marries *Emma*, whom the *Saxons* call *Elgiva*, Daughter of *Richard* Duke of

Malmsb.

Normandy. With him *Ethelred* formerly had War or no good correſpondence, as appears

Calviſius.

by a Letter of Pope *John* the 15ᵗʰ, who made peace between them about eleaven years before; puſt up now with his ſuppos'd acceſs of ſtrength by this Affinity, he caus'd the *Danes*

Florent.

all over *England*, though now living peace-

Hunting.

ably, in one day perfidiouſly to be maſſacherd, both Men, Woemen and Children; ſending private Letters to every Town and Citty, wherby they might be ready all at the ſame hour; which till the appointed time (being

Calviſius.

the 9ᵗʰ of *July*) was conceal'd with great ſilence, and perform'd with much unanimity; ſo generally hated were the *Danes. Mat. Weſt.* writes, that this Execution upon the *Danes* was ten years after ; that *Huna* one of *Ethelreds* Chief Captains, complaining of the *Daniſh* Inſolencies in time of Peace, thir Pride, thir raviſhing of Matrons and Virgins, incited

the

the King to this Maſſacher, which in the mad-
neſs of Rage made no difference of innocent
or nocent.   Among theſe, *Gunhildis* the Siſter
of *Swane* was not ſpar'd, though much deſerv-
ing not pitty only, but all protection : ſhe with
her Husband Earl *Palingus*, coming to live in
England, and receaving Chriſtianity, had her
Husband and young Son ſlain before her face,
her ſelf then beheaded, foretelling and de-
nouncing that her blood would coſt *England*
dear.   Some ſay this was done by the Tray-   *Mat. Weſt.*
tor *Edric*, to whoſe cuſtody ſhe was committed ; but the Maſſacher was ſom years before
Edric's advancement; and if it were done by
him afterward, it ſeems to contradict the private correſpondence which he was thought to
hold with the *Danes*.   For *Swane* breathing   1003.
revenge, haſted the next year into *England*,   *Sim. Dun.*
and by the treaſon or negligence of Count
Hugh, whom *Emma* had recommended to the
Government of *Devonſhire*, ſack'd the City of
Exeter, her Wall from Eaſt to Weſt-gate,
brok'n down : after this waſting *Wiltſhire*, the
People of that County, and of *Hamſhire*, came
together in great numbers with reſolution
ſtoutly to oppoſe him, but *Alfric* thir General, whoſe Sons Eyes the King had lately put
out, madly thinking to revenge himſelf on the
King, by ruining his own Country, when he
ſhould have order'd his Battel, the Enemy being at hand, fain'd himſelf tak'n with a vomit-
ing ; wherby his Army in great diſcontent,
deſtitute of a Commander, turn'd from the E-
nemy ; who ſtreight took *Wilton* and *Salsbu-*

ry,

ry, carrying the pillage thereof to his Ships.
Thence the next year landing on the Coast of
Norfolk, he wasted the Country, and set Nor-
wich on fire; Ulfketel Duke of the East-Angles, a man of great valour, not having space
to gather his Forces, after Consultation had,
thought it best to make Peace with the Dane,
which he breaking within three weeks, issued silently out of his Ships, came to Thetford, staid there a night, and in the Morning
left it flameing. Ulfketel hearing this, commanded some to go and break, or burn his
Ships; but they not dareing or neglecting,
he in the mean while with what secresie
and speed was possible, drawing together his
Forces, went out against the Enemy, and
gave them a feirce Onset retreating to thir
Ships; but much inferiour in number, many
of the Chief East-Angles, there lost thir lives.
Nor did the Danes come off without great
slaughter of thir own ; confessing that they
never met in England with so rough a charge.
The next year, whom Warr could not, a
great Famin drove Swane out of the Land.
But the Summer following, another great
Fleet of Danes enter'd the Port of Sandwich,
thence powr'd out over all Kent and Sussex,
made prey of what they found. The King
levying an Army out of Mercia, and the
West-Saxons, took on him for once the Manhood to go out and face them ; But they who
held it safer to live by Rapine, than to hazard a Battel, shifting lightly from place to
place, frustrated the slow motions of a heavy
Camp,

1004.
Sim. Dun.

1005.
Sim. Dun.

1006.
Sim. Dun.

Camp, following thir wonted courſe of rob-
bery, then running to thir Ships.   Thus all
Autumn they wearied out the Kings Army,
wᶜʰ gone home to winter, they carried all thir
pillage to the Ile of *Wight*, and there ſtaid till
Chriſtmas; at which time the King being in
Shropſhire, and but ill imploy'd (for by the
procurement of *Edric*, he cauſ'd, as is thought,
Alfhelm a Noble Duke, treacherouſly to be   *Florent.*
ſlain, and the Eyes of his two Sons to be put
out) they came forth again, over-running
Hamſhire, and *Barkſhire*, as far as *Reading* and
Wallingford : thence to *Aſhdune*, and other
places thereabout, neither known nor of tolerable pronuntiation; and returning by another way, found many of the People in Arms
by the River *Kenet*; but making thir way
through, they got ſafe with vaſt booty to thir
Ships.   The King and his Courtiers wearied   1007.
out with thir laſt Summers jaunt after the   *Sim. Dun.*
nimble *Danes* to no purpoſe, which by proof
they found too toilſome for thir ſoft Bones,
more us'd to Beds and Couches, had recourſe
to thir laſt and only remedy, thir Cofers; and
ſend now the fourth time to buy a diſhonour-
able peace, every time ſtill dearer, not to be
had now under thirty ſix thouſand pound (for
the *Danes* knew how to milk ſuch eaſie Kine)
in name of Tribute and expences : which out
of the People over all *England*, already half
begger'd, was extorted and paid.   About the
ſame time *Ethelred* advanc'd *Edric*, ſurnam'd
Streon, from obſcure condition to be Duke of
Mercia, and marry *Edgitha* the Kings Daugh-
T 3   ter.

ter. The cause of his advancement, *Florent* of *Worster*, and *Mat. West.* attribute to his great wealth, gott'n by fine policies and a plausible tongue : he prov'd a main accessory to the ruin of *England*, as his actions will soon declare. *Ethelred* the next year somewhat rowsing himself, ordain'd that every three hundred and ten Hides (a Hide is so much Land as one Plow can sufficiently Till) should set out a Ship or Gally, and every nine Hides find a Corslet and Head-peice : new Ships in every Port were builded, vittl'd, fraught with stout Mariners and Souldiers, and appointed to meet all at *Sandwich*. A man might now think that all would go well ; when suddenly a new mischief sprung up, dissention among the great ones ; which brought all this diligence to as little success as at other times before. *Bithric* the Brother of *Edric*, falsly accus'd *Wulnoth* a great Officer set over the *South-Saxons*, who fearing the potency of his Enemies, with twenty Ships got to Sea, and practis'd piracy on the Coast. Against whom, reported to be in a place where he might be easily surpris'd, *Bithric* sets forth with eighty Ships ; all which driv'n back by a Tempest and wrackt upon the shoar, were burnt soon after by *Wulnoth*. Disheart'nd with this misfortune, the King returns to *London* ; the rest of his Navy after him ; and all this great preparation to nothing. Whereupon *Turkill*, a *Danish* Earl, came with a Navy to the Ile of *Tanet*, and in *August* a far greater, led by *Heming* and *Ilaf* joyn'd with him. Thence coasting to *Sandwich*,

1008.
Sim. Dun.

1009.
Sim. Dun.

Sandwich, and landed, they went onward and began to affault *Canterbury*, but the Citizens and Eaft *Kentiſh* men, coming to compofition with them for three thoufand pound, they departed thence to the Ile of *Wight*, robbing and burning by the way. Againſt thefe the King levies an Army through all the Land, and in feveral quarters places them nigh the Sea, but fo unſkillfully or unfuccefsfully, that the *Danes* were not thereby hinderd from exercifeing thir wonted Robberies. It happ'nd that the *Danes* one day were gone up into the Country, far from thir Ships, the King having notice thereof, thought to intercept them in thir return ; his men were refolute to overcome or die, time and place advantagious ; but where courage and fortune was not wanting, there wanted Loyalty among them. *Edric* with futtle arguments that had a fhew of deep policy, difputed and perfwaded the fimplicity of his Fellow Counfellers, that it would be beſt confulted at that time to let the *Danes* pafs without ambuſh or interception. The *Danes* where they expected danger, finding none, pafs'd on with great joy and booty to thir Ships. After this, failing about *Kent*, they lay that Winter in the *Thames*, forcing *Kent* and *Eſſex* to Contribution, oft-times attempting the City of *London*, but repulſ't as oft to thir great lofs. Spring begun, leaving thir Ships, they pafs'd through *Chiltern* Wood into *Oxfordſhire*, burnt the City, and thence returning with divided Forces waſted on both fides the *Thames* ; but hearing, that an Army

1010.
Sim. Dun.
Florent.

from

from *London* was marcht out against them, they on the North-side, passing the River at *Stanes*, join'd with them on the South into one body, and enrich't with great spoils, came back through *Surrey* to thir Ships; which all the Lent-time they repair'd. After *Easter*, sailing to the *East-Angles* they arriv'd at *Ipswich*, and came to a place call'd *Ringmere*, where they heard that *Ulfketel* with his Forces lay, who with a sharp encounter soon entertain'd them; but his men at length giving back, through the suttlety of a *Danish* Servant among them who began the flight, lost the field, though the Men of *Cambridgeshire* stood to it valiantly. In this Battel *Ethelstan* the Kings Son in Law, with many other Noblemen, was slain; wherby the *Danes* without more resistance, three months together had the spoiling of those Countries and all the Fenns, burnt *Thetford* and *Grantbrig*, or *Cambridge*; thence to a hilly place not far off, called by *Huntingdon Balesham*, by *Camden Gogmagog* Hills, and the Villages therabout they turn'd thir fury, slaying all they met save one man, who getting up into a Steeple, is said to have defended himself against the whole *Danish* Army. They therefore so leaving him, thir Foot by Sea, thir Horse by Land through *Essex*, return'd back lad'n to thir Ships left in the *Thames*. But many dayes pass'd not between, when sallying again out of thir Ships as out of Savage Denns, they plunder'd over again all *Oxfordshire*, and added to thir prey

Hunting. *Buckingham*, *Bedford*, and *Hertfordshire*; then

like

like wild Beasts glutted, returning to their
Caves.   A third excursion they made into
Northamptonshire, burnt *Northampton*, ransack-
ing the Country round; then as to fresh pa-
sture betook them to the *West-Saxons*, and in
like sort harrasing all *Wiltshire*, return'd, as I
said before, like wild Beasts, or rather Sea-
Monsters to thir Water-stables, accomplish-
ing by *Christmas* the Circuit of their whole
years good Deeds; an unjust and inhumane
Nation, who receaving or not receaving tribute where none was owing them, made such
destruction of mankind, and rapine of their
lively-hood, as is a misery to read.   Yet here
they ceas'd not, for the next year repeating
the same Cruelties on both sides the *Thames*,
one way as far as *Huntingdon*, the other as far
as *Wiltshire* and *Southampton*, follicited again
by the King for Peace, and receaving thir demands both of Tribute and Contribution, they
slighted thir Faith; and in the beginning of
September laid seige to *Canterbury*.   On the
20th day, by the treachery of *Almere* the Arch-
deacon, they took part of it and burnt it, committing all sorts of massacher as a sport; some
they threw over the wall, others into the fire,
hung some by the privy members, Infants pul-
led from their mothers breasts, were either
tost on Spears, or Carts drawn over them;
Matrons and Virgins by the hair drag'd and
ravish't.   *Alfage* the grave Arch-bishop, above
others hated of the *Danes*, as in all Counsells
and Actions to his might thir known opposer,
tak'n, wounded, imprison'd in a noisom Ship;
the

1011.

Sim. Dun.

Eadmer.
Malmsb.
Eadmer.

the multitude are tith'd, and every tenth only
1012. spar'd. Early the next year before *Easter*,
Sim. Dun. while *Ethelred* and his Peers were assembl'd
at *London*, to raise now the fifth Tribute a-
mounting to forty eight thousand pound, the
Eadmer. *Danes* at *Canterbury* propose to the Arch-bishop, who had bin now seav'n months thir
Prisoner, life and liberty, if he pay them three
thousand pound; which he refuseing as not
able of himself, and not willing to extort it
from his Tennants, is permitted till the next
Sunday to consider; then hal'd before their
Counsel, of whom *Turkill* was Chief, and still
refuseing, they rise most of them being drunk,
and beat him with the blunt side of thir Axes,
then thrust forth deliver him to be pelted with
stones; till one *Thrum* a converted *Dane*, pittying him half dead, to put him out of pain;
with a pious impiety, at one stroak of his Axe
on the head dispatch'd him. His Body was
carried to *London*, and there buried, thence
afterward remov'd to *Canterbury*. By this time
the Tribute paid, and Peace so oft'n violated
sworn again by the *Danes*, they dispers'd thir
Fleet; forty five of them, and *Turkill* thir
Cheif staid at *London* with the King, swore
him Allegeance to defend his Land against all
Strangers, on condition only to be fed and
cloath'd by him. But this voluntary friendship of *Turkill* was thought to be deceitfull,
that staying under this pretence he gave intelligence to *Swane*, when it would be most sea-
1013. sonable to come. In *July* therfore of the next
Sim. Dun. year, King *Swane* arriving at *Sandwich*, made

no

no stay there, but sailing first to *Humber*, thence
into *Trent*, landed and encamp'd at *Gainsbur-
row* : whither without delay repair'd to him
the *Northumbrians*, with *Uthred* thir Earl;
those of *Lindsey* also, then those of *Fisburg*,
and lastly all on the North of *Watling-street*
(which is a high way from East to West Sea)
gave Oath and Hostages to obey him. From
whom he commanded Horses and Provision
for his Army, taking with him besides Bands
and Companies of thir Choicest Men; and
committing to his Son *Canute* the care of his
Fleet and Hostages; he marches towards the
South Mercians, commanding his Souldiers to
exercise all Acts of Hostility; with the terrour whereof fully executed, he took in few
dayes the City of *Oxford*, then *Winchester*;
thence tending to *London*, in his hasty passage over the *Thames*, without seeking Bridge
or Ford, lost many of his men. Nor was his
Expedition against *London* prosperous; for
assaying all means by force or wile to take the
City, wherin the King then was, and *Turkill*
with his *Danes*, he was stoutly beat'n off as
at other times. Thence back to *Wallingford*
and *Bath*, directing his course, after usual havock made, he sate a while and refresh'd his
Army. There *Ethelm* an Earl of *Devonshire*,
and other great Officers in the West yielded
him subjection. These things flowing to his
wish, he betook him to his Navy, from that
time stil'd and accounted King of *England*, if
a Tyrant, saith *Simeon*, may be call'd a King.
The *Londoners* also sent him Hostages, and
made

made thir Peace, for they fear'd his Fury. *E-thelred* thus reduc't to narrow compaſs, ſent *Emma* his Queen, with his two Sons had by her, and all his Treaſure tò *Richard* the 11ᵈ her Brother, Duke of *Normandy*; himſelf with his *Daniſh* Fleet abode ſome while at *Greenwich*, then ſailing to the Ile of *Wight*, paſs'd after *Chriſtmas* into *Normandy*; where he was honourably receav'd at *Roan* by the Duke, though known to have born himſelf

Malmsb. churliſhly and proudly towards *Emma* his Siſter, beſides his diſſolute Company with other Woemen. Mean while *Swane* ceas'd not to exact almoſt inſupportable tribute of the People, ſpoiling them when he liſted; beſides, the

1014. like did *Turkill* at *Greenwich*. The next year

Sim. Dun. beginning, *Swane* ſickens and dies; ſome ſay

Mat. Weſt. terrifi'd and ſmitt'n by an appearing ſhape of Sᵗ *Edmund* arm'd, whoſe Church at *Bury* he had threat'nd to demoliſh; but the Authority hereof relies only upon the Legend of Sᵗ *Edmund*. After his death the *Daniſh* Army and Fleet made his Son *Canute* thir King; but the Nobility and States of *England* ſent Meſſengers to *Ethelred*, declareing that they preferr'd none before thir Native Sovran, if he would promiſe to govern them better than he had done, and with more Clemency. Wherat the King rejoicing, ſends over his Son *Edward* with Embaſſadors to Court both high and low, and win thir Love, promiſing largly to be thir mild and devoted Lord, to conſent in all things to thir will, follow thir counſel, and whatever had been done or ſpok'n by any man againſt

against him, freely to pardon; if they would loyally restore him to be thir King. To this the People cheerfully answer'd, and Amity was both promis'd and confirm'd on both sides. An Embassey of Lords is sent to bring back the King honourably; he returns in *Lent* and is joyfully receav'd of the People, marches with a strong Army against *Canute*; who having got Horses and joyn'd with the men of *Lindsey*, was preparing to make spoil in the Countries adjoyning; but by *Ethelred* unexpectedly coming upon him, was soon driv'n to his Ships, and his Confederates of *Lindsey* left to the anger of thir Country-men, executed without mercy both by Fire and Sword. *Canute* in all hast sailing back to *Sandwich*, took the Hostages giv'n to his Father from all parts of *England*, and with slit Noses, Ears cropt, and Hands chop't off, setting them ashore, departed into *Denmark.* Yet the People were not disburd'nd, for the King rais'd out of them thirty thousand pound to pay his Fleet of *Danes* at *Greenwich.* To these Evils the Sea in *October* pass'd his bounds, overwhelming many Towns in *England*, and of thir Inhabitants many thousands. The year following, an Assembly being at *Oxford*, *Edric* of *Streon*, having invited two Noblemen, *Sigeferth*, and *Morcar*, the Sons of *Earngrun* of *Seav'nburg* to his Lodging, secretly murder'd them: the King, for what cause is unknown, seis'd thir Estates, and caus'd *Algith* the Wife of *Sigeferth* to be kept at *Maidulfsburg*, now *Malmsbury*; whom *Edmund* the Prince there married against

1015.
Sim. Dun.

againſt his Fathers minde, then went and poſſeſs'd thir Lands, making the People there
ſubject to him. *Mat. Weſt.* ſaith, that theſe
two were of the *Danes* who had ſeated themſelves in *Northumberland*, ſlain by *Edric* under

Malmsb. colour of Treaſon laid to thir charge. They
who attended them without, tumulting at the
death of thir Maiſters, were beat'n back; and
driv'n into a Church, and defending themſelves were burnt there in the Steeple. Mean
while *Canute* returning from *Denmark* with a

Leges Ed. great Navy, two hundred Ships richly gilded
Conſ. Tit. and adorn'd, well fraught with Arms and all
deduct. Proviſion; and, which *Encomium Emmæ* men-
Norman. tions not, two other Kings, *Lachman* of *Sweden*, *Olav* of *Norway*, arriv'd at *Sandwich*; and
as the ſame Authour then living writes, ſent
out ſpies to diſcover what reſiſtance on Land
was to be expected; who return'd with certain report, that a great Army of *Engliſh* was
in readineſs to oppoſe them. *Turkill*, who upon the arrival of theſe *Daniſh* Powers, kept
faith no longer with the *Engliſh*, but joyning
now with *Canute*, as it were to reingratiate

Encom.Em. himſelf after his revolt, whether real or com-
plotted, counſell'd him (being yet young) not
to land, but leave to him the management of
this firſt Battel; the King aſſented, and he
with the Forces which he had brought, and
part of thoſe which arriv'd with *Canute*, landing to thir wiſh encounter'd the *Engliſh*, though
double in number, at a place call'd *Scoraſtan*,
and was at firſt beaten back with much loſs.
But at length animating his Men with Rage
only

only and Despair, obtain'd a clear Victory, which won him great reward and possessions from *Canute*. But of this Action no other writer makes mention : from *Sandwich* therfore sailing about to the River *Frome*, and there landing, over all *Dorset*, *Summerset*, and *Wiltshire*, he spread wastfull hostility. The King *Camden*. lay then sick at *Cosham* in this County ; though it may seem strange how he could lie sick there in the midst of his Enemies. Howbeit *Edmund* in one part, and *Edric* of *Streon* in another, rais'd Forces by themselves ; but so soon as both Armies were united, the Traytor *Edric* being found to practice against the Life of *Edmund*, he remov'd with his Army from him ; whereof the Enemy took great advantage. *Edric* easily enticeing the forty Ships of *Danes* to side with him, revolted to *Canute*, the *West-Saxons* also gave pledges and furnished him with Horses. By which means the 1016. year ensuing, he with *Edric* the Traytor, pas- *Sim. Dun.* sing the *Thames* at *Creclad*, about twelftide, enter'd into *Mercia*, and especially *Warwickshire*, depopulating all places in thir way. Against these, Prince *Edmund*, for his hardiness call'd *Ironside*, gather'd an Army ; but the *Mercians* refus'd to fight unless *Ethelred* with the *Londoners* came to aid them ; and so every man return'd home. After the Festival, *Edmund* gathering another Army besought his Father to come with the *Londoners*, and what force besides he was able ; they came with great strength gott'n together, but being come, and in a hopefull way of good success,

it

it was told the King; that unless he took the better heed, some of his own Forces would fall off and betray him. The King daunted with this perhaps cunning whisper of the Enemy, disbanding his Army, returns to *London*. *Edmund* betook him into *Northumberland*, as some thought to raise fresh Forces; but he with Earl *Uthred* on the one side, and *Canute* with *Edric* on the other, did little else but wast the Provinces; *Canute* to Conquer them, *Edmund* to punish them, who stood neuter; for which cause *Stafford, Shropshire*, and *Lestershire*, felt heavily his hand; while *Canute*, who was ruineing the more Southern Shires, at length march'd into *Northumberland*; which *Edmund* hearing dismiss'd his Forces, and came to *London*. *Uthred* the Earl hasted back to *Northumberland*, and finding no other remedy, submitted himself with all the *Northumbrians*, giving hostages to *Canute*. Nevertheless by his command or connivence, and the hand of one *Turebrand* a *Danish* Lord; *Uthred* was slain, and *Iric* another *Dane* made Earl in his stead. This *Uthred* Son of *Walteof*, as *Simeon* writes, in his treatise of the Seige of *Durham*, in his youth obtain'd a great Victory against *Malcolm* Son of *Kened* King of *Scots*, who with the whole Power of his Kingdome was fall'n into *Northumberland*, and laid seige to *Durham*. *Walteof* the old Earl unable to resist, had secur'd himself in *Bebbanburg*, a strong Town, but *Uthred* gathering an Army rais'd the Seige, slew most of the *Scots*, thir King narrowly escaping, and with the heads

of

of thir flain fixt upon Poles befet round the Walls of *Durham.* The year of this exploit *Simeon* cleers not, for in 969, and in the Reign of *Ethelred* as he affirms, it could not be. *Canute* by another way returning Southward, joyfull of his fuccefs, before *Eafter* came back with all the Army to his Fleet. About the end of *April* enfueing, *Ethelred* after a long, troublefome and ill govern'd Reign, ended his dayes at *London,* and was buried in the Church of St *Paul.*

Edmund Ironfide.

AFter the deceafe of *Ethelred,* they of the Nobility who were then at *London* together with the Citizens, chofe *Edmund* his Son (not by *Emma,* but a former Wife the Daughter of Earl *Thored*) in his Fathers room; but the Arch-bifhops, Abbots, and many of the Nobles affembling together elected *Canute*; and coming to *Southampton* where he then remain'd, renounc'd before him all the Race of *Ethelred,* and fwore him fidelity : he alfo fwore to them, in matters both Religious and Secular, to be thir faithfull Lord. But *Edmund* with all fpeed going to the *Weft-Saxons,* was joyfully receav'd of them as thir King, and of many other Provinces by thir example. Mean while *Canute* about mid *May* came with his whole Fleet up the River to *London* ; then caufing a great Dike to be made on *Surrey* fide, turn'd the ftream and drew his

Florent.
Aelred in the life of *Ed. Conf.*

Florent.
Sim. Duns

V   Ships

Ships thether West of the Bridge; then be-
girting the City with a broad and deep trench,
assail'd it on every side; but repulst as before
by the valourous Defendants, and in despair
of success at that time, leaving part of his
Army for the defence of his Ships, with the
rest sped him to the *West-Saxons*, e're *Edmund*
could have time to assemble all his Powers:
who yet with such as were at hand invoking
Divine Aid, encounter'd the *Danes* at *Pen* by
Gillingham in *Dorsetshire*, and put him to flight.
After Mid-summer, encreast with new Forces,
he met with him again at a place call'd *She-*
rastan, now *Sharstan*; but *Edric*, *Almar*, and
Algar, with the *Hampshire* and *Wiltshire* Men,
then siding with the *Danes*, he only maintain'd the fight, obstinately fought on both
sides, till night and weariness parted them.
Day light returning renu'd the Conflict;
wherein the *Danes* appearing inferiour, *Edric*
to disheart'n the *English* cuts off the Head of
one *Osmer*, in countnance and hair somewhat
resembling the King, and holding it up, cries
aloud to the *English*, that *Edmund* being slain
and this his Head, it was time for them to
flie; which fallacy *Edmund* perceaving, and
op'nly shewing himself to his Souldiers, by
Malmsb. a Spear thrown at *Edric*, that missing him
yet slew one next him, and through him another behinde, they recover'd heart, and lay
sore upon the *Danes* till night parted them
as before: for e're the third morn, *Canute*
sensible of his loss, march'd away by stealth
to his Ships at *London*, renuing there his
Leagre.

Leagre. Some would have this Battel at *She-raſtan* the ſame with that at *Scoraſtan* before mention'd, but the circumſtance of time per-mits not that, having bin before the landing of *Canute*, this a good while after, as by the Proceſs of things appears: from *Sheraſtan* or *Sharſtan*, *Edmund* return'd to the *Weſt-Sax-ons*, whoſe Valour *Edric* fearing, leſt it might prevail againſt the *Danes*, ſought pardon of his Revolt, and obtaining it ſwore Loyalty to the King, who now the third time com-ing with an Army from the *Weſt-Saxons* to *London*, rais'd the Seige, chaſeing *Canute* and his *Danes* to thir Ships. Then after two dayes paſſing the *Thames* at *Branford*, and ſo coming on thir backs, kept them ſo turn'd, and obtain'd the Victory : then returns again to his *Weſt-Saxons*, and *Canute* to his Seige, but ſtill in vain ; riſing therefore thence, he enter'd with his Ships a River then call'd *A-renne* ; and from the Banks therof waſted *Mer-cia* ; thence thir Horſe by Land, thir Foot by Ship came to *Medway*. *Edmund* in the mean while with multipli'd Forces out of many Shires, croſſing again at *Branford*, came in-to *Kent*, ſeeking *Canute* ; encounter'd him at *Otford*, and ſo defeated, that of his Horſe, they who eſcap'd fled to the Ile of *Sheppey* ; and a full Victory he had gain'd, had not *E-dric* ſtill the Traytor by ſome wile or other detain'd his perſuit : and *Edmund* who never wanted courage, here wanted prudence to be ſo miſled, ever after forſak'n of his wonted Fortune. *Canute* croſſing with his Army into

Essex, thence wasted *Mercia* worse than before, and with heavy prey return'd to his Ships: them *Edmund* with a collected Army persueing, overtook at a place call'd *Assandune*, or *Asseshill*, now *Ashdown* in *Essex*; the Battel on either side was fought with great vehemence; but perfidious *Edric* perceaving the Victory to incline towards *Edmund*, with that part of the Army which was under him, fled, as he had promis'd *Canute*, and left the King over-match't with numbers: by which desertion the *English* were overthrown, Duke *Alfric*, Duke *Godwin*, and *Ulfketel* the valiant Duke of *East-Angles*, with a great part of the Nobility slain, so as the *English* of a long time had not receav'd a greater blow. Yet after a while *Edmund* not absurdly call'd *Ironside*, preparing to try again his Fortune in another Field, was hinder'd by *Edric* and others of his Faction, adviseing him to make Peace and divide the Kingdome with *Canute*. To which *Edmund* over-rul'd, a Treaty appointed, and Pledges mutually giv'n, both Kings met together at a place call'd *Deorhirst* in *Glostershire*; *Edmund* on the West side of *Severn*, *Canute* on the East with thir Armies, then both in person wasted into an Iland, at that time call'd *Olanege*, now *Alney* in the midst of the River; swearing Amity and Brother-hood, they parted the Kingdome between them. Then interchanging Armes and the habit they wore, assessing also what pay should be allotted to the Navy; they departed each his way. Concerning this interview, and the cause therof,

Camden.

Camden.

Camden.

therof, others write otherwife; *Malmsbury*, that *Edmund* grieving at the lofs of fo much blood fpilt for the ambition only of two men ftriveing who fhould Reign, of his own accord fent to *Canute*, offering him fingle Combate, to prevent in thir own Caufe the effufion of more blood than thir own; that *Canute* though of courage anough, yet not unwifely doubting to adventure his body of fmall Timber, againft a man of Iron fides, refus'd the Combate, offring to divide the Kingdome; this offer pleafing both Armies, *Edmund* was not difficult to confent; and the decifion was, that he as his Hereditary Kingdome fhould Rule the *Weft-Saxons*, and all the *South*, *Canute* the *Mercians*, and the *North*. *Huntingdon* follow'd by *Mat. Weft*. relates, That the Peers on every fide wearied out with continual Warfare, and not refraining to affirm op'nly, that they two who expected to Reign fingly, had moft reafon to fight fingly, the Kings were content; the Iland was thir Lifts, the Combate Knightly; till *Knute* finding himfelf too weak, began to parle, which ended as is faid before. After which the *Londoners* bought thir Peace of the *Danes*, and permitted them to winter in the City. But King *Edmund* about the feaft of St *Andrew*, unexpectedly deceas'd at *London*, and was buried neer to *Edgar* his Grand-father at *Glafton*. The caufe of his fo fudden death is uncertain; common Fame, faith *Malmsbury*, laies the guilt therof upon *Edric*, who to pleafe *Canute*, allur'd with promife of Reward two

of

of the Kings Privy Chamber, though at firſt
abhorring the fact, to aſſaſſinate him at the
Stool, by thruſting a ſharp Iron into his hinder parts. *Huntingdon*, and *Mat. Weſt*. relate it done at *Oxford* by the Son of *Edric*,
and ſomething vary in the manner, not worth
recital. *Edmund* dead, *Canute* meaning to
Reign ſole King of *England*, calls to him all
the Dukes, Barons, and Biſhops of the Land,
cunningly demanding of them who were witneſſes what agreement was made between
him and *Edmund* dividing the Kingdom, whether the Sons and Brothers of *Edmund* were
to govern the *Weſt-Saxons* after him, *Canute*
living? they who underſtood his meaning, and
fear'd to undergo his anger, timorouſly anſwer'd, that *Edmund* they knew had left no
part therof to his Sons or Brethren, living or
dying; but that he intended *Canute* ſhould be
thir Guardian, till they came to age of Reigning. *Simeon* affirms, that for fear or hope of
Reward they atteſted what was not true:
notwithſtanding which he put many of them
to death not long after.

Canute, or *Knute*.

1017.
Sim. Dun.
Sax. Ann.

CAnute having thus founded the Nobility,
and by them underſtood, receav'd thir
Oath of fealty, they the pledge of his bare
hand, and Oath from the *Daniſh* Nobles;
whereupon the Houſe of *Edmund* was renounc't, and *Canute* Crown'd. Then they
enacted,

enacted, that *Edwi* Brother of *Edmund*, a Prince of great hope, fhould be banifh't the Realm. But *Canute* not thinking himfelf fecure while *Edwi* liv'd, confulted with *Edric* how to make him away; who told him of one *Ethelward* a decay'd Nobleman, likelieft to do the work. *Ethelward* fent for, and tempted by the King in private, with largeft rewards, but abhorring in his mind the deed, promis'd to do it when he faw his opportunity; and fo ftill deferr'd it. But *Edwi* afterwards receav'd into favour as a fnare, was by him or fome other of his falfe friends, *Canute* contriving it, the fame year flain. *Edric* alfo counfel'd him to difpatch *Edward* and *Edmund*, the Sons of *Ironfide*; but the King doubting that the Fact would feem too foul done in *England*, fent them to the King of *Sweden*, with like intent; but he difdaining the Office, fent them for better fafety to *Solomon* King of *Hungary*; where *Edmund* at length dy'd, but *Edward* married *Agatha* Daughter to *Henry* the *German* Emperour. A digreffion in the Lawes of *Edward* Confeffor under the Title of *Lex Noricorum* faith, that this *Edward* for fear of *Canute*, fled of his own accord to *Malefclot* King of the *Rugians*, who receav'd him honourably, and of that Countrey gave him a Wife. *Canute* fettl'd in his Throne, divided the Government of his Kingdom into fowr parts; the *Weft-Saxons* to himfelf, the *Eaft-Angles* to Earl *Turkill*, the *Mercians* to *Edric*, the *Northumbrians* to *Eric*; then made Peace with all Princes round about

bout him, and his former Wife being dead, in
July married *Emma* the Widow of King *E-
thelred*. The *Christmas* following was an ill
Feast to *Edric*, of whose Treason, the King
having now made use as much as serv'd his
turn, and fearing himself to be the next betray'd, caus'd him to be slain at *London* in the
Palace, thrown over the City Wall, and there
to lie unburied; the head of *Edric* fixt on a
Pole, he commanded to be set on the highest
Tower of *London*, as in a double fence he had
promis'd him, for the murder of King *Edmund* to exalt him above all the Peers of *England*. *Huntingdon*, *Malmsbury*, and *Mat.
West.* write, that suspecting the Kings intention to degrade him from his *Mercian* Duke-
dome, and upbraiding him with his Merits,
the King enrag'd, caus'd him to be strangl'd
in the room, and out at a Window thrown
into the *Thames*. Another writes, that *Eric*
at the Kings command struck off his head. O-
*Encom.Em.
Ingulf.* ther great men though without fault, as Duke
Norman the Son of *Leofwin*, *Ethelward* Son of
Duke *Agelmar*, he put to death at the same
time, jealous of their Power or Familiarity
with *Edric*: and notwithstanding Peace, kept
1018. still his Army; to maintain which, the next
Sim. Dun. year he squees'd out of the *English*, though
Hunting. now his Subjects, not his Enemies, seventy
Mat. West. two, some say, eighty two thousand pound,
besides fifteen thousand out of *London*. Mean
while great Warr arose at *Carr*, between
Uthred Son of *Waldef*, Earl of *Northumberland*, and *Malcolm* Son of *Kened* King of
Scots,

Scots, with whom held *Eugenius* King of *Lo-thian*. But heer *Simeon* the relater seems to have committed some mistake, having slain *Uthred* by *Canute* two years before, and set *Eric* in his place : *Eric* therfore it must needs be, not *Uthred*, who manag'd this Warr a-gainst the *Scots*. About which time in a Con-vention of *Danes* at *Oxford*, it was agreed on both Parties to keep the Laws of *Edgar*; *Mat. West.* saith, of *Edward* the Elder. The next year *Canute* sail'd into *Denmarke*, and there abode all Winter. *Huntingdon* and *Mat. West.* say, he went thether to repress the *Swedes*, and that the night before a Battel to be fought with them, *Godwin* stealing out of the Camp with his *English*, assaulted the *Swedes*, and had got the Victory ere *Canute* in the morning knew of any fight. For which bold enter-prise, though against Discipline, he had the *English* in more esteem ever after. In the Spring at his return into *England*, he held in the time of *Easter* a great Assembly at *Chir-chester*, and the same year was with *Turkill* the *Dane* at the Dedication of a Church by them built at *Assendune*, in the place of that great Victory which won him the Crown. But suspecting his Greatness, the year following banish'd him the Realm, and found occasion to do the like by *Eric* the *Northumbrian* Earl upon the same jealousie. Nor yet content with his Conquest of *England*, though now a-bove ten years enjoy'd, he pass'd with fifty Ships into *Norway*, dispossess'd *Olave* their King, and subdu'd the Land, first with great

1019.
Sim. Dun.

'1020.
Sim. Dun.

1021.
Sim. Dun.
Malmsb.
1028.
Sim. Dun.

summes

summes of money sent the year before to gain him a Party, then coming with an Army to

1029.
Sim. Dun.

compell the rest. Thence returning King of *England, Denmarke,* and *Norway,* yet not secure in his mind, under colour of an Embassey he sent into banishment *Hacun* a powerfull *Dane,* who had married the Daughter of his Sister *Gunildis,* having conceav'd some suspicion of his practices against him : but such course was tak'n, that he never came back; either perishing at Sea, or slain by contrivance the next year in *Orkney.* *Canute*

1030.
Sim. Dun.
1031.
Sim. Dun.

therefore having thus establish't himself by bloodshed and oppression, to wash away, as he thought, the guilt thereof, sailing again into *Denmarke,* went thence to *Rome,* and offer'd there to St *Peter* great guifts of Gold and Silver, and other precious things; besides the usual Tribute of *Romscot,* giving

Hunting.

great Alms by the way, both thether and back again, freeing many places of Custome and Toll with great expence, where strangers were wont to pay, having vow'd great amendment of life at the Sepulchre of *Peter* and *Paul,* and to his whole People in a large

1032.
Sim. Dun.

Letter writt'n from *Rome* yet extant. At his return therefore he built and dedicated a Church to St *Edmund* at *Bury,* whom his Ancestors had slain, threw out the Secular Priests who had intruded there, and plac'd Monks in thir stead; then going into *Scotland,*

Hunting.
1035.
Sim. Dun.

subdu'd and receav'd homage of *Malcolm,* and two other Kings there, *Melbeath,* and *Jermare.* Three years after having

made

made *Swane* his suppos'd Son by *Algiva* of
Northampton, Duke *Alfhelms* Daughter (for
others say the Son of a Priest whom *Algiva*
barren had got ready at the time of her feign-
ed labour) King of *Norway*, and *Hardecnute* *Florent.*
his Son by *Emma* King of *Denmarke*, and design'd *Harold* his Son by *Algiva* of *Northampton* King of *England*, dy'd at *Shaftsbury*, and
was buried at *Winchester* in the old Monastery.
This King, as appears, ended better than he *Florent.*
began, for though he seems to have had no
hand in the death of *Ironside*, but detested the
fact, and bringing the murderers, who came
to him in hope of great reward, forth among
his Courtiers, as it were to receave thanks,
after they had op'nly related the manner of
thir killing him, deliver'd them to deserved
punishment, yet he spar'd *Edric* whom he
knew to be the prime Authour of that dete-
stable fact; till willing to be rid of him,
grown importune upon the confidence of his
Merits, and upbraided by him that he had
first relinquisht, then extinguisht *Edmund* for
his sake; angry to be so upbraided, therfore
said he with a chang'd countnance, Traytor
to God and to me, thou shalt die; thine own
mouth accuses thee to have slain thy Master
my Confederate Brother, and the Lords A-
nointed.   Whereupon although present and *Malmsb.*
privat Execution was in rage done upon *Edric*,
yet he himself in cool blood scrupl'd not to
make away the Brother and Childern of *Edmund*, who had better right to be the Lords
Anointed heer than himself.   When he had
obtain'd

obtain'd in *England* what he defir'd, no wonder if he fought the Love of his conquer'd Subjects for the love of his own quiet, the maintainers of his Wealth and State, for his own profit. For the like reafon he is thought to have married *Emma*, and that *Richard* Duke of *Normandy* her Brother might the lefs care what became of *Elfred* and *Edward*, her Sons by King *Ethelred*. He commanded to be obferv'd the Ancient *Saxon* Laws, call'd afterwards the Laws of *Edward* the Confeffor, not that he made them, but ftrictly obferv'd them. His Letter from *Rome* profeffes, if he had done aught amifs in his Youth, through negligence or want of due temper, full refolution with the help of God to make amends, by governing juftly and pioufly for the future; charges and adjures all his Officers and Vicounts, that neither for Fear of him, or Favour of any perfon, or to enrich the King, they fuffer injuftice to be done in the Land; commands his Treafurers to pay all his Debts ere his return home, which was by *Denmark*, to compofe matters there; and what his Letter profefs'd, he perform'd all his life after. But it is a fond conceit in many great Ones, and pernicious in the end, to ceafe from no violence till they have attain'd the utmoft of their ambitions and defires; then to think God appeas'd by their feeking to bribe him with a fhare however large of their ill-gott'n fpoils, and then laftly to grow zealous of doing right, when they have no longer need to do wrong. Howbeit *Canute* was Famous through

through Europe, and much honour'd of Conrade the Emperour, then at Rome, with rich guifts and many grants of what he there demanded for the freeing of paſſages from Toll and Cuſtome. I muſt not omit one remarkable action done by him, as Huntingdon reports it, with great Scene of circumſtance, and emphatical expreſſion, to ſhew the ſmall Power of Kings in reſpect of God; which, unleſs to Court-Paraſites, needed no ſuch laborious demonſtration. He caus'd his Royal Seat to be ſet on the ſhoar, while the Tide was coming in; and with all the State that Royalty could put into his countnance, ſaid thus to the Sea: Thou Sea belongſt to me, and the Land wheron I ſit is mine; nor hath any one unpuniſh't reſiſted my Commands: I charge thee come no furder upon my Land, neither preſume to wet the Feet of thy Sovran Lord. But the Sea, as before, came rowling on, and without reverence both wet and daſhed him. Wherat the King quickly riſeing, wiſh'd all about him to behold and conſider the weak and frivolous Power of a King, and that none indeed deſerv'd the name of a King, but he whoſe Eternal Laws both Heav'n, Earth, and Sea obey. A truth ſo evident of it ſelf, as I ſaid before, that unleſs to ſhame his Court Flatterers who would not elſe be convin't, Canute needed not to have gone wet-ſhod home: The beſt is, from that time forth he never would wear a Crown, eſteeming Earthly Royalty contemptible and vain.

Harold.

Harold.

Florent.
Bromton.
Hunting.
Mat. West.

Mat. West.

Encom.Em.

1036.
Sim. Dun.

Harold for his swiftness surnam'd *Hare-foot*, the Son of *Canute* by *Algiva* of *Northampton* (though some speak doubtfully as if she bore him not, but had him of a Shoomakers Wife, as *Swane* before of a Priest; others of a Maid-Servant, to conceal her barrenness) in a great Assembly at *Oxford*, was by Duke *Leofric* and the *Mercians*, with the *Londoners*, according to his Fathers Testament, elected King; but without the Regal Habiliments, which *Ælnot* the Arch-bishop having in his Custody, refus'd to deliver up, but to the Sons of *Emma*, for which *Harold* ever after hated the Clergy; and (as the Clergy are wont thence to inferr) all Religion. *Godwin* Earl of *Kent*, and the *West-Saxons* with him, stood for *Hardecnute*. *Malmsbury* saith, that the Contest was between *Dane* and *English*; that the *Danes* and *Londoners* grown now in a manner *Danish*, were all for *Hardecnute*; but he being then in *Denmarke*, *Harold* prevail'd, yet so as that the Kingdome should be divided between them; the West and South part reserv'd by *Emma* for *Hardecnute*, till his return. But *Harold* once advan't into the Throne, banish'd *Emma* his Mother-in-law, seis'd on his Fathers Treasure at *Winchester*, and there remain'd. *Emma* not holding it safe to abide in *Normandy* while Duke *William* the Bastard was yet under Age,

retir'd

retir'd to *Baldwin* Earl of *Flanders*. In the
mean while *Alfred* and *Edward* Sons of *Ethelred*, accompanied with a small number of
Norman Souldiers in a few Ships, coming to
visit their Mother *Emma* not yet departed
the Land, and perhaps to see how the People
were inclin'd to restore them their Right;
Elfred was sent for by the King then at *London*; but in his way met at *Guilford* by Earl
Godwin, who with all seeming friendship entertain'd him, was in the night surpris'd and
made Prisner, most of his Company put to
various sorts of cruel death, decimated twice
over, then brought to *London*, was by the
King sent bound to *Eely*, had his Eyes put
out by the way, and deliver'd to the Monks
there, dy'd soon after in thir Custody. *Malmsbury* gives little credit to this Story of *Elfred*, as not Chronicl'd in his time, but rumour'd only. Which *Emma* however hearing, sent away her Son *Edward*, who by good
hap accompanied not his Brother, with all
speed into *Normandy*. But the Authour of
Encomium Emmæ, who seems plainly (though
nameless) to have been some Monk, yet
liv'd, and perhaps wrote within the same
year when these things were done; by his
relation differing from all others, much ag-
gravates the cruelty of *Harold*, that he not
content to have practis'd in secret (for op'n-
ly he durst not) against the life of *Emma*,
sought many treacherous wayes to get her
Son within his Power; and resolv'd at length
to forge a Letter in the name of their Mother,

ther, inviting them into *England*, the Copy of which Letter he produces writt'n to this purpose.

EMma *in name only Queen, to her Sons* Edward *and* Alfrid *imparts Motherly Salutation. While we severally bewail the death of our Lord the King, most Dear Sons, and while daily ye are depriv'd more and more of the Kingdome your Inheritance* ; *I admire what Counsel yee take, knowing that your intermitted delay; is a daily strengthning to the Reign of your Usurper, who incessantly goes about from Town to City, gaining the Chief Nobles to his Party, either by Gifts, Prayers, or Threats. But they had much rather one of you should Reign over them, than to be held under the Power of him who now Over-rules them. I entreat therefore that one of you come to me speedily, and privately* ; *to receive from me wholesome Counsel, and to know how the business which I intend shall be accomplisht. By this Messenger present, send back what you determine. Farewell, as dear both as my own Heart.*

These Letters were sent to the Princes then in *Normandy*, by express Messengers, with Presents also as from their Mother ; which they joyfully receiving, return word by the same Messengers, that one of them will be with her shortly ; naming both the time and place. *Alfrid* therefore the younger (for so it was thought best) at the appointed time, with a few Ships and small numbers

about

about him appearing on the Coast, no sooner came ashore but fell into the snare of Earl *Godwin*, sent on purpose to betray him; as above was related. *Emma* greatly sorrowing for the loss of her Son, thus cruelly made away, fled immediatly with some of the Nobles her faithfullest adherents into *Flanders*, had her dwelling assign'd at *Bruges* by the Earl; where having remain'd about two years, she was visited out of *Denmarke* by *Hardecnute* her Son; and he not long had remain'd with her there, when *Harold* in *England*, having done nothing the while worth memory, save the Taxing of every Port at eight Marks of Silver to sixteen Ships, dy'd at *London*, some say at *Oxford*, and was buried at *Winchester*. After which, most of the Nobility, both *Danes* and *English* now agreeing, send Embassadors to *Hardecnute* still at *Bruges* with his Mother, entreating him to come and receave as his Right the Scepter, who before Midsomer came with sixty Ships, and many Souldiers out of *Denmark*.

1039.
Sim. Dun.

Hunting.
1040.
Sim. Dun.
Malmsb.

Hardecnute.

HArdecnute receav'd with Acclamation, and seated in the Throne, first call'd to mind the injuries done to him or his Mother *Emma* in the time of *Harold*; sent *Alfric* Arch-bishop of *Yorke*, *Godwin* and others, with *Troud* his Executioner to *London*, commanding them to dig up the body

X
of

of King *Harold*, and throw it into a Ditch; but by a fecond order, into the *Thames*. Whence tak'n up by a Fifherman, and convei'd to a Church-yard in *London*, belonging to the *Danes*, it was enterr'd again with honour. This done he levied a fore Tax, that eight Marks to every Rower, and twelve to every Officer in his Fleet fhould be paid throughout *England*; by which time they who were fo forward to call him over, had anough of him; for he, as they thought, had too much of theirs. After this he call'd to account *Godwin* Earl of *Kent*, and *Leving* Bifhop of *Worfter*, about the death of *Elfred* his half Brother, which *Alfric* the Arch-bifhop laid to thir charge; the King depriv'd *Leving* of his Bifhoprick, and gave it to his accufer: but the year following, pacifi'd with

Malmsb.   a round fumme reftor'd it to *Leving*. *Godwin* made his Peace by a fumptuous Prefent, a gally with a guilded ftem bravely rigg'd, and eighty Souldiers in her, every one with Bracelets of Gold on each Arm, weighing fixteen ounces, Helmet, Corflet, and Hilts of his Sword guilded; a *Danifh* Curtax lifted with Gold or Silver, hung on his left fhoulder, a Shield with bofs and nailes guilded in his left hand, in his right a Launce: befides this, he took his Oath before the King, that neither of his own counfel or will, but by the command of *Harold* he had done what he did, to the putting out of *Elfreds* Eyes. The like

1041.   Oath took moft of the Nobility for them-
Sim. Dun.   felves or in his behalf. The next year, *Hardecnute*

decnute fending his Houfecarles, fo they call'd
his Officers, to gather the Tribute impos'd;
two of them rigorous in their Office, were
flain at *Worfter* by the People; whereat the
King enrag'd, fent *Leofric* Duke of *Mercia*,
and *Seward* of *Northumberland*, with great
Forces and Commiffion to flay the Cittizens,
rifle and burn the City, waft the whole Province. Affrighted with fuch news, all the
People fled; the Countreymen whither they
could, the Cittizens to a fmall Iland in *Severn*, call'd *Beverege*, which they fortifi'd and
defended ftoutly, till Peace was granted them,
and freely to return home. But their City
they found fack't and burnt; wherewith the
King was appeas'd. This was commendable
in him, however cruel to others, that toward
his half Brethren, though Rivals of his Crown,
he fhew'd himfelf alwayes tenderly affection'd; as now towards *Edward*, who without fear came to him out of *Normandy*, and
with unfeigned kindnefs receav'd, remain'd
fafely and honourably in his Court. But *Har-*   1042.
decnute the year following, at a Feaft where-   *Sim. Dun.*
in *Ofgod* a great *Danifh* Lord gave his Daughter in Marriage at *Lambeth*, to *Prudon* another Potent *Dane*; in the midft of his mirth,
found and healthfull to fight, while he was
drinking fell down fpeechlefs, and fo dying,
was buried at *Winchefter* befide his Father. He
was it feems a great lover of good chere; fitting at Table four times a day, with great variety of Difhes, and fuperfluity to all Com-
mers. Whereas, faith *Huntingdon*, in our

Time

Time Princes in their Houses made but one meal a day. He gave his Sister *Gunildis*, a Virgin of rare Beauty, in marriage to *Henry* the *Alman* Emperour; and to send her forth pompously, all the Nobility contributed thir Jewels and richest Ornaments. But it may seem a wonder that our Historians, if they deserve that name, should in a matter so remarkable, and so neer thir own time, so much differ. *Huntingdon* relates against the credit of all other records, that *Hardecnute* thus dead, the *English* rejoycing at this unexpected riddance of the *Danish* yoke, sent over to *Elfrid* the Elder Son of *Emma* by King *Ethelred*, of whom we heard but now, that he dy'd Prisner at *Eely*, sent thether by *Harold* six years before; that he came now out of *Normandy*, with a great number of men to receave the Crown; that Earl *Godwin* aiming to have his Daughter Queen of *England* by marrying her to *Edward* a simple youth, for he thought *Elfred* of a higher Spirit than to accept her, perswaded the Nobles that *Elfred* had brought over too many *Normans*, had promis'd them Lands here, that it was not safe to suffer a Warlike and suttle Nation to take root in the Land, that these were to be so handl'd as none of them might dare for the future to flock hither, upon pretence of relation to the King; thereupon by common consent of the Nobles, both *Elfred* and his Company were dealt with as was above related; that they then sent for *Edward* out of *Normandy*, with hostages to be left there of

their

their faithfull intentions to make him King,
and their desires not to bring over with him
many *Normans*; that *Edward* at their call
came then first out of *Normandy*; whereas
all others agree that he came voluntarily over
to visit *Hardecnute*, as is before said, and was
remaining in the Court at the time of his
death. For *Hardecnute* dead, saith *Malmsbury*, *Edward* doubting greatly his own safety, determin'd to rely wholly on the advice
and favour of Earl *Godwin*, desiring therfore
by Messengers to have private speech with
him, the Earl a while deliberated: at last af-
senting, Prince *Edward* came, and would
have fall'n at his feet; but that not permitted, told him the danger wherein he thought
himself at present, and in great perplexity
besought his help to convey him some whither out of the Land. *Godwin* soon apprehending the fair occasion that now as it were
prompted him how to advance himself and
his Family, cherfully exhorted him to remember himself the Son of *Ethelred*, the Grand-
child of *Edgar*, right Heir to the Crown, at
full Age; not to think of flying but of reigning, which might easily be brought about if
he would follow his Counsel; then setting
forth the Power and Authority which he had
in *England*, promis'd it should be all his to
set him on the Throne, if he on his part would
promise and swear to be for ever his friend,
to preserve the honour of his House, and to
marry his Daughter. *Edward*, as his necessity then was, consented easily, and swore to

whatever

whatever *Godwin* requir'd. An Assembly of
States thereupon met *Gillingham*, where *Edward* pleaded his right; and by the powerful
influence of *Godwin* was accepted. Others,
as *Bromton*, with no probability write, that
Godwin at this time was fled into *Denmarke*,
for what he had done to *Elfred*, return'd and
submitted himself to *Edward* then King, was
by him charg'd op'nly with the death of *Elfred*, and not without much ado, by the intercession of *Leofric* and other Peers, receav'd
at length into favour.

Edward the Confessor.

GLad were the *English* deliver'd so unexpectedly from their *Danish* Maisters,
and little thought how neer another Conquest
was hanging over them. *Edward*, the *Easter*
following, Crown'd at *Winchester*, the same
year accompanied with Earl *Godwin*, *Leofric*,
and *Siward*, came again thether on a sudden,
and by their Counsel seis'd on the Treasure of
his Mother *Emma*. The cause alleg'd is, that
she was hard to him in the time of his banishment; and indeed she is said not much to
have lov'd *Ethelred* her former Husband, and
therafter the Childern by him; she was moreover noted to be very covetous, hard to the
poor, and profuse to Monasteries. About
this time also King *Edward*, according to promise, took to Wife *Edith* or *Egith* Earl *Godwins* Daughter, commended much for Beauty,

margin notes:
1043.
Sim. Dun.

Malmsb.

ty, Modesty, and, beyond what is requisite in a Woeman, Learning. *Ingulf* then a youth lodging in the Court with his Father, saw her oft, and coming from the School, was sometimes met by her and pos'd, not in Grammar only, but in Logic. *Edward* the next year but one, made ready a strong Navy at *Sandwich* against *Magnus* King of *Norway*, who threat'nd an Invasion; had not *Swane* King of *Denmarke* diverted him by a War at home to defend his own Land, not out of good will to *Edward*, as may be suppos'd, who at the same time expres'd none to the *Danes*, banishing *Gunildis* the Neece of *Canute* with her two Sons, and *Osgod* by sirname *Clapa*, out of the Realm. *Swane* overpowred by *Magnus*, sent the next year to entreat Aid of King *Edward*; *Godwin* gave counsel to send him fifty Ships fraught with Souldiers; but *Leofric* and the general voice gain-saying, none were sent. The next year *Harold Harvager* King of *Norway* sending Embassadors, made Peace with King *Edward*; but an Earthquake at *Worster* and *Darby*, Pestilence and Famine in many places, much lesse'nd the enjoyment thereof. The next year *Henry* the Emperour displeas'd with *Baldwin* Earl of *Flanders*, had streit'nd him with a great Army by Land; and sending to King *Edward*, desir'd him with his Ships to hinder what he might, his escape by Sea. The King therfore with a great Navy coming to *Sandwich*, there staid till the Emperour came to an agreement with Earl *Baldwin*. Mean while

1045.
Sim. Dun.

1046.
Sim. Dun.

1047.
Sim. Dun.

1048.
Sim. Dun.

1049.
Sim. Dun.

while *Swane* Son of Earl *Godwin*, who not permitted to marry *Edgiva* the Abbeſs of *Cheſter* by him deflour'd, had left the Land, came out of *Denmarke* with eight Ships, feigning a deſire to return into the Kings favour ; and *Beorn* his Couſin German, who commanded part of the Kings Navy, promis'd to intercede that his Earldome might be reſtor'd him. *Godwin* therfore and *Beorn* with a few Ships, the reſt of the Fleet gone home, coming to *Pevenſey* (but *Godwin* ſoon departing thence in perſuit of twenty nine *Daniſh* Ships who had got much booty on the Coaſt of *Eſſex*, and periſh'd by tempeſt in their return) *Swane* with his Ships comes to *Beorn* at *Pevenſey*, guilefully requeſts him to ſail with him to *Sandwich*, and reconcile him to the King, as he had promis'd. *Beorn* miſtruſting no evil where he intended good, went with him in his Ship attended by three only of his Servants : but *Swane* ſet upon barbarous cruelty, not reconciliation with the King, took *Beorn* now in his power and bound him ; then coming to *Dertmouth*, ſlew and buried him in a deep Ditch. After which, the men of *Haſtings* took ſix of his Ships and brought them to the King at *Sandwich* ; with the other two he eſcap'd into *Flanders*, there remaining till *Aldred* Biſhop of *Worſter* by earneſt mediation wrought his Peace with the King. About this time King *Edward* ſent to Pope *Leo*, deſiring abſolution from a vow, which he had made in his younger years, to take a journey to *Rome*, if God voutſaf'd him to Reign in *England* ;

Mat. Weſt.

gland ;

gland; the Pope difpenc'd with his Vow, but not without the expence of his journey giv'n to the poor, and a Monaftery built or re edifi'd to St *Peter* : who in a Vifion to a Monk, as is faid, chofe *Weftminfter*, which King *Edward* thereupon rebuilding endow'd with large privileges and revennues. The fame year, faith *Florent* of *Worfter*, certain *Irifh* Pirats with thirty fix Ships enter'd the mouth of *Severn*, and with the Aid of *Griffin* Prince of *South-Wales*, did fome hurt in thofe parts : then paffing the River *Wey*, burnt *Dunedham*, and flew all the Inhabitants they found. Againft whom *Aldred* Bifhop of *Worfter*, with a few out of *Glofter* and *Herefordfhire*, went out in haft : but *Griffin* to whom the *Welfh* and *Irifh* had privily fent Meffengers, came down upon the *Englifh* with his whole power by night, and early in the morning fuddenly affaulting them, flew many, and put the reft to flight. The next year but one, King *Edward* remitted the *Danifh* Tax, which had continu'd thirty eight years heavy upon the Land fince *Ethelred* firft paid it to the *Danes*, and what remain'd thereof in his treafury he fent back to the owners : but through imprudence laid the foundation of a far worfe mifchief to the *Englifh*; while ftudying gratitude to thofe *Normans*, who to him in exile had bin helpfull; he call'd them over to public Offices here, whom better he might have repaid out of his private purfe ; by this means exafperating either Nation one againft the other, and making way by degrees to the *Norman* Conqueft.

1051.

Sim. Dun.

Ingulf.

Conqueſt. *Robert* a Monk of that Country, who had bin ſerviceable to him there in time of need, he made Biſhop, firſt of *London*, then of *Canterbury*; *William* his Chaplain Biſhop of *Dorcheſter*. Then began the *Engliſh* to lay aſide thir own Ancient Cuſtomes, and in many things to imitate *French* Manners, the great Peers to ſpeak *French* in thir Houſes, in *French* to write thir Bills and Letters, as a great piece of Gentility, aſham'd of thir own: a preſage of thir ſubjection ſhortly to that people, whoſe Faſhions and Language they affected ſo ſlaviſhly: But that which gave beginning to many Troubles enſueing, happ'nd this year, and upon this occaſion. *Euſtace* Earl of *Boloign*, Father of the Famous *Godfrey* who won *Jeruſalem* from the *Saracens*, and Husband to *Goda* the Kings Siſter, having bin to viſit King *Edward*, and returning by *Canterbury* to take Ship at *Dover*, one of his Harbingers inſolently ſeeking to lodge by Force in a Houſe there, provok'd ſo the Maſter thereof, as by chance or heat of anger to kill him. The Count with his whole Train going to the Houſe where his Servant had bin kill'd, ſlew both the ſlayer and eighteen more who defended him. But the Townſmen running to Arms, requited him with the ſlaughter of twenty one more of his Servants, wounded moſt of the reſt; he himſelf with one or two hardly eſcaping; ran back with clamour to the King; whom ſeconded by other *Norman* Courtiers, he ſtirr'd up to great anger againſt the Cittizens of *Canterbury*.

Earl

Ingulf.

Malmsb.

Earl *Godwin* in haft is fent for, the caufe related and much aggravated by the King againft
that City, the Earl commanded to raife Forces, and ufe the Cittizens thereof as Enemies.
Godwin, forry to fee Strangers more favour'd
of the King than his Native People, anfwer'd,
that it were better to fummon firft the Chief
Men of the Town into the Kings Court, to
charge them with Sedition, where both Parties might be heard, that not found in fault
they might be acquitted, if otherwife, by fine
or lofs of life might fatisfie the King whofe
peace they had brok'n, and the Count whom
they had injur'd; till this were done refufe-
ing to profecute with hoftile punifhment them
of his own Country unheard, whom his Office was rather to defend. The King difplea-
fed with his refufal, and not knowing how to
compell him, appointed an Affembly of all
the Peers to be held at *Glofter*, where the matter might be fully try'd; the Affembly was
full and frequent according to fummons; but
Godwin miftrufting his own Caufe, or the violence of his Adverfaries; with his two Sons,
Swane and *Harold*, and a great Power gather-
ed out of his own and his Sons Earldomes,
which contein'd moft of the South-Eaft and
Weft parts of *England*, came no furder than
Beverftan, giving out that their Forces were
to go againft the *Welfh*, who intended an irruption into *Herefordfhire*; and *Swane* under
that pretence lay with part of his Army therabout. The *Welfh* underftanding this device,
and with all diligence clearing themfelves before

fore the King, left *Godwin* detected of false
accusation in great hatred to all the Assembly. *Leofric* therefore and *Siward* Dukes of
great Power, the former in *Mercia*, the other in all parts beyond *Humber*, both ever
faithfull to the King, send privily with speed
to raise the Forces of thir Provinces. Which
Godwin not knowing, sent boldly to King *Edward*, demanding Count *Eustace* and his Followers, together with those *Boloignians*, who
as *Simeon* writes, held a Castle in the Jurisdiction of *Canterbury*. The King as then having but little Force at hand, entertain'd him
a while with treaties and delays, till his summon'd Army drew nigh, then rejected his
demands. *Godwin* thus match'd, commanded his Sons not to begin fight against the
King; begun with, not to give ground. The
Kings Forces were the flower of those Counties whence they came, and eager to fall on:
But *Leofric* and the wiser sort detesting Civil
War, brought the matter to this accord, that
Hostages giv'n on either side, the whole Cause
should be again debated at *London*. Thether
the King and Lords coming with thir Army,
sent to *Godwin* and his Sons (who with their
Powers were come as far as *Southwark*) commanding their appearance unarm'd with only twelve Attendants, and that the rest of
their Souldiers they should deliver over to
the King. They to appear without pledges
before an adverse faction deny'd; but to dismiss their Souldiers refus'd not, nor in ought
else to obey the King as far as might stand
with

Sim. Dun.

with honour and the juſt regard of thir ſafety. This anſwer not pleaſing the King, an
Edict was preſently iſſu'd forth, that *Godwin*
and his Sons within five dayes depart the
Land. He who perceav'd now his numbers
to diminiſh, readily obey'd, and with his
Wife and three Sons, *Toſti, Swane,* and *Gyrtha,* with as much Treaſure as their Ship
could carry, embarking at *Thorney,* ſail'd into *Flanders* to Earl *Baldwin,* whoſe Daughter *Judith Toſti* had married : for *Wulnod* his
fourth Son was then hoſtage to the King in
Normandy ; his other two, *Harold* and *Leofwin,* taking Ship at *Briſtow,* in a Veſſel that
lay ready there belonging to *Swane,* paſs'd
into *Ireland.* King *Edward* perſueing his diſpleaſure, divorc'd his Wife *Edith* Earl *Godwins* Daughter, ſending her deſpoil'd of all her
Ornaments to *Warewel* with one waiting Maid,
to be kept in cuſtody by his Siſter the Abbeſs there. His reaſon of ſo doing was as *Malmſb.*
harſh as his act, that ſhe only, while her near-
eſt Relations were in baniſhment, might not,
though innocent, enjoy eaſe at home. After
this, *William* Duke of *Normandy* with a great
number of Followers coming into *England,*
was by King *Edward* honourably entertain'd
and led about the Cities, and Caſtles, as it
were to ſhew him what ere long was to be
his own (though at that time, ſaith *Ingulf,*
no mention thereof paſs'd between them)
then after ſome time of his abode here, pre-
ſented richly and diſmiſs'd, he return'd home.
The next year Queen *Emma* dy'd, and was
buried

buried at *Winchester.* The Chronicle attributed to *John Bromton* a *Yorkshire* Abbot, but rather of some namelefs Author living under *Edward* the Third, or later, reports that the year before, by *Robert* the Arch-bishop she was accus'd both of confenting to the death of her Son *Alfred,* and of prepareing poyfon for *Edward* alfo; laftly of too much familiarity with *Alwin* Bishop of *Winchester*; that to approve her innocence, praying over-night to St *Swithun,* she offer'd to pafs blind-fold between certain Plow-shares red hot, according to the Ordalian Law, which without harm she perform'd; that the King therupon receav'd her to honour, and from her and the Bishop, penance for his credulity; that the Arch-bishop asham'd of his Accufation fled out of *England :* which befides the filence of Ancienter Authours (for the Bishop fled not till a year after) brings the whole ftory into fufpicion, in this more probable, if it can be proov'd, that in memory of this deliverance from the Nine burning Plowshares, Queen *Emma* gave to the Abbey of Saint *Swithune* nine Mannors, and Bishop *Alwin* other nine. About this time *Griffin* Prince of *South-Wales* wafted *Herefordshire*; to oppofe whom the People of that Country with many *Normans,* garrifond in the Caftle of *Hereford,* went out in Armes, but were put to the worfe, many flain, and much booty driv'n away by the *Welsh.* Soon after which, *Harold* and *Leofwin,* Sons of *Godwin,* coming into *Severn* with many Ships, in
the

the Confines of *Somerset* and *Dorsetshire*, spoil-
ed many Villages, and resisted by those of *Somerset* and *Devonshire*, slew in fight more
than thirty of thir pricipal men, many of the
common sort, and return'd with much booty
to thir Fleet.   King *Edward* on the other side *Malmsb.*
made ready above sixty Ships at *Sandwich*
well stor'd with Men and Provision, under the
Conduct of *Odo* and *Radulf* two of his *Norman*
Kindred, enjoyning them to find out *Godwin*,
whom he heard to be at Sea.   To quick'n
them, he himself lay on ship-board, oft-times
watch'd and sail'd up and down in search of
those Pirats.   But *Godwin*, whether in a mist,
or by other accident, passing by them, arri-
ved in another part of *Kent*, and dispersing
secret messengers abroad, by fair words allu-
red the Chief Men of *Kent*, *Sussex*, *Surrey*, and
Essex to his Party ; which news coming to the
Kings Fleet at *Sandwich*, they hasted to find
him out ; but missing of him again, came up
without effect to *London*.   *Godwin* advertis'd
of this, forthwith sail'd to the Ile of *Wight* ;
where at length his two Sons *Harold* and *Leofwin* finding him, with thir united Navy lay
on the Coast, forbearing other hostility than
to furnish themselves with fresh victual from
Land as they needed.   Thence as one Fleet
they set forward to *Sandwich*, using all fair
means by the way to encrease their numbers
both of Mariners and Souldiers.   The King
then at *London*, startl'd at these tydings, gave
speedy order to raise Forces in all parts which
had not revolted from him ; but now too late,
for

for *Godwin* within a few dayes after with his Ships or Gallies came up the River *Thames* to *Southwark*, and till the Tide return'd had conference with the *Londoners*; whom by fair speeches, for he was held a good Speaker in those times, he brought to his bent. The Tide returning, and none upon the Bridge hindring, he row'd up in his Gallies along the South bank; where his Land-army, now come to him, in array of battel stood on the shore, then turning toward the North side of the River, where the Kings Gallies lay in some readiness, and Land-forces also not far off, he made shew as offring to fight; but they understood one another, and the Souldiers on either side soon declar'd thir resolution not to fight *English* against *English*. Thence coming to Treaty, the King and the Earl reconcil'd, both Armies were dissolv'd, *Godwin* and his Sons restor'd to their former Dignities, except *Swane*, who touch't in conscience for the slaughter of *Beorn* his Kinsman, was gone barefoot to *Jerusalem*, and returning home, dy'd by sickness or *Saracens* in *Lycia*; his Wife *Edith*, *Godwins* Daughter, King *Edward* took to him again, dignify'd as before. Then were the *Normans*, who had done many unjust things under the Kings Authority, and giv'n him ill counsel against his People, banish't the Realm, some of them not blameable permitted to stay. *Robert* Arch-bishop of *Canterbury*, *William* of *London*, *Ulf* of *Lincoln*, all *Normans*, hardly escaping with thir followers, got to Sea. The Archbishop went with his complaint to *Rome*; but
returning,

returning, dy'd in *Normandy* at the same Monasterie from whence he came. *Osbern* and *Hugh* surrender'd thir Castles, and by permission of *Leofric* pass'd through his Counties with thir *Normans* to *Macbeth* King of *Scotland*. The year following *Rhese* Brother to *Griffin*, Prince of *South-Wales*, who by inrodes had done much damage to the *English*, tak'n at *Bulendun*, was put to death by the Kings appointment, and his head brought to him at *Glofter*. The same year at *Winchefter* on the second holy-day of *Eafter*, Earl *Godwin* fitting with the King at Table, funk down suddenly in his feat as dead : his three Sons *Harold*, *Tofti*, and *Gyrtha*, forthwith carried him into the Kings Chamber, hoping he might revive : but the malady had fo feis'd him, that the 5th day after he expir'd. The *Normans* who hated *Godwin* give out, faith *Malmsbury*, that mention happ'ning to be made of *Elfred*, and the King thereat looking fowerly upon *Godwin*, he to vindicate himfelf, utter'd thefe words, Thou, O King, at every mention made of thy Brother *Elfred*, look'ft frowningly upon me : but let God not fuffer me to fwallow this morfel, if I be guilty of ought done againft his life or thy advantage; that after thefe words, choak't with the morfel tak'n, he funk down and recover'd not. His firft Wife was the Sifter of *Canute*, a Woman of much infamy for the trade fhe drove of buying up *English* Youths and Maids to fell in *Denmark*, wherof fhe made great gain; but e're long was ftruck with thunder, and dy'd. The

1053.
Sim. Dun.

Y
year

1054.
Sim. Dun.

year enfuing, *Siward* Earl of *Northumberland*, with a great number of Horfe and Foot, attended alfo by a ftrong Fleet at the Kings appointment, made an expedition into *Scotland*, vanquifh't the Tyrant *Macbeth*, flaying many thoufands of *Scots* with thofe *Normans* that went thether, and plac'd *Malcolm* Son of the *Cumbrian* King in his ftead; yet not without lofs of his own Son, and many other both *English* and *Danes*. Told of his Sons death, he

Hunting.

afk'd whether he receav'd his deaths wound before or behind? when it was anfwer'd before, I am glad, faith he; and fhould not elfe have thought him, though my Son, worthy of Burial. In the mean while King *Edward* being without Iffue to fucceed him, fent *Aldred* Bifhop of *Winchefter* with great Prefents to the Emperour, entreating him to prevail with the King of *Hungary*, that *Edward* the remaining Son of his Brother *Edmund Ironfide*, might be

1055.
Sim. Dun.

fent into *England*. *Siward* but one year furviving his great Victory, dy'd at *York*; reported by *Huntingdon* a man of Giant like ftature, and by his own demeanour at point of death manifefted, of a rough and meer fouldierly mind. For much difdaining to die in bed by a difeafe, not in the field fighting with his enemies, he caus'd himfelf compleatly arm'd, and weapon'd with Battel-ax and Shield to be fet in a chair, whether to fight with death, if he could be fo vain, or to meet him (when far other weapons and preparations were needful) in a Martial bravery; but true fortitude glories not in the feats of War, as they

are

are such, but as they serve to end War soonest by a victorious Peace. His Earldom the King bestow'd on *Tosti* the Son of Earl *Godwin :* and soon after in a Convention held at *London,* banish'd without visible cause, *Huntingdon* saith for treason, *Algar* the Son of *Loofric ;* who passing into *Ireland,* soon return'd with eighteen ships to *Griffin* Prince of *South-Wales,* requesting his Aid against King *Edward.* He assembling his Powers, enter'd with him into *Hereford-shire ;* whom *Radulf* a timorous Captain, Son to the Kings Sister, not by *Eustace,* but a former Husband, met two miles distant from *Hereford ;* and having horsed the *English* who knew better to fight on foot, without stroke he with his *French* and *Normans* beginning to flie, taught the *English* by his example. *Griffin* and *Algar* following the chase, slew many, wounded more, enter'd *Hereford,* slew seven Canons defending the Minster, burnt the Monasterie and Reliques, then the City ; killing some, leading captive others of the Citizens, return'd with great spoils ; whereof King *Edward* having notice, gather'd a great Army at *Gloster* under the Conduct of *Harold* now Earl of *Kent ;* who strenuously pursuing *Griffin,* enter'd *Wales,* and encamp'd beyond *Straddale.* But the enemy flying before him farther into the Countrey, leaving there the greater part of his Army with such as had charge to fight, if occasion were offer'd, with the rest he return'd, and fortifi'd *Hereford* with a Wall and Gates. Mean while *Griffin* and *Algar* dreading the di-

ligence

ligence of *Harold*, after many messages to and fro, concluded a Peace with him. *Algar* discharging his Fleet with pay at *West-Chester*, came to the King, and was restor'd to his Earldom. But *Griffin* with breach of Faith, the

1056.
Sim. Dun.

next year set upon *Leofgar* the Bishop of *Hereford* and his Clerks then at a place call'd *Glastbrig* with *Agelnoth* Vicount of the Shire, and slew them; but *Leofric, Harold*, and King *Edward* by force, as is likeliest, though it be not said how, reduc'd him to Peace. The

1057.
Sim. Dun.

next year *Edward* Son of *Edmund Ironside*, for whom his Uncle King *Edward* had sent to the Emperour, came out of *Hungary*, design'd Successor to the Crown; but within a few dayes after his coming dy'd at *London*, leaving behind him *Edgar Atheling* his Son, *Margaret* and *Christina* his Daughters. About the same time also dy'd Earl *Leofric* in a good old age, a man of no less Vertue than Power in his time, Religious, Prudent and Faithful to his Country, happily wedded to *Godiva* a Woman

1058.
Sim. Dun.

of great praise. His Son *Algar* found less favour with King *Edward*, again banish't the year after his Fathers death; but he again by the aid of *Griffin*, and a Fleet from *Norway*, maugre the King, soon recover'd his Earldom.

1059.
Sim. Dun.

The next year *Malcolm* King of *Scots* coming to visit King *Edward*, was brought on his way by *Tosti* the *Northumbrian* Earl, to whom he

1061.
Sim. Dun.

swore Brotherhood: yet the next year but one, while *Tosti* was gone to *Rome* with *Aldred* Arch-bishop of *York* for his Pall, this sworn Brother taking advantage of his absence, roughly

roughly harrass'd *Northumberland*. The year passing to an end without other matter of moment, save the frequent inrodes and robberies of *Griffin*, whom no bonds of Faith could restrain, King *Edmard* sent against him after *Christmas Harold* now Duke of *West-Saxons* with no great body of Horse from *Gloster*, where he then kept his Court, whose coming heard of, *Griffin* not daring to abide, nor in any part of his Land holding himself secure, escap't hardly by Sea, e're *Harold* coming to *Rudeland*, burnt his Palace and Ships there, returning to *Gloster* the same day : But by the middle of *May* setting out with a Fleet from *Bristow*, he sail'd about the most part of *Wales*, and met by his Brother *Tosti* with many Troops of Horse, as the King had appointed, began to waste the Countrey ; but the *Welsh* giving pledges, yeilded themselves, promis'd to become tributary, and banish *Griffin* thir Prince ; who lurking somewhere, was the next year tak'n and slain by *Griffin* Prince of *North-Wales* ; his Head, with the head and tackle of his Ship sent to *Harold*, by him to the King, who of his gentleness made *Blechgent* and *Rithwallon* or *Rivallon* his two Brothers Princes in his stead ; they to *Harold* in behalf of the King swore Fealty and Tribute. Yet the next year *Harold* having built a fair house at a place call'd *Portascith* in *Monmouth-shire*, and stor'd it with provision, that the King might lodge there in time of hunting, *Caradoc* the Son of *Griffin* slain the year before, came with a number of men, slew all he found there, and took

1062.
Sim. Dun.

1063.
Sim. Dun.

1064.
Sim. Dun.

1065.
Sim. Dun.
Camden.

Y 3 away

away the provision. Soon after which the *Nor-thumbrians* in a tumult at *York*, beset the Palace of *Tosti* thir Earl, slew more than two hundred of his Souldiers and Servants, pillaged his Treasure, and put him to flie for his life. The cause of this Insurrection they alledg'd to be, for that the Queen *Edith* had commanded in her Brother *Tosti*'s behalf, *Gospatric* a Noble Man of that Countrey to be treacherously slain in the Kings Court; and that *Tosti* himself the year before with like treachery had caus'd to be slain in his Chamber *Gamel* and *Ulf* two other of thir Noble Men, besides his intolerable exactions and oppressions. Then in a manner the whole Country coming up to complain of thir grievances, met with *Harold* at *Northampton*, whom the King at *Tosti*'s request had sent to pacifie the *Northumbrians*; but they laying op'n the cruelty of his Government, and thir own birth-right of freedom not to endure the tyrannie of any Governour whatsoever, with absolute refusal to admit him again, and *Harold* hearing reason, all the accomplices of *Tosti* were expell'd the Earldom. He himself banish't the Realm, went into *Flanders*; *Morcar* the Son of *Algar* made Earl in his stead. *Huntingdon* tells another cause of *Tosti*'s banishment, that one day at *Windsor*, while *Harold* reach'd the Cup to King *Edward*, *Tosti* envying to see his younger Brother in greater favour than himself, could not forbear to run furiously upon him, catching hold of his Hair, the scuffle was soon parted by other attendants rushing

rushing between, and *Tosti* forbidd'n the Court. He with continu'd fury rideing to *Hereford*, where *Harold* had many Servants, preparing an entertainment for the King, came to the House and set upon them with his followers; then lopping off Hands, Arms, Legs of some, Heads of others, threw them into Butts of Wine, Meath, or Ale, which were laid in for the Kings drinking : and at his going away charg'd them to send him this word, that of other fresh meats he might bring with him to his Farm what he pleas'd, but of Sous he should find plenty provided ready for him : that for this barbarous Act the King pronounced him banisht ; that the *Northumbrians* taking advantage at the Kings displeasure and sentence against him, rose also to be reveng'd of his cruelties done to themselves; but this no way agrees, for why then should *Harold* or the King so much labour with the *Northumbrians* to re-admit him, if he were a banisht man for his Crimes done before ? About this time it happ'd that *Harold* putting to Sea one *Malmsb.* day for his pleasure, in a Fisher Boat, from his Mannor at *Boseham* in *Sussex*, caught with a Tempest too far off Land, was carried into *Normandy* ; and by the Earl of *Pontiew*, on whose Coast he was drv'n, at his own request brought to Duke *William* ; who entertaining him with great courtesie, so far won him, as to promise the Duke by Oath of his own accord, not only the Castle of *Dover* then in his tenure, but the Kingdom also after King *Edwards* death to his utmost endeavour, therup-

on

on betrothing the Dukes Daughter then too young for marriage, and departing richly presented. Others fay, that King *Edward* himself after the death of *Edward* his Nephew, sent *Harold* thether, on purpose to acquaint Duke *William* with his intention to bequeath him his Kingdom : but *Malmsbury* accounts the former story to be the truer. *Ingulf* writes, that King *Edward* now grown old, and perceaving *Edgar* his Nephew both in body and mind unfit to Govern, especially against the pride and insolence of *Godwins* Sons, who would never obey him ; Duke *William* on the other side of high Merit, and his Kinsman by the Mother, had sent *Robert* Arch-bishop of *Canterbury*, to acquaint the Duke with his purpose, not long before *Harold* came thether. The former part may be true, that King *Edward* upon such considerations had sent one or other ; but Arch-bishop *Robert* was fled the Land, and dead many years before. *Eadmer* and *Simeon* write, that *Harold* went of his own accord into *Normandy*, by the Kings permission or connivence, to get free his Brother *Wulnod* and Nephew *Hacun* the Son of *Swane*, whom the King had tak'n hostages of *Godwin* and sent into *Normandy*; that King *Edward* foretold *Harold*, his journey thether would be to the detriment of all *England* and his own reproach ; that Duke *William* then acquainted *Harold*, how *Edward* e're his coming to the Crown had promis'd, if ever he attain'd it, to leave Duke *William* Successor after him. Last of these *Mathew Paris* writes, that *Harold*

Leges Ed.
Conf. Tit.
Lex Noric.

rold

rold to get free of Duke *William*, affirm'd his coming thether not to have bin by accident or force of Tempeſt, but on ſet purpoſe, in that private manner to enter with him into ſecret confederacie; ſo variouſly are theſe things reported. After this King *Edward* grew ſickly, yet as he was able kept his *Chriſtmas* at *London*, and was at the Dedication of Sᵗ *Peter*'s Church in *Weſtminſter*, which he had rebuilt; but on the Eve of *Epiphanie*, or *Twelftide*, deceas'd much lamented, and in the Church was Entoomb'd. That he was harmleſs and ſimple, is conjectur'd by his words in anger to a Peaſant who had croſs'd his Game (for with Hunting and Hawking he was much delighted) By God and Gods Mother, ſaid he, I ſhall do you as ſhrew'd a turn if I can; obſerving that Law-Maxime, the beſt of all his Succeſſors, that the King of *England* can do no wrong. The ſoftneſs of his Nature gave growth to Factions of thoſe about him, *Normans* eſpecially and *Engliſh*; theſe complaining that *Robert* the Arch-biſhop was a ſower of diſſention between the King and his People, a traducer of the *Engliſh*; the other ſide, that *Godwin* and his Sons bore themſelves arrogantly and proudly towards the King, Uſurping to themſelves equall ſhare in the Government; oft-times making ſport with his ſimplicity, that through their Power in the Land, they made no ſcruple to kill men of whoſe Inheritance they took a likeing, and ſo to take poſſeſſion. The truth is, that *Godwin* and his Sons did many things boiſtrouſly

and

1066.

Sim. Dun.

Hunting.

and violently, much against the Kings mind; which not able to resist, he had, as some say, his Wife *Edith Godwins* Daughter in such a-versation, as in bed never to have touch'd her; whether for this cause or mistak'n Chastitie, not commendable; to enquire further is not material. His Lawes held good and just, and long after desir'd by the *English* of thir *Norman* Kings, are yet extant. He is said to be at Table not excessive, at Festivals nothing puft up with the costly Robes he wore, which his Queen with curious Art had woven for him in Gold. He was full of Alms-deeds, and exhorted the Monks to like Charitie. He is said to be the first of *English* Kings that cur'd the Disease call'd thence the Kings Evil; yet *Malmsbury* blames them who attribute that Cure to his Royaltie, not to his Sanctitie; said also to have cur'd certain blind men with the water wherin he had wash'd his hands. A little before his death, lying speechless two days, the third day after a deep sleep, he was heard to pray, that if it were a true Vision, not an Illusion which he had seen, God would give him strength to utter it, otherwise not. Then he related how he had seen two devout Monks, whom he knew in *Normandy*, to have liv'd and dy'd well, who appearing told him they were sent Messengers from God to foretell, that because the great Ones of *England*, Dukes, Lords, Bishops, and Abbots, were not Ministers of God but of the Devil, God had deliver'd the Land to thir Enemies; and when

he

he desir'd that he might reveal this Vision, to the end they might repent, it was answer'd; they neither will repent, neither will God pardon them; at this relation others trembling, *Stigand* the Simonious Arch-bishop, whom *Edward* much to blame had suffer'd many years to sit Primate in the Church, is said to have laught, as at the feavourish Dream of a doteing Old Man; but the event prov'd it true.

Harold Son of Earl *Godwin.*

Harold, whether by King *Edward* a little before his death ordain'd Successor to the Crown, as *Simeon* of *Durham,* and others affirm; or by the prevalence of his Faction, excluding *Edgar* the right Heir, Grandchild to *Edmund Ironside,* as *Malmsbury* and *Huntingdon* agree, no sooner was the Funeral of King *Edward* ended, but on the same day was Elected and Crown'd King : and no sooner plac't in the Throne, but began to frame himself by all manner of compliances to gain affection, endeavour'd to make good Laws, repeal'd bad, became a great Patron to Church and Church-men, courteous and affable to all reputed good, a hater of evil doers, charg'd all his Officers to punish Theeves, Robbers, and all disturbers of the Peace, while he himself by Sea and Land labour'd in the defence of his Countrey : so good an actor is ambition. In the mean while

Hoved.

Florent.

a blazing

a blazing Star, feven Mornings together, about the end of *April*, was feen to ftream terribly, not only over *England*, but other parts of the World; foretelling heer, as was thought, the great Changes approaching: plainlieft prognofticated by *Elmer* a Monk of *Malmsbury*, who could not forefee, when time was, the breaking of his own Legs for foaring too high. He in his youth ftrangely afpiring, had made and fitted Wings to his Hands and Feet; with thefe on the top of a Tower, fpread out to gather Air, he flew more than a Furlong; but the wind being too high, came fluttering down, to the maiming of all his Limbs; yet fo conceited of his Art, that he attributed the caufe of his fall to the want of a Tail, as Birds have, which he forgot to make to his hinder parts. This ftory, though feeming otherwife too light in the midft of a fad narration, yet for the ftrangenefs thereof, I thought worthy anough the placing as I found it plac't in my Authour. But to digrefs no farder, *Tofti* the Kings Brother coming from *Flanders*, full of Envy at his younger Brothers advancement to the Crown, refolv'd what he might to trouble his Reign; forcing therfore them of *Wight Ile* to Contribution, he fail'd thence to *Sandwich*, committing Piracies on the Coaft between. *Harold* then refiding at *London*, with a great number of Ships drawn together, and of Horfe Troops by Land, prepares in

Malmsb. perfon for *Sandwich*: whereof *Tofti* having notice, directs his courfe with fixty Ships towards *Lindfey*, taking with him all the Seamen

men he found, willing or unwilling : where
he burnt many Villages, and flew many of the
Inhabitants ; but *Edwin* the *Mercian* Duke,
and *Morcar* his Brother, the *Northumbrian*
Earl, with thir Forces on either fide, foon
drove him out of the Countrey. Who thence
betook him to *Malcolm* the *Scottifh* King, and
with him abode the whole Summer. About
the fame time Duke *William* fending Embaffadors to admonifh *Harold* of his Promife and
Oath, to affift him in his Plea to the Kingdom, he made anfwer, that by the death of
his Daughter betroth'd to him on that condition, he was abfolv'd of his Oath, or not   *Eadmer.*
dead, he could not take her now an Out-
landifh woman, without confent of the Realm ;
that it was prefumptuoufly done, and not to
be perfifted in, if without confent or knowledge of the States, he had fworn away the
right of the Kingdome ; that what he fwore
was to gain his Liberty, being in a manner
then his Prifner ; that it was unreafonable in
the Duke to require or expect of him the
foregoing of a Kingdome, conferr'd upon him
with univerfal favour and acclamation of the
People : To this flat denial he added contempt, fending the Meffengers back, faith
Mathew Paris, on maim'd Horfes. The Duke
thus contemptuoufly put off, addreffes himfelf to the Pope, fetting forth the Juftice of
his Caufe, which *Harold*, whether through
haughtinefs of mind, or diftruft, or that the
wayes to *Rome* were ftop'd, fought not to do.
Duke *William*, befides the Promife and Oath
of

of *Harold*, alledg'd that King *Edward* by the advice of *Seward*, *Godwin* himself, and *Stigand* the Arch-bishop, had given him the Right of Succession, and had sent him the Son and Nephew of *Godwin*, pledges of the guift; the Pope sent to Duke *William*, after this demonstration of his Right, a Consecrated Banner. Wherupon he having with great care and choice got an Army of tall and stout Souldiers, under Captains of great skill and mature Age, came in *August* to the Port of St *Valerie*. Mean while *Harold* from *London* comes to *Sandwich*, there expecting his Navy; which also coming, he sails to the *Ile* of *Wight*; and having heard of Duke *William*'s preparations and readiness to invade him, kept good watch on the Coast, and Foot Forces every where in fit places to guard the shoar. But e're the middle of *September*, provision failing when it was most needed, both Fleet and Army return home. When on a sudden, *Harold Harvager* King of *Norway*, with a Navy of more than five hunderd great Ships, (others less'n them by two hunderd, others augment them to a thousand) appears at the mouth of *Tine*; to whom Earl *Tosti* with his Ships came as was agreed between them; whence both uniting, set sail with all speed, and enter'd the River *Humber*. Thence turning into *Ouse*, as far as *Rical*, landed; and won *Torke* by assault. At these tideings *Harold* with all his Power hasts thetherward; but e're his coming, *Edwin* and *Morcar* at *Fulford* by *Torke*, on the North side of *Ouse*, about the Feast

Malmsb.
Mathew
Paris.

Feaſt of St *Mathew* had giv'n them Battel; ſucceſsfully at firſt, but over-born at length with
numbers, and forc't to turn their backs,
more of them periſh'd in the River, than in
the Fight. The *Norwegians* taking with them
five hunderd Hoſtages out of *York*, and leaving there one hundred and fifty of their own,
retir'd to their Ships. But the fifth day after, King *Harold* with a great and well appointed Army, coming to *York*, and at *Stam-* *Camden.*
ford-Bridge, or *Battell*-Bridge on *Darwent*,
aſſailing the *Norwegians*, after much blood-
ſhed on both ſides, cut off the greateſt part
of them with *Harfager* their King, and *To-*
ſti his own Brother. But *Olave* the Kings
Son, and *Paul* Earl of *Orkney*, left with many Souldiers to guard the Ships, ſurrendring
themſelves with Hoſtages and Oath giv'n never to return as Enemies, he ſuffer'd freely
to depart with twenty Ships, and the ſmall
remnant of their Army. One man of the *Malmsb.*
Norwegians is not to be forgott'n, who with
incredible valour keeping the Bridge a long
hour againſt the whole *Engliſh* Army, with
his ſingle reſiſtance delai'd their Victorie;
and ſcorning offer'd life, till in the end no
man dareing to graple with him, either dreaded as too ſtrong, or contemned as one de-
ſperate, he was at length ſhot dead with an
Arrow; and by his fall op'nd the paſſage of
perſuit to a compleat Victorie. Wherewith
Harold lifted up in minde, and forgetting
now his former ſhews of popularitie, defrauded his Souldiers their due, and well deſerved
ſhare

share of the spoils. While these things thus
past in *Northumberland*, Duke *William* lay still
at Saint *Valerie*; his Ships were readie, but
the wind serv'd not for many days; which put
the Souldierie into much discouragement and
murmur, taking this for an unlucky signe of
thir success; at last the wind came favourable,
the Duke first under sail awaited the rest at
Anchor, till all coming forth, the whole Fleet
of nine hunderd Ships, with a prosperous

Sim. Dun. gale arriv'd at *Hastings.* At his going out
of the Boat by a slip falling on his hands, to
correct the Omen, a Souldier standing by
said aloud, that their Duke had tak'n possession of *England.* Landed, he restrein'd his
Army from waste and spoil, saying, that they
ought to spare what was thir own. But these
are things related of *Alexander* and *Cæsar*,
and I doubt thence borrow'd by the Monks
to inlay their Story. The Duke for fifteen
dayes after landing kept his Men quiet within the Camp, having tak'n the Castle of *Hastings*, or built a Fortress there. *Harold* secure
the while, and proud of his new Victorie,
thought all his Enemies now under foot: but
sitting jollily at dinner, news is brought him,
that Duke *William* of *Normandy* with a great
multitude of Horse and Foot, Slingers and
Archers, besides other choice Auxiliaries
wch he had hir'd in *France*, was arriv'd at *Pe-
vensey*. *Harold* who had expected him all the
Summer, but not so late in the year as now it
was, for it was *October*; with his Forces much
diminish't after two sore Conflicts, and the
departing

departing of many others from him difcon-
tented, in great haft marches to *London.*
Thence not tarrying for fupplies which were
on thir way towards him, hurries into *Suffex*
(for he was always in haft fince the day of his
Coronation) and e're the third part of his Army could be well put in order, finds the Duke
about nine mile from *Haftings*, and now drawing nigh, fent fpies before him to furvey the
ftrength and number of his Enemies : them,
difcover'd fuch, the Duke caufing to be led
about, and after well fill'd with meat and
drink fent back. They not over-wife, brought
word that the Dukes Army were moft of
them Priefts ; for they faw their faces all o-
ver fhav'n ; the *Englifh* then ufeing to let
grow on their upper-lip large Muftachio's, as
did anciently the *Britans.* The King laugh-
ing, anfwer'd, That they were not Priefts,
but valiant and hardy Souldiers. Therefore
faid *Girtha* his Brother, a Youth of noble courage and underftanding above his Age, Forbear thou thy felf to fight, who art obnoxious to Duke *William* by Oath, let us unfworn
undergo the hazard of Battel, who may juftly fight in the defence of our Country ; thou
referv'd to fitter time, may'ft either reunite
us flying, or revenge us dead. The King not
hark'ning to this, left it might feem to argue Fear in him, or a Bad Caufe, with like
Refolution rejected the Offers of Duke *William* fent to him by a Monk before the Battel, with this only Anfwer haftily deliver'd,
Let God judge between us. The Offers were
Z   thefe,

thefe, That *Harold* would either lay down the
Scepter, or hold it of him, or try his Title
with him by fingle Combate in the fight of
both Armies, or referr it to the Pope. Thefe
rejected, both fides prepar'd to fight the next
morning, the *Englifh* from finging and drinking all night, the *Normans* from confeffion of
thir fins, and communion of the Hoft. The
Englifh were in a ftreit difadvantagious place,
fo that many difcourag'd with thir ill ordering, fcarce having room where to ftand, flip'd
away before the Onfet, the reft in clofe order with thir Battel-Axes and Shields, made
an impenetrable Squadron : the King himfelf with his Brothers on foot ftood by the
Royal Standard, wherein the figure of a man
fighting was inwov'n with Gold and precious
Stones. The *Norman* Foot, moft Bowmen,
made the formoft Front, on either fide Wings
of Horfe fomewhat behind. The Duke Arming, and his Corflet giv'n him on the wrong
fide, faid pleafantly, *The ftrength of my Duke-
dom will be turn'd now into a Kingdom.* Then
the whole Army finging the Song of *Rowland*,
the remembrance of whofe Exploits might
heart'n them, imploring laftly Divine help,
the Battel began ; and was fought forely on
either fide ; but the main Body of *Englifh* Foot
by no means would be brok'n, till the Duke
caufing his men to feign flight, drew them
out with defire of purfuit into op'n diforder,
then turn'd fuddenly upon them fo routed
by themfelves, which wrought thir overthrow ; yet fo they dy'd not unmanfully, but
turning

turning oft upon thir Enemies, by the advantage of an upper ground, beat them down by heaps, and fill'd up a great Ditch with thir Carcasses. Thus hung the Victory wavering on either side, from the third hour of day to Evening; when *Harold* having maintain'd the fight with unspeakable courage and personal valour, shot into the head with an Arrow, fell at length, and left his Souldiers without heart longer to withstand the unwearied Enemy. With *Harold* fell also his two Brothers, *Leofwin*, and *Girtha*, with them greatest part of the *English* Nobility. His Body lying dead a Knight or Souldier wounding on the thigh, was by the Duke presently turn'd out of military service. Of *Normans* and *French* were slain no small number; the Duke himself also that day not a little hazarded his person, having had three choice Horses kill'd under him. Victory obtain'd, and his dead carefully buried, the *English* also by permission, he sent the body of *Harold* to his Mother without ransom, though she offer'd very much to redeem it, which having receav'd, she buried at *Waltham*, in a Church built there by *Harold*. In the mean while, *Edwin* and *Morcar*, who had withdrawn themselves from *Harold*, hearing of his death, came to *London*; sending *Aldgith* the Queen thir Sister with all speed to *West-Chester*. *Aldred* Arch-bishop of *York*, and many of the Nobles, with the *Londoners* would have set up *Edgar* the right Heir, and prepar'd themselves to fight for him; but *Morcar* and *Edwin* not likeing the choice, who each of them expected to have been chos'n before him, withdrew thir Forces and return-

Sim. Dun.

ed home. Duke *William* contrary to his former Resolution, if *Florent* of *Worster*, and they who follow him say true, wasting, burning, and slaying all in his way, or rather, as saith *Malmsbury*, not in Hostile but in Regal manner came up to *London*, met at *Barcham* by *Edgar*, with the Nobles, Bishops, Citizens, and at length *Edwin* and *Morcar*, who all submitted to him, gave Hostages, and swore Fidelity, he to them promis'd Peace and Defence; yet permitted his Men the while to burn and make prey. Coming to *London* with all his Army, he was on *Christmaß* day solemnly Crown'd in the great Church at *Westminster*, by *Aldred* Arch-bishop of *York*, having first giv'n his Oath at the Altar in presence of all the People, to Defend the Church, well Govern the People, Maintain Right Law; prohibit Rapine and unjust Judgment. Thus the *English*, while they agreed not about the choice of thir Native King, were constrein'd to take the Yoke of an Out-landish Conquerour. With what minds, and by what course of life they had fitted themselves for this Servitude, *William* of *Malmsbury* spares not to lay op'n. Not a few years before the *Normans* came, the Clergy, though in *Edward* the Confessors daies, had lost all good Literature and Religion, scarse able to read and understand thir Latin Service : He was a miracle to others who knew his Grammar. The Monks went clad in fine Stuffs, and made no

difference

difference what they eat; which though in it self no fault, yet to thir Consciences was irreligious. The Great Men giv'n to Gluttony and dissolute Life, made a prey of the Common People, abuseing thir Daughters whom they had in Service, then turning them off to the Stews; the meaner sort tipling together night and day, spent all they had in Drunkenness, attended with other Vices which effeminate mens minds. Whence it came to pass, that carried on with fury and rashness more than any true fortitude or skill of War, they gave to *William* their Conquerour so easie a Conquest. Not but that some few of all sorts were much better among them; but such was the generality. And as the long suffering of God permits bad men to enjoy prosperous daies with the good, so his severity oft-times exempts not good men from thir share in evil times with the bad.

If these were the Causes of such Misery and Thraldom to those our Ancestors, with what better close can be Concluded, than here in fit season to remember this Age in the midst of her Security, to fear from like Vices without amendment the Revolution of like Calamities.

F I N I S.

AN
INDEX

Of all the Chief Persons and Material Passages contained in the foregoing HISTORY.

A

Z 4   Albania,

The Table.

The Table.

The Table.

a Con-

The Table.

Bonosus

The Table.

The Table.

C.   Cadwal-

The Table.

C.

Capis

The Table.

The Table.

A a Coillus

The Table.

The Table.

D.

The Table.

E, Eadbald

The Table.

E.

The Table.

A a 4   Ec-

The Table.

The Table.

Edric

The Table.

The Table.

The Table.

The Table.

The Table.

The Table.

F.

B b   *Brother*

The Table.

Godwin

The Table.

Bb 2 Griffin

The Table.

The Table.

H.

Bb 3 Harold

The Table.

Henninus

The Table.

I.

Immanuentius

The Table.

Julius

The Table.

K.

The Table.

The Table.

Keorle

The Table.

L. Learning

The Table.

L.

The Table.

The Table.

The Table.

O.

The Table.

Oslac

The Table.

The Table.

Portfmouth

The Table.

Cc 3

The Table.

S.

Saxons

The Table.

The Table.

Suidhelm

The Table.

T.

The Table.

Trinobantes

V.

The Table.

W.

The Table.

The Table.

Y.

FINIS.

Mr John Miltons

CHARACTER

OF THE

𝕷𝖔𝖓𝖌 𝕻𝖆𝖗𝖑𝖎𝖆𝖒𝖊𝖓𝖙

AND

ASSEMBLY of DIVINES.

In MDCXLI.

Omitted in his other Works, and never before Printed,
And very seasonable for these times.

LONDON:

Printed for *Henry Brome*, at the *Gun* at the West-
end of St. *Pauls*. 1 6 8 1.

TO THE
READER.

THE Reader may take notice, That this Character of Mr. Miltons was a part of his History of Britain, and by him designed to be Printed: But out of tenderness to a Party, [whom neither this nor much more Lenity has had the luck to oblige] it was struck out for some harshness, being only such a Digression, as the History it self would not be discomposed by its omission: which I suppose will be easily discerned, by reading over the beginning of the Third Book of the said History, very near which place this Character is to come in.

It is reported (and from the fore-going Character it seems probable) that Mr. Milton had lent most of his Personal Estate upon the Publick Faith; which when he somewhat earnestly and warmly pressed to have restored [observing how all in Offices had not only feathered their own Nests, but had enricht many of their Relations and Creatures, before the Publick Debts were

A 2

dis-

To the Reader.

discharged] *after a long and chargeable Atten-dance, met with very sharp Rebukes ; upon which at last despairing of any Success in this Affair, he was forced to return from them poor and friend-less , having spent all his Money , and wearied all his Friends. And he had not probably men-ded his worldly condition in those days , but by performing such Service for them , as afterwards he did , for which scarce any thing would appear too great.*

Mr.

Mr. *JOHN MILTONS* Character

OF THE

LongParliament

In 1641.

OF thefe who fway'd moft in the late Troubles, few words as to this point may fuffice. They had Arms , Leaders, and Succeffes to their wifh ; but to make ufe of fo great an Advantage was not their skill. To *other* caufes therefore, and not to the want of Force, or Warlick Manhood in the *Britains*, both thofe, and thefe lately, we muft impute the ill Husbanding of thofe fair Opportunities, which might feem to have put Liberty fo long defired , like a Bridle into their hands. Of which other caufes equally belonging to Ruler , Prieft , and People, above hath been related : which , as they brought *thofe Antient Natives* to Mifery and Ruine, by Liberty, which, rightly ufed, might have made them happy ; fo brought they *thefe of late*, after many Labours, much Blood-fhed, and vaft expence,

pence, to Ridiculous Frustration: in whom the like defects, the like Miscarriages notoriously appeared, with Vices not less hateful or inexcusable.

For a Parliament being call'd, to Redress many things, as 'twas thought, the People with great Courage, and expectation to be eased of what Discontented them, chose to their behoof in Parliament, such as they thought best affected to the Publick Good, and some indeed Men of *Wisdom* and *Integrity*; the rest, [to be sure the greater part,] whom Wealth or ample Possessions, or bold and active Ambition [rather than Merit] had commended to the same place.

But when once the superficial Zeal and Popular Fumes that acted their *New Magistracy* were cool'd, and spent in them, straight every one betook himself, setting the Common-wealth behind, his private Ends before, to do as his own profit or ambition led him. Then was Justice delayed, and soon after deny'd: Spight and Favour determined all: Hence Faction, thence Treachery, both at home and in the Field: Every where Wrong, and Oppression: Foul and Horrid Deeds committed daily, or maintain'd, in secret, or in open. Some who had been called
led

led from Shops and Ware-houses, without o-
ther Merit, to sit in Supreme Councels and Com-
mittees, [as their Breeding was] fell to Huckster the Common-wealth. Others did thereafter as Men could sooth and humour them best ;
so he who would give most, or under Covert
of Hypocritical Zeal, insinuate basest, enjoyed
unworthily the Rewards of Learning and Fidelity ; or escaped the punishment of his
Crimes and Misdeeds. Their Votes and Or-
dinances, which Men lookt should have contained the Repealing of Bad Laws, and the immediate Constiturion of better, resounded with
nothing else, but new Impositions, Taxes, Ex-
cises ; Yearly, Monthly, Weekly. Not to
reckon the Offices, Gifts, and Preferments be-
stowed and shared among themselves : They
in the mean while, who were ever faithfullest
to this Cause, and freely aided them in Person, or
with their Substance, when they durst not compel either, slighted, and bereaved after, of their
just Debts by greedy Sequestrations, were tos-
sed up and down after miserable Attendance
from one Committee to another with Petitions
in their hands, yet either mist the obtaining of
their suit, or though it were at length granted,
[mere shame and reason oft-times extorting
from

from them at least a shew of Justice] yet by their Sequestratours and Sub-committees abroad, Men for the most part of insatiable hands, and noted Disloyalty, those Orders were commonly disobeyed: which for certain durst not have been, without secret complyance, if not compact with some Superiours able to bear them out. Thus were their Friends confiscate in their Enemies, while they forfeited their Debtours to the State, as they called it, but indeed to the Ravening Seizure of innumerable Thieves in Office: Yet were withal no less burthened in all extraordinary Assesments and Oppressions, than those whom they took to be disaffected: Nor were we happier Creditours to what we call'd the State, than to them who were Sequestred as the States Enemies.

For that Faith which ought to have been kept as Sacred and Inviolable as any thing holy, *The Publick Faith*, after infinite Sums received, and all the Wealth of the Church not better imploy'd, but swallowed up into a private *Gulph*, was not ere long ashamed to confess Bankrupt. And now besides the sweetness of Bribery, and other gain, with the love of Rule, their own Guiltiness, and the dreaded name

of

of *juſt Account*, which the People had long call'd for, diſcovered plainly that there were of their own number, who ſecretly contrived and fomented thoſe Troubles and Combuſtions in the Land, which openly they ſate to remedy; and would continually finde ſuch work, as ſhould keep them from being ever brought to that *Terrible ſtand*, of laying down their Authority for lack of new buſineſs, or not drawing it out to any length of Time, tho' upon the Ruine of a whole Nation.

And if the *State* were in this plight, *Religion* was not in much better; to Reform which, a certain number of Divines were called, neither choſen by any Rule or Cuſtome Eccleſiaſtical, nor eminent for either Piety or Knowledge above others left out; only as each Member of Parliament in his private Fancy thought fit, ſo elected one by one. The moſt part of them were ſuch, as had Preach'd and cryed down, with great ſhew of Zeal, the Avarice and Pluralities of Biſhops and Prelates; that one Cure of Souls was a full Employment for one Spiritual Paſtour how able ſoever, if not a charge rather above humane ſtrength. Yet theſe Conſci-

B encious

entious men (ere any part of the work done
for which they came together, and that on
the Publick Salary) wanted not boldneſs, to
the Ignominy and Scandal of their Paſtor-like
Profeſſion, and eſpecially of their boaſted
Reformation, to ſeize into their hands, or
not unwillingly to accept [beſides one, ſome-
times two or more of the beſt Livings] Col-
legiate Maſterſhips in the Univerſities, rich
Lectures in the City, ſetting Sail to all Winds
that might blow Gain into their covetous
Boſoms: By which means theſe great Rebu-
kers of Non-Reſidence, among ſo many di-
ſtant Cures, were not aſhamed to be ſeen ſo
quickly Pluraliſts and Non-Reſidents themſelves, to a fearful Condemnation doubtleſs
by their own Mouths. And yet the main
Doctrine for which they took ſuch pay, and
inſiſted upon with more vehemence than
Goſpel, was but to tell us in effect, that their
Doctrine was worth nothing, and the Spiritual Power of their Miniſtry leſs available
than Bodily Compulſion; perſwading the
Magiſtrate to uſe it, as a ſtronger means to
ſubdue and bring in Conſcience, than Evangelical perſwaſion: Diſtruſting the Virtue of
their own Spiritual weapons, which were given
them,

them, if they be rightly called, with full warrant of sufficiency to pull down all thoughts and imaginations that exalt themselves against God. But while they taught compulsion without convincement, which not long before they complained of, as executed unchristianly, against themselves, these intents are clear to have been no better than Antichristian : setting up a Spiritual Tyranny by a Secular power, to the advancing of their own Authority above the Magistrate, whom they would have made their Executioner, to punish Church-Delinquencies, whereof Civil Laws have no cognizance.

And well did their Disciples manifest themselves to be no better principled than their Teachers, trusted with Committeeships and other gainful Offices, upon their commendations for Zealous, [and as they stickt not to term them] Godly men ; but executing their places like Children of the Devil, unfaithfully, unjustly, unmercifully, and where not corruptly, stupidly. So that between them the Teachers, and these the Disciples, there hath not been a more ignominious and mortal wound to Faith, to Piety, to the work of Reformation,

B 2   nor

nor more cause of Blaspheming given to the
Enemies of God and Truth , since the first
Preaching of Reformation.

The People therefore looking one while on
the Statists , whom they beheld without con-
stancy or firmness , labouring doubtfully beneath the weight of their own too high undertakings, busiest in petty things, trifling in the
main, deluded and quite alienated , expressed
divers ways their disaffection ; some despising
whom before they honoured, some deserting,
some inveighing, some conspiring against them.
Then looking on the *Church-men*, whom they
saw under subtle Hypocrisie to have Preached
their own Follies , most of them not the Gospel, Time-servers, Covetous,Illiterate Persecu-
tors , not lovers of the Truth , like in most
things whereof they accused their Predecessors :
Looking on all this, the People which had been
kept warm a while with the counterfeit zeal of
their Pulpits , after a false heat, became more
cold and obdurate than before , some turning
to Lewdness, some to flat Atheism, put beside
their old Religion , and foully scandalized in
what they expected should be new.

Thus

Thus they who of late were extoll'd as our greateſt Deliverers, and had the People wholly at their Devotion, by ſo diſcharging their Truſt as we ſee, did not only weaken and unfit themſelves to be diſpenſers of what Liberty they pretended, but unfitted alſo the People, now grown worſe and more diſordinate, to receive or to digeſt any Liberty at all. For Stories teach us, that Liberty ſought out of ſeaſon, in a corrupt and degenerate Age, brought *Rome* itſelf into a farther Slavery: For Liberty hath a ſharp and double edge, fit only to be handled by Juſt and Vertuous Men; to bad and diſſolute, it becomes a miſchief unweildy in their own hands: neither is it compleatly given, but by them who have the happy skill to know what is grievance, and unjuſt to a People, and how to remove it wiſely; what good Laws are wanting, and how to frame them ſubſtantially, that good Men may enjoy the freedom which they merit, and the bad the Curb which they need. But to do this, and to know theſe exquiſite proportions, the *Heroick Wiſdom* which is required, ſurmounted far the Principles of theſe narrow Politicians: what wonder then if they ſunk as theſe unfortunate *Britains* before them, entangled and oppreſt with things too
hard

hard, and generous above their strain and temper ? For *Britain*, to speak a truth not often spoken, as it is a Land fruitful enough of Men stout and courageous in War, so is it naturally not over-fertile of Men able to govern justly and prudently in Peace, trusting only in their Mother-Wit ; who consider not justly, that Civility, Prudence, love of the Publick good, more than of Money or vain Honour, are to this Soyl in a manner Outlandish ; grow not here, but in minds well implanted with solid and elaborate Breeding, too impolitick else and rude, if not headstrong and intractable to the industry and vertue either of executing or understanding true Civil Government. Valiant indeed, and prosperous to win a field ; but to know the end and Reason of winning, unjudicious and unwise : in good or bad Success alike unteachable. For the Sun which we want, ripens Wits as well as Fruits ; and as Wine and Oyl are Imported to us from abroad : so must ripe Understanding, and many civil Vertues, be imported into our minds from Forreign Writings, and examples of best Ages, we shall else miscarry still, and come short in the attempts of any great Enterpise. Hence did their Victories prove as fruitless, as their losses dan-

dangerous ; and left them still conquering under the same grievances, that men suffer conquered : which was indeed unlikely to go otherwise , unless men more than vulgar bred up, as few of them were, in the knowledge of Antient and Illustrious Deeds , invincible against many and vain Titles, impartial to Friendships and Relations , had conducted their Affairs : but then from the Chapman to the Retailer , many whose Ignorance was more audacious than the rest, were admitted with all their sordid Rudiments to bear no mean sway among them, both in Church and State.

From the confluence of all their Errors, Mischiefs, and Misdemeanous, what in the eyes of Man could be expected , but what befel those Antient Inhabitants whom they so much resembled, Confusion in the end ?

But on these things, and this Parallel, having enough insisted , I return to the story which gave us matter of this Digression.

F I N I S.

APPENDIX II

Milton jotted down a number of possible subjects for British Tragedies while writing *The History of Britain*. They are preserved in the Cambridge Manuscript at Trinity College, Cambridge (ms 583). The whole manuscript was published in facsimile, edited by W. Aldis Wright, in 1899. The spelling has been modernised.

1. Venutius husband to Cartismandua. 1a. The cloister king Constans set up by Vortigern.

2. Vortimer poisoned by Rowena. Vortiger marrying Rowena. See Speed. Reproved by Vodin, archbishop of London.

3. Vortiger immured. The massacre of the Britons by Hengist in their cups at Salisbury Plain. Malmesbury.

4. Sigher of the East Saxons revolted from the faith, and reclaimed by Jarumanus.

5. Ethelbert of the East Angles slain by Offa the Mercian king. See Holinshed. Speed in the life of Offa and Ethelbert.

6. Sebert slain by Penda after he had left his kingdom. See Holinshed.

7. Wulfer slaying his two sons for being Christians.

8. Osbert of Northumberland slain for ravishing the wife of Bernbocard and the Danes brought in. See Stow, Holinshed and Speed.

9. Edmund the last king of the East Angles martyred by Hinguar the Dane. See Speed.

10. Siegbert, tyrant of the West Saxons, slain by a swineherd.

11. Edmund, brother of Athelstan, slain by a thief at his own table. Malmesbury.

12. Edwin, son to Edward the younger, for lust deprived of his kingdom. Or rather, by faction of monks whom he hated, together with the impostor Dunstan.

13. Edward, son of Edgar, murdered by his stepmother, to which may be inserted the tragedy stirred up betwixt the monks and priests about marriage.

14. Ethelred, son of Edgar, a slothful king, the ruin of his land by the Danes.

15. Ceaulin, king of the West Saxons, for tyranny deposed and banished, and dying.

16. The slaughter of the monks of Bangor by Edelfride, stirred up as is said by Ethelbert, and he by Austin the monk because the Britons could not receive the rites of the Roman church, See Bede, Geoffrey of Monmouth and Holinshed. Which must begin with the convocation of British clergy by Austin to determine superfluous points which by them were refused.

17. Edwin by vision promised the kingdom of Northumberland on promise of his conversion, and therein established by Rodoald, king of the East Angles.

18. Oswin, king of Deira, slain by Oswie his friend, king of Bernitia, through instigation of flatterers.

19. Sigibert of the East Angles keeping company with a person excommunicated, slain by the same man in his house, according as the bishop Cedda had foretold.

20. Egfrid, king of the Northumbers, slain in battle against the Picts, having before wasted Ireland and made war for no reason on men that ever loved the English, forewarned also by Cuthbert not to fight with the Picts.

21. Kinewulf, king of the West Saxons, slain by Kineard in the house of one of his concubines.

22. Gunthildis, the Danish lady, with her husband Palingus and her son slain by appointment of the traitor Edric in King Ethelred's days. Holinshed, together with the massacre of the Danes at Oxford. Speed.

23. Brightrick of the West Saxons poisoned by his wife Ethelburga, Offa's daughter, who dies miserably also in beggary after adultery in a nunnery. Speed.

24. Alfred in disguise of a minstrel discovers the Danes' negligence; sets on with a mighty slaughter. About the same time, the Devonshire men rout Hubba and slay him. A Heroical Poem may be founded somewhere in Alfred's reign, especially at his issuing out of Edelingsey on the Danes; whose actions are well like those of Ulysses.

25. Athelstan exposing his brother Edwin to the sea, and repenting.

26. Edgar slaying Ethelwold for false play in wooing, wherein may be set out his pride, lust, which he thought to close by favouring monks and

building monasteries. Also the disposition of woman in Elfrida towards her husband.

27. Swain besieging London and Ethelred repulsed by the Londoners.

28. Harold slain in battle by William the Norman. The first scene may begin with the ghost of Alfred, the second son of Ethelred, slain in cruel manner by Godwin, Harold's father, his mother and brother dissuading him.

29. Edmund Ironside defeating the Danes at Brentford, with his combat with Canute.

30. Edmund Ironside murdered by Edric the traitor and revenged by Canute.

31. Gunhilda, daughter to King Canute and Emma, wife to Henry the third emperor, accused of unchastity, is defended by her English page in combat against a giant-like adversary, who by him at two blows is slain. Speed, in the life of Canute.

32. Hardicanute dying in his cups, an example to riot.

33. Edward Confessor's divorcing and imprisoning his noble wife Editha, Godwin's daughter, wherein is showed his over-affection to strangers, the cause of Godwin's insurrection; his slackness to redress the corrupt clergy and superstitious pretence of chastity. Wherein Godwin's forbearance of battle praised, and the English moderation of both sides magnified.